CONTESTED KNOWLEDGE

CONTESTED KNOWLEDGE

Social Theory Today

Fifth Edition

Steven Seidman

A John Wiley & Sons, Ltd., Publication

This edition first published 2013
© 2013 John Wiley & Sons, Ltd

Edition history: Blackwell Publishing Ltd (1e, 1994, 2e, 1998, 3e, 2003, and 4e, 2008)

Wiley-Blackwell is an imprint of John Wiley & Sons, formed by the merger of Wiley's global Scientific, Technical and Medical business with Blackwell Publishing.

Registered Office
John Wiley & Sons, Ltd, The Atrium, Southern Gate, Chichester, West Sussex, PO19 8SQ, UK

Editorial Offices
350 Main Street, Malden, MA 02148-5020, USA
9600 Garsington Road, Oxford, OX4 2DQ, UK
The Atrium, Southern Gate, Chichester, West Sussex, PO19 8SQ, UK

For details of our global editorial offices, for customer services, and for information about how to apply for permission to reuse the copyright material in this book please see our website at www.wiley.com/wiley-blackwell.

Library of Congress Cataloging-in-Publication Data

Seidman, Steven.
    Contested knowledge : social theory today / Steven Seidman. – 5th ed.
      p.   cm.
    Includes bibliographical references and index.
    ISBN 978-1-118-22790-9 (pbk.)
1. Sociology–Methodology.   2. Postmodernism–Social aspects.   I. Title.
    HM585.S44 2013
    301.01–dc23
                                                          2011051687

A catalogue record for this book is available from the British Library.

Set in 10/12.5pt Galliard by SPi Publisher Services, Pondicherry, India
Printed in Singapore by Ho Printing Singapore Pte Ltd

2   2013

Contents

Preface

I am very much a child of the sixties. I dropped out of college, looked to my body as a source of pleasure and rebellion, and marched to change the world. I imagined the social sphere as a field of enormous possibilities for self- and collective renewal. As the sixties dead-ended in drugs, violence, and either political extremism or liberal accommodation, I followed the hordes of the middle class into graduate school. I looked to sociology as a discipline that would help make sense of my individual and collective world while also contributing to envisioning a different and better future.

I recall the disillusionment of my first few years as a sociologist. I expected my colleagues to share my moral vision of sociology. The reality was sobering. My colleagues, whom I admired for their research skills and their accomplishments, hardly read outside of their specialty areas; few of them deliberately linked their scholarship to public debates and controversies; much of the culture of sociology in the 1980s and 1990s seemed parochial – a world where "scientific" talk and status anxieties produced an insulated expert culture. I was distraught at the wreckage of professionalization: smart, well-intentioned individuals with good values, whose intellect was disciplined by a culture that often ignored history, non-American and non-"Western" cultures, and that lacked strong ties to a public world of moral and political debate.

I rebelled. I turned to the roots of modern social thought in order to call sociology to task for abandoning its moral promise. In the 1980s, I undertook a study of the Enlightenment origins of European social theory. The passion that previously went into personal and social rebellion was now channeled into a quest to reform sociology. I hoped to find in the original inspiration of modern social theory a warrant for approaching sociology as having a moral and political purpose. I found what I was looking for: the *philosophes* and the classics viewed social analysis as a vehicle of social critique and change.

As the memories of the 1960s faded, my own writings became obscure. In the apolitical spirit of America in the 1980s, I was absorbing the disciplinary culture of sociology. I started thinking of myself as a "theorist," as if theory had its own problems and value apart from social analysis and critique. I was losing myself in "theory" discussions. My work was starting to feel sterile and pointless. I felt alienated from my original moral and political motives for becoming a sociologist.

The AIDS crisis jolted me. It was 1981. I remember reading of the mysterious disease that was taking the lives of gay men. I recall the media hysteria, the homophobic public response, and the governmental neglect. I was living in New Mexico trying to finish a book on the classical social theorists. As I was preoccupied with Marx's *Capital* or Durkheim's *Suicide*, the fatalities from AIDS seemed to be growing exponentially. The AIDS epidemic fed into a backlash against the social rebellions of the 1960s. America, once again, seemed in the throes of a major political and cultural war. As a leftist and gay man, my life felt raw and vulnerable. The progressive culture that I valued was under attack. AIDS was an enemy killing off my friends and threatening me personally. In the midst of this social and personal upheaval, my work on classical sociology felt more and more pointless, as did the field of sociology in general.

In a manner of speaking, I took leave of sociology in the early 1980s. I finished the book on classical social theory. But my focus had definitely shifted. AIDS and the backlash against the progressive movements of the 1960s gripped me. I began clipping out everything that appeared in the press on AIDS and the social backlash. I stopped reading sociology and sociological theory. As the politics of the body, sexuality, gender, and knowledge moved to the center of my life, I found myself absorbed in the texts of feminism, gay and lesbian studies, race theory, poststructuralism, and cultural studies. In the course of reading and writing in these areas, I had for all practical purposes ceased being part of the sociological community.

And yet, I have returned to sociology. I write this book, in part, as a sociologist. Why?

Perhaps I was drawn back to the discipline the way a young adult, having achieved a certain independence and individuality, returns to his or her original family with a newfound sense of belonging. Sociology was the community that originally nourished me and provided me with new ways of thinking about myself and the social world. I have learned that, as much as I resist sociology, I am ever drawn to it. I have realized that this discipline is a home of sorts for me. I like to think of sociology as a sort of extended family or, better yet, a church. We quarrel with passion and sometimes fury, because many of our deepest beliefs and values are attached to our social ideas and because we care dearly about each other, if not always in an intimate way, then as individuals who share a similar disciplinary history and culture.

I have returned to sociology, but I am not quite the same person that I was before my "travels." Like anyone who spends considerable time in an alien culture, I have come to see my native land as just one among many cultures. I have relativized the premises, concepts, and knowledges of sociology. In particular, I have come to see the theory debates among postwar sociologists as simply one tradition of debate about "the social world." Sociological theorists have wrongly imagined that their central problems, for example, the logic of social action and order, the dispute over the validity of conflict versus order paradigms, or the question of the relation between the micro and macro levels of analysis, pertain to the very nature of "the social." The presumption is that if anyone, at any time, were to think seriously about the social world he or she would end up centering reflection on these issues. This is, as anthropologists would say, an example of ethnocentrism, a practice that claims universality and validity for the particular values and ideas of one group. For example, postwar Western feminists have not defined these theory problems as central. Instead, feminist debate has revolved around questions of the natural and social aspects of gender, the concept of gender as a master category of social explanation, the origins of male dominance, the relation between the private and public realm, the nature of identity and difference, and the multiple character of domination and resistance.

Relativizing sociological theory does not mean denying its importance. There is much in sociological theory that is valuable and worth defending; in particular its social understanding of the self, its rich conceptual language for understanding institutions and whole societies, its accounts of social development, order, and crisis, and its tradition of cultural social studies. And yet, sociological theory has all too often, especially in the last few decades, become isolated from public life and has chased the idol of science to a point of its own obscurity. Much sociological theory has abandoned a moral and political intention to engage the world as a medium of critical analysis and change.

I return to sociology as I initially came to the discipline, with the hope of finding a home where social analysis is valued because it is inspired by a will to make a better world. This does not mean giving up empirical analysis; nor does it mean abandoning analytical perspectives. However, I do believe that the purpose of sociology is not to accumulate knowledge, establish a science of society, or build a system of sociology, but to be part of the ongoing conversation and conflict over the present and future shape of the social world. The hope that has guided sociology and modern social theory for some 200 years is that knowledge can make a difference in our lives and that its chief value lies in the kinds of lives it imagines and helps to create. This hope is what inspired this volume.

Acknowledgments

It is a pleasure to recognize the many individuals (some anonymous) who commented on drafts of the chapters or otherwise contributed to the making of *Contested Knowledge*. Many thanks to Pat Akard, Jeff Alexander, Bob Antonio, Molefi Asante, Zygmunt Bauman, Robert Bellah, Roslyn Bologh, Judith Butler, Craig Calhoun, Patricia Clough, Edith Kurzweil, Richard Lachmann, Michelle Lamont, Barbara Laslett, Charles Lemert, Linda Nicholson, Dorothy Smith, Stephen Turner, David Wagner, and Jeffrey Weeks. A special thanks to Jeff Alexander and especially Linda Nicholson, with whom I have had the good fortune to carry on a conversation about these matters for many years.

Introduction

Modern social theory has been inspired by a noble purpose: to advance human freedom. By conceiving of the human condition as fundamentally social and historical, the social sciences anticipated the possibility that societies could rationally fashion their own destiny. If social customs and institutions are understood as products of human actions, not natural or divine law, couldn't they be shaped to benefit all of humanity?

The social scientist was imagined as a public educator whose chief task was public enlightenment. In their quest for truth, social scientists would illuminate the social dangers to freedom and the prospects for progress. The pioneers of the social sciences, thinkers such as Montesquieu, Condorcet, Marx, Comte, Weber, Charlotte Perkins Gilman, and W. E. B. Du Bois, invented new and imaginative ways of understanding the origin and organization of the social world. Their ideas addressed matters of considerable moral and political significance, for example, the origins of inequality, the bureaucratic threat to freedom, the state of the Negro in society, and the exploitation of women. For the founding figures of the social sciences, knowledge was valued as a means of promoting social progress.

Contemporary sociological theory has not abandoned this social purpose. Sociologists continue to provide critical perspectives on the present that aim to enlighten a broad public. Yet sociological theory and, to a lesser extent, sociology in general, have become more and more isolated from public life, to the detriment of both sociology and public life. As sociological theorists have retreated from their role as public educators, their ideas have lost social relevance. Moreover, the general public suffers from theorists' diminishing social authority. Sociological theory has been a catalyst of public debate and an important provider of critical social perspectives. As theorists and many sociologists become preoccupied with insular disciplinary concerns, public officials, activists, policy-makers, journalists, and media commentators have assumed the chief role of public intellectuals. Unfortunately, these individuals, though often thoughtful and insightful, are usually focused narrowly on specific issues

Contested Knowledge: Social Theory Today, Fifth Edition. Steven Seidman.
© 2013 John Wiley & Sons, Ltd. Published 2013 by John Wiley & Sons, Ltd.

or political events such as gays in the military or the Middle East conflicts or electoral politics; they are pressured to meet commercial deadlines and standards. Accordingly, their social ideas often lack the conceptual and historical depth that has been part of the social sciences. A vigorous democratic public culture is nourished by the social ideas crafted by sociologists and critical social scientists.

Why has sociological theory become increasingly isolated from public life? Sociology continues to produce theorists of impressive talent, but its culture is more and more removed from a general public culture. The growing insularity of sociological theory reflects, in part, the fact that theorists are often oriented to members of their own expert culture. Much of current sociological theory simply does not speak a broad public language; the conventions and concerns of this disciplinary culture render their ideas either inaccessible to a general public or irrelevant to the ways in which the moral and political issues of the day are discussed in everyday life. The sad truth is that sociological theory, especially in the United States, is hardly read today beyond a small circle of academic theorists.

If sociological theory is in trouble, one reason is the quest for an overarching theory of society and history. From Comte through Parsons, Habermas, and Randall Collins, theorists have tried to discover the underlying principles of social order and social change. These theorists believe that there are very general problems such as the nature of social action and social order or the relationship between the individual and social institutions that are at the core of social knowledge. It is the task of theory to settle these so-called foundational issues or to uncover the universal principles of social life. A core of theoretical principles would then guide social research and social analysis. Unfortunately, theorists have been unable to achieve anything approaching consensus on the core premises, concepts, and explanatory models of social knowledge. And, sadly, theorists' aspiration to provide secure foundations for social knowledge has often led them into a series of arcane conceptual and methodological debates that have largely proved fruitless. Sociological theorists are in danger of losing the attention of both researchers and the public.

Sociology needs to recover its role as public educator in order to contribute to a more measured and thoughtful public discussion. In this regard, I would like to see sociological theory regain its focus on issues of broad public significance. Instead of being driven by narrow disciplinary conventions and disputes, theorists should seriously try to address the key social and political debates of our time, and in an accessible language. Theorists need to recover the moral impulse at the heart of social theory, and to see themselves, once again, as public educators engaging the issues of the day. *Contested Knowledge* is animated by the original promise of modern social thinking: the idea that social theory can produce ideas that would help create a better world.

CONFLICTING VIEWS OF SOCIAL THEORY

Since the Enlightenment, the very meaning of social theory has been debated. Three views of theory have been at the center of debate: theory as scientific, philosophical, and moral.

Scientific social theory assumes that science is the only method capable of achieving reliable social knowledge. Our common-sense ideas about society as well as the social understandings of poets and novelists, journalists and social commentators, are said to express personal values and opinions. Science tells us what is real and true. The ideal of the social sciences is to discover ideas that mirror the world; by contrast, the ideas of ordinary folk mirror personal beliefs or political ideology.

Scientific theorists aim to discover laws or principles that apply to human behavior in all societies, past and present. For example, Auguste Comte searched and thought he found the laws that govern how societies establish order and change; Marx wanted to uncover the laws of capitalism; the American sociologists Randall Collins and Peter Blau tried to gather together the principles that govern key aspects of social life, for example, social conflict, order, change, peace, and war. For these theorists, the sciences of physics or biology serve as models for social theory. True knowledge requires that observations, research, and facts be organized as general principles or laws that are proven through repeated testing.

Philosophical approaches share with scientific theorists the aim to reveal timeless social truths. In some ways, philosophically oriented theorists are even more ambitious than scientific ones. Not content with uncovering general principles or social laws, philosophical theorists aspire to develop sweeping, overarching theories of human behavior and social evolution. However, instead of developing their ideas from observations and facts, philosophical theorists believe that research must be preceded by rigorous conceptual thinking. Before we can observe and record social life we must have certain ideas about the nature of social life. Do we focus on the individual or on social groups? Are individuals agents who shape society or do individuals mostly adapt to social forces? And, which social forces – religion, the economy, class, or bureaucracy – are the most important in shaping social life? In short, philosophical theorists aim to establish the core categories and ideas about human behavior and social life that would guide researchers. Perhaps the two greatest thinkers in this tradition are Talcott Parsons and Jürgen Habermas. As we'll see, they approach theory as a serious discursive project. Theory involves reasoning about the most basic aspects of social life, for example, how is social order possible or is there a pattern to social change across centuries? The aim of theory, say the philosophical theorists, is to provide the foundational concepts and ideas that will guide the work of researchers and social analysts.

The styles of scientific and philosophical theorists are very different. Scientific theorists work primarily with the observations and facts produced by researchers. They aim to organize empirical research into a set of social principles or laws. By contrast, philosophical theorists spend considerable time thinking about the ideas of other thinkers as they develop their own views about human behavior and social life. Parsons' major work, *The Structure of Social Action*, was a study of the ideas of several European thinkers; no research was discussed. His aim was to develop a general theory of social action. Similarly, Habermas's *A Theory of Communicative Action* is a virtual tour through European and American philosophy and social theory from the mid-nineteenth century to the present; he aspired to reveal the essential structure of human communication as the foundation for a general theory of society.

Theorists have tried not only to understand but to change society. While many thinkers believe that their social role should be confined to revealing social truths, others maintain that theory should contribute to changing social life. These thinkers endorse a *moral vision of social theory*. From this point of view, social knowledge is valuable because of its potential to make the world a better place to live.

Approaching theory as a moral or critical practice has been a key part of modern social thinking. Many theorists have crafted powerful social views that advocate specific social and political responses to threats to freedom and democracy. Theorists have proposed powerful critical analyses of class conflict, male dominance, the decline of religious faith, the crisis of solidarity, and the bureaucratization of society. The aim of a morally inspired theory is to alert the public to a social danger in order to prompt and sometimes guide political action.

Think of Marx's exposé of capitalism as a class-divided, exploitative type of society. His critique of capitalism aimed to contribute to a working-class social revolt. Or, to take another example, Robert Bellah and his colleagues composed *Habits of the Heart*, an empirically rich social analysis of the US, in order to alert Americans to the dangers of a culture that championed individual self-interest at the expense of community values. Feminists and queer theorists have offered critical social perspectives that challenge male and heterosexual dominance; their critiques played a pivotal role in the making of movements for gender and sexual justice.

A moral approach to theory and social analysis does not mean giving up a commitment to truth or empirical knowledge. However, thinkers who emphasize the political and moral meaning of social thinking may not necessarily view theory or research as always capable of producing hard and fast truths. These thinkers defend a distinct role for sociologists: social analysis as social criticism. For these thinkers, truths may be possible, but we cannot and should not abandon our moral and political commitment to a better world.

Despite the prominence of scientific and philosophical approaches, most theorists have in fact not given up on a moral vision of social science. Most theorists would still, if push came to shove, concede that social knowledge finds its ultimate value in whatever good for humanity comes of it. The tribe of theorists and social scientists are, by and large, a good lot, who care about people and believe that their efforts should be socially beneficial. Yet the sad truth is that this moral hope is often not acknowledged as an important criterion in judging the worth of social research and theory. It is, for most social scientists, simply a hope, a heartfelt hope, but one that is not supposed to influence decisions about methods, concepts, explanations, and research aims. This does not mean that the values and moral vision of the social scientist do not find a prominent place in social research. No matter how much a social scientist may wish to expunge moral commitments from his or her work, they remain. Unfortunately, though, while moral commitments shape social science, they are often not acknowledged or reflected upon in the work we do.

These three views of social theory are *styles* of theorizing. Often, thinkers combine these styles. Marx simultaneously engaged in a philosophical analysis of concepts, sought to uncover the laws of capitalism, and was a fierce critic of modern societies. Talcott Parsons' *The Structure of Social Action* was a philosophical analysis of the concept of social action. Subsequently, Parsons sought to apply his theoretical ideas by offering empirical explanations of Nazism, family dynamics, and modern racism. And, this tireless defender of social truth was also a relentless champion of American liberal pluralism against the socialist left and a conservative right.

There are, though, tensions among these approaches. For example, scientific approaches are hostile to the intrusion of values or political convictions into social analysis. Yet as much as scientific approaches want to stick to "just the facts," facts and observations often cannot adjudicate between different conceptual approaches. A philosophical analysis of concepts is often necessary to get at the deeper conceptual underpinnings of empirical disputes about the social world. Or, in its quest for logically compelling foundational concepts, a philosophical approach often becomes entangled in obscure debates that are far removed from the concerns of researchers and activists or policy makers. And those who embrace a moral style must struggle with reconciling partisanship with the ideals of scholarship. Even strong advocates of a moral vision of human studies must concede that the very effectiveness of their ideas may depend on their public authority, an authority that may be weakened by their partisanship. The vital tension between a scientific, philosophical, and a moral vision will be examined as we analyze the contemporary significance of social theory.

Part I

The Rise of the Classical Tradition

Introduction to Part I

Every group and society seems to develop its own views of human behavior. Perhaps this reflects our reliance on planning rather than instinct to survive; or perhaps it's inherent in a species that uses language to think and communicate. In any event, we find that, throughout history, human association has been accompanied by ideas about human motivation, social interaction, and social order. However, not all societies have produced "social thought" or something like a deliberate and methodical effort to provide secular explanations of social life. Similarly, not all societies have created social institutions (e.g., universities, publishing companies, journals) and social roles (e.g., professors, social critics, and commentators) whose purpose is to analyze and debate the truthfulness of social ideas.

It is impossible to locate the origins of social thought. In many of the so-called ancient civilizations (China, Egypt, Greco-Roman), we observe diverse traditions of social thought. For example, in ancient Greece, Plato, Aristotle, and Thucydides crafted social analyses of war, the origins of the family and the state, and the relation between religion and the government. Aristotle's *Politics* offers a rich social account of the formation of different political systems and the interconnections between the individual, family, culture, and politics. Although thinkers like Plato and Aristotle were insightful about humanity and society, most historians do not credit them as founding figures of the social sciences.

What makes the social thought of premodern times different from social science? Perhaps it's that the social sciences hold different assumptions about the world and about social knowledge than do the traditions of premodern social thought. Ancient and Christian social thought often viewed the universe as an unchanging hierarchical order in which all beings, human and otherwise, had a more or less fixed and proper place and purpose. Premodern social thought often approached human behavior as part of a conception of the overall natural and moral structure of the universe. For example, Aristotle's social thought was less concerned with explaining social patterns

Contested Knowledge: Social Theory Today, Fifth Edition. Steven Seidman.
© 2013 John Wiley & Sons, Ltd. Published 2013 by John Wiley & Sons, Ltd.

such as the role of social class in shaping politics than with sketching an ideal society in the context of a comprehensive philosophy of life. Social science has abandoned the static, hierarchical world view of its Greek and Christian predecessors. Modern social scientists have, in the main, abandoned the effort to craft a comprehensive philosophy of life. Social science occupies a different world of ideas than premodern "Western" social thought.

In the next four chapters, we take a first glance at the world of modern social thinking. Eighteenth- and early-nineteenth-century Europe was the principal home for the birth of social science. Beginning with the ideas of the Enlightenment, we trace the development of modern social theory in the work of Auguste Comte, Karl Marx, Emile Durkheim, and Max Weber. These thinkers make up the core of what is considered the classical tradition of modern social theory.

The Idea of a Science of Society
The Enlightenment and Auguste Comte

Eighteenth-century Europe gave rise to some remarkable social thinkers, including Voltaire, Hume, Adam Ferguson, Condorcet, Montesquieu, Adam Smith, and Mary Wollstonecraft. Although they wrote widely on philosophy, natural science, and literature, they produced an impressive body of social ideas. Of particular importance, Enlightenment social thinkers (Enlighteners) broke away from the Greek and Christian traditions of social thought. They pioneered a new science of society.

Although the Enlighteners took up the cause of science with the enthusiasm of crusaders, they were not its original creators. The great breakthroughs to a scientific world view occurred from the fifteenth through the seventeenth centuries, the result of the efforts of Copernicus, Kepler, Galileo, and Newton. From the perspective of that time period, the commitment to science amounted to a serious challenge to the prevailing Aristotelian–Christian world view. In early modern Europe, the universe was seen as a hierarchical order in which every being (human, animal, plant, spiritual) had a rightful place and purpose in a divinely created and ordered universe. The natural and social worlds were viewed as being spiritually infused with value, meaning, and purpose. By contrast, the scientific revolution conceived of the universe as a mechanical system composed of matter in motion that obeyed natural laws. Both divine purpose and human will became peripheral, indeed unnecessary, features of the scientific world view.

If the Enlighteners were not the creators of the scientific revolution, they were its great popularizers and propagandists. Through their writing and speeches, they proved indispensable in introducing science to educated Europeans. Moreover, they were themselves innovators, less in their efforts in the natural sciences than in the study of human behavior. They dismissed much of previous social thought as based on prejudice, opinion, revelation, philosophical reasoning, and tradition; true knowledge, they asserted, can only rest on the solid ground of fact and scientific method. Departing from views of society as a divine or natural order, the Enlighteners

Contested Knowledge: Social Theory Today, Fifth Edition. Steven Seidman.
© 2013 John Wiley & Sons, Ltd. Published 2013 by John Wiley & Sons, Ltd.

understood society as a "field" of individual interaction responsive to human intentions. The Enlighteners created a social world view that has become dominant in the modern West. At its core is the notion that humans create society; through our actions we shape a world of institutions which in turn shape us; the interplay between individuals and social institutions determines the history and future of humanity. The aim of a science of society is to reveal the common patterns of human association across different societies.

The Enlighteners championed the scientific world view, but only after they had altered it to suit their own purpose. Like many educated men and women of the time, they saw in the scientific world view a triumph of reason over prejudice. However, they were troubled by this revolution in thinking to the extent that science projected the universe as a purely materialistic, mechanical place with no room for freedom and morality. It was perhaps the genius of Montesquieu, Adam Smith, and Condorcet that they were able to wed science to a liberal humanistic world view. This was achieved by conceiving human history as a product of individual actions yet patterned in a law-like way. Thus, in his great work *The Spirit of the Laws*, Montesquieu traced the variations in political systems to both natural and social factors such as geography, climate, and religion while claiming to demonstrate that this variation was limited by the constraints of human nature.[1] Similarly, in his grand vision of history as the march of human progress, Condorcet believed that the drive to human freedom explains why some societies progress more quickly than others; at the same time, he believed that our common human nature creates important similarities between different societies.[2]

The thinkers of the Enlightenment aimed both to understand human behavior and to use science to promote freedom and progress. But, how can science be both a morally neutral instrument of knowledge and a vehicle of social progress? In a *Sketch for a Historical Picture of the Progress of the Human Mind*, Condorcet argued that the very nature of science – its reliance upon facts and observation, its openness to criticism and revision – promotes individualism, tolerance, equality, and democracy. Accordingly, he thought that the progress of science automatically translates into social progress. Today, in the aftermath of Nazism, Hiroshima, and widespread revelations about scientific torture and control through medicine and psychiatry, we would surely question whether science is necessarily wedded to liberal and humanistic values. Is it not possible that the Enlighteners read their own liberal values into science? Many Enlightenment thinkers held that, by discerning the laws of history, social science would have insight into the correct social norms and social policies. But how do we guard against the possibility that the so-called objective laws of history might, in fact, be colored by the social values and interests of the scientist? If social knowledge is to guide social affairs, we need to be certain that our social ideas truly mirror the objective, not our subjective, world. But how can we be certain of this?

The social motivation of Enlightenment thinkers raises further suspicions that their scientific vision was not innocent of moral and political meanings. The figures of the Enlightenment lived in a period of social turmoil. European societies were divided between social groups that defended social hierarchy and the status quo (the church and landed aristocracy) and groups such as commercial entrepreneurs and peasants and laborers who struggled for freedom, equality, and democracy. The Enlighteners were mostly from socially privileged backgrounds (sons of nobility or parliamentarians) but were typically not members of the ruling clerical and aristocratic elite. Their livelihood was guaranteed neither by the ruling elite nor by an independent university system of the kind that developed in the twentieth century. As educated men with few social privileges, their sympathies generally were with those who wanted to bring about social change.

The Enlighteners were participants in the social struggles of the time. Their activities as polemicists and social critics carried serious risk, from fines and economic insecurity, to exile, imprisonment, even execution. Indeed, many of them wrote under assumed names, or penned essays in which the critical message was carefully camouflaged by humor or parody. Since they were typically not landowners or members of parliament, their battle site was culture. They fought against the beliefs and social norms that upheld a society organized around social hierarchy, intolerance, and inequality. In eighteenth-century France, the struggle was primarily against the Catholic hierarchy. At one level, Enlightenment thinkers fought for freedoms relating to public expression, free speech, and tolerance of dissent. At another level, their battles were centered on the very issue of which beliefs, values, and social norms should prevail in society. In other words, the Enlighteners challenged the very basis of the landed aristocracy and church hierarchy by disputing the legitimacy of a society organized on the basis of a Christian religious culture. In this regard, they took up the cause of science as a key part of their struggle to shape the future of Europe and humanity.

In light of the breakthroughs to a scientific world view by their predecessors, it is hardly surprising that the Enlighteners seized on science as a vehicle to challenge the Christian culture. Through the persecution of Galileo and other innovators of science for heresy, the public associated science with social rebellion. Moreover, the scientific world view was interpreted by both the church and its detractors as a grave threat to the Christian cosmology. In a universe that was viewed as governed by mechanical laws, God was rendered as little more than a peripheral, detached observer. As the role of God in natural and human affairs was reduced to that of a spectator, the social role of the church would diminish accordingly.

The world view of science challenged the public authority of the church. Science projected a universe in which all beings were reducible to matter in motion; the only differences that counted were those related to shape, force, mass, or velocity. Fundamental Christian beliefs about the existence of spiritual beings and actions (e.g., angels or divine incarnations) and about the very notion of a human soul differentiating us from animals were placed in doubt. Similarly, to the extent that science assumed that true knowledge is based on observations, facts, and scientific method, Christian knowledge founded upon revelation, tradition, and the authority of the church was discredited. Finally, we should notice the close tie between the social values associated with modern Western science and those of the Enlighteners. For example, the Newtonian universe placed all beings on an equal footing; scientific knowledge itself was not an inherited right or gift but a product of education and effort; natural laws apply to all beings in the universe. In short, the scientific revolution seemed in tune with modern liberal values and the social agenda of those groups who wanted social reform. It was not, however, the generation of Galileo or Newton that translated the scientific cosmology into a social world view; it was the Enlighteners.

Whereas the first phase of the scientific revolution (from the fifteenth to the seventeenth centuries) still left God and the church in charge, in the second phase, initiated by the Enlighteners, God was a matter of personal belief and the church, a human institution deserving of no special public authority. The Enlighteners directly challenged the social power of the church and the landed aristocracy by criticizing religion as the source of knowledge, social norms, and public values. If true knowledge is based on observation and fact, then religion, which is based on revelation or tradition, is mere opinion or an illusion. Indeed, many Enlighteners accused the church of inventing Christianity in order to gain social privileges by keeping the masses in a state of awe, fear, and ignorance. The existing social order, with its alliance of the church hierarchy, monarch, and landed aristocracy, was viewed as a fragile artifice resting upon rather shaky religious foundations.

By championing the cause of science, the Enlighteners were able to mount a frontal assault upon the social status quo. Yet the very style of their criticism can just as easily be turned against them. If the church forged a world view that masked its desire for social power, is not the same true for the Enlighteners? Didn't they intend to replace religion with science and priests with scientists? Is the claim that only science ensures true knowledge and guarantees social progress simply another ruse on the part of a rising social elite wishing to legitimate their desire for power?

Our suspicions gain credibility when we note that, for all their rhetoric of science as based on facts, observations, and method, the Enlighteners ignored the point that science, just like religion, rests upon ideas that cannot be scientifically proven. For example, the claims that humans are natural beings, that nature is uniform and lawlike, that observations yield knowledge, and that history is patterned and goal-directed cannot be proven by science. These beliefs are in the end matters of faith. Moreover, despite reassurances that their social explanations rested upon a bedrock of fact, their contemporaries and successive generations have raised grave doubts. For example, insisting on his scientific approach, Montesquieu declared: "I have not drawn my principles [of social organization] from my prejudices, but from the nature of things."[3] But did "the nature of things" reveal that climate, as Montesquieu believed, rather than religion or social class, is the main determinant of political systems? When Montesquieu proposed that cold climates produce individuals who are courageous, generous, and insensitive to pain, when he explained the "Englishmen's love of liberty" by the impatience produced by cold weather, was he simply giving voice to "the nature of things," or to his prejudices? Perhaps even more telling of the moral patterning of Enlightenment social thought are their grand stories of the march of human progress and the triumph of reason over superstition. These narratives look suspiciously like secular versions of Christian millennialism. We are, in short, left with the impression that the Enlightenment practice of science is as weak a guarantor of truth as religion. The cultural clash between the backers of religion and the proponents of science appears to be a battle over the shape of society and the right to legislate social norms and ideals.

For all their celebration of science as a medium of truth, the Enlighteners used science as a powerful instrument of social change. There is no reason to doubt the sincerity of their belief in science as the path to true knowledge. They accepted the equation that science equals truth precisely the way their predecessors professed Christianity – as a faith. Beliefs harden into a faith when they become the common-sense understandings of large segments of society. By the mid to late eighteenth century, science was already a central part of a secular humanistic world view that was valued by many educated Europeans. Moreover, many Europeans perceived science as both a symbol of a new enlightened era and a force of social progress. To champion science was to be in step with the march of human progress. Christianity may have been the object of the Enlightenment's derision, but its faith that truth will bring salvation continued to animate even the enlightened mind.

The Age of Enlightenment may not have been the great turning point in human history that its greatest thinkers and many of their successors believed, but it was a period of great turmoil and change. The outlines of a new or "modern" type of society were visible in the expansion of commerce, the formation of liberal political institutions, and the emerging class organization of European societies. For many individuals, especially in the West, these changes were understood as representing major human progress. And, from this perspective, science stands as both a symbol of progress and a chief cause.

The champions of the Enlightenment had their detractors. Not everyone in the eighteenth century was an enthusiast of the Enlightenment. Critics disputed the equation that science equals truth and that the modern era points to inevitable human progress. The Enlightenment provoked a counter-Enlightenment. As in the former movement, the latter exhibited a great deal of diversity. "Romantic" critics such as the English poets Wordsworth and Coleridge championed intuition and affect, spiritual longings and the unity of nature, humanity and God.[4] The great "conservative" social critics Edmund Burke and Joseph de Maistre insisted on a social ideal that valued religion and tradition.[5] Revolutionary critics such as the French radicals Gracchus Babeuf and Charles Fourier defended egalitarian values that were tied to a pastoral, agrarian social ideal.[6] Common to these varied strains of the counter-Enlightenment was a deep hostility towards economic individualism, the secularization of culture, the scientization of knowledge, and the doctrine of social progress.

As the new spirit of freedom and social change swept through Europe and the United States, the ideological conflicts among Enlighteners, and between them and counter-Enlightenment critics, intensified and moved into the center of public life. The question of the meaning and social significance of science was at the heart of these cultural clashes.

Successors to the Enlightenment science of society inherited the Enlighteners' faith in science. They absorbed the great moral hopes that were attached to science. However, the heirs to the Enlightenment could hardly ignore the sobering realities of the excesses of the French Revolution or the many critics of Enlightenment secular humanism. At the start of the nineteenth century, it was the clash over ideas about science, society, and historical change that underlay the grand visions of the classics.

AUGUSTE COMTE

Comte lived in a period of extreme social upheaval in France. The high hopes many Europeans had of the French Revolution (1789) were dashed by its recourse to political terrorism and the failure to realize a new France. However, the ardent faith in liberty and progress inspired by the Age of Enlightenment did not disappear in the aftermath of the revolution. Comte shared in this Enlightenment faith. Like many of his contemporaries, he was dismayed by the restoration of monarchical rule in the early decades of the nineteenth century. Comte's social thought was formed in a France that was torn between Enlighteners and revolutionaries on the one side and supporters of empire and monarchy on the other.

Comte observed that France in the first half of the nineteenth century was in a state of social crisis. The Enlightenment and the French Revolution went a long way towards undermining the old France, that had been dominated by the church and a wealthy, landed aristocracy. The revolution failed, however, to create a new France. The Enlighteners, especially the more radical elements who inspired the revolution (e.g., Rousseau and Robespierre) were right to expose the oppressive state of the peasants and laborers, and criticize the corruption of the church and aristocracy. Unfortunately, their utopian social hopes could not be translated into a realistic agenda of social reform. It was no accident that, once the revolutionaries had assumed power, their rule rapidly degenerated into fierce power struggles and violence, and brutal repression replaced reason and law. In this regard, Comte thought that the critics of the Enlightenment, mostly voices of conservative tradition and Catholic orthodoxy, were correct in criticizing the Enlightenment thinkers for failing to understand that social change has to be anchored in custom and tradition. However, these conservative critics voiced only one option: to defend the status quo against the chaos they anticipated being unleashed by the reforms of the Enlighteners. Comte did not think that this position was defensible in light of the far-reaching social changes that had occurred in the previous century. France was a nation on its way to becoming a modern industrial society; this was irreversible and a sign of social progress.

Auguste Comte (1798–1857) was born in Montpellier, France. Comte's ideas were formed during the upheavals of the French Revolution and counter-revolutions. It's not surprising then that Comte was especially concerned with how societies establish social order and how they change. Comte argued that societies evolved through a series of three stages. The driving force of social evolution was the ruling ideas of the time. The final stage, which Comte termed the positive stage, was guided by scientific knowledge. Comte imagined sociology to be the ultimate fruit of the age of science. Sociology would reveal the laws of social life, making possible great social progress.

France was in a transitional social state. The old France was dying. Restoring the monarchy and the power of the church and aristocracy would only incite social chaos. Change was inevitable. Yet the new France imagined by the revolutionaries – a society of universal rights, equality, mass democracy, and secular humanism – was an invitation to social disorder. Contrary to the faith of the Enlighteners, a new society could not be fashioned according to the dictates of a reason that legislates the laws and institutions of an ideal social order. Society is not a mere slab of clay that we can mold to our desires. Comte was convinced that it was this rationalist faith of the Enlighteners that resulted in the failure of the French Revolution. Social change must be anchored in the living traditions of a nation's past and in an understanding of the principles of social order.

France was in a social crisis; it was polarized between advocates of radical change and defenders of a social order in decline. This made for a remarkably unstable social condition, as was manifest in the flip-flop in nineteenth-century France between republic, empire, and monarchy. Comte himself lived through seven different political regimes, from short-lived republican governments to restored monarchs and a Napoleonic empire. The social unrest was not just political; France was undergoing intensive industrialization, which created enormous social strains in a still largely agrarian society. The clerical and aristocratic ruling elite was being challenged by a powerful stratum of industrialists and bankers who were, in turn, threatened by discontented peasants, laborers, and craftsmen.

Comte wished to find a way out of this social impasse. He proposed a program of social reform that offered a social vision of France marching to the tune of social progress. The vehicle for this social reformation was to be a new science of society, which Comte called sociology.

Comte's scientific vision of sociology

Comte felt that the current era was a turning point in history. Whereas some Europeans interpreted the current social crisis as symbolizing social decline, Comte understood it as marking the birth pangs of a new era of unlimited human progress.

In essence, the current crisis was cultural. France, like all of Europe, was in the throes of a great cultural change that would eventually shape the destiny of all societies. Humanity was about to undergo a great transformation in its cultural foundations. The change involved a shift from a religious and metaphysical to a scientific world view. The cultural collision between the religious, metaphysical, and scientific world views had reached a climax in nineteenth-century France. Underlying Comte's perspective on the cultural crisis of Europe was a grand vision of the evolution of the human mind.

Comte thought that he had discovered a law governing the progress of the human mind. According to the so-called Law of the Three Stages, the human mind passes through three stages of thought: the theological, the metaphysical, and the positive. In the first stage, the theological, the human mind explains the origin and ultimate purpose of phenomena by reference to supernatural entities (e.g., spirits, divine beings, gods). A Christian world view would exemplify the theological stage. In the second stage, the metaphysical, human thought continues its search to uncover the first and final cause of things but appeals to essences or abstract forces (e.g., human reason or natural law). The philosophical systems of Descartes or Leibniz illustrate the metaphysical stage. The final stage, the positive, abandons the search for essences, first causes, and final purposes in favor of explaining the interconnection and succession of facts. Philosophical or religious speculation gives way to the discovery of natural and social laws. The positive stage represents the era of the modern sciences.

Comte is not simply sketching a series of changes, but a progressive historical development. The sciences represent not just a successor world view to religion and philosophy, but a breakthrough from speculation to truth. As an heir to the Enlightenment, Comte believed that the discovery of a language of truth is a turning point for humanity. Truth will liberate humankind from the web of ignorance, illusion, and error that has slowed, sometimes to a halt, the march of human progress.

Comte believed that each science passes through these three stages, but at varying rates depending on their degree of difficulty. The most general and simple of the sciences precede those that are more concrete and complex. Thus, Comte proposed that mathematics and astronomy would reach the positive stage prior to physics, chemistry, biology and sociology. In other words, Comte thought that humankind would first be able to free itself from religious and metaphysical ideas in matters remote from human considerations (e.g., mathematics or astronomy or physics). Once our ideas about nature were freed from religious and metaphysical beliefs, it would be possible to apply a scientific approach to human affairs. Accordingly, sociology, as the study of humanity, is the last science to develop because it is the most complex and concrete.

Sociology is the queen of the sciences. Unlike the other sciences, which analyze one narrow segment of life, sociology integrates all knowledge about humanity. Comte relied upon biology for his guiding social imagery and language. Society is visualized in organic terms, as a system whose "needs" are met by the normal operation of its functionally interdependent parts. Like any organism, society grows in a slow, continuous, and linear way, exhibiting a movement from simplicity to complexity and from potentiality to self-realization. Sociology was to be *the* science of society; its aim was to discover the universal laws that govern the organization and evolution of humanity.

Comte conceived of sociology as consisting of two parts: statics and dynamics. Social statics analyzes the structure and functioning of society; it describes the elementary parts of society, their functions and interconnections. Social dynamics investigates the evolution of humanity; it reveals the source of change and its stages and direction. Comte's aim was nothing less than to sketch the universal laws of social statics and dynamics, a project that he began in *The Course of Positive Philosophy* (1830–42) and completed in the *System of Positive Polity* (1851–4).[7]

Comte's sociology began with the premise that every science has its own separate subject matter. Departing from the conventional wisdom of many Enlightenment thinkers, Comte thought that it was a mistake to conceive of society as a collection of individuals. Instead, he believed that society consisted of social interaction, social rules, and institutions that are independent of the psychology of individuals. Social statistics investigate the structure and functioning of this social world. The chief problem is to explain social order, especially in modern societies. Given the emphasis upon individualism promoted by an industrializing society, how is self-interest curbed to permit social stability? Comte emphasized the role of the family, government, and religion in explaining social order. The family provides the initial and sustaining formative moral milieu for the individual; the idea of the self-sufficient, independent individual is a myth, as we are born and formed in families. Where the moral influence of the family comes up short, religion compensates. Religion furnishes a common creed which strengthens our social bonds and loyalties to social and political institutions.

Comte introduced the idea of social dynamics to explain the laws of social evolution. He elaborated a grand vision of the progression of humanity towards perfection. Comte envisioned humanity as passing through fixed, invariable stages, each successive one representing a higher level of human development. Although all societies would pass through the same stages simultaneously if there were no interferences, accidents (e.g., natural disasters) result in social change proceeding at different rates. Thus, the differences among societies that we can observe across history are interpreted as exhibiting all of the successive stages of human evolution. From this perspective, we can locate all societies somewhere on a hierarchy of human development, from lower to higher social types.

Social change is viewed as a linear, directional progressive process. Humanity is moving towards the same goal or endpoint, even if at varying rates. Driving social development is the evolution of the human mind. Changes in social and political institutions are correlated with cultural evolution. Thus, the theological stage is dominated by priests and military institutions. In the metaphysical stage, which corresponds roughly to the early modern period (1300–1700), it is lawyers and clergy who govern society. Finally, the positive stage, an era just coming into view in European societies, will witness the growing social authority of industrialists and scientists. Comte held that all humanity evolves through these three social stages; history culminates in the positive age.

Comte believed that human evolution has reached a turning point. The crisis in France and Europe was the result of a great collision between these three social systems and world views. The Enlighteners represented the metaphysical stage, although some strains of Enlightenment thought were indicative of the positive era; their arch enemies, the conservative defenders of the status quo, exemplified the theological stage. In the breakthroughs in science over the past few centuries, Comte detected the ascending spirit of the positive stage. Comte's sociology was intended to provide a diagnosis of the contemporary crisis and to suggest a remedy: the consolidation of the "positive" or industrial-scientific order. According to the Law of the Three Stages, social evolution points irreversibly towards the positive era. In his opinion, the destiny of France was to serve as the midwife to the birth of the new world order. And, as we will see, Comte was equally convinced that it was to be the fate of sociology to show France its appointed historical role.

Comte's heavenly vision of sociology

There is a paradox at the heart of Comte's sociology. His scientific vision of sociology was animated by a moral passion that eventually came to dominate his work. Comte frankly admitted the moral motivations of his science. He wished to provide humankind with an understanding of the laws of humanity which would serve as moral guidelines for social reform. If sociology could reveal the underlying principles of social order and change, true knowledge could guide social reform.

Like many Enlightenment social thinkers, Comte thought that the role of science in producing social truths could be separated from its moral role. However, Comte himself failed to maintain the separation of science and morality.

Comte imagined sociology as resting on a firm bedrock of observation and facts, even though he held that facts are made coherent by a broad intellectual perspective. Comte never clarified, though, the origins of these interpretive perspectives or their relation to "facts." If the theories that guide observation originate in a particular cultural world view, how can we be sure that they are not biased by the values and social interests of their social origin? If theories guide the selection and interconnection of facts, how can we avoid the suspicion that theorists select and interpret facts in ways that confirm the theory? Consider Comte's own social ideas. The guiding ideas of his sociology, for example, assumptions about the uniformity of human nature, the continuous, linear, directional process of history, and the progress of humanity, are little more than leaps of faith akin to a religious and philosophical cast of mind. What facts could possibly confirm or disconfirm a theory as grand as the Law of the Three Stages? How can we avoid the conclusion that Comte's evolutionary theory betrays the prejudices of a modern Western, largely secular man inspired by a faith in progress? The entire non-Western world is reduced by Comte to little more than a bit player in human history. Is this not the conceit of the modern West? Comte's vision of humanity is deeply millennial, exhibiting standard Judeo-Christian themes, most impressively the anticipation of a period of world peace and human perfection.

In the end, Comte's moral vision bursts through his rhetoric of science. A central aim of Comte's sociology was to lay bare not only the principles of social order and change but provide a blueprint of the good society. Whereas his first major work, *The Course of Positive Philosophy*, intended to uncover the universal laws of social statics and dynamics, his later work, a *System of Positive Polity*, addressed the moral role of sociology. In the fully realized positive society, industrialists would share power with scientists. Whereas the former would have priority in the mundane sphere of institutional functioning, the latter would govern spiritual matters. The sciences would furnish the core beliefs of the new society. The creators of science such as Galileo, Newton, and Comte himself would be deified; cults would form around these sacred figures. In particular, to the extent that sociology provided a unifying social vision, sociologists would become the high priests of the positive society! Sociologists would furnish the moral guidelines of the positive society, and specify the duties, obligations, and social roles that have to be fulfilled in order for social harmony to prevail.

Twentieth-century sociologists inspired by the scientific vision have been embarrassed by Comte's wish to make science into a religion. They have tried to dismiss this prophetic, religious impulse as either a reflection of his gradual mental deterioration or at least as separable from his scientific achievements. But Comte was, at heart, a visionary sociologist. His moral vision was built into the very core of his sociology.

Suggested Readings

Peter Gay, *The Enlightenment* (New York: W. W. Norton, 1977).
Robert Nesbit, *The Sociological Tradition* (New York: Basic Books, 1966).
Mary Pickering, *Auguste Comte* (Cambridge: Cambridge University Press, 1993).
Ken Tucker, *Classical Social Theory* (Cambridge, MA: Blackwell, 2001).

References

1   Baron de Montesquieu, *The Spirit of the Laws* (New York: Hafner Press, 1975).
2   Marquis de Condorcet, *Sketch for a Historical Picture of the Progress of the Human Mind* (New York: Noonday Press, 1955).
3   Montesquieu, The Spirit of the Laws, p. lxvii.
4   Regarding the romantic critique of the Enlightenment, the reader should consult M. H. Abrams, *Natural Supernaturalism* (New York: Norton, 1971); Charles Taylor, *Hegel* (Cambridge: Cambridge University Press, 1979); and Alvin Gouldner, "Romanticism and Classicism: Deep Structures in Social Science," in *For Sociology* (New York: Basic Books, 1973).
5   For an overview of conservative social thought in this period, see Karl Mannheim, "Conservative Thought," in *From Karl Mannheim*, ed. J. Wolff (New York: Oxford University Press, 1971) and Robert Nesbet, *The Sociological Tradition* (New York: Basic Books, 1966).
6   Regarding the revolutionary critics of the Enlightenment, see G. H. Cole, *Socialist Thought* (New York: St. Martin's Press, 1962); J. L. Talmon, *The Rise of Totalitarian Democracy* (Boston: Beacon Press, 1952); and George Lichtheim, *The Origins of Socialism* (New York: Praeger, 1969).
7   Auguste Comte, *The Course of Positive Philosophy*, 3 vols. (London: George Bell and Sons, 1876 [1830–42]); *System of Positive Polity*, 4 vols. (New York: Burt Franklin, 1875 [1851–4]).

2

The Revolutionary Theory of Karl Marx

Marx never met Comte. His few belittling comments on his somewhat older contemporary suggest that he thought of Comte as a bit of a crank. In truth, Marx himself was reportedly quite quarrelsome and irascible, especially with intellectual competitors. And, in the first half of the nineteenth century, Comte had made a name for himself among educated Europeans, while Marx, for most of his life, labored in relative obscurity. In fact, Comte and Marx had much in common, in particular, a hope that a new era was dawning that would liberate humanity. Like Comte, Marx ardently believed that social knowledge had a key role to play in creating this new age.

THE UNITY OF THEORY AND PRACTICE

Comte developed his social ideas in the context of postrevolutionary France. France was divided between a tradition of Enlightenment imbued with millenarian hopes of humankind's capacity to make the future according to its own will, and social groups that steadfastly defended the authority of the past. Underlying this clash of world views was a conflict between a nascent middle class and an established landed nobility and clerical elite. Comte's sociology aimed to integrate these antagonistic elements by proclaiming that progress can be achieved only through gradual, orderly change that is respectful of the past. This was a message that had special appeal to the middle classes, who feared both a restoration of the old regime and a revolution from below.

Germany did not experience a revolution comparable to the revolutions in France or the American colonies. Moreover, whereas France was viewed by many educated Germans as a dynamic, even if intensely conflicted, society, Germany seemed static and backward by comparison. Politically, Germany was divided into many independent states. German unification came in 1871 and only as a result of the military and economic power of Prussia and the diplomatic skill of Bismarck. Economically,

Contested Knowledge: Social Theory Today, Fifth Edition. Steven Seidman.
© 2013 John Wiley & Sons, Ltd. Published 2013 by John Wiley & Sons, Ltd.

Karl Marx (1818–83) was born in Trier, Germany. He was educated at the University of Bonn and later at the University of Berlin where he studied philosophy, law, and history. Marx left Germany for France in 1843. In 1847, the socialist group "The League of the Just" commissioned Marx and his longtime collaborator, Frederick Engels, to write "The Communist Manifesto." In the Manifesto, Marx identified the class struggle as the motor of history; he predicted the end of capitalism through a revolution of the working class. In a socialist society, there would be individual differences but not great social inequalities. Marx eventually relocated to London where he wrote *Capital* and became active in the International Working Men's Association.

Germany was largely agrarian, with spurts of industrialization frustrated by government regulation and an anti-business culture. Socially, Germany was dominated by a highly conservative landed nobility that permitted little freedom and social innovation. Given this view of Germany's social backwardness in relation to France, it was not surprising that the German middle classes were politically weak and admiring of the martial, paternalistic spirit of the landed aristocracy.

Germany was, however, influenced by the new spirit of change in Europe. The ideas of the Enlightenment took hold in Germany, especially in educated circles. Many German cultural and political elites took over the Enlightenment spirit of progress. They did so, however, in a society where there were few real prospects of social change. Unlike in France and England, where the middle class played a crucial role in promoting liberal social change, the German middle classes aspired to imitate, rather than to overthrow, the aristocracy. Lacking an identifiable social group that could bring about social change, many progressive Germans assumed that the real forces of change were intellectuals and their ideas. Instead of approaching society as an arena of social conflict, German intellectuals imagined the collision of world views as the real source of social change. History was understood as the story of the development of reason through the clash of ideas.

As a child of the Enlightenment, Marx came of age in a Germany largely hostile to change. There was no viable middle-class movement motivated to challenge the social status quo. Discontent among peasants and laborers was unorganized in the first decades of the nineteenth century. In his early writings, Marx raised the following questions: What are the prospects for social change in Germany? What social forces are positioned to bring about change? What role does social theory or science have in promoting social change? Finally, what kinds of changes are possible and desirable? In addressing these questions, Marx often went beyond liberal social ideas towards a revolutionary perspective.

As he surveyed the German political scene, Marx noted two social groups that were interested in bringing about social change: liberal reformers and idealist philosophers.

Liberal reformers believed that change required piecemeal administrative and legislative actions. Science might be useful in analyzing particular problems or supplying information about specific issues, but, these reformers believed, there was no need for a theory of society or history. Marx disagreed. He argued that, in order to effect change, it is necessary to understand the social forces – institutions, cultural traditions, social groups – that stand in its way. This requires a theoretical perspective. Moreover, Marx thought that German traditions that emphasize a religious duty to submit to authority obstructed change. He thought that social change required that this religious culture must be weakened to allow for new ideas favoring social progress. Social criticism has a pivotal role to play in undermining the authority of this anti-Enlightenment cultural tradition.

Marx's sympathy was with the idealist philosophers. In fact, the young Marx was a member of a group of brilliant theorists who were inspired by the German idealist tradition. They drew on the philosophy of Kant and Hegel to articulate their own vision of enlightened change. Their aim was to replace German religious culture by a secular–humanistic culture that promoted roughly speaking liberal ideas. The way to bring about cultural change was to challenge the truth of the religious underpinnings of German national culture and substitute a secular humanistic philosophy.

Marx was a member of the idealist circle, but he was impatient with the limits of their vision. The critical philosophers, Marx argued, were right to insist upon the importance of theory to change consciousness. They were naive, though, to think that simply appealing to the truth of their ideas would transform German culture. Marx proposed what was to become a controversial tenet of his thought: Individuals do not act on ideas primarily because they are true but on the basis of their self-interest. Ideas may shape our actions, but our social interests determine which ideas we adopt. Moreover, our social interests are determined by our social position, in particular, our class status. It follows that, if ideas are rooted in class structure, only by changing this social condition can there be cultural change. Criticizing culture – the realm of ideas, values, meanings – is important, but one must also criticize the social conditions that produce and sustain this culture. Marx was moving away from an idealist philosophy preoccupied with intellectual critique; he was gravitating toward a "materialist" perspective that viewed the real source of social change in the clash of social interests arising from social inequities.

Marx also took issue with the way the idealists imagined that their critical ideas would change society. Idealists assumed that the power of reason to discover the truth was sufficient to bring about change. Once truths were revealed, the public would, they thought, be moved to act by these ideas. Marx held that it is social interests, not abstract theories, that motivate behavior. People believe what their self-interest dictates. This does not mean that theory has no role to play in promoting social change. Quite the contrary: theory can become a force of change only if it appeals to individuals whose self-interest is to change social conditions. In other words, if theory expresses the social interests of individuals who are socially positioned as oppressed, it can become a force of change. To the extent that individuals take over a theoretical perspective as their own, to that extent they understand the world through the lens of that theory. And, "theory ... becomes a material force once it has gripped the masses."[1] Theory can help transform a mass of isolated individuals into a group with a common political identity and agenda. To take a contemporary example, as women adopted a feminist perspective in the 1970s, their understanding of themselves, men, and society was dramatically altered; these women were transformed into a social and ideological bloc of feminists mobilized for political action.

Although Marx had high expectations of the role of theory as a political force, he did not believe that theory by itself could bring about change. Theory could be a force for change only if there existed individuals who, because of their class position, had an interest in changing society. It was one's class status – for example, as wage laborers – that created the potential for social discontent and an interest in changing social conditions. Theory by itself could not create the social conditions of discontent nor the interest in change. It could, however, give voice to social discontents and direct its political expression. If the social conditions conducive to change were absent, theory would be powerless. Marx's point seems to be that, while it is individuals who create change, this occurs only when they are propelled by self-interest which, in turn, depends on underlying social conditions of inequality. Individuals who are socially disadvantaged will have an interest in social change. Theory cannot create the underlying conditions ripe for change or the interest in change, but it can make individuals aware that their discontent is social in origin and that change can come about only through political struggle.

Marx saw few prospects for substantial social change in Germany's near future. However, he was aware of the big changes that were happening throughout Europe. While industrialization was slow in Germany, in France, Britain, America, Belgium, and Spain, the appearance of factories, the spread of commerce, and the emergence of new banking and financial institutions were transforming the social landscape. Moreover, accompanying industrialization were giant steps towards secularization (the separation of state and church) and democratization (e.g., the rise of political parties, constitutional governments, the extension of civil and political rights). Marx viewed these changes positively. While he believed that the middle classes were the driving force of the initial phase of modernization, Marx was convinced that they would oppose broad social change. His stint as a journalist in the early 1840s and his subsequent stay in Paris from 1843 to 1845 exposed him to the ruthless treatment of peasants and laborers by capitalists who, fearing social rebellion from below, often aligned themselves with the aristocratic old guard. In Paris, he became aware of the centrality of the conflicts between capitalists and laborers as he read the new writings of British and French political economists and met with socialists and radical workers. Gradually, Marx would see in the laboring class the vehicle to transform Germany, Europe, and indeed humanity.

Marx never gave up his Enlightenment faith in the coming of a new era. He did, though, abandon his youthful idealist philosophy with its faith in the power of reason to change the world. He gradually developed an original theoretical perspective whose aim was to provide an understanding of present-day society for the purpose of social revolution. The agents of change were not the middle classes, a group that was not only weak in Germany but had already showed its true colors in its ruthless oppression of peasants and laborers. The true carriers of revolution were to be the working classes, the mass of laborers whose poverty, insecurity, and degradation would propel them to social rebellion. Marx intended to wed his new science of society, which he called "historical materialism," with oppressed laborers to create a revolutionary ferment powerful enough to liberate humanity.

HISTORICAL MATERIALISM: A REVOLUTIONARY SCIENCE

Marx's growing political radicalism went hand in hand with his turn to social theory. As we have seen, Marx insisted that an agenda for social change must rely upon a theoretical perspective that highlights the social sources of political conflict and the groups likely to bring about change. Drawing on the writings of British and French political economists and historians, Marx had already come to the conclusion that the idealist philosophy needed to give way to a "materialist" social theory, i.e., a theory that analyzed the political economy of society. Throughout the 1840s, Marx sketched what a critical social theory anchored in political economy might look like.

In *The German Ideology*, Marx, along with his friend and collaborator, Engels, had his final intellectual reckoning with the idealist philosophy.[2] Marx and Engels aimed to shift the focus of social criticism from the analysis of consciousness and the evolution of ideas to that of the development of social institutions and social conflicts.

The German idealists held that what is unique about humans is that we have the capacity to reason and think. Although many idealists focused primarily on the nature of human consciousness or the structure of reason, they did outline a social perspective. They held that human thought produces beliefs, values, and norms. Every society is said to have its own unique world views, values, standards of truth, rightness, beauty, and its own social ideals. Culture was the dynamic core of society. The cultural system shapes the structure of society. The evolution of society reflects the evolution of its culture. It follows that the key to analyzing society lies in understanding its culture. The major social conflicts involve a clash of ideas. History is understood as the evolution of the mind towards higher levels of intellectual and social advancement.

Marx bought into more of idealism than he cared to admit. For example, he borrowed from idealists a view of society as a contradictory organic whole which evolves through stages of development. Yet he was so intent on breaking from the idealists that he frequently stated his position in extreme terms, a strategy that has made Marx an easy target of criticism.

Marx acknowledged that humans are "rational" in that we form thoughts that have varying levels of coherence and consistency. However, it is a mistake to take our deliberate, reasoning capacities as the essence of what it means to be human. The idealist premise ignores one crucial fact: The human species is a part of nature. Our conscious, rational life presupposes our physical, material existence. Humans are capable of a conscious, reasoning life but only if we first maintain ourselves as natural beings with bodies and real physical needs. Idealists mistakenly abstract our conscious, thinking life from our material life. Humans are a part of nature; our conscious lives reside in our bodies; material neediness and want is our destiny. Before we can be in a position to reason and create culture, we must maintain ourselves as natural beings. The reproduction of material life precedes the production of culture.

Humans are not self-maintaining; our bodies do not produce the resources they need to reproduce. The natural environment, moreover, does not provide us with what we need to live. Humans must not only look to nature to survive but must alter it in order to satisfy our bodily needs. In other words, humans do not simply live off nature but transform it. The activity by means of which we maintain this interchange with the natural environment Marx calls, somewhat ambiguously, labor or productive activity. Moreover, as we transform the natural environment to survive, we shape our own human nature. It is precisely the fact that humans make their own nature (e.g., our needs, wants, desires, and consciousness) through their laboring practices that Marx takes to be truly unique to humankind. It follows that human consciousness and its products – culture – should be grasped in relation to our material productive life.

Underlying Marx's concept of human nature is a powerful Enlightenment secular–humanistic vision. Humankind creates its own nature through its own actions. We alone have the potential to purposefully fashion our lives. The fate of humanity is in our own hands, not dictated by God or the laws of nature. Marx believed, however, that throughout history humans have not shaped their fate in a purposeful, rational way. Quite the contrary: the history of humanity reveals a sad tale of humankind submitting to the control of the very forces it has created. As a man of the Enlightenment, Marx hopes that this can change. Indeed, Marx enlists science to provide humanity with the vision and the instrument to allow us to seize control of our destiny. The tale of human sorrow is about to turn into a story of hope and wonder, but, to understand Marx's prophetic role, we must grasp the rudiments of his science of society.

The starting point of a theory of society should be the labor or productive activity of a society. Assuming, as Marx seems to, that productive activity means economic labor or paid (in kind or money) labor, social analysis should initially focus on the dominant means of economic production of a society. In other words, why does a particular society organize its economic labor or its means of production (land, raw material, technology, human labor power) the way it does? Marx discounts geographical and technological explanations since such factors are unable to account for social variations in socioeconomic systems. What makes Marx an important social theorist is his social explanation: class dynamics shape the organization of socioeconomic life, which, in turn, determines the structure and direction of the whole society. This is, at bottom, the core of historical materialism.

Marx proposed a class theory of society. As he declared in "The Communist Manifesto": "The history of all hitherto existing society is the history of class struggles. Freeman and slave, patrician and plebeian, lord and serf, guildmaster and journeyman, in a word, oppressor and oppressed, stood in opposition to one another."[3] All societies, past and present, have been divided between individuals who own and control the "means of production" (i.e., raw materials, technology, and money or the resources to hire or buy labor) and individuals who own only their capacity to labor. In short, all societies have been stratified, roughly speaking, between a propertied and a laboring class. Except for periods of social revolution, the propertied class has had more power due to its economic resources. Accordingly, it has been able to shape to a considerable degree the organization of labor, i.e., what is produced, how, and who does what. Most importantly, the propertied class has the power to control the distribution of wealth in society.

What makes the propertied class a key social force is that it is able to translate its immense economic power into control over political, cultural, and social institutions. For example, its wealth, considerable leisure time, organizational skills, education, and social connections give it the upper hand in struggles to control the government. These same resources allow the propertied class to take control over cultural institutions (e.g., schools, the church, and mass media) and to shape what ideas have authority and social influence. "The class which has the means of material production at its disposal, consequently, also controls the means of mental production, so that … the ruling ideas are nothing more than the ideal expression of the dominant [social class]."[4] The economic, political, and cultural power of the propertied class is directed to promoting its social interests and protecting the basis of its power, i.e., private property. In a word, the propertied class becomes a ruling class shaping the whole society in its own image.

Marx was convinced that the power of the ruling class is never total, and its efforts to exert complete control over society fail. Not only are there divisions within the ruling class (e.g., different segments of the propertied class may clash) but, more importantly, the mass of laborers do not meekly submit to social rule from above. Despite efforts by the ruling class to impose their own rule on the whole society, segments of the working class develop their own culture which expresses their class interests. Antagonistic interests lead to class conflict. The propertied ruling class is interested in a cheap, insecure, and docile labor force; it wishes to preserve its social privileges and power by maintaining the social status quo. In contrast, the interests of the laborers are to raise their wages, improve their work and nonwork conditions, and enhance their role in society. Beneath the surface calm of all societies are deep contradictions that inevitably surface in battles over work conditions and at times erupt into open class warfare. This signals a period of transition to a new society. Human history unfolds as a series of epochal changes driven by the suffering and struggle of oppressed social classes.

Marx's vision of history has a definite Enlightenment cast. History is patterned and meaningful; the succession of individual societies that pass in and out of existence reveals a story of human progress. Marx's stage theory of history begins with the "primitive tribal community," to be succeeded by the "ancient communal type," the "feudal type," and finally the "capitalist-bourgeois" society, which is destined to give way to "communism." These changes speak to the progress of humanity from a state of simplicity and underdevelopment in which human affairs are governed by nonrational forces (e.g., myth, religion, class conflict) to a state of complexity, individualism, and cultural development. In the communist stage, humanity will be governed by conscious choice and reason; freedom will coincide with moral order and social harmony. The vehicle to inaugurate this new era of freedom was the working class. Inspired by the high ideals of liberal society, yet driven to revolt by its massive deprivation, the working class would smash the iron grip of capitalism while preserving its marvels of technological and social progress. Marx envisioned a cataclysmic worldwide revolution bringing forth a new era of communist freedom.

DAS KAPITAL: THE LOGIC OF SOCIAL REVOLUTION

During his stay in Paris (1843–5), Marx had arrived at the conclusion that the working class would be the agent of revolution in the era of modern capitalism. He was convinced that this revolution would be the last major historical change. It would bring to an end the succession of class-based revolutions that have been at the center of history. The working class, unlike the bourgeois-capitalist class or the feudal nobility before it, would not set itself up as a new ruling class. The working class would be the first class in history to truly represent the interests of all humanity. The conflict between the working class and capitalists is seen as a struggle over the ultimate destiny of humanity; the triumph of the working class anticipated an era free of class division and gross social inequality.

In Marx's early writings, his vision of working-class revolution was presented as a conclusion of his science of society. Drawing on the writings of classical economists such as Adam Smith and David Ricardo, Marx pushed their liberal perspective on industrial capitalism in a radical direction. For example, in some notes that were posthumously published under the title of *The Economic and Philosophical Manuscripts of 1844*, Marx interpreted the division of labor as creating a class-structured society, rather than, according to the liberal economists, as providing the engine of social progress.[5] The immense wealth produced under capitalism, Marx argued, simultaneously created a rich capitalist class and extreme poverty and deprivation for the masses. Marx thought that the material and spiritual impoverishment of the laborers, in the context of a rich society inspired by the ideals of human liberty, would eventually incite them to revolt. However, by the mid-1850s, it was clear, even to Marx, that a working-class revolt was not imminent. Marx did not abandon his belief in social revolution. Rather, he assumed that social revolution would occur as a result of the very logic of capitalist development. Marx's humanistic vision of laborers rising up in revolt against social injustice gave way to a much more structural view of social revolution. Marx's search for the logic of social revolution lay at the very heart of his unfinished masterpiece, *Capital: A Critique of Political Economy*.[6]

Capital starts with an analysis of the commodity. In capitalist societies, wealth assumes the form of a vast production and circulation of commodities. A commodity is a good produced for the purpose of exchange. Accordingly, it has both a "use value" or a value by virtue of satisfying a need and an "exchange value" or a value at which it is exchanged or, to simplify, a price. The source of exchange value and its magnitude is the amount of time it takes, on average, to produce a commodity. For example, assuming that one hour of labor produces a value of $5, then an eight-hour workday would produce a value of $40. The so-called labor theory of value explains why different commodities are exchanged in different proportions or prices. If we pay $50 for shoes, it is because there is an equivalence of labor time represented in the $50 and in the shoes.

Capitalism is not the only commodity-producing society. It is, however, the only society that produces commodities for the purpose of making profit. Why else would an entrepreneur risk starting a business unless profit was anticipated? A central question for understanding capitalism is: Where does profit come from? Marx did not think it came from cheating the consumer by charging a higher price for the good than its actual value. Moreover, Marx rejected the view that profit came from the risk-taking decisions of the capitalist. Marx proposed that profit originates from the exploitation of the laborer by the capitalist.

To grasp Marx's view of profit as exploitation, it is helpful to see the world from the vantage point of the capitalist. A business is started with the intention of realizing a profit. To go into business, the capitalist must purchase the necessary means of production. A series of exchanges occur; the aspiring entrepreneur purchases raw materials and technology from other capitalists. The exchange is fair in that there is an equivalence between the value of the goods purchased and the money paid. A business does not function on raw material and technology alone; capitalists need human labor power to set the work process in motion. Interestingly, says Marx, labor power is for sale just like any other commodity. Laborers sell their ability to labor or "labor power" as the only commodity that they own. Its price or exchange value is, like that of all commodities, equal to the amount of time it takes, on average, to produce a living wage, i.e., to maintain human life from day to day. If it takes eight hours to produce a value of $50, which is sufficient to maintain the laborer for a day, then that is the cost of labor. Now, says Marx, when the capitalist and the laborer meet on the market, they enter into an ostensibly free and fair contractual agreement. The capitalist agrees to pay the laborer a wage equal to his/her exchange value for which, in return, the capitalist gets to use the laborer for an agreed-upon number of hours. Accordingly, our entrepreneur purchases not only raw materials and technology but enough labor power for the business to operate productively.

Viewed from the vantage point of these economic exchanges, capitalism seems to epitomize fairness and freedom. However, if we look at the exchange between the capitalist and the laborer from the latter's vantage point, its exploitive character is revealed. The laborer *must* sell his/her labor power in order to survive. It is true, though, that the capitalist pays the laborer a fair wage, i.e., a wage equal to the exchange value of labor power. In return for this wage, the laborer must work for the capitalist for the amount of time they agreed upon. But, what if the laborer produces a value for the capitalist in excess of the value paid to him or her in the form of a wage? This "discrepancy" or exploitation, as Marx calls it, is the origin of profit.

Let's say that a worker contracts with a capitalist to work ten hours for a fair wage of $50. During this work time, the worker creates a value of $60. Who gets the extra $10? The wage contract states only that the capitalist agrees to pay the worker a wage equal to the exchange value of labor power, not a wage equal to the amount of value created by the worker. So long as the capitalist pays the laborer the agreed-upon wage, whatever value the laborer creates belongs to the capitalist. The extra $10 belongs, fair and square, according to the wage contract, to the capitalist. But, you ask, why doesn't the laborer protest at this exploitation? From the laborer's point of view, it seems like he or she is getting paid for each hour worked. If the laborer works ten hours for a wage of $50, it appears that he or she is being paid $5 per hour. The laborer doesn't realize that, after eight hours, a value equal to her or his wage ($50) is created and that two additional hours is profit for the capitalist. The laborer doesn't perceive exploitation because this unpaid work time is obscured by the hourly wage system. Moreover, exploitation is concealed by the capitalist ideology which asserts that everyone gets paid for their work and that profit comes from the risks, hard work, and managerial skills of the capitalist. In contrast to the social surface of capitalist society with its apparent equal and just exchanges between free individuals, Marx argued that capitalism is founded upon class inequality and exploitation.

Initially, the mass of laborers do not see their own exploitation; they do not pierce through the capitalist ideology which asserts a society based on individual freedom, equality, and justice. Their social discontent is directed at machines that threaten to replace them or at other workers who compete for their jobs. Gradually, the mass of laborers is transformed into a working-class political movement advocating the overthrow of capitalism. How does this social transformation of the workers, and of capitalism, transpire?

The nature of capitalism is to realize profit. Capitalists have no choice. If one starts a business, regardless of personal motives or values, a profit must be made. No profit, no livelihood. Profit-making must, moreover, permit economic modernization. If capitalists don't make enough profit to modernize the work process, they risk losing a share of the market to the competition. The logic of capitalism demands that individual entrepreneurs make profits and continuously modernize, or else face economic and social failure. This same logic has grave social and political implications for workers. Economic modernization means not only devising new and better products, but making the labor process more efficient, keeping wages down, and maximizing worker productivity. In other words, just as the laborers must sell their capacity to labor to capitalists to survive, capitalists have little choice but to exploit and oppress laborers.

Marx does not criticize the capitalists for being greedy or lacking social conscience. The logic of capitalism forces them to make a profit, modernize, and exploit labor. *Capital* is a story of a social system that controls the lives of all individuals. Moreover, Marx is not saying that the system is without redeeming value. Marx had great admiration for the capacity of capitalism to produce wealth, stimulate technological, social, and cultural innovation, and create the conditions for democracy. Capitalism creates social conditions that make human freedom possible, but, at the same time, it undermines that potential by creating gross social inequalities; only the business class truly benefits from capitalism's remarkable productivity. In order for everyone to prosper and be free, capitalism must be changed. Marx thought he had discovered the logic of social revolution in the very dynamics of capitalism.

Driven by competition, capitalists are compelled to modernize. While this permits the survival of individual entrepreneurs, it also signals the beginning of the end of capitalism. Economic modernization contributes to transforming the mass of laborers into a politically aware working class. Rationalizing the workplace further disempowers workers; it often results in depressed wages, worker insecurity as machines replace workers, and extreme specialization, which strips work of all its skill and imagination. In a word, every effort by capitalists to increase profits intensifies worker degradation and discontent. The progress of capitalism and the immense social opportunities for individual development it creates are experienced by workers as a kind of social and spiritual impoverishment. Their work lives are bereft of freedom and creativity; their families are often torn apart as both parents and children work; their communities are devastated by poverty and social instability. The visible disparity between the lives of capitalists and the stagnation or worse of the laborers awakens their political will. Initially, their struggles are focused on work conditions, the length of the workday, wages, or child labor laws. Gradually, they come to view the source of their discontent in the very nature of capitalism.

Social revolution does not occur, however, until the system offers no other choice to workers. The stimulus to this ultimate act of revolt is a series of socioeconomic crises that escalate in intensity and rapidity. Regular cycles of depression and recession expose the irrational nature of capitalism. Capitalists modernize to survive. This dynamic means leaps in productivity but also recurring social crises. Consumption must expand to absorb the increased flow of goods. This spurs the internationalization of capitalism and the widening of the domestic market by commercializing hitherto noncommercial sectors (e.g., leisure, recreation, sports). Unfortunately, no matter how fast new markets are created, the rapid shifts in capital investment inevitably give rise to periodic gluts in the market, massive layoffs, and far-reaching social dislocations. For example, computer sales get hot; capital is poured into computer production without any idea of what the market will hold; at some point, production will exceed demand; computer production slows or halts; workers are laid off; families and communities suffer. Marx maintained that regular economic crises undermine workers' faith in the system as their lives and those of their families deteriorate.

Laborers become political agents in order to survive and preserve their human dignity. Because they work and live together, and because they share similar interests and ideas, their discontent coalesces into a unified working-class consciousness. Attacks against machinery and capitalists give way to union organizing and the formation of socialist or labor political parties. Inspired by a socialist ideology that speaks to their experience, the working class directs its political activity towards socializing the economy and democratizing social institutions. The socialist revolution, peacefully accomplished wherever the ballot box is accessible but violent if it is not, is potentially of world historical significance. It may signal a shift from a social condition where individuals are controlled by forces beyond their control to a society where we can purposefully shape our historical destiny.

TENSIONS BETWEEN A SCIENTIFIC AND MORAL VISION

The chief aim of Marx's theorizing was to change society. As he stated in his "Theses on Feuerbach," "philosophers have only interpreted the world, the point is to change it."[7] Social change is always about moral values and social ideals. Marx offered a radical Enlightenment social vision. He took liberal ideals of individualism, liberty, and equality seriously; he was convinced that Western capitalist societies realized these ideals but in partial, incomplete ways. For example, capitalist society cherished individualism, but, as a class-based society, it extended real freedom only to the business class. Similarly, legal equality was an advance over a feudal system of legalized social hierarchy, but it left intact gross social inequalities. Marx wished to realize yet also transform the social dreams of liberalism; this required the overthrow of capitalism. Marx championed the working class as carriers of this revolutionary moral hope.

Social theory and social change went hand in hand. Science not only provided an understanding of society but could become an actual force in changing society. Marx believed that science could become a force of change if its social understandings were accepted by individuals and groups interested in change. A social scientific perspective might serve as the lens through which individuals viewed their personal and social reality. As such, theory can politicize people. This was the belief that inspired *Capital*. Marx thought that the mass of laborers had an interest in change. He intended *Capital* to become a lens through which laborers would view themselves as an exploited, oppressed social class. *Capital* provided a social explanation of worker discontent that targeted the system of capitalism as its source and socialist political practice as the remedy. *Capital* was intended to be a part of the moral and political struggles of the time.

Although Marx never denied the moral impulse behind his social theorizing, from the mid-1840s, he began to see himself as a scientist. For example, in *The German Ideology*, Marx claimed that his perspective on history was a breakthrough to a true science of society. In contrast to ideologists who offered biased, one-sided social ideas, Marx declared that historical materialism provided an objective under-standing of social reality. Marx was persuaded that the premises, basic concepts, and explanations of his social perspective were universally valid. Yet nowhere did he clarify the standards of truth that guided his judgment. Marx did offer some rationales for his claims, but they are, by and large, rather feeble. For example, his claim that human nature is not uniform and fixed but that humans make and remake their nature through their actions is asserted, not demonstrated. We can just as easily argue that human nature is constant and uniform though humans change their beliefs and values. Assumptions about human nature as fixed or changeable or good or bad are akin to religious or metaphysical beliefs. Similarly, Marx's claim that economic productive activity is more important than culture in structuring society is little more than a statement of faith or a strategic political claim. How would one know which is causally prior? Indeed, it is not at all clear that Marx's claim is coherent. Can there be produc-tive activity that is not already shaped by norms and beliefs? Finally, exactly how are we supposed to distinguish productive, laboring activity from symbolic, religious, domestic, or reproductive practices?

Marx's premises appear to be little more than beliefs, not obvious truths. This does not mean that his social ideas are fictitious or lack value. The usefulness of ideas and their truthfulness are not necessarily correlated. Ideas may be true but useless; they may be wrong but useful. If Marx intended to shape the political awareness of the laborers into a critical force through his social ideas, the "success" of his efforts should be judged by this practical standard, not by whether or not his ideas are true in some absolute sense. Unfortunately, Marx aspired to justify his social ideas solely on the grounds of their correspondence to the world "out there." This is unfortunate, not only because it was unnecessary and probably impossible, but because it has undesirable consequences. By defending his social and political ideas solely on the basis of their empirical truth, Marx avoided having to advance serious arguments defending the moral and political values that inform his social perspective. Marx simply invoked the laws of history and society to authorize his social values (e.g., socialism, democracy, and individualism).

Marx's critical attitude towards Western industrial societies did not extend to his faith in science and its power to liberate humanity. No less than his ideological opponents, Marx was a captive of the Enlightenment faith that science can reveal truths that are liberating. He saw himself as the Newton of social science. *Capital* was to be to the social sciences what Darwin's *On the Origin of Species* was to the natural sciences. Such grandiose claims have not been peculiar to Marx in the history of social science. Condorcet and Comte before Marx, and Spencer, Durkheim, and virtually every major twentieth-century theorist from Parsons to Habermas, have made similar auspicious announcements. The claim that a set of social ideas are scientific, rather than ideological, might appropriately be viewed as a strategy to confer public authority on these ideas. By the mid-nineteenth century, if not sooner, science carried authority; to speak in the name of science was to speak the language of truth. Science gave legitimacy to the social cause in whose name it spoke. Science conferred social status and power on social ideas and those who produced and supported them. From this perspective, Marx's claim to scientific status was, in part, a political strategy, an effort to promote a particular social and political world view.

Marx's vision of a science of society was powerful and surely drove his thinking. Yet, however much he wanted to wrap his ideas in the mantle of science, he was driven to offer a majestic vision of history and the future. This vision has proven to be aesthetically, morally, emotionally, and politically captivating, as the history of the twentieth century makes clear. As much as Marx may have wished to separate his values and social hopes from his science, they are built into his basic premises, concepts, and explanations. For example, assumptions regarding the changeable nature of humanity or the linear movement of history towards communism are directly wedded to his social agenda. Similarly, while *Capital* purports to offer an objective view of current Western societies, its basic assumptions, concepts, and explanations reflect a critical attitude. Profit equals exploitation only if one accepts the labor theory of value and rejects the value additive role of managerial, risk-taking behavior. Finally, his vision of history as a movement from simplicity to complexity, from the dominance of the group to individualism, from a social state controlled by unconscious forces to one directed by deliberate, reasoned action is akin, in its moral reach, to those of the great world religions.

The irony of Marx is that this great social visionary, a figure who truly rivals the Judeo-Christian prophets in fashioning a powerful moral vision aimed at redeeming humanity by a great transformation, could delude himself into believing that his social ideas were merely a revelation of scientific reason. How odd it is that great modern minds such as Comte and Marx, men of immense insight and observation, could be so unaware of how they offered beautiful and socially powerful empirical, moral, and political visions in the name of science. Perhaps it is because, in Western societies, the

belief in science as liberating humankind from myth and oppression is itself one of the chief illusions of our era.

Suggested Readings

Shlomo Avineri, *The Social and Political Thought of Karl Marx* (Cambridge: Cambridge University Press, 1978).

Jon Elster, *Making Sense of Marx* (Cambridge: Cambridge University Press, 1985).

David McLellan, *Karl Marx* (New York: Harper Colophon, 1973).

Tom Rockmore, *Marx After Marxism* (Oxford: Blackwell, 2002).

Jonathan Wolff, *Why Read Marx Today?* (Oxford: Oxford University Press, 2002).

References

1   Karl Marx, "A Contribution to the Critique of Hegel's Philosophy of Right. Introduction," in *Early Writings* (New York: Random House, 1975), p. 251.

2   Karl Marx and Friedrich Engels, *The German Ideology*, in *Collected Works*, vol. 5 (New York: International, 1975).

3   Karl Marx, "The Communist Manifesto," in *The Revolutions of 1848*, edited by David Fernbach (New York: Random House, 1974), pp. 67–8.

4   Marx and Engels, *The German Ideology*, in *Collected Works*, vol. 5, p. 59.

5   Karl Marx, *The Economic and Philosophical Manuscripts of 1844* (New York: International, 1964).

6   Karl Marx, *Capital: : A Critique of Political Economy*, vols. 1–3 (New York: International, 1967–73).

7   Marx, "Theses on Feuerbach," in Marx and Engels, *Collected Works*, vol. 5, p. 5.

The Promise of Sociology
Emile Durkheim

Neither Comte nor Marx were university professors. Although trained as academics, their ideas were formed outside of the academy. Comte and Marx crafted powerful critical social perspectives, but they were also creators of social movements whose aim was to transform society. Like the great Judeo-Christian prophets, Comte and Marx fashioned grand visions of history and human freedom. By contrast, Durkheim – and Weber, as we'll see in the next chapter – were professors more or less throughout their lives. They were the first generation of social thinkers to write as sociologists. Sociology was understood as a specialized discipline rather than as a general theory of humanity. Unlike Comte and Marx, Durkheim and Weber wrote research-oriented studies. Durkheim's study of suicide and Weber's analysis of Protestantism and capitalism are still considered models of modern sociology. Nevertheless, neither Durkheim nor Weber abandoned the wish to craft a sweeping view of history, nor did they abandon the moral hope that science could contribute to bringing about social change. Whereas Comte and Marx wore their moral commitments on their sleeves, Durkheim and Weber wove their moral vision into the very premises, concepts, and empirical explanations of their social studies.

In the course of the nineteenth century, France had changed considerably. Through the first half of the century, France was largely an agrarian society of peasants, divided by language, social custom, and regional disputes and was ruled by the Catholic Church, the landed nobility, and the monarchy. By the turn of the century, France was well on the way to becoming a modern, secular, industrial nation. Nevertheless, in one important respect very little had changed. France remained socially and politically unstable. Just as Comte faced a nation polarized between the forces of revolution and tradition, Durkheim also came of age in a period of intense social division. Durkheim wished to defend a social liberal worldviewagainst the ideological agendas of the Right and Left. He shared Comte's hope that sociology could contribute to the social reconstruction of France.

Contested Knowledge: Social Theory Today, Fifth Edition. Steven Seidman.
© 2013 John Wiley & Sons, Ltd. Published 2013 by John Wiley & Sons, Ltd.

Emile Durkheim (1858–1917) was born in Epinal, France. He studied at the prestigious Ecole Normale Supérieure. Durkheim taught at the University of Bordeaux and at the Sorbonne. He spent much of his career trying to establish sociology as a legitimate science. Durkheim aimed to show that "society" could be studied in the same way that psychologists study the individual mind and behavior. In *Suicide*, Durkheim believed he demonstrated that scientific methods could be applied to the study of group life. Durkheim's efforts to establish sociology as a scientific discipline were rewarded in 1913 when the name of his Chair changed from "Professor of the Science of Education" to "Professor of the Science of Education and Sociology." Durkheim was the first official sociologist in Europe.

Durkheim came of age at a critical juncture in French history. The Third French Republic had established itself as the longest-surviving liberal political regime in French history. Whatever optimism existed among supporters of the Republic, however, was tempered by the organized opposition of the conservative Right and the radical Left. On the one hand, France remained a society tied to an agrarian, patriarchal, and Catholic culture; the church, landed aristocracy, and military elites resisted secularism, individualism, and the free market ideology of middle-class liberals. On the other hand, modernization brought forth a new social force equally opposed to liberalism: a socialist Left rooted in the discontent of laborers and, to a lesser extent, a revolutionary feminism anchored in the disempowerment of women. Whereas the Right attacked liberalism for supposedly unleashing moral and social anarchy, the Left assailed liberalism for leaving social inequality in place. Turn-of-the-century France may have succeeded in fashioning a modern, somewhat democratic social order, but its fate was very much in doubt.

Durkheim's sympathy lay with the Third Republic. He was, by all accounts, personally uncomfortable with radical change, whether forward looking or backward looking. He was not, though, a simple-minded apologist for the business and professional strata for whom social liberalization often meant a social policy of unrestrained capitalism. Durkheim wished to preserve a republican France, but only if it was inspired by the high ideals of the French Revolution – *liberté*, *égalité*, and *fraternité*.

Durkheim's liberalism shared little with the British and American defense of an unbridled economic individualism. His liberalism fused the British and American respect for individualism with the European concern with moral order and civic virtue; it affirmed economic freedom but only if socially regulated; he defended individualism but only if the individual was firmly rooted in social institutions; he valued cultural pluralism but only in a society that had a clear moral center. In short, to end the bitter conflicts in France, Durkheim reached for a social vision that would integrate the spirit of liberalism (individualism), radicalism (social justice), and conservatism (moral order). Durkheim's liberal social values shaped the core of his empirical sociology. His moral vision is at the heart of two of his most important sociological studies: *The Division of Labor in Society* and *Suicide*.[1]

DURKHEIM'S LIBERAL VISION OF HISTORY AND MODERNITY

In the course of the nineteenth century, science had become an important language of moral and political argumentation. Appeals to scientific facts, explanations, or principles justified moral and political preferences. Thus, Comte invoked the Law of the Three Stages as proof of the inevitability and desirability of his view of an ideal industrial society. Marx sought to justify his own social values by identifying them with the laws of history. If the laws of society require particular social institutions, they are said to be objective rather than merely personal or ideological preferences. Durkheim likewise wished to use science to support his moral and political convictions. His sociology, at one level, was meant to show that social liberal values and politics were rooted in the very structure of contemporary society.

In *The Division of Labor in Society*, Durkheim presented a social liberal ideal that took the form of an evolutionary theory of society. He set out to write a story of the development of humanity from humankind's "primitive" stage to the "advanced" modern era.

Durkheim distinguishes two types of society: segmental or traditional societies that are unified by "mechanical solidarity" and organized or modern societies that feature "organic solidarity." The history of humanity is charted as the movement from a "primitive," segmental to a "modern, organized" type of society.

"Primitive" societies exhibit a fundamental simplicity and uniformity in their social structure. Typically, they are composed of a series of kinship groupings whose structure and functioning are more or less identical. Each individual is born into a kin group that assigns specific social roles in the course of the individual's life cycle. The kin group defines and regulates the behavior of its members. There are minimal social exchanges between these groups as each kin unit is largely socially self-sufficient. This lack of social differentiation between kin units is what Durkheim means by a segmental social structure. The social units (kin groupings) replicate one another in terms of their organization.

If primitive societies feature a segmental social structure, what is their source of social solidarity? If each kin group is self-sufficient, what social force knits them together into an identifiable, coherent social whole? Durkheim's answer is that primitive societies are unified by a religiously based common culture. In a society where individual experiences exhibit a pronounced uniformity, kin units develop similar beliefs and values. In a primitive culture, most individuals share the same beliefs, values, and norms. Moreover, because primitives are unable to understand the social and natural forces that shape their lives, they imagine a universe governed by supernatural forces; the core of primitive culture is religious. Primitives view the human order as a sacred order filled with supernatural beings. It is precisely this religious culture that brings the disparate social segments together into a coherent social whole.

To the extent that primitive societies are unified by a common culture, we can expect them to be conservative. If it is a common culture that keeps society integrated, then any cultural transgression would be a threat to social unity. Accordingly, deviance is treated harshly; deviants are subject to severe social and legal repression. Durkheim is proposing a sort of unconscious social logic: individuals act as the unwitting vehicles of social forces. Primitives repress deviance because it is unconsciously felt as a threat to personal and social coherence. Like Comte and Marx, Durkheim believed that, in primitive societies, humankind is under the control of social forces that are not understood. As we will see, the story Durkheim relates is one of humanity evolving towards a condition of rational understanding and social control. Western modernity signals the key turning point in human evolution; science destroys the illusions of supernatural powers, giving to humanity the potential to fashion its own destiny.

Societies organized in a segmental way are inherently unstable. Drawing from Darwinism, Durkheim reasons that the very social insularity and parochialism of primitive societies limits their capacity to respond effectively to changes in their natural and social environments. Social invasions, encounters with foreign civilizations, changes in natural resources, climate, or population compel primitive societies to change in order to survive. Social adaptation requires introducing more social complexity and differentiation. For example, kinship groups could adapt by learning to specialize in their economic practice. However, once humanity starts down the path of social differentiation, social evolution will undermine kin-based societies. In other words, natural and social events set in motion an inexorable dynamic, pushing humanity forward. The endpoint of social evolution is a modern type of society characterized by an "organized" social structure and "organic" type of solidarity.

Modern societies are said to be characterized by a highly differentiated social structure. Whereas the basic social units of primitive societies reveal a high level of structural and functional uniformity, in modern societies, they are differentiated. Large encompassing multifunctional kin groups are replaced by a multitude of specialized social institutions (e.g., the economy, polity, family, welfare, military, educational), each regulating a sector of individual behavior. For example, primitive kin groups satisfied a range of political, emotional, economic, religious, and educational needs. The modern Western family specializes in attending to the emotional and psychological needs of the individual. Nonfamilial institutions develop and specialize in economic, political, or educational functions. Social differentiation and specialization is internal to institutions as well. Thus, the production of knowledge becomes a specialized role of the educational system, but, within this system, a process of differentiation transpires. Knowledge is broken down into disciplines, specialties, and subspecialties.

The evolution of society towards increased social differentiation is paralleled by a dynamic of cultural pluralism. In a modern, differentiated society, individual experiences exhibit a wide variation depending on social class, nationality, religion, occupation, age, or regional location. As individuals are allowed more latitude in shaping their ideas, the range of culture held in common shrinks. Moreover, those beliefs and values held in common will be highly general and abstract. For example, moderns may share a general belief in the value of the individual but disagree about the meaning and social role of the individual. Indeed, Durkheim was convinced that, as modern culture becomes pluralistic, one of the few beliefs we share is individualism. Moderns make the individual sacred; individualism is our public religion. Despite the deification of the individual, modern culture undergoes a thorough process of secularization. The world of natural and human events is more clearly differentiated from the world of supernatural forces. Whereas the former sphere is, in principle, intelligible through science, the latter sphere is a matter of private faith. Modern culture projects a human-centered world; institutions are judged by their value to the individual and society.

The evolution of humanity towards a modern society is accompanied by a process of individualism. Durkheim observes two powerful social forces promoting individualism. First, the advance in the division of labor requires that individuals be given more freedom to regulate their institutional behavior. In a differentiated society, neither the state nor the church has the capacity to regulate institutions as varied as the economy, the state, family, school, and the military. Their daily regulation must be left to individuals who occupy social roles in those institutions. This institutional pressure to permit greater individualism is reinforced by cultural pluralism. If there are fewer common ideas in modern societies, then society *must* rely more on individuals than on institutional authorities such as the state or church to create social rules and norms. The very survival of society depends upon permitting the individual more freedom to make rules and regulate social affairs. To translate this empirical proposition into moral terms, Durkheim is appealing to a sociological argument about modern society in order to justify individualism and cultural pluralism.

A final question remains. Assuming that modernization entails social differentiation, cultural pluralism, secularism, and individualism, how are modern societies unified? What prevents such societies from being wrenched apart by the centrifugal forces of modernization? Contrary to some Leftist thinkers of his time, Durkheim does not believe that the modern state can impose moral order in a society where social rules and norms are decentralized and heterogeneous. Against conservatives, Durkheim argues that any effort to impose a religious order will create disorder. Social order must arise from the very organization of modern society. How does this happen? In its routine, everyday functioning, institutional differentiation and specialization (the social division of labor) create an interdependent, socially integrated, and unified society.

Durkheim argues that the division of labor functions not only as an economic but as a moral force. Specialization and interdependence of social roles and a corresponding system of moral rights, duties, and exchanges create social bonds. Durkheim explains:

> Where society relies most completely upon the division of labor, it does not become a jumble of juxtaposed atoms. . . . Rather the members are united by ties which extend deeper and far beyond the short moments during which exchange is made. Each of the functions that they [individuals] exercise is . . . dependent upon others, and with them forms a solitary system. . . . Because we fill some . . . social function, we are involved in a complex of obligations. . . . There is, above all, . . . the state . . . [which] is entrusted with the duty of reminding us of the sentiment of common solidarity.[2]

Modern social institutions – the family, economy, government, church, educational system – are mutually dependent; they are locked into a network of exchanges that bind them together through functional interdependency, shared social norms, and the moral authority of the state into an integrated system. For example, the economy depends upon the family to socialize individuals into disciplined, motivated workers. Similarly, the family depends upon the economy to provide jobs and income that make a family possible. Only a well-functioning, productive economy makes it possible for individuals to set up independent households. The functional and moral interconnectedness of modern societies is, moreover, more stable and durable than the culturally enforced solidarity of primitive societies because they are more adaptable to environmental changes. Thus, contrary to critics on the Right and Left, Durkheim held that, in principle, modern societies successfully combine economic dynamism, cultural creativity, individualism, and a stable, coherent social order.

Durkheim was aware that the actual state of social affairs in France and Europe did not mirror his social ideal. There was endemic social conflict, economic crises, and moral disarray across the continent. In fact, he wrote *The Division of Labor in Society* to provide a perspective on current social problems that would be an alternative to the ideas of socialists, conservatives, and individualistic liberals. For example, the socialist Left described economic crises as symptomatic of the inherent contradictions of capitalism; what was needed, they said, was socialism. By contrast, Durkheim believed that such economic crises were related to the lack of effective coordination of production and consumption; and this was a result of the rapidity of economic changes in the past few decades. In other words, in the initial phases of economic modernization, especially as substantial spatial separation between producers and consumers is introduced, producers are unclear about market demand. Regular communication between producers and consumers will allow producers to adjust levels of production to market needs. Similarly, conservatives denounced modern individualism and secularism for causing social chaos; they called for a restoration of the power of religion. By contrast, Durkheim viewed much of the social turmoil of the time as short-term, as the inevitable by-product of the birth of a new order. In a modern society, a period of adjustment is needed in order to determine the appropriate social rules, norms, rights, and obligations, for the stable, effective functioning of institutions.

Although Durkheim defended modern Western social developments against critics from the Left and Right, he was equally critical of certain liberals. British-styled liberals uncritically celebrated Western modernity. They defined individual freedom and creativity as the very essence of social modernization. They held that unrestrained individual freedom yields productivity, civic harmony, and advances the public welfare. These liberals advocated a free market unencumbered by governmental regulation. Durkheim believed that they were blind to the realities of coercion, social domination, and moral disruption that accompany modernization. For example, these individualistic liberals championed the market system for unleashing individual freedom but did not consider the division of labor, which compels individuals to exchange; they saw only individual opportunity but not the inequalities of social classes. Durkheim did. He did not, though, follow the Marxist view of class conflict. Rather, he believed that a rigid class system would disappear as modernity was democratized. Durkheim was convinced that social democratization, by which he meant equal opportunity for individual advancement in economic, political, and educational institutions, was an intrinsic aspect of modernization. He advocated reforms that would equalize social competition (e.g., abolishing inherited property) and promote a condition of social justice.

Durkheim sketched a broad social perspective for a liberal society that he intended to defend without becoming an apologist for a narrow economic liberalism. Unlike individualistic liberals, Durkheim acknowledged serious problems in the present. In particular, he was alarmed at the potential personal and social costs of individualism. Whereas, in *The Division of Labor*, his focus was on social structure and the problem of social order, subsequently, his attention shifted somewhat to the social and moral meaning of individualism. Durkheim never retreated from his commitment to individualism, but he wished to defend the individual as part of a stable moral and social order. This rethinking of individualism, which was fundamental to Durkheim's social liberalism, is clarified in a major study, *Suicide*.

SUICIDE: INDIVIDUALISM AND COMMUNITY REVISITED

Durkheim disagreed with conservatives who criticized modern society for promoting individualism at the expense of moral and social order. In *The Division of Labor in Society*, Durkheim argued that social differentiation, cultural pluralism, and secularism stimulate individualism. In modern societies, individuals must have more freedom to create the social rules that regulate their lives. Far from undermining social coherence, individual freedom makes it possible because social norms and values cannot be legislated by the state, church, or family. Modern society creates the individual as an active social agent because freedom is necessary for its ongoing social functioning.

The social importance of the individual in modern societies is symbolized by the reverence surrounding the individual. Durkheim argued that, when intense group feelings are attached to an idea or object, and these feelings are expressed in shared beliefs and social practices, we are witnessing what is in essence a religion. Despite the secularity of modernity, as evidenced in the separation of the church and state and in the decline of Judeo-Christian dogma, it evolves its own religion of humanity. The individual functions as a sacred object; laws, social institutions, and customs create and protect the rights and dignity of the individual. Subsequent to *The Division of Labor*, Durkheim emphasized the contribution of this religious culture of individualism to social coherence.

Durkheim distinguished his own defense of individualism from British-style liberalism which celebrated individualism freed from institutional constraints. Unbridled individualism was supposed to guarantee social progress. For example, economic greed was said to promote the public welfare by producing more and better goods at a cheaper price for the consumer or by encouraging the virtues of hard work, self-sacrifice, and risk taking. Durkheim disagreed. Championing a form of individualism that rejected all social limits is harmful to the individual and society. Individualism is to be valued only when it occurs within a social and moral framework. This moral claim was what Durkheim intended to prove in the book that has been hailed as the first work of scientific sociology: *Suicide*.

Durkheim's decision to study suicide was a calculated, even if provocative, gesture. His reasons were twofold. First, Durkheim was struggling to legitimate sociology as a science. At the time, sociology was a fledgling field of study that had no academic status. In early-twentieth-century France, sociology was not a recognized science. Few sociology courses were taught, and professors advocating sociology were in a bitter struggle with their colleagues. Chief among the enemies of sociology were humanists (secular and religious) who believed that sociology denied free will and therefore undermined moral responsibility. Perhaps an even more formidable opponent were social scientists, for whom society was at bottom a matter of individual psychology and behavior. To legitimate sociology as a science, Durkheim had to persuade his detractors that society is a reality irreducible to the psychology of the individual. What better way to make his case than to show that suicide, an act that seemed so obviously explainable by individual psychology, was a social fact. At the same time, a study of suicide could show the social dangers of unbridled individualism. *Suicide* would be an ideal vehicle for promoting his social liberal vision and doing so in the name of science.

Durkheim does not deny that psychological distress prompts individuals to take their own lives. Rather, his chief claim is that social conditions produce this suicidal disposition. Durkheim's three basic types of suicide (egoistic, altruistic, anomic) indicate different social conditions of integration and regulation. I will provide an overview of each type with an eye to spotlighting Durkheim's social liberal values.

In egoistic suicide, individuals take their lives because of the psychological distress that stems from their lack of social integration:

> In this case the bond attaching man to life relaxes because that attaching him to society is itself slack. The incidents of private life which . . . are considered its [suicide's] determining causes are in reality only incidental causes. The individual yields to the slightest shock of circumstance because the state of society has made him a ready prey to suicide.[3]

Durkheim explores the dynamics of egoistic suicide through an empirical case study relating religion and suicide. He observes that statistical portraits of suicides in Western industrial nations consistently show that Protestants have higher suicide rates than do Catholics. There is no credible reason to assume that these two groups differ in any significant psychological way. Moreover, both denominations condemn suicide. However, Durkheim notes some key social differences. In particular, Protestantism is highly individualistic. Protestants arrive at their faith through an appeal to individual conscience. They share few common beliefs and practices; accordingly, they are less socially integrated into their religious community. By contrast, the centralized bureaucratic organization of Catholicism imposes a unified faith on its practitioners. Catholics share many of the same beliefs and practices; accordingly, they are strongly integrated into their religious social community.

Durkheim infers a general social principle: suicide rates increase as social integration decreases. Why? Because, lacking close social ties, the individual loses moral purpose and falls prey to ennui and a deadly melancholic isolation:

> Social man necessarily presupposes a society which he expresses and serves. If this dissolves . . . we are bereft of reasons for existence. . . . In this sense it is true to say that our activity needs an object [social goal] transcending it.[4]

Translating this "scientific principle" into a moral language, Durkheim is suggesting that if individuals lack a stable social framework they will suffer harm.

Although Durkheim's analysis of egoistic suicide trumpeted the message that unrestrained individualism is undesirable, he insisted that too much social integration is equally harmful. This moral view is developed in his comments on altruistic suicide. Altruism is the flip side of egoism. It indicates a condition of too much social integration; the needs, interests, and identity of the group overwhelm and extinguish a separate individual existence. If the individual's life is so completely fused with the well-being of the group, any disturbances in group life threaten individual well-being. Suicide is one response to the disruption or weakening of group solidarity. Given the pronounced individualism of modern societies, altruistic suicide is rare; it is almost exclusively confined to the military. War situations in particular provide the clearest illustration. Inspired by the spirit of intense group identification and nationalism, individuals perform heroic acts of self-sacrifice. The moral message here is that too much group control is unhealthy, at least in modern societies.

Social integration represents one social axis of suicide; the other is social regulation. Anomic suicide illustrates a condition in which the individual lacks sufficient social direction. Durkheim assumed that society defines and directs individual wants, desires, and goals. Lacking adequate social regulation, individuals cannot organize their lives in a stable and coherent way. Durkheim's example of anomic suicide is the documented rise in suicide rates during economic crises. This social phenomenon, he argued, is less the product of economic decline (since it affects upwardly and down-wardly mobile individuals) than the result of the moral disorder that accompanies abrupt socioeconomic change. As individuals quickly shift their socioeconomic status (up or down), there occurs, at least temporarily, a disruption in expectations and goals as social opportunities are dramatically altered. Suicide is one expected outcome of the moral confusion and distress experienced in an anomic state. Interpreted from a moral perspective, Durkheim's analysis of anomic suicide contains an unpleasant message to British-styled liberals and to the socialist Left. Despite their good intentions of wanting to free the individual from repressive social controls, too much freedom results in distress, possibly suicide. Durkheim concludes that individuals require a stable, intact social and moral framework to set limits and to give direction and purpose to their behavior.

Durkheim insisted upon the scientific status of his analysis, but is it merely coincidental that the principles he claims to have discovered coincide precisely with his own social liberal values? *Suicide* served Durkheim as a medium through which to engage current public debates regarding the proper relation between the individual and the social community. Against conservatives, he insisted upon individualism as a condition of a healthy society. Against individualistic liberals and socialists, he maintained the necessity of social and moral regulation as a condition of a healthy individualism.

If Durkheim's social agenda is not entirely clear in the analysis of types of suicide, it is spelled out in the concluding section where he assumes the explicit role of social reformer. If suicide rates indicate a social disturbance in the relation of the individual to the group, the remedy must be social. Durkheim believed that neither the family, church, or state could offset currents of egoism and anomie in modern societies. For example, secularization has weakened the social role of the church; the loss of many of its social functions has similarly weakened the family; the removal of the state from daily affairs has rendered it incapable of directly regulating individual behavior. Durkheim imagined that, as the workplace becomes central to modern life, new forms of community and moral regulation will crystalize, providing a kind of moral and social center for the individual. As in *The Division of Labor in Society*, *Suicide* served Durkheim as a vehicle to recommend a society that combined individualism, moral coherence, and social justice.

SCIENCE, TRUTH, AND MORAL HOPE

Durkheim made it clear that science would have little value if it did not contribute to advancing human welfare: "We should judge our researches to have no worth at all if they were to have only a speculative interest. If we separate carefully the theoretical from the practical problems, it is not to the neglect of the latter; but, on the contrary, to be in a better position to solve them."[5] In his sociological studies of the division of labor, suicide, the family, education, and religion, Durkheim never restricted social analysis to stating facts and proposing explanations or theories. He always offered a moral and often political perspective on social affairs. For example, in the first two major sections of *The Division of Labor in Society*, Durkheim sets out the social facts pertaining to the evolution of humankind from a primitive to a modern society. He sketches an ideal of modern society that allows him to pass judgment on current developments. In the third section of *Division*, entitled "Abnormal Forms," Durkheim tells us what is wrong with the current social division of labor and what reforms would be appropriate.[6] For example, as we've seen, present economic crises are interpreted as temporary maladjustments to rapid social change, requiring expanded communication between producers and consumers, not the transformation of capitalism into socialism. For Durkheim, science, morality, and social policy go hand in hand, though they remain distinct aspects of social analysis.

Durkheim offered a justification for this sociological approach in *The Rules of Sociological Method*.[7] He outlined the rules of sociological analysis. His strategy was, broadly speaking, to distinguish the establishment of scientific facts and explanations from ideology for the purpose of making moral and social policy recommendations.

Durkheim defines the subject matter of sociology as those shared institutions, cultural beliefs, and social conventions that are irreducible to individual psychology. He calls these phenomena "social facts." Their key feature is that, though produced by individuals, they exist external to us and constrain our behavior. For example, the division of labor is a social fact in that it constrains our behavior (e.g., we must specialize in our social roles), seemingly irrespective of our personal wishes.

Sociology studies social facts as if, in Durkheim's phrase, they were "things." Durkheim counsels that we view social facts dispassionately – without feelings or preconceptions. Our ideas of social facts should come from the world as it is, not from our individual biases. By immersing ourselves in the study of facts, we can avoid contaminating our sociological ideas with personal values. The sociologist aims to establish social facts, relate them to their appropriate societal type (e.g., primitive, feudal, or modern), and offer historical, causal, and functional explanations. This allows sociology to ascertain the "normal" structure and functioning of social facts. Durkheim believed that the normality of social facts is a function of their being "general" to a given social type and useful or contributing to its stability. For example, since individualism in a modern differentiated society is both general and socially useful, it is normal. By contrast, individualism would be abnormal in a primitive society because it would be exceptional and dysfunctional.

Durkheim asserted that his methodological rules made it possible for science to produce universal truths about social facts. This would permit sociologists to make objective moral judgments. He was, I am convinced, badly mistaken.

His claim that sociologists can somehow set aside their prejudices and preconceptions in order to gain access to social reality "as it actually is" ignores the important role that social interests and values play in social knowledge. Contrary to Durkheim's recommendation that "all preconceptions must be eradicated,"[8] our preconceptions guide our perceptions. They tell us what is important, how to relate perceptions to form concepts and to frame relations between concepts, and make it possible to fashion disparate bits of information into a coherent social story or picture. Durkheim thought that, if we could open ourselves to the world, it would impress its essential nature upon us. However, the world is always experienced as meaningful. We can never get around our preconceptions to get to a world that exists as raw experience. To the extent that our social perceptions are guided by our interests and preconceptions, our social ideas are structured by our particular social interests, values, and culturally biased assumptions. Consider Durkheim's social evolutionary theory. Durkheim's image of primitive society exhibits the standard Western stereotypes of the time, for example, primitive society as socially simple, culturally homogeneous, mired in supernatural religiosity, anti-individualistic, socially intolerant, and resistant to change. His concept of modernity is no less stereotyped, even if in an idealized way; for example, modernity as socially complex, secular, culturally pluralistic, individualistic, tolerant, and socially dynamic. If there is any doubt that this "typology" is little more than a thinly disguised story of human progress, the subtitle of *Division*, "A Study of the Organization of Superior Societies," betrays Durkheim's modern, European, middle-class values.

Durkheim imagined an intimate tie between scientific knowledge and morality. Science was not only to serve moral ends but was to give morality an objective status. Yet Durkheim also wished to maintain the separation between science, morality, and politics. In the end, he did not succeed. For example, his retreat into a view that assumes an unambiguous separation between the scientist and society in order to justify a value-neutral, objective view of science is contradicted by his insistence on the social formation of consciousness. If the culture of a society is shaped by its social structure, then doesn't this hold true for the sociologist as well? As we have seen, Durkheim's ideas about social knowledge, social evolution, and modernity look suspiciously like the social values and ideas of a modern, middle-class, liberal Frenchman.

His moral vision bursts into center stage in his last great work, *The Elementary Forms of Religious Life*.[9] Durkheim attempted to explain the origin and nature of religion. His thesis was that religious beliefs are really symbolic ways of understanding the power of society to fashion the individual; religious rituals are interpreted as socially integrating practices. Prior to the advent of the Enlightenment, humankind lacked the power of reason to grasp that the supernatural and spiritual forces that they assumed governed human affairs were really social forces (e.g., the division of labor, cultural beliefs, law). Modern science destroys this illusion; science forces humanity to confront a reality governed by human and natural forces. In particular, sociology steps forward as the successor to religious social beliefs and ethics. The sociologist occupies the social role previously held by shamans, prophets, and priests. Clearly, there are strong echoes of Comte's fusion of sociology and religion. Durkheim seems to open up the possibility that by uncovering the true reality of society as a transcendent power that provides coherence and purpose to our lives sociology may become the centerpiece of a religious cult.

Suggested Readings

Jeffrey Alexander, *Theoretical Logic in Sociology*, vol. 3 (Berkeley: University of California Press, 1983).

Robert Jones, *Emile Durkheim* (Newbury Park, CA: Sage, 1985).

Jennifer Lehman, *Deconstructing Durkheim* (New York: Routledge, 1993).

Steven Lukes, *Emile Durkheim* (New York: Penguin, 1977).

Robert Nesbit, *The Sociology of Emile Durkheim* (New York: Oxford University Press, 1974).

References

1   Emile Durkheim, *Suicide* (New York: Free Press, 1951); *The Division of Labor in Society* (New York: Free Press, 1933).

2   Durkheim, *The Division of Labor in Society*, p. 227.

3   Durkheim, *Suicide*, pp. 214–15.

4   Durkheim, *Suicide*, p. 213.

5   Durkheim, *The Division of Labor in Society*, p. 33.

6   Durkheim, *The Division of Labor in Society*, Book 3, "Abnormal Forms."

7   Emile Durkheim, *The Rules of Sociological Method* (New York: Free Press, 1966).

8   Durkheim, *The Rules of Sociological Method*, p. 31.

9   Emile Durkheim, *The Elementary Forms of Religious Life* (New York: Free Press, 1954).

4

The Ironic Social Theory of Max Weber

Weber shared with Emile Durkheim the view that the period between 1890 and World War I was crucial in shaping the fate of individual freedom. In both France and Germany, industrialization, national unification and bureaucratization, the formation of a secular educational system, the establishment of constitutional government, and the rule of law signaled the triumph of modernization. While Durkheim and Weber defended modernization against critics, they were sensitive to the dangers to freedom in the modern world. For example, a centralized bureaucratic state may be necessary for economic development and national security, but it threatens to become a new type of despotic rule.

In contrast to many liberals, Weber did not believe that economic modernization automatically translates into social and political liberalization. Whereas in Britain and the United States a liberal political culture accompanied industrial capitalist development, German industrialization coexisted with a hierarchical and authoritarian social and political culture. Despite the phenomenal success of the German economy in the second half of the nineteenth century, social and political power remained in the hands of a feudal-styled class of Prussian landowners called the "Junkers."

Germany was unified as a result of the iron will of Bismarck, who made the Prussian state into a dominant national force. Prussia was, moreover, ruled by the Junkers. They were a landed aristocracy who aggressively supported nationalistic and militaristic values. Unlike in France and Britain, where capitalist development was paralleled by the economic and political decline of the landed aristocracy, the Junker class adapted either by becoming successful capitalists, or, where they lost economic power, by managing to retain their social and political authority. If the Junkers didn't dominate Germany in a direct political way, their social authority allowed them to imprint on society their bellicose nationalism, economic protectionism, support of church orthodoxy, and anti-labor sentiment. The Prussian Junkers, with the support

Contested Knowledge: Social Theory Today, Fifth Edition. Steven Seidman.
© 2013 John Wiley & Sons, Ltd. Published 2013 by John Wiley & Sons, Ltd.

Max Weber (1864–1920) was born in Frankfurt, Germany. He studied law at the University of Heidelberg and the University of Berlin. In 1889, he completed his doctorate in economic and legal history. Unlike Marx and Durkheim, Weber was deeply pessimistic about the prospects for individual freedom in the modern world. He feared a bureaucratic world that valued order and security over freedom and individuality. He worried about a bureaucratic government run by career professionals and officials, rather than by true leaders. From the vantage point of the present, who do you think provided the more realistic judgment of our world: Marx or Weber?

of a religious and a humanistic cultural elite deeply hostile to Enlightenment values, exercised considerable public authority in Germany through World War I.

Weber came of age in a Germany that was deeply divided. There were conflicts between the defenders of modernization and its detractors, who nostalgically looked backward. Moreover, defenders of social modernization split into hostile camps. There were individualistic liberals who advocated a free market system, conservative nationalists who backed an activist state that could weave together economic development and military national strength, and revolutionary socialists who rejected both capitalism and nationalism. These ideological divisions expressed deep-seated antagonisms between the middle class, the landed aristocracy, and the working class. The similarity with Durkheim's France is striking except – and this is a big exception – that there was no German counterpart to the Third French Republic. There was, in fact, no German counterpart to the French Revolution or to the English or American revolutions; there was no middle-class revolution in Germany. Although the German middle class prospered, it did not challenge the social and political power of the Junkers. Instead of becoming a political force mobilized to overthrow Junker rule, the German middle classes took over their conservative, nationalistic values.

Whereas Marx, a generation earlier, gave up any hope of the middle class becoming a force of social reform in Germany, Weber did not. Weber was convinced that only the middle classes had the social authority and resources to deal the death blow to the Junkers. However, Weber did not imagine that middle-class rule would bring about inexorable social progress. It is not that Weber put his social faith in the working class; he did not. Rather, Weber never fully bought into the social faith of the Enlightenment. Although he was committed to many Enlightenment values, Weber never abandoned some counter-Enlightenment ideas. Curiously, he held on to more of the conservative nationalism of the Junker class than he realized. Whatever hopes he harbored for human progress were tempered by a streak of pessimism and *Realpolitik* he took over from the Prussian, Lutheran culture that he otherwise detested. Lacking in Weber is the strong sense of social hope we observed in the Enlightenment and in Comte, Marx, and Durkheim. Weber's social vision blends a championing of individualism with an equally passionate commitment to nationalism.

PURITANISM AND THE MAKING OF THE MIDDLE CLASS

The future of Germany was tied to the destiny of the middle class. Weber believed that only a strong, politically aggressive middle class could succeed in both modernizing Germany and making this nation into a world power. He was not very hopeful. The German middle class had a history of retreating from political struggle. In his early writings, Weber sought to explain the political immaturity of the German middle class. He also sought to awaken the political will of the German bourgeoisie.

This moral and political motivation underlies Weber's first great work of sociology, *The Protestant Ethic and the Spirit of Capitalism.*[1] Although its chief theme revolves around the link between Protestantism and capitalism, the subtext is Weber's appeal to the disillusioned, hard-working, inner-directed Puritan as an ideal for the German middle class.

The Protestant Ethic explores the religious origins of the "spirit" or culture of capitalism. Weber believed that modern capitalism would not have developed without certain psychological attitudes. In order for individuals to risk the capital investment involved in starting up an enterprise, and in order for workers to accept the disciplined, specialized labor of industrial capitalism, this behavior had to be made meaningful and valuable. Why should an entrepreneur work hard and sacrifice in the present for an uncertain future payoff? Of course, once capitalism was established, entrepreneurs would be compelled to accumulate wealth and reinvest profits in order to be competitive. However, in the early stages of capitalist development, there was no market mechanism that enforced self-sacrificing, risk-taking behavior. Weber wanted to understand why individuals would become entrepreneurs.

Weber identified a cultural milieu in European societies that contributed to the rise of modern capitalism. This culture valued discipline, hard work, frugality, deferred gratification, the accumulation of wealth without ostentatious consumption, and a pride in economic success. Unlike many European liberals who maintained that humans are naturally competitive, hard working, greedy, and economically motivated, Weber argued that this behavior is learned. And while Weber agreed with socialists that competition enforces entrepreneurial behavior once capitalism is established, they did not identify the social forces that initially encouraged this behavior.

Weber proposed what at first glance seemed like a far-fetched thesis: Protestantism played a key role in the cultural origins of capitalism. Of course, Protestants were not motivated by economic interests. Quite the contrary, the Protestant Reformation was a movement of spiritual renewal in revolt against the materialism and secularism of the Catholic Church. Its salvationist doctrine, however, unintentionally propelled entrepreneurial activity. Weber's story is sadly ironic. The intense spiritual hopes that drove Protestantism unwittingly created a vast materialistic, secular civilization devoid of morally elevated values.

In ascetic Protestant sects such as Calvinism, Pietism, Methodism, Baptism, and Congregationalism, Weber found a cultural world view that placed a *religious* value upon entrepreneurial behavior. Weber's most famous example is Calvinism. Calvin enunciated the doctrine of predestination: God predetermined who was saved at the moment of creation. Moreover, priests were not privileged to act as the chief messengers of divine judgment. The clergy had no special insight into the purpose of creation nor into the calculus of salvation. Good works, charity, monetary contributions, or prayer did not guarantee salvation; each individual was alone with his or her own doubts about personal salvation. In response to the heightened feelings of anxiety that spread throughout the religious community, Calvinists appealed to external signs to interpret the fate of their souls. Economic success served as a chief marker of religious fate. Accordingly, economic behavior was imbued with transcendent religious significance. To work hard at an occupation and to signal one's success by a prosperous business or career achievement, rather than by conspicuous consumption, was perceived by the community as a clear indicator of a saved soul. The salvationist religious meanings attached to entrepreneurial behavior formed the cultural matrix for the rise of modern capitalism.

The full irony – and pathos – of Weber's tale is revealed in the finale of *The Protestant Ethic*. The very success of Protestantism in stimulating capitalism would result in its death knell. Once capitalism was established, competition would enforce entrepreneurial behavior; religious motivations would be replaced by secular, utilitarian ones. The Protestant work ethic would give way to motivations based on survival, status, and power.

Weber's understanding of the emerging modern capitalist civilization shared little of the celebratory spirit of the Enlightenment. In contrast to liberals and socialists who championed industrial development for making possible a new era of individualism and social progress, Weber laments the decline of a culture of moral virtue and individualism. Inspired by religious values that emphasized actively engaging in worldly affairs, the Protestant in the seventeenth and eighteenth centuries was a genuine individualist. His or her nineteenth- and twentieth-century heir is trapped in a capitalist, bureaucratic system, what Weber called an "iron cage."[2]

The Protestant Ethic did not offer an entirely pessimistic social vision. Although the full glory of Protestant individualism can never be recaptured, Weber hoped that the Puritan spirit of worldly activism might be an inspiration to the German middle classes. The self-made Puritan who struggled relentlessly to refashion the world in his or her own image was precisely what was lacking among Weber's contemporaries. The German middle class seemed to aspire to little more than staking out their own small share of Germany's wealth and prestige by accommodating to Prussian rule. *The Protestant Ethic* offered a partial explanation of this phenomenon. In Germany, it was not the activist ethic of Calvinism that shaped its culture but a Lutheran "accommodationist" spirit that was dominant. Lutheranism enjoined the individual to fulfill the duties of the occupation or social station one occupied; its spirit is one of world accommodation rather than transformation. Lutheranism shaped a culture that produced a placid, other-directed individual. The contrast between the inner-directed Puritan who struggles to refashion the world and the other-directed, socially accommodating Lutheran was intended to stimulate self-awareness and social activism on the part of the German middle classes.

EXPLAINING WESTERN MODERNITY AND THE IRONY OF HISTORY

The Protestant ethic thesis originally appeared as an essay in 1904. Subsequently, Weber pursued the broader theme of explaining Western modernization in a series of comparative studies. Investigations of Greco-Roman and Mesopotamian civilizations, followed by studies of China, India, Ancient Judaism, Islam, and medieval Christian civilization analyzing the development of law, religion, cities, and political structures, comprised his two master works, *Economy and Society* and the *Collected Essays in the Sociology of Religion*.[3] In each study, Weber asks, "Why did modernization initially occur in the West and not in Eastern civilizations?" For example, why did modern science originate in the West? Why did a rational-legal system first develop in Roman civilization? Why did modern capitalism arise in the West? How to explain the Western political formation of constitutional government, the rule of law, parliamentary bodies, civil rights, and political parties?

Weber's sociology of modernity avoided explanations that appealed to human nature, individual psychology, climate, or geography. He rejected explanations of social development that relied on one factor, for example, the economy, population, or ideas. Although Weber did not avoid an evolutionary story of humankind that views change as patterned and meaningful, he did not assume a set of fixed stages humanity passes through towards a predetermined endpoint. Nor did Weber relate a story of the progress of humanity from a lowly beginning to a higher, liberated endpoint. Nevertheless, Weber's sociology of civilizations reveals a vision of the meaning of history that centers on the fatefulness of modernity. To illustrate Weber's sociology of modernity, I will consider his study of Chinese civilization, *The Religion of China*.[4]

At various times in its history, social conditions in China were favorable to modernization. Despite the accumulation of economic wealth and the formation of trade companies and merchant associations in China, modern capitalism never developed. Despite its technological superiority over the West through the early modern period, modern science remained foreign to Chinese soil. Despite the formation of a political empire, Chinese bureaucracy remained highly traditionalistic. Weber wanted to explain the absence of modernization in China.

Weber offered a snapshot picture of China. Chinese unification in 221 BC proved fateful. Rule by warring feudal lords was replaced by a bureaucratic empire ruled by an emperor and a cultural elite (mandarins) who administered the empire. The mandarins were the principal carriers of the state ideology: Confucianism. State and ideological social control from above was reinforced by control over the individual in daily village life by a rigid kinship system. Weber held that each of these social forces (the bureaucratic state, the Confucian ideology, the village kinship system) contributed to blocking Chinese modernization.

The emperor was the symbolic ruler of China. The class of mandarins who administered the bureaucratic state effectively ruled China for some 2,000 years. Weber distinguishes the "patrimonial" bureaucracy of China from the modern Western bureaucratic state by its essentially personalistic character. For example, the emperor, in principle, owns and has unlimited control over all bureaucratic offices, personnel, and resources; officials serve at the emperor's discretion; their loyalty is to the emperor, not to their office or to an ideal of bureaucratic professionalism. The Chinese patrimonial state avoided both "refeudalization" and modernization. By limiting terms of office, routinely circulating officials, implementing a system of surveillance, and instituting an examination system that fostered an identification of the mandarins with the imperial state, the emperor sought to avoid decentralization. However, political modernization was opposed by the mandarins since a modern bureaucratic ethic of expertise, specialization, and technical training would undermine their legitimacy. The mandarins' opposition to political modernization was also supported by the emperor, for whom a modern bureaucratic order would restrict imperial power.

The patrimonial bureaucratic state also impeded social and economic modernization. For example, Weber argues that the imperial state favored a more personalistic legal system that gave wide latitude to the decisions of the judge. By contrast, a modern legal code operates according to rules of evidence and precedent that greatly restrict the discretion of the judge. In the West, the development of a modern juridical code (e.g., in Rome) was made possible by the existence of an independent stratum of jurists and lawyers. Imperial China opposed the rise of such a group as a restriction on the emperor's rule. Similarly, the imperial state favored state-financed and -controlled businesses over a free market because it feared the development of an independent merchant class. In Weber's view, the patrimonial Chinese state suppressed the very forces that could have been the vehicles of social modernization.

The only countervailing social force to the imperial state was the village clan. Despite the ambitions of the imperial state to exercise total control over society, the expanse and diversity of China made that impossible. Village life was more or less free from state rule but was dominated by the local kinship system. Instead of creating space for social innovation, the clan reinforced Chinese traditionalism by exerting strict control over the individual and village social life. Anchored in a culture of ancestor worship and the rule of the elders that made tradition and social customs sacred, the village clan enforced a conservative way of life, for example, by greatly restricting occupational choice, individual mobility, and the accumulation of individual wealth.

Imperial rule was, ultimately, in the hands of the mandarins. This cultural elite administered the bureaucratic state on a daily basis; they shaped the political culture of China. It was the mandarins who made Confucianism into a state ideology.

From the perspective of the Judeo-Christian tradition, Confucianism appears less as a religion than as a cultural ideal. For example, Confucianism lacks a concept of a creator God with whom individuals have a personal relationship. Confucianism imagines the universe as an ordered cosmos in which all beings have a fixed place and purpose in a hierarchical order. Cosmic harmony is to be maintained by individuals establishing an equilibrium internally (psychologically) and externally (socially). Confucianism encourages an ethic of individual control over feelings and behavior as a way to maintain emotional and social balance. Its social ethic emphasizes family piety, literary cultivation, and public service. Private wealth and power are important but only if they are achieved through public office; private enterprise was thought to disturb inner and outer poise. The Confucian ethic directs the individual to accommodate to the world as it is, to fulfill the duties of one's social station. Material comfort, familial honor and security, and a public office carrying status are the earthly rewards to be expected from following a Confucian ethic. Foreign to Confucianism is the Puritan struggle to refashion the world according to a moral vision.

As in his studies of India, ancient Judaism, or ancient Far Eastern civilizations, Weber's study of China purported to be a scientific analysis of the divergent paths of the West and the East. Weber catalogues the factors that stimulated the break-through to modernity in the West and obstructed modernization in the East. For example, the worldly activist ethic of Protestantism promoted modernization, whereas the Confucian ethic of world accommodation, in combination with the imperial bureaucracy and the village clan system, impeded modernization in China. As much as Weber tried to document his perspective on modernization by painstaking empiri-cal comparisons and tentative causal sketches, his sociology discloses a moral vision suggesting a tragic human drama.

The standard Enlightenment historical narrative envisioned a progressive movement of humankind from a simple underdeveloped social state where the individual was dominated by the group, myth, and nature to a complex advanced society where, with the aid of science, the individual reigned supreme over nature and history. The perspectives of Comte, Marx, and Durkheim are variations on this story of social progress. It was not Weber's vision. His view of social evolution originates with the bureaucratic civilizations of the ancient Far Eastern and Roman civilizations. Although Weber admires their achievements of national unity and military prowess, this is bought at the price of individual freedom and social dynamism. Whether Weber is discussing the empires of ancient Rome, Egypt, or China, he underscores the bureau-cratic stifling of social pluralism and individualism and, ultimately, their social decline. Political liberalization and social modernization go hand in hand; where institutional pluralism and individualism are permitted, a prosperous and dynamic social order flourishes. For example, the overriding theme of Weber's sociology of China is that modernization failed, in large part, because the imperial bureaucracy suppressed countervailing social forces. By contrast, in the West state bureaucracy had to contend with multiple power centers, e.g., the church, jurists, and lawyers, an independent merchant class, cities freed from centralized state authority where social and cultural innovations were encouraged. Weber's vision is decidedly liberal: social pluralism and individualism promote an innovative, dynamic society.

Weber does not, however, fashion this liberal theme into a narrative of moderniza-tion as social progress. The story he tells is that of the movement of the West from bureaucratic empire to social liberalization to the present day where European nations are potentially returning to some form of bureaucratic empire. Modernization is described, so to speak, as consisting of two phases. The first phase, roughly from the sixteenth to the mid-nineteenth century, was the dynamic phase. Western societies created modern science, free market capitalism, the inner-directed individualism exemplified by the Puritan and political democratic structures such as rule of law, constitutionalism, civil rights, and parliamentary government. However, social developments from the late nineteenth century on threatened to undermine this liberal, individualistic society. In particular, the spread of bureaucracy and its utilitarian, status-oriented culture to all modern institutions fashioned a society of other-directed, spiritually bland, and apolitical individuals ruled by a soulless bureaucracy. In other words, Weber saw in China not simply the past from which Western modernization departed but the possible future of the West and humanity. The tragic irony in Weber's vision of history is that the future of humanity may be less the utopian visions of the Enlighteners than the dystopian reality of bureaucratic despotism. Distracted and dazed by modern utopian dreams, Enlighteners, tragically, are not even aware of the dystopian world that humankind is entering. Whether this blocked vision was the tragedy of Enlighteners or whether the tragedy was Weber's inability to see that he projected the worst features of Germany onto humanity's future is crucial in assessing his social vision.

CHARISMA AND BUREAUCRACY: THE MODERN DREAM TURNED NIGHTMARE

Unlike his Enlightenment predecessors and contemporaries, Weber does not relate a story of humankind's continuous march forward. Weber imagines a perpetual conflict between the forces of order that threaten to squash individual freedom and those that support social innovation and change. If bureaucracy represents the exemplary force of order, charisma is a chief source of change. Weber charts a movement from bureaucratic empires to social modernization in the West in which charismatic movements played a key role.[5]

Weber puzzled over how to explain social change in the face of the conservative power exercised by bureaucratic empires. In the concept of charismatic movements, he identified a force whose social intensity could offset bureaucratic social paralysis.

Charisma is the magical supernatural power that an individual claims to possess. The charismatic leader commands public authority by virtue of claiming to possess extraordinary powers. Between the charismatic leader and the disciple, there are powerful moral and emotional bonds; the leader fashions a social mission that the disciple pledges to enact. Charismatic movements are potentially revolutionary social forces in that the personal loyalty that the disciple owes the leader is to be demonstrated by pursuing an agenda of social change. Despite the fact that charismatic movements inevitably either dissipate or are routinized (i.e., evolve their own stable social life), Weber believed that they have been key forces in loosening or destroying the social strangulation of bureaucracy.

In another ironic twist, Weber believed that, while charismatic movements were pivotal in engendering modernization, the latter environment is hostile to charisma. For example, the secularity of modern culture diminishes the credibility of individual claims to possess magical powers. Similarly, capitalism fosters a utilitarian culture inimical to charismatic authority. Perhaps the most significant obstacle to charisma is modern bureaucracy, which encourages individuals to value a secure and orderly social environment. In fact, Weber thought that the defining feature of Western modernity was the spread of bureaucracy, along with its conservative culture, to all social spheres. The bureaucratization of society anticipated a bleak future for humanity. To the extent that social modernization went hand in hand with bureaucratization, the advance of science, democracy, law, and so on promised to inaugurate a stultifying era of bureaucratic domination.

The very social forces that have created a dynamic modern society have stimulated bureaucratization. For example, capitalism introduces a dynamic market system, but its need for a massive infrastructure of transportation and communication, and a legal administrative apparatus that ensures that contracts are enforced, encourage the bureaucratization of the state. Similarly, market competition inevitably leads to the development of giant corporations which, with their high capital investment, coordination of massive resources, and planning, stimulates economic bureaucratization. Modernization also entails political democratization (e.g., the spread of civil rights, political parties, representational political bodies) which, in turn, requires bureaucratic administrative structures to sustain it. Gradually, but inevitably, bureaucracy spreads to virtually every social sphere – the economy, government, political parties, church, welfare, military, education, and science.

Bureaucratization involves a unique administrative and social order; social institutions are organized according to a spirit of impersonality and professionalism. Bureaucratic institutions are divided into offices, each defined by a specific function and social role; offices are arranged in a hierarchical way so that there is a kind of top-down command system; individuals are assigned specific roles with clearly marked duties and authority. Bureaucratic business is carried out according to a set of impersonal rules and procedures that aim to exclude personal considerations and conflicts from interfering with institutional operations. Finally, bureaucracy creates a new type of worker, the official or white collar worker, who is a technically skilled, specialized professional hired on the basis of qualifications.

Weber maintained that bureaucracy's spirit of impersonality and professionalism makes it the most efficient mode of administration in modern societies. Its spread is inevitable and irreversible. For example, bureaucratization makes possible mass democracy and national social planning. Moreover, bureaucracy promotes social justice and equality, as individuals – as both clients and officials – are, in principle, treated equally and fairly. The same features that make bureaucracy efficient and socially beneficial, however, render it a truly ominous social force. Weber left little doubt that bureaucracy was the most powerful social force in modernity, one that threatened humanity with a bleak future.

Bureaucracy is said to reduce individual freedom. In a bureaucratic society, individuals lose control over the means to satisfy their needs. For example, in a bureaucratic economy, whether capitalist or socialist, most individuals do not control access to the means of production (technology, raw material, labor) which, given their sheer size, technical complexity, and cost, are either bureaucratically administered or beyond the resources of most individuals. We are dependent on economic institutions for our livelihood. Similarly, the bureaucratization of the means of scientific and scholarly research means that individuals gain access to research technology and textual materials only as members of universities or research centers. As these institutions own the means of scientific production, they exercise control over science and scholarship.

Weber concluded that as institutions are bureaucratized, and individuals lose direct control over the means (e.g., economic, educational, military) to shape their own lives, they become dependent on bureaucracy to satisfy many of their needs. Bureaucratization fosters a social world where individuals are dependent and power-less. It cultivates an other-directed type of individual who values cooperative and approval-seeking behavior, the very opposite of the inner-directed, Puritan self who sought to refashion the world.

Bureaucracy foreshadows a political calamity. As individuals become dependent on bureaucracy, they believe that their fate is sealed by it. Ironically, modern citizens lose interest in politics, even as they are empowered by civil rights, political parties, and parliamentary bodies. Moreover, politicians find themselves dependent on the technical knowledge and skills of bureaucrats in order to formulate and implement public policy. The reliance of policy makers on the technical knowledge of bureaucratic officials and their limited public accountability encourage high-level bureaucrats to take control of the policy-making powers of politicians. The expanding political role of the bureaucracy is, according to Weber, unfortunate; democracy suffers because citizens lose power; bureaucracies are not accountable to citizens. And, the power interests of the nation suffer because bureaucrats are not leaders with political vision but career-oriented and driven by narrow, parochial interests.

Weber paints a bleak picture of the development of modern Western modernity. The initial dynamic phase of modernization fosters widespread bureaucratization, which threatens to thwart individuality, freedom, and democracy. In the face of the bureaucratization of society, the two dominant social ideologies become obsolete. Classical individualistic liberalism, with its championing of unrestrained individual-ism, a free market, and minimal government, is increasingly irrelevant since it ignores the social power of bureaucratization. The socialist promise of freedom through state economic regulation and mass democracy would unintentionally encourage the spread of bureaucratization and political authoritarianism.

What can be done? Like the Puritan that he so admired, Weber counsels that we face facts: The evil today is neither capitalism nor socialism but bureaucracy. Neither nostalgia for the past nor a utopian flight from the present (e.g., socialism) are responsible reactions to *irreversible social bureaucratization*. "Where administration has been completely bureaucratized, the resulting system of domination is practically indestructible."[6] Weber offers a sobering view of our social prospects. Bureaucracy is permanent, but, if we promote conflicting bureaucracies, some aspects of social dynamism and freedom can be preserved. Thus, Weber defended capitalism against the socialist Left less because he disagreed with their critique of its class inequalities than because he believed that capitalism preserves the tension between state elites, business owners, and unions that promotes social dynamism and freedom. Weber was especially worried that the bureaucratization of politics would give rise to mediocre, conservative leaders who would be either guided by parochial social interests or ruled by the bureaucracy. In the context of the ongoing conflict among world powers, Weber feared that weak political leaders would diminish national power and pose a danger of political or economic colonization. He recommended a political arrangement that would encourage the rise of charismatic leaders to offset the bureaucratization of the state and the political parties. Toward the end of his life, he defended a political system in which political leaders would be selected directly by the citizens. Ignoring the potential for abuse, Weber hoped that this would permit the rise of charismatic leaders who would otherwise be repressed by bureaucratized political parties and interest groups.

SCIENCE, TRUTH, AND VALUES

Weber crafted a theoretical perspective on social life that was filled with contradictions and irony. He was an Enlightener who passionately believed in the power of reason and science. He was an ardent defender of modernity against its critics. Yet Weber's vision of modernity is bleak. He imagined advanced phases of modernization resembling the stultifying empires of the ancient East: authoritarian bureaucracies dominating public life and a retreat into cult movements or narrowly private lives.

Despite his dark vision of humankind's future, Weber never relinquished an Enlightenment faith in science. Unlike conservative or romantic critics of modernity who viewed science, like other aspects of modernity, as socially destructive, Weber's faith in science was never shaken. Even in the face of humanity's imminent descent into darkness, Weber imagined himself as remaining soberly engaged with the world as it is. Like the Puritans he so admired, Weber would not take flight in prophecy or ideological fancy. If science had to abandon its dream of a resurrected humanity, it must not forsake its role of compelling us to take a sober, responsible look at ourselves.

To the extent that Weber preserved an Enlightenment faith in science, it was a sobering faith compared with that of many of his predecessors and contemporaries. For Condorcet and Comte or Marx and Durkheim, science was a catalyst of modernization and social progress. Science destroyed the myths and superstitions that constrained our lives and originated from ignorance, error, or priestly manipulation. Science freed us from prejudice to see reality as it is; it revealed humanity as the active agent in shaping the social world. Finally, science promised to uncover the principles of social organization and laws of history; it made possible a rational organization of society by providing moral and policy guidelines based on social knowledge.

Weber shared a belief in the disillusioning power of science. Science can force us to take responsibility for our behavior. By viewing the social world as a creation of individual actions, science compels individuals to grasp their own actions as socially consequential. Weber even imagines a "moral" role for science: by clarifying the personal and social implications of our values, science can exert pressure on us to act in a morally responsible way. Science cannot, though, illuminate the meaning and purpose of history; it cannot provide us with directives for social action since moral decisions are always subject to contention and ultimately are matters of conscience.[7] In this regard, Weber criticizes Enlighteners who wish to go beyond viewing science as a medium of social disillusionment to constructing new world views. Efforts to replace a religious with a scientific world view (e.g., Comte or Marx) are doomed to failure because of their artificial, merely intellectual character. Moreover, Weber was insistent that science forfeits its credibility when it goes beyond interpreting facts to assigning meaning and value to social events.

Reacting to the tendency of many social scientists to blur the line between science and morality and to make science into almost a religion, Weber advanced the doctrine of value neutrality. Social science should confine itself to establishing facts and causal relationships and proposing general models and sociological principles. Value judgments and proposals for social reform belong in the realm of private life and politics. Why? Because, though it is possible to have knowledge about social facts and their causal relations, judgments about their value are a matter of opinion or ideology. It is a matter of empirical science that capitalism involves private property and the production of commodities; it is a matter of ideology as to whether capitalism is good because it expands freedom or bad because it creates inequalities. Science and ideology, factual knowledge, and moral judgment are, in Weber's view, separate intellectual spheres.

In Weber's more considered reflections on science, however, he is compelled by the logic of his own analysis to throw suspicion around this neat division between science and morality. This point deserves clarification.

The scientist, says Weber, never approaches reality with a blank mind. Reality is always filtered through a conceptual lens. We always know the world from a particular standpoint. A standpoint involves a series of assumptions about the nature of the world. For example, an image of the social world as a hierarchical purposeful order, a social organism, an aggregate of self-interested individuals, a dynamic contradictory system, or images of society as driven by economic or class dynamics, religious ideas, or nation-state conflicts, frame what we can know. These overarching, cohering frameworks are products of a specific social milieu and cannot be directly subject to empirical verification or proof. Yet their role is pivotal in scientific research. They guide our problem selection; they frame what we see, how we see the world, and the significance and role that "facts" or "events" play in social knowledge. These overarching frameworks are translated into a series of concepts, typologies, and causal models that make possible a scientific or empirical-analytical ordering of reality.

Our broad intellectual standpoint governs the major changes in scientific theories. As a standpoint shifts, so will its empirical and conceptual apparatus, including what problems are considered important, the underlying concepts, causal models, and so on. Weber makes it perfectly clear, moreover, that it is not specialized scientific research that drives these broad shifts in the standpoint and conceptual structure of science, but changes in the broader social context. Broad social changes alter our basic images of society and social values which, in turn, get translated into new areas of interest, problems to study, and new conceptual and empirical approaches.

All research in the cultural [social] sciences in an age of specialization, once it is oriented towards a given subject matter through particular settings of problems and has established its methodological principles, will consider the analysis of the data as an end in itself. . . . It will lose its awareness of its ultimate rootedness in value ideas in general. . . . But there comes a moment when the atmosphere changes. The significance of the unreflectively utilized viewpoints becomes uncertain. . . . The light of the great cultural problems moves on. Then science too prepares to change its standpoint and its analytical apparatus.[8]

Is not Weber saying that it is social interests and values that structure science, that govern its problem selection, conceptual approaches, and transformation? It is this understanding of the social structuring of science that compelled Weber, despite his principled declaration of the separation of science and morality, to conclude that it is but a "hair-line that separates science from faith."[9] Weber still hedged. He was convinced that values inform science in its problem selection, concept formation, methodological criteria (e.g., economy, precision, consistency), and interpretive function. Moreover, if broad social interests and values are the prime movers of social scientific change, perhaps Weber should have surmised, with his usual sober and disillusioning candor, that the idea of science as a pure sphere of knowledge is itself an illusion of the modern West!

Suggested Readings

Reinhard Bendix, *Max Weber* (New York: Doubleday, 1962).
Roslyn Bologh, *Love or Greatness* (London: Unwin Hyman, 1990).
Randall Collins, *Weberian Social Theory* (Cambridge: Cambridge University Press, 1984).
Wolfgang Mommsen, *The Age of Bureaucracy* (New York: Blackwell, 1983).
Lawrence Scaff, *Fleeing the Iron Cage* (Berkeley: University of California Press, 1989).

References

1   Max Weber, *The Protestant Ethic and the Spirit of Capitalism* (New York: Free Press, 1958).
2   Weber, *The Protestant Ethic and the Spirit of Capitalism*, p. 181.
3   Max Weber, *Economy and Society*, vols. 1–3 (New York: Bedminster Press, 1968); *Gesammelte Aufsätze zur Religionssoziologie*, vols. 1–3 (Stuttgart: Verlag: 1988 [1920]).
4   Max Weber, *The Religion of China: Confucianism and Taoism* (New York: Free Press, 1951).
5   Max Weber, "Charisma and Its Transformation," in *Economy and Society*, vol. 3.
6   Max Weber, "Bureaucracy," in *Economy and Society*, vol. 3, p. 987.
7   Max Weber, "Science as a Vocation," in *From Max Weber: Essays in Sociology*, edited by Hans Gerth and C. W. Mills (New York: Oxford University Press, 1946).
8   Max Weber, "Objectivity in Social Science and Social Policy," in *The Methodology of the Social Sciences* (New York: Free Press, 1949), p. 112.
9   Weber, *The Methodology of the Social Sciences*, p. 110.

Afterword to Part I

Why do we still read and think about the classics? Let me suggest two reasons.

First, from Adam Smith or Voltaire to Weber, these thinkers fashioned compelling social visions of humanity. The human condition is understood as fundamentally social and historical. If you want to understand social inequality, poverty, economic growth, nationalism, love and gender roles, the classics say you must examine social factors such as social class, religion, or population dynamics. Why is this important? A consistently social approach to human behavior allows us to purposefully bring about a better social world. Instead of assuming that nature or God control the fate of humanity, the classics hold that humans can deliberately shape their own future. At the core of classical social thinking is the hope that social knowledge can contribute to a freer, more rational individual and collective life.

Second, the classics crafted imaginative images of social life and the modern world. These social maps continue to be useful as many of us try to make sense of our lives and try to make a world where there is less suffering and injustice.

Against views of society as a collection of individuals, Comte thought of society as an organic whole welded together by shared religious and moral beliefs. Comte alerted us to the dangers of celebrating individualism without considering the effects of too much individualism on social and moral order. Like Durkheim, Comte believed that a healthy society is one that is made coherent and unified by common beliefs and values. Comte forced us to consider society as a sort of independent reality apart from the individual. Individual freedom is important but so too is the unity and coherence of the whole society.

Marx shared with Comte a view of society as something more than a collection of individuals. However, Marx emphasized political and economic dynamics, not religion and culture. He thought of society as organized around the clash of social interests anchored in social class. Whether an individual is a laborer or a business owner matters, not just in terms of standard of living but in terms of beliefs, political

Contested Knowledge: Social Theory Today, Fifth Edition. Steven Seidman.
© 2013 John Wiley & Sons, Ltd. Published 2013 by John Wiley & Sons, Ltd.

power, social opportunities, and so on. Drawing from a limited stock of categories (e.g., labor, mode of production, social class, ideology), he fashioned a magnificent synthetic view of society and history. Marx related a social drama of epoch proportions that not only is useful in making sense of inequalities and social conflicts but tells us how to create a more just society. More than that of any other social thinker, Marx's vision of society and modernity has moved the world.

Durkheim and Weber are the heirs of Comte and Marx. They took over the idea of the social character of humanity; they offered views of social life that were sometimes deeply at odds with what many of us believe. In particular, instead of seeing society as produced by individuals, they considered individualism to be a product of social forces.

For example, the social shaping of the self is a chief motif in Durkheim's sociology. In *Suicide*, he argues that the act of self-destruction, an act often imagined as psychologically driven, is explained by social conditions, for example, the degree to which an individual is socially integrated or regulated. Accordingly, the remedy to suicide is less individual than social reform. In *The Division of Labor in Society*, he proposes that individualism is a product of social forces. In industrial societies, the individual becomes a common cultural belief and value. This makes possible legal protections for the self and a wide latitude for subjective choice and expression. In contrast to individualistic notions of social life, Durkheim approaches the individual as embedded in social institutions and emphasizes the importance of shared cultural beliefs and values as a condition of freedom and social unity. A good society, Durkheim held, is one where the individual is anchored in stable communities, where individual needs and purposes are made clear and limited, and where a condition of social justice prevails. Despite his aspirations to make sociology into a respectable science, Durkheim did not shy away from proposing a notion of the good society and telling us how to achieve this state.

Weber emphasized the cultural construction of the self. This was a key point in *The Protestant Ethic and the Spirit of Capitalism*. Prior to Weber's time, it was often assumed that individuals are naturally motivated to compete for economic goods and accumulate wealth. Capitalism is often regarded as an expression of human nature. Aren't people greedy and self-interested by nature? Against this view, Weber held that capitalist economic behavior, which entails work specialization, career success, accumulating wealth, and delayed gratification, is in part a result of social beliefs and values. Weber traced a capitalistic economic ethic to the Reformation. It was the religious significance of economic behavior among Protestants that drove people to their obsession with money and wealth. He arrived at the paradoxical conclusion that it wasn't human nature that produced capitalism but the spiritual longing of Puritans, who assigned to capitalist behavior a religious, redemptive value. In other words, Weber asserted the cultural formation of individualistic economic behavior. And far from celebrating modern life for setting the individual free, Weber observed a growing trend toward bureaucratization that could crush individual freedom. Today, we are all Weberians in the sense that while bureaucracy is embraced for its efficiency, we are keenly aware of the threat it presents to freedom and democracy.

Whether its Marx's vision of a modern world in the throes of class conflict or Weber's image of individuals in the iron-clad grip of bureaucracy, it is almost impossible to think about our world without drawing on the ideas of the classics. We read them because they have helped shape our world and remain indispensable for understanding it.

Still, Marx and Comte, Durkheim and Weber are very much the children of their time. Their grand stories of human history always begin and end in the West; men step forward as the chief actors on the scene of history; despite their claims to objectivity, they offered social visions that clearly marked out good and bad, evil and redemption. Today, we can appreciate that their faith in science, reason, individualism, progress, and the West contributed to the making of modern colonial empires and men's dominance, but also in producing powerful moral and political visions filled with social hope for a better world.

Part II

Rethinking the Classical Tradition: American Sociology

Introduction to Part II

Marx created Marxism, a tradition that understood theory to be in the service of social change. Marxism's success as a theory is related to its becoming part of a world-wide movement to bring about a socialist revolution. In the United States and in virtually every European nation, a working-class movement took shape in the mid to late nineteenth century that forever changed the political landscape. By the early twentieth century, the ideas of Marx were being absorbed into universities across the globe. Marxism was now a reference point for all serious social thinkers. For example, the sociological ideas of Durkheim and Weber took shape in a critical dialogue with Marxism. While a socialist movement championing a Marxist ideology did not have the presence in the United States that it had in many European nations, Marx's writings were being read by social critics and by academics. By the post-World War II period, Marxism was likely the leading social perspective in the world. It was no longer possible to theorize or do sociology without engaging the ideas of Marx and his successors.

The sociological theory of Comte, Durkheim, and Weber didn't fare nearly as well. Comte was a prominent thinker through much of the nineteenth century. Indeed, he had a considerable following in Britain and the United States even through the first decades of the twentieth century. But, by the mid-twentieth century, he was almost a forgotten figure. Even though his ideas lost favor among academics, his vision of a natural science of society has been periodically revived and championed, as we'll see in the case of Randall Collins and Peter Blau.

Durkheim established himself in France as a thinker of the first rank. He was an important figure in French academic and public intellectual life. He commented on public affairs and was the driving force in institutionalizing sociology in France. His social ideas spawned disciples and he created a Durkheimian school of sociology. By the early twentieth century, Durkheim was increasingly recognized in France and elsewhere as a master social thinker.

Contested Knowledge: Social Theory Today, Fifth Edition. Steven Seidman.
© 2013 John Wiley & Sons, Ltd. Published 2013 by John Wiley & Sons, Ltd.

Weber fared much the same as Durkheim. Recognized as one of the most learned thinkers of his time, Weber was also a public figure. He was in great demand by public officials and politicians for counsel in political matters. But Weber neither created a movement nor a school of social thinking. There was no Weberian sociology after his death. His ideas were widely discussed in Germany but not beyond its borders, at least through the early decades of the twentieth century.

In the first half of the twentieth century, Marx, Weber, and Durkheim were not the towering figures they became by the 1960s. Aside from Marx, few academics and even fewer in the general public even would have heard of Durkheim or Weber. Their writings were not translated. In fact, it was Comte and the great English social evolutionary theorist Herbert Spencer who were the key figures shaping American sociology. Some of the most important American thinkers of the time such as William Graham Sumner and Lester Ward drew heavily on the ideas of Comte and Spencer to explain the great changes surrounding industrialization, urbanism, migration, and immigration that were taking place no less in America then in Europe.

So, how is it that Marx, Durkheim, and Weber came to be viewed as "classics" or as the founding figures of modern social theory? These European thinkers might not have become the core of a classical tradition had it not been for the prestige of French and especially Germany universities in the early twentieth century. Remember, research-oriented universities were relatively new in America, while in Europe they reached back centuries. Many of the key social thinkers in America studied in European universities. They followed the debates that were raging in France and Germany around the origin of capitalism, the nature of secularism, the prospects for revolutionary change and democracy, and so on. And, Marx, Durkheim, and Weber were among the key figures they read. The debates over these large social issues were taking on a new relevance in the United States as the Great Depression, fascism and Nazism, and social movements associated with feminism and black civil rights generated great turmoil and change in America. In other words, as America began to experience many of the same upheavals experienced by Europe, such as economic crises, class conflict, and left- and right-wing challenges to a liberal society, Comtean- and Spencerian-styled evolutionary theories lost credibility. American thinkers began to look for ideas that spoke to their changing social reality, especially ideas that addressed serious social dangers and conflicts. Many thinkers began to turn to the master thinkers of Europe.

The chief figure in shifting American social theory away from Comte and Spencer to Marx, Durkheim, and Weber was Talcott Parsons. Parsons studied in Germany and when he returned to Harvard he brought with him the European focus on capitalism and the ideas of Marx and his sociological counterparts. As we'll see, Parsons's *The Structure of Social Action* was a pivotal text in the making of a classical tradition that placed Marx, Durkheim, and Weber at its center.

Parsons dominated American sociology and social theory from the 1950s through the end of the 1960s. However, as America was in the throes of new social conflicts, Parsons's ideas struck many as out of sync with the times. Parsonian sociology was attacked as thinkers looked to fashion new social maps to make sense of a changing social world. Curiously, though, critics of Parsons did not abandon his canonizing of

Marx, Weber, and Durkheim. Instead, many of these critics sought to reinterpret the "classics" as they developed new theoretical perspectives.

From the 1950s to the present, American social theory, especially sociological theory, has often taken shape through interpreting or building on the work of the classics, which until recently has been associated almost exclusively with these European thinkers. For example, C. Wright Mills, perhaps Parsons's most formidable critic, fashioned a critical social theory by building on Marx and Weber. Or, one of the most far-reaching efforts to develop a new social theory, but one that built considerably on the classics, was *The Social Construction of Reality* by Peter Berger and Thomas Luckmann. Though lacking Parsons's methodical elaboration of ideas into a system, Berger and Luckmann offered an outline of a theory of society that rivals Parsons in its sweep and elegance. But, the conflict sociology of Randall Collins and, as we'll see, the moral sociology of Robert Bellah are no less inspired by the classics in fashioning their own social vision.

5

The Grand Theory of Talcott Parsons, Peter Berger, and Thomas Luckmann

TALCOTT PARSONS

After spending a year at the London School of Economics, Parsons took his doctorate from the University of Heidelberg, Germany. It was not, I think, fortuitous that his dissertation was on German perspectives on modern capitalism. The success of the Russian Revolution gave enhanced credibility to the Marxist critique of capitalism and Western liberalism as deeply flawed and destined to decline. Parsons hoped to find in the German sociologists an alternative to the Marxist critique. In the next decade, Parsons's project would go beyond the defense of capitalism. In the face of the Great Depression and the rise of Nazism, Parsons aimed to provide a compelling defense of Western liberal civilization. He turned to European sociology in order to find a new foundation for a general theory of society and history that would support his liberal world view.

Parsons's intellectual strategy was bold. He largely ignored his American predecessors and contemporaries, and instead attempted a wholesale switch to a distinctively European-centered sociology. But, Comte and Spencer were to be replaced as the core of the classical tradition by Weber and Durkheim. This was the intention of his first major work, *The Structure of Social Action*, a book that was largely ignored by his contemporaries but that has since become a "classic" text in sociological theory – a measure indeed of Parsons's success in shaping sociology.[1]

The Structure of Social Action may strike us as a rather odd book to write in the 1930s. In the face of a devastating economic depression, a communist revolution in Russia, the rise of fascism and Nazism, Parsons delivers a massive 800-page book whose primary question is: "What is the general, indeed universal, structure of social action?" Why would Parsons choose to engage in a seemingly philosophical investigation of the nature of social action as the world was reeling from cataclysmic, epoch-shaping social

Contested Knowledge: Social Theory Today, Fifth Edition. Steven Seidman.
© 2013 John Wiley & Sons, Ltd. Published 2013 by John Wiley & Sons, Ltd.

Talcott Parsons (1902–79) was born in Colorado Springs, USA. Parsons studied in Germany at the University of Heidelberg. He spent his entire career at Harvard and became the dominant American social theorist in the postwar period. Parsons fashioned a new image of society as a "social system." The parts of the system such as the family and the economy had specific roles and were interdependent. If one part or "subsystem" broke down, the system would experience social dysfunctions. Parsons was optimistic about the future of humankind. He imagined America leading the world into a new era of freedom and democracy.

changes? Parsons's book is studiously academic; it is composed of painstakingly detailed textual analyses of European thinkers with an eye not to their perspectives on capitalism or politics but to their most general ideas about the self, social action, and society.

Is this the case of an academic retreating into the calm civility of bookish learning in the face of discomforting realities? Perhaps not. Like many of his contemporaries, Parsons thought that the crisis of Western liberalism was more than a social crisis; it was an intellectual crisis. If Western societies were tumbling down the road of self-destruction, it was not unreasonable to suppose that this reflected, in part, certain habits of thought. A crisis that so fundamentally challenged Western civilization warranted a study of our most elementary social ideas. Underlying this philosophical or theoretical inquiry was a hope: the possibility that social theory could contribute to reestablishing secure foundations for Western liberal civilization.

Why focus on the structure of social action? Parsons believed that our assumptions about social action are the most elementary social ideas. Concepts of human motivation, behavior, and goals shape in far-reaching ways the way we think about social institutions, politics, and social change. This is true not only for social theorists but for all of us; each of us holds ideas about the individual and social action, and these shape our broad perception of politics and society. Moreover, everyday social ideas are shaped by the broad intellectual perspectives created by academics and intellectuals. To the extent that social reform requires changes in the way people think about the self and society, theoretical inquiry aimed at changing social ideas would have a moral and political significance.

Parsons was convinced that the principal Western cultural traditions held to contradictory views of society. On the one hand, there were perspectives (e.g., utilitarianism, behaviorism, Marxism, social Darwinism) which conceived of the individual as adapting to physical or social forces beyond her or his immediate control; these forces drove individuals to act in specific ways. For example, instinct theories such as Freudian psychology described individuals as propelled by biological drives; behaviorists explained human conduct by mechanistic stimulus-response patterns; many sociologists explain behavior by appealing to market forces or class position. The key feature of these theories of social action is that the individual merely adapts to objective conditions (biological, psychological, or sociological) which determine our social behavior. Parsons calls this social perspective, at times, positivism, utilitarianism, or materialism. On the other hand, Parsons notes opposing perspectives (e.g., German idealism, historicism, American pragmatism) that conceive of the individual as the originator and director of his or her own action. Such perspectives involve explanations of behavior that refer to the values or beliefs of the individual. An example is Weber's account of capitalist behavior in terms of the religious vision of the Puritan. Parsons calls social action that is interpreted as expressing subjective motivations and meanings "idealism."

Western culture has been divided between materialist and idealist social ideas. Parsons believed that each perspective has its advantages and drawbacks. For example, idealism views the individual as an active agent who can shape her or his own social destiny. However, idealism may be interpreted as blaming individuals for their own misfortunes. Materialism may make society responsible for individual misfortune, but it conceives of the individual as passive or as a product of forces beyond individual control. This may legitimate a culture of social engineering. Parsons argued that the division between materialism and idealism was at the core of social theory and Western culture; it contributed to social and ideological discord and to the present social crisis. In *The Structure of Social Action*, Parsons hoped to fashion a perspective that integrated subjective freedom and objective determinism in order to establish stable intellectual foundations for Western liberalism.

The Structure of Social Action is occupied with detailed textual analyses of the key sociological works of Pareto (Italy), Weber (Germany), Durkheim (France), and Marshall (England). Underlying these interpretive sketches is a far-reaching claim: despite their different national settings, divergent empirical concerns, and varied ideological commitments, each of these social theorists, almost uncannily, gravitated toward a common theoretical standpoint that involved the integration of materialism and idealism. Classical European social theory converged towards what Parsons calls a "voluntaristic theory of action." Parsons aimed to clarify this new theoretical foundation for sociology and, indeed, Western social thought.

At the core of the voluntarist theory of action is an understanding of human action as involving both freedom and necessity, or individual choice and social constraint. Individuals, argued Parsons, do not simply adapt to objective conditions, but direct their own behavior in ways that express their subjective interests and values. Approaching human action as involving individual choice requires that the basic social concepts and explanations of sociology make reference to a realm of subjective meanings. Yet a sociology that explains human action only as an expression of individual choice is inadequate since our conduct is always constrained by objective conditions, e.g., our physical and psychological makeup or social class position. Although some of these conditions may be able to be manipulated by the individual, many of them cannot, at least not in the immediate course of action. Accordingly, we need a conceptual vocabulary that speaks to the experience of subjective choice and to the social constraints on action. Formally stated, the voluntaristic theory of action assumes an *actor* who exerts *effort* in a *situation* in which some aspects are unalterable (*conditions of action*), while other aspects can be used as *means* to achieve *goals*; both the selection of means and goals are guided by *norms*.

The Structure of Social Action was an exercise in general theory. It was intended to clarify the conceptual premises of a general theory of society. Parsons urges that, in place of either one-sided materialist or idealist premises, our starting point should be an integrated "voluntaristic theory of action." Social action is imagined as combining both subjective choice and objective constraint. Although he asserts that this theoretical standpoint is empirically superior to either materialism or idealism, Parsons makes no attempt in this work to specify what empirical concepts, models, or social explanations might derive from his theory of action. The aim of the *Structure* was to set out the foundations for a general theory of society.

The stock market crash came in 1929; in 1933, the Nazis seized power. Parsons spent the decade at work on *The Structure of Social Action*, a book framing social thought as anchored in its image of social action. Yet Parsons was oddly silent when it came to spelling out its moral and political gains. Parsons thought that an investigation into the elementary premises of social thought could speak to the current social crisis; however, he never clarified in what ways this was so.

If Parsons did not feel compelled to give any moral or political account of his theorizing, perhaps it was because he believed that this would force him to acknowledge the moral vision that shaped his work. If Parsons defended the value of the voluntaristic theory of action on strictly conceptual grounds, perhaps it was because he realized that any other justification would push him into moral and political argumentation. No matter how much Parsons wished to frame his theory of action in a "pure" theoretical language (actor, effort, goals, conditions of action), the plain truth is that he is making a moral argument about human behavior and social ideals. Whether individual behavior is viewed as "free" or "determined" or as involving subjective choice or necessity is at some level a statement of values. Parsons's preference for imagining human action as voluntary yet constrained is a statement of liberal social hope, the hope that society values choice and diversity within responsible limits. Parsons refused to concede the moral underpinnings of his theorizing. Perhaps he felt that such a concession would undermine the authority of his argument. Thus, he cloaked his moral vision in a language of value-neutral, objective theory. Indeed, the highly abstract, general character of his theorizing seems to remove theory from any moral or political taint. It was as if he believed that the authority of his ideas depended on their being seen as an expression of pure theory.

Functionalist sociology as liberal advocacy

After *The Structure of Social Action*, Parsons's writings went in two directions. He turned to more empirical concerns, as he sought to address current developments.[2] He also articulated his ideas about action into a set of premises and concepts that could serve as the basis for a general theory of society. Specifically, Parsons developed a model of society as a functioning social system. It is to this general theory that we briefly turn. I focus on his most important theoretical statement, *The Social System*.[3]

The Social System shifted from the individual actor to patterns of interaction or what he calls "the social system." Parsons wished though to retain the dual emphasis on subjective choice and objective conditions. At the heart of *The Social System* is a systems model: society is composed of three analytically distinct systems (the personality system is composed of individual needs and motivations; the cultural system relates to shared beliefs and values; and the social system consists of a plurality of social roles and norms). It is important to keep in mind that these systems are not actual entities but represent analytical dimensions of social life. Individual needs, social roles, norms, and cultural values are always interrelated. Consider a baseball team. To be a member of the team each player must make the team value of winning (cultural system) his or her own; each player must know what behavior is expected of him or her (social system) in order to promote a goal; finally, each player must identify with the team or have his or her needs met by membership (personality system). A systems approach to a base-ball team would, accordingly, propose a multidimensional explanation analyzing the interrelations between the personality, social, and cultural systems. Parsons imagined that his general systems model would form the foundations of a comprehensive science of humanity. Particular sciences would specialize in one "system," e.g., psy-chology would focus on the personality system and anthropology on the cultural system. In this grand scheme, sociology was the study of the social system.

Inspired by this grand theoretical vision, Parsons viewed *The Social System* as laying out the basic concepts that would unify and guide sociologists in analyzing social systems. By social systems, Parsons meant virtually any pattern of interaction that has achieved sufficient continuity to have evolved social roles, statuses, social expectations, and norms, e.g., a baseball team, hospital, university, club, friendship, family, or political party. The key question in analyzing social systems is to explain social integration. Assuming that social systems are composed of a multitude of roles, norms, statuses, obligations, and authority relations and that they are subject to conflict and change, how is social stability routinely achieved?

Parsons disputed explanations of social order that appealed to notions of a human inclination to civic order or a process of natural selection and survival; individualistic accounts do not explain the coordination of conflicting interests. Similarly, he took issue with perspectives that explained social order as a result of domination, for example, the coercive power of the state or a ruling social class; such accounts leave no room for subjective choice and social consensus. For Parsons, social order was made possible by a series of complex processes of social coordination and cultural consensus.

Proceeding from the simple to the complex, Parsons argued that well-functioning social systems require a "fit" between the needs and motivations of the individual and the role requirements of the institution or social unit. For example, if professors are expected to concentrate on research, but universities value teaching, there would be a great deal of institutional discontent, conflict, and instability. A stable university pre-supposes that the expectations of professors and university administrators coincide. What Parsons called the "complementarity of expectations" must occur in a multitude of social interactions or role relations in order for social systems to achieve routine order. Thus, not only must there be a fit between professors and administrators but overlap in expectations between professors and students, professors and staff, profes-sors and parents of students, among professors, and so on.

If routine social order presupposes a complementarity of expectations, how does this come about? Parsons's account draws heavily on a notion of cultural consensus. Let me explain. In order for there to be a fit between personal and institutional needs and between individuals and social roles, there must be a minimal level of shared understandings and values. If individuals occupied sharply different worlds of meaning and value, social interaction and institutional functioning would be embroiled in continuous conflicts. But how does cultural integration translate into social integration? Parsons spoke of "internalization," by which he meant a socialization process where cultural meanings become part of the self; the individual, as it were, takes into him or herself the beliefs, norms, and values of the society. To the extent that there is a shared culture and to the extent that socialization is roughly successful, individuals grow up with similar understandings and motivations. Social order will, accordingly, exhibit a consensual aspect, i.e., individuals obey social norms and rules because they believe in them, because they express who they are and what they want society to be. To explain routine order, Parsons introduced a second key concept: "institutionalization." Whereas internalization refers to culture becoming a part of the self, institutionalization is a parallel process of culture becoming a part of the institutional order, i.e., defining roles, statuses, norms, and goals. If the same cultural patterns that define the needs and expectations of the individual also define institutional environments, we would expect a fit between individuals and institutions and the achievement of social integration.

Parsons was aware that all of these conditions – the complementarity of expectations, cultural consensus, successful socialization and institutionalization – are never fully present in any society. Social stability is rarely achieved in the absence of a great deal of social conflict. For example, in societies characterized by individualism and social pluralism, cultural consensus and therefore social integration will be precarious. If society permits substantial divergence with respect to ideologies, we would expect conflicting understandings of needs, expectations, social norms, and therefore institutional conflict. Indeed, Parsons expected endemic social disturbances stemming from everyday disruptions in socialization and institutionalization. These strains in the "fit" between the individual, culture, and institutional roles may be "functional" if they encourage social innovation.

There are, however, more threatening sources of social conflict. Parsons spoke of social disturbances stemming from "allocative" conflicts. Social systems are, in essence, concerned with the allocation of social resources, personnel, and rewards. If social resources and rewards are scarce, division over who gets what and how much is inevitable. Social systems must evolve mechanisms to allocate resources (e.g., technology and personnel) and rewards (e.g., money and prestige) so that basic social requirements are satisfied. Viewed from the vantage point of allocation, problems of social system integration take on a more "materialist" or structural aspect. Are social systems distributing the social, technical, and human resources of society in a way that ensures individual and social reproduction? For example, is society producing enough food and housing? Is the educational system producing the kinds of skills needed in the economy? Is society producing enough technicians, physicians, or farm workers? Social system integration presupposes not only that the right resources are being produced and distributed at the needed levels, but that the allocation of resources, rewards, and personnel effectively keeps individuals satisfied and avoids major social divisions. In other words, social systems evolve mechanisms (i.e., norms of justice, performative standards) that determine how social rewards (e.g., money and prestige) are distributed among personnel. Widespread social perceptions that these allocative mechanisms are unfair will produce the kinds of social conflicts that Marx thought were integral to property-based societies.

Social system strains and conflicts are endemic and inevitable. Disruptions in social-ization and institutionalization are unavoidable. Individuals who, for whatever reason, grow up angry toward society will likely rebel against institutional expectations. Cultural diversity inevitably translates into conflicting interpretations of needs, social norms, and roles. Moreover, because social systems must allocate scarce resources, it is inevitable that the enormous problem of coordinating resources, ensuring that social functions receive the right level of inputs and yield the right level of outputs, will result, from time to time, in deficits. Similarly, the allocation of rewards to personnel can hardly avoid strains. If segments of a society perceive that the allocation of resources and rewards is unfair, if people feel that their level of prestige is unjust, further discon-tent over allocation norms and mechanisms will threaten serious social conflict. Should integration break down because of problems of socialization or allocation, social systems have recourse to the coercive force of the state, e.g., the law, police, military.

The Social System was published in 1951. In his subsequent writing, Parsons elabo-rated this systems approach in a decidedly more functionalist and formalistic direc-tion.[4] Social systems were now understood as having four functional requirements or needs: adaptation, goal attainment, integration, and pattern maintenance. Considering a whole society (e.g., the United States) as a type of social system, Parsons imagined four subsystems emerging to satisfy the four functional needs. Thus, the economy specializes in securing the material conditions of society (adaptation); political institu-tions prioritize the goals of society and ensure that they are attained by mobilizing social resources (goal attainment); the legal system plays a key role in maintaining social regulation and solidarity (integration); and the family, religion, and education aim to produce individuals who have the appropriate needs, values, motives, and skills (pattern maintenance). Each subsystem (e.g., the economy or the family), moreover, must handle these same four survival problems. For example, the family has problems of adaptation (economic maintenance), goal attainment (making major decisions), integration (coordinating family relationships), and pattern maintenance (transmit-ting family values to children).

By the early 1960s, Parsons had evolved a formalistic systems theory whose focus was on functional requirements, cybernetic flows, input/output processes, and interchanges between systems and subsystems. Although Parsons's systems theory took a decidedly antihumanistic turn, a language of systems imperatives crowding out a language of indi-vidual action and subjectivity, his social perspective involved an aggressive defense of Western liberalism. Nowhere is this clearer than in his theory of social evolution.

Liberal America: the end of history

Parsons's *The Structure of Social Action* and *The Social System* were written against the backdrop of social events that threatened Western liberalism, for example, the Russian Revolution, the Great Depression, European fascism, and World War II. In the postwar period, however, American liberal hegemony at home and abroad was consolidated. The renewed economic prosperity of the 1950s and the rise of state bureaucratic welfare systems focused on economic and domestic management raised the hope for many Americans that an era of social peace was beginning. This hope for social harmony was shared by many intellectuals, who expressed a strong disillusionment with radical ideologies and movements. Parsons shared this hope. Indeed, he recast this liberal social dream into an evolutionary theory in which an idealized contemporary America marks the virtual endpoint of history.[5]

Parsons outlined a vision of humanity evolving from "primitive" to modern societies. The key to change is a process of social differentiation. This refers to (1) the separation and relative autonomy of institutional spheres (e.g., family, economy, law, government, religion); (2) their functional specialization (e.g., family as a socializing agent); and (3) their interdependence (e.g., the family provides the economy with adult workers which, in turn, makes possible the material basis of the family). Social differentiation propels social evolution on a trajectory of social progress. Progress means that, in the course of social evolution, structures emerge that make possible higher levels of social adaptation for all of humankind, i.e., permit greater control over the environment. Parsons calls these structures "evolutionary universals." For example, a money economy, bureaucratic organization, and universalistic norms enhance social adaptation by permitting higher levels of material productivity, more efficient social coordination of resources, and the social inclusion of diverse social groups. In addition, progress means that history reveals a movement towards greater levels of individual freedom, democracy, and social integration. Parsons's perspective on social change as social progress can be clarified by turning briefly to his analysis of modernization.[6]

Parsons conceives of modernization as marking an epochal change in history. In premodern periods, "society" was experienced as a natural force determining the fate of individuals; modernity renders society an active, ongoing creation of individuals.

The ruling institutions of early modern Europe, for example, the monarchy, aristocracy, church, the corporate estate system, meant that individuals experienced society as if it were a fixed, closed, natural force. Individuals were born into a particular status (e.g., serf or noble) that determined their social destiny. There was little mobility or variation in social experience. Society was experienced as constricted, weighted with burdensome duties, obligations, customs, traditions, and responsibilities. This hierarchical, closed social system was destroyed by three successive revolutions: the industrial, democratic, and educational.

Beginning in the late eighteenth century, the industrial revolution brought about the differentiation of the household and the economy. In western Europe and the United States, this entailed the emergence of a market economy separate from the activities of the family household. This had two major consequences for social evolution. First, it enhanced the adaptive capacity of Western societies in that material production was enormously more efficient and productive. Second, it greatly expanded individual freedom; individuals had greater choice over occupational decisions which, in turn, meant greater latitude over personal matters, e.g., residence, intimate, and family arrangements. At a social level, the enhanced levels of freedom and mobility rendered the experience of society as more of a medium for individual choice than as a natural force fixing an individual's fate. The experience of society as something created by and for individuals was reinforced by the modern democratic revolutions. Whereas tradition and custom ruled early modern life, the democratic revolutions rendered society, in principle, as the intentional creation of individuals. Insofar as individuals are bearers of political and civil rights, society exists only through their consent. Citizenship gives individuals a feeling of society as their own, as responsive to human purpose and ideals. Of course, citizenship does not make individuals free if social resources are controlled by an elite or ruling class; society would still be experienced as oppressive, as something to escape from. Thus, the educational revolution is of the highest importance; it breaks down rigid barriers to individual mobility and opens up the social environment to the free play of individual talent and effort. The educational revolution of the twentieth century equalizes social competition; as individual social status reflects personal talent and effort, the experience of society is that of a hospitable field of individual action or a vehicle responsive to the needs and efforts of the self.

Parsons envisions modernization as creating an open, mobile, democratic social order. Central to modernization is the experience of society as an active, ongoing creation of its social members. Individuals feel an identification or a sense of "ownership" with the society as a whole. Nowhere is this social identification more evident than in the development of what Parsons calls a "societal community." Beyond particular attachments to specific class, ethnic, racial, or religious groups, modernity encourages the individual to feel a sense of belonging to a national community, a community of abstract national citizens. The creation of a societal community, of a society-wide moral community beyond particular moral groupings, makes possible high levels of individualism, pluralism, and social competition without threatening to devolve into social disorder.

Parsons thought that the United States had gone furthest in institutionalizing a modern societal community animated by an activist social ethos. America was settled as a multiethnic, multireligious society while creating an encompassing societal community. For example, religious freedom was established as a private choice; the state was to protect and guarantee freedom of belief by prohibiting the establishment of a state religion. Religious faith was, accordingly, perceived as irrelevant as a factor in national identity and inclusion. Similarly, ethnic group affiliation and identity were encouraged, even celebrated, in America, but as a personal choice, not a condition of national inclusion or citizenship. In principle, religious, ethnic, racial, or class affiliation is irrelevant for being an American. This is another way of saying that the United States created a social community apart from and above that of particular attachments, a community to which all Americans belong, as national citizens. A point of contrast would be Israel, where religious status (being Jewish) defines national citizenship. Institutionalizing a coherent societal community renders conflicts over ethnicity or religion less socially divisive as these are not, in principle, conflicts over national identity and inclusion. Moreover, to the extent that particularistic group attachments are not so socially weighted, individuals would be permitted more latitude in such decisions.

Parsons's social imagery is inspiring, even dreamy. For example, contrary to the many critics of modern society, Parsons highlights the real advance of personal liberties with modernization. "American society – and most modern societies without dictatorial regimes – has institutionalized a far broader range of freedoms than had any previous society." He continues:

> Perhaps they can be said to begin with freedom from some of the exigencies of physical life: ill health, short life, geographical circumscription, and the like. They certainly include reduced exposure to violence for most of the population most of the time. Higher incomes and extensive markets enhance freedom of choice in consumption. Then there is an immense range of free access to various services like education, public accommodations, and the like. There is widespread freedom of marital choice, of occupation, of religious adherence, of political allegiance, of thought, of speech and expression.[7]

Modern society is experienced as an open, fluid environment that permits individuals to interact in a relatively free, empowering way. Far from society being imagined as oppressive, as burdened with the weight of tradition and coercion, it provides a secure space for individuals.

The autonomy of theory

Parsons frankly confessed that he was an "uncurable theorist." He approached theory as an effort to grasp the most abstract, fundamental, and universal features of society and to weave them into a general theory of society, all and every society.

Parsons had a truly Olympian image of theory. To aspire to the heights of universal knowledge, theory had to be thoroughly disengaged from current social and political conflicts. The theorist should be interested in nothing more than truth. Whether Parsons was theorizing about social action, the social system, social evolution, or the human condition, his aim was to lay bare the most abstract, elementary, and universal aspects of social processes. He aspired to reach for a concept of the social that was purged of all particular, historical social aspects. Parsons offered a vision of theory as an autonomous, intellectual enterprise, unsullied by social interests or moral advocacy.

Parsons viewed theory as a foundational exercise. Its aim was to clarify the most basic premises, concepts, and explanatory models of sociology and, indeed, social science. Theory was to unify and guide empirical science. Much of Parsons's theorizing aimed to provide conceptual foundations, to legislate a set of concepts and explanatory logics for the human sciences. Parsons wished to elaborate this conceptual foundation into a general theory of society and history; he aspired to an encompassing theoretical system that would, in effect, render his heirs little more than disciples whose work would amount to smoothing out the rough edges of Parsons's grand synthesis. Somewhere in this project is a hope that theory and science will benefit humanity. Unfortunately, nowhere is such a moral aim articulated; nowhere does Parsons clarify the moral or political meaning of his theorizing or offer moral rationales for his theories. In Parsons, theory is intended to be cut loose from its moral and political moorings; whatever moral vision animated him, it was buried beneath layers of morally purged vocabularies, muted by the dogma of value-neutrality, objectivity, general theory, and social knowledge.

PETER BERGER AND THOMAS LUCKMANN

Parsons's voluntaristic theory of social action was intended to provide an alternative to Marxist views of society and modernity. Parsons argued that subjective beliefs and shared meanings are integral to the human condition. If all social behavior is guided by norms, values, and moral ideals, a materialist view of society is exposed as one-sided. Parsons argued, moreover, that society is not just a struggle for economic gain and power but involves individuals fabricating shared worlds of meaning, engaging in rituals that create forms of solidarity and community, and aspiring to social ideals and transcendent goals, for example, salvation, justice, self-fulfillment, or autonomy.

Parsons imagined the possibility of a culture-centered sociology or a sociology that took seriously processes of identity formation, the making of social solidarities, the role of ritual and common values in social integration. In this regard, Parsons challenged the dominant image of modernity as a secular, rational, economic, materialist universe. Although he never surrendered a deeply Enlightenment vision of modern societies as marching down a path of social progress, he imagined modernity as an epoch with its own myths, rituals, solidarities, sacred beliefs, and redemptive hopes. Against the current of much Enlightenment thinking, Parsons, like Freud and Nietzsche, and Weber and Durkheim, before him, found a place in his social perspective for the nonrational, for the deeply emotional and volatile aspects of the human condition.

As Parsonian thinking came under attack in the 1960s and 1970s, many social thinkers and sociologists abandoned his strong interest in cultural analysis. Considering, for example, the conflict theory, exchange theory, rational choice theory, and neo-Marxist approaches that came to dominate sociology in the 1970s and after, the analysis of cultural meanings is either absent or decidedly secondary. One social thinker who both made culture central to social analysis and aspired to a social theory as far-reaching as that of Parsons was Peter Berger. With his sometime collaborator,

Peter Berger was born in Vienna, Austria, in 1929. He was educated at the New School for Social Research in New York. Berger taught sociology at the New School for Social Research, Rutgers University, and Boston College. **Thomas Luckmann** was a German sociologist. Together, Berger and Luckmann developed a theory of the social world as a human accomplishment. The social world, according to Berger and Luckmann, is constructed by individuals in interaction. We give meaning and purpose to people, things, and events. Berger was a pioneer in the sociology of religion as well. He examined the fate of religion in the modern secular world. Religion doesn't disappear, he thought, but it becomes private and has diminishing impact on social life. Berger wrote before the great movements of religious fundamentalism swept our world. What do you suppose he'd say now?

Thomas Luckmann, Berger wrote one of the monumental statements of social theory in the postwar years, *The Social Construction of Reality*.[8]

The irony of Marxism and functionalism, say Berger and Luckmann, was that though their social ideas were inspired by the high ideals of the Enlightenment, their social theories sketched a process of social evolution in which individual choice counted for very little. Berger and Luckmann were convinced that something has gone terribly wrong when Enlightenment thinkers defend an antihumanistic social theory.

Berger and Luckmann wished to bring real individuals back into the center of social thinking. They aimed to replace mechanistic social imagery with a view of society as a precariously negotiated, fluid order that ultimately resides in the interactions of individuals. The very title of their major work, *The Social Construction of Reality*, underscored the power of the individual to shape society and the open-ended character of history. Paralleling the shift to a more individualistic and dynamic view of social realities in symbolic interactionism and conflict theory, Berger and Luckmann approached social life as produced and reproduced in individual interaction. They sought to recover the "voluntaristic" dimension of social life that was integral to the early works of Marx and Parsons but was submerged in their later, more socially deterministic, perspectives.

The subtitle of *The Social Construction of Reality*, *A Treatise in the Sociology of Knowledge*, signals the unique approach of the authors. The sociology of knowledge was at the time defined as an inquiry into the social origin and role of ideas, in particular religion, theoretical ideas, and political ideologies. Instead of describing ideas as pure expressions of reason, their sociology of knowledge approach understood ideas as closely tied to social interests and conflicts, for example, as instruments of class domination. Berger and Luckmann aimed to redefine the sociology of knowledge. Instead of a specialized study of the social role of ideologies, they proposed that it become an inquiry into the ways in which everyday ideas about reality are created and maintained. They reasoned that cultural elites are not alone in defining what is real; ordinary individuals draw on bodies of knowledge to fashion reality. The sociology of knowledge should be centered on understanding the way that everyday realities are socially constructed. It was Berger and Luckmann's aim to make the sociology of knowledge into a general sociological theory focused on the everyday social construction of reality.

Berger and Luckmann proposed a dramatic departure from Marxism and function-alism. Unlike Marx, who described the social world as produced through labor and class struggle, or Parsons, who imagined society as a system governed by functional prerequisites, Berger and Luckmann perceived society as a cultural or symbolic con-struction. Society is neither a system, mechanism, or an organic form; it is a symbolic construct or a mindful artifice composed of ideas, meanings, and language. Here is one formulation of their outlook: "Human existence is ... an ongoing externalization. As man externalizes himself, he constructs the world.... . In the process of externaliza-tion, he projects his own meanings into reality. Symbolic universes, which proclaim that *all* reality is humanly meaningful and call upon the *entire* cosmos to signify the validity of human existence, constitute the farthest reaches of this projection."[9] Their underlying premise is that ideas about society, including ordinary bodies of knowledge (e.g., proverbs, stereotypes, shared expectations, folk wisdom), are the very stuff of the social world. For Berger and Luckmann, society is a fluid, precarious, negotiated field of loosely connected activities. It is held together, ultimately, by the thin threads of shared understandings and a common language.

Berger and Luckmann set themselves two tasks. First, they would clarify the main premises and concepts that allowed us to grasp the nature of everyday life. Drawing from the phenomenological philosophy of Edmund Husserl and Alfred Schutz, they introduced a range of foundational concepts such as intentional consciousness, multiple realities, the practical attitude, intersubjectivity, and so on. Their intent was to frame everyday life as a fluid, precariously negotiated achievement of individuals in interaction. Their second and chief aim was to offer a general theory of the social origins and reproduction of social institutions. Their principal thesis was that individuals in interaction create social worlds through their linguistic, symbolic activity for the purpose of giving coherence and purpose to an essentially open-ended, unformed human existence.

Berger and Luckmann's sociological theory synthesized the existential philosophy associated with Jean-Paul Sartre and Albert Camus and the classical sociological tradition. From the former, they argued that people construct social worlds to give order and meaning to their lives in the face of an awareness of the ultimate meaninglessness of existence. The threat of metaphysical anguish never entirely disappears since the social worlds we create are fragile and events threaten to reveal the chaos and meaninglessness that lurk below a surface of order and purpose. Drawing on classical sociological themes, Berger and Luckmann also argued that the social worlds we create always threaten to dominate us. These philosophical themes are worked into a sociological theory of social institutions.

Social institutions have their origin in individual interaction. Berger and Luckmann described the origin of social institutions as a process of externalization. In *The Sacred Canopy: Elements of a Sociological Theory of Religion*, Peter Berger outlined this process as follows:

> The fundamental dialectic process of society consists of three moments, or steps. These are externalization, objectivation, and internalization. … Externalization is the ongoing outpouring of human being into the world, both in the physical and the mental activity of men. Objectivation is the attainment by the products of this activity … of a reality that confronts its original producers as a facticity external to and other than themselves. Internalization is the reappropriation by men of this same reality, transforming it once again from structures of the objective world into structures of the subjective consciousness. It is through externalization that society is a human product. It is through objectivation that society becomes a reality sui generis. It is through internalization that man is a product of society.[10]

Human neediness propels individuals into social interaction; recurring social exchanges give rise to patterns of expectations and social norms. Social institutions are little more than recurring patterns of interaction anchored in shared understandings and expectations. Curiously, their argument is decidedly functionalist. Social institutions are functional in that they fix needs, provide a predictable, orderly setting for behavior.

Following Marx, Berger and Luckmann maintained that humans make their own nature through their social practices. The plastic, open-ended character of human nature is given form and purpose by social processes. Institutions are not necessarily forces of domination but are functional. However, we can become alienated from the social worlds that we create. Alienation is not, as in Marx, a condition of humankind dominated by a real world of objects (e.g., commodities); rather, it appears as an almost natural, inevitable property of the social worlds that we create to take on an object-like character. Berger and Luckmann refer to a process of objectivation. The origin of institutions as an ongoing negotiated achievement between individuals is, so to speak, forgotten as the social world is experienced as an objectively coherent order. Alienation, or what Berger and Luckmann called "reification," occurs when the institutional order is assumed to have taken on a life of its own independently of human intentions and needs; society is felt to be a thing apart from its creators and is perceived as controlling human behavior. Reification is an inevitable result of generational dynamics. As a new generation is socialized into a preexisting, taken-for-granted social order, the social world is experienced as natural. Socialization is described as the process by which the objective world of social institutions is made into the paramount subjective reality. In effect, the socially produced institutional world is internalized by the individual as an objective, natural order.

Paralleling Marxist approaches, Berger and Luckmann maintained that reification is never completely successful. Humans reclaim their social creations and themselves as active, creative agents. How so? Between generations, there are different experiences, values, and hopes. Generational discord results in challenges by the younger cohort to the legitimacy and necessity of the existing institutional order. Moreover, routine social events (e.g., intersocietal contacts, social conflicts, illness, and death) disrupt the natural, taken-for-granted character of the institutional order. Social order is always precarious; the merely contingent human origin of social worlds threatens to break through the illusion of its naturalness and objectivity. This, in turn, threatens to confront us with the chaotic and meaningless nature of human existence, an awareness that could undermine social authority and incite social disorder.

The susceptibility to disruption of the social worlds we make calls forth fortifying strategies. Although Berger and Luckmann mentioned coercive means to maintain social order, their focus is on what they call legitimations. In the face of events that threaten to render our social experience fragile and purposeless, individuals react by developing symbolic systems. Their purpose is to reassert the objectivity of social institutions. This is accomplished by viewing the social order as part of a suprahuman order fixed by nature or God. Social institutions are granted authority not by mere human will but by divine decree, natural law, or historical destiny. Religion, philosophy, myth, and science have been the chief symbolic sources of social legitimation. They aim to reassure us that established everyday perceptions of the social world are part of an objective order; this order secures our subjective sense of the world as orderly, coherent, and purposeful. Of course, legitimations may be questioned. In fact, Berger and Luckmann believe that, in contemporary Western pluralistic societies, legitimations are perpetually contested. It is precisely modern Western experiences of perpetual epistemological uncertainty, experiences that generate relativism and subjectivism, that have made possible insights into the social construction of reality. Where once legitimations were understood as statements of social reality to be accepted at face value, today we view them as interpretations subject to debate. In the modern world, the conflict of interpretations is unavoidable and is at bottom a conflict over the will to power.

Despite rejecting Parsons's functionalist sociology, Berger and Luckmann shared his ambitious vision of sociological theory. They sought to uncover the universal features of social life, to offer a set of premises, concepts, and explanatory schemas that could account for social life – anywhere and anytime. They described social life as both an objective order and a subjectively meaningful experience. They produced a general theory of the social origin, structure, and change of institutions.

No less than Parsons, a moral impulse and vision lay at the heart of Berger and Luckmann's theoretical effort. Their work was framed in the language of science, cleansed of explicit moral judgment. Yet, Berger and Luckmann fashioned a liberal, fiercely antiutopian, moral vision forged against the dark history of Nazi Germany. Its liberalism is that of a commitment to the value of the individual as an active, creative force and to social institutions that protect individual freedom. It is a cautious and guarded liberalism. Institutions must carry sufficient authority to prevent individualism from deteriorating into chaos and anarchy. Berger and Luckmann were all too aware of the dark forces that lie in our hearts. Institutions must serve as a check and control when these passions are incited. Their thinking is decidedly antiutopian. Although humans make and remake themselves and their social worlds, the social order needs to have enough solidity and authority to constrain the sometimes wild passions and dreams of individuals and groups. Against all utopian impulses, Berger and Luckmann underscore the dangers of viewing institutions as simply domination and of the wish for a freedom without institutional constraint; this hubris throws open the floodgate of dangerous passions. Like many liberals living in the shadow of fascism, Berger and Luckmann no longer put their faith in a self-regulating human reason; in a post-Christian world, only social authorities have the power to channel aggressiveness in socially beneficial ways. In the absence of the possibility of a religiously based social order, they pinned their hopes on society to maintain the fragile balance between freedom and moral order.

Suggested Readings

Jeffrey Alexander, *Twenty Lectures* (New York: Columbia University Press, 1987).

Peter Berger, *An Invitation to Sociology* (New York: Doubleday, 1963).

Dorothy Ross, *The Origins of American Social Science* (Cambridge: Cambridge University Press, 1991).

Arthur Vidich and Stanford Lyman, *American Sociology* (New Haven, CT: Yale University Press, 1985).

References

1   Talcott Parsons, *The Structure of Social Action: A Study in Social Theory with Special Reference to a Group of Recent European Writers* (New York: Free Press, 1968 [1937]).

2   Many of his early empirical writings are collected in Talcott Parsons, *Essays in Sociological Theory* (New York: Free Press, 1954).

3   Talcott Parsons, *The Social System* (Glencoe, IL: Free Press, 1951).

4   Talcott Parsons, *Social Systems and the Evolution of Action Theory* (New York: Free Press, 1977).

5   Talcott Parsons, *Societies: Evolutionary and Comparative Perspectives* (Englewood Cliffs, NJ: Prentice-Hall, 1966).

6   Talcott Parsons, *The System of Modern Societies* (Englewood Cliffs, NJ: Prentice-Hall, 1971).

7   Parsons, *The System of Modern Societies*, p. 114.

8   Peter Berger and Thomas Luckmann, *The Social Construction of Reality: A Treatise in the Sociology of Knowledge* (New York: Anchor, 1967).

9   Berger and Luckmann, *The Social Construction of Reality*, p. 104.

10   Peter Berger, *The Sacred Canopy: Elements of a Sociological Theory of Religion* (New York: Anchor, 1967), p. 4.

6

The Scientific Theory of Randall Collins and Peter Blau

The struggle over functionalism was more or less over by the late 1960s, even though the polemics continued well into the 1970s. In place of functionalist dominance came the era of the warring schools of sociology. Theorists stepped forward, claiming for their particular theoretical synthesis (e.g., conflict theory, exchange theory, symbolic interactionism, ethnomethodology, phenomenological sociology, Marxism) a successor status to functionalism.

The era of warring schools expressed something of the state of America. The United States was racked by social conflict: young against old, Black against White, gay against straight, women against men, and Vietnam war protesters against the political and military establishment. The movements linked to Black, Latino, native American, gay, and women's liberation, to student and youth rebellion, challenged America's basic institutions. New voices of social thought and criticism were being heard – feminist, gay and lesbian, Latino, and African-American. Simultaneously, radical perspectives of social criticism drawn from European neo-Marxism (e.g., the Frankfurt school, structural Marxism) were making an impact, particularly among young sociologists who sought a sophisticated language of social criticism.

Mainstream sociology was not immune to these critical voices. For example, neo-Marxism, feminism, radical sociology, and dependency theory became new, even if peripheral, forces in sociology in the 1970s. Moreover, the social conflicts of the period made their way into mainstream sociological theory through the incorporation of the themes of conflict, power, diversity, and inequality. However, while some sociological theorists took over the humanistic, critical impulse of the times, many reacted against this politicization and embraced a narrow model of scientific theory. These scientific theorists viewed theory as a body of knowledge that could be put in the service of empirical research. The hope was that a close link between theory and research would result in the "takeoff" of sociology as a truly scientific discipline. Scientific theorists abandoned the grand theories of their predecessors in favor of

Contested Knowledge: Social Theory Today, Fifth Edition. Steven Seidman.
© 2013 John Wiley & Sons, Ltd. Published 2013 by John Wiley & Sons, Ltd.

more narrowly empirical and explanatory theories. Two sociologists whose theories exemplify this aspiration to develop a natural science of society are Randall Collins and Peter Blau.

RANDALL COLLINS

Taking his doctorate in Berkeley in the late 1960s, Randall Collins translated the spirit of the period into a no-nonsense scientific theory that he called "conflict theory." In his major work, *Conflict Sociology: Towards an Explanatory Science,* Collins locates his own theoretical efforts in critical relation to the state of the discipline and of theory.[1] The discipline, thought Collins, is doing well; sociological research has accumulated an impressive body of knowledge. However, sociology's achievements have not been widely recognized by the public nor by many sociologists. One reason is that socio-logical research is dispersed across various specialty fields (e.g., crime, organization, social psychology, medicine, family); few sociologists have sought conceptual integra-tion. Collins was especially critical of sociological theorists whose humanistic aspira-tions have left them either indifferent to, or ignorant of, sociological research. The result is an uncoupling of theory from research, to the detriment of both. Collins aimed to reconnect theory and research, and conflict theory was to be the vehicle to fulfill the promise of sociology.

Conflict sociology aspires to be a genuine science. The essence of science, in Collins's view, is to explain empirical reality. Not all types of explanations count as science; only those that account for variations in social behavior across space and time and take the form of general principles or social laws are truly scientific.

> The scientific ideal is to explain everything, and to do it by making causal statements which are ultimately based upon experience. ... Science is a way of finding the common principles that transcend particular situations, of extrapolating from things we know to things we do not, as a way of seeing the novel as another arrangement of the familiar. This aim is no different when applied to sociology than to physics.[2]

Science must rely on painstaking empirical research, especially comparative research that permits the development of general explanations about social behavior. Drawing on available empirical work, Collins's *Conflict Sociology* proposed hundreds of explan-atory principles.

Collins wished to convince the sociological community that conflict theory is the only basis for a science of society. His immodesty is not peculiar among theorists. I would be hard pressed to think of any modern social theorist – from Comte, Marx, and Durkheim to Parsons, Dahrendorf, and Coleman – who has not claimed for his or her theory a breakthrough to a true science. Theorists have competed for the privilege of declaring themselves the Newton of the social sciences.

The claim to the mantle of science for conflict theory rests, however, on exceed-ingly fragile foundations. Collins rests his case for conflict theory on dubious, largely rhetorical, appeals to realism. For example, he proposes that social structure be

Randall Collins, born in 1941, has taught at the University of California at San Diego and at the University of Virginia, and currently teaches at the University of Pennsylvania. Collins is known for his conflict theory. Social life is structured by conflicts that produce domination and subordination as people struggle for scarce but valued goods – power, prestige, and wealth. He views stratification as occurring in three spheres that correspond to the valued goods in societies. Groups that gain more power dominate in the political sphere. Groups that gain more prestige dominate the cultural sphere. And, finally, groups that gain more wealth control the economic sphere. Critics say that this view of social life expresses the specific culture of American individualism and capitalism. What do you think?

conceptualized as recurring patterns of individual interaction, rather than as an independent reality. Collins might have justified this approach on the grounds that it opens up new possibilities for research or resolves certain conceptual problems or encourages liberal social values. Instead he claims that an individualistic approach to social life is true in the sense of mirroring social reality. Collins appeals to common-sense knowledge that only individuals exist and that conflict is the real stuff of social life. "I believe that the only viable path to a comprehensive explanatory sociology is a conflict perspective. ... [It] grounds explanations in real people pursuing real interests. ..."[3] Conflict theory is recommended because its premises correspond to reality as we ordinarily observe and know it. But how do we know that only individuals exist in a state of conflict? After all, how we know reality depends on the concepts and perspectives that structure our perceptions. Is the "individual" merely the "body," or does this concept imply thinking, feeling, and behavioral practices? Are not the thoughts and feelings of an "individual" derived from "society"? If, as most sociologists concede, individuals are penetrated by society in the sense of internalizing social beliefs and values, the distinction between the individual and society would seem to be an analytical one, i.e., perhaps useful for certain reasons but not mirroring reality.

Collins's distaste for the kind of philosophical reasoning that his theoretical claims seem to demand does not mean that conflict theory does not merit serious consideration. His strongest defense of conflict theory centers on his assertion of its explanatory power. Also, Collins believed that conflict theory could organize empirical research into a coherent body of scientifically valid knowledge.

Conflict Sociology begins with the premise that social life consists of individuals who are motivated to satisfy their own needs and wants. Individuals use whatever material (e.g., wealth or physical strength) and cultural (e.g., education or verbal skills) resources are available to secure their goals. Moreover, individuals pursue their self-interest in social encounters in which there is an unequal distribution of resources, i.e., individuals have more or less physical strength, attractiveness, wealth, education, or occupational prestige. Insofar as the desired goods (e.g., wealth, deference, and power) are scarce, and assuming that individuals will use their available and unequal resources to achieve their goals, all social encounters will involve conflict and be structured by relations of domination and subordination. The institutional and cultural structure of a society will reflect the unequal distribution of power. Social life is a field of struggle and conflict.

> For conflict theory, the basic insight is that human beings are sociable but conflict-prone animals. Why is there conflict? Above all else, there is conflict because violent coercion is always a potential resource. ... What we do know firmly is that being coerced is an intrinsically unpleasant experience, and hence ... calls forth conflict in the form of antagonism to being dominated. Add to this the fact that coercive power, especially as represented in the state, can be used to bring one economic goods and emotional gratification – and to deny them to others – and we can see that the availability of coercion as a resource ramifies conflicts throughout the entire society.[4]

Individuals maneuver for advantage. They deploy whatever symbolic and ideological means are available to press their social advantage; they form alliances with other individuals to gain social dominance. In this regard, Collins's conflict model comes closer to Weber than to Marx. Instead of viewing the *whole society* as divided into two social classes anchored in the possession or lack of property, Collins conceived of society as involving heterogeneous conflicts between groups whose individual membership may not involve significant overlap. He described social stratification as occurring along three dimensions: economic (or between occupational classes), cultural (or between status groups), and political (or between political parties). Although some individuals might be members of the "dominant" group in each of these conflicts, typically, individuals who are members of a cultural elite will not necessarily be members of the economic or political elite. Moreover, there is no necessary coherence between the social interests of elites in these three spheres. For example, business elites may very well be at odds with cultural elites over a range of social issues. Collins offered a Nietzschean vision of individuals struggling for power but reconfigured into an essentially individualistic liberal social perspective.

Collins translated his theory of social conflict into a sociological research program. He recommended that sociologists focus on the "power" factor. Conceiving of power as an empirically useful variable, Collins suggested that by analyzing the (material and cultural) resources that individuals possess we can explain a great deal of social behavior in a range of social spheres (e.g., organizational, political, economic, familial). Collins proposed that the level of resources that individuals command – along with other secondary factors (e.g., social contacts) – directly affects their possession or lack of power which, in turn, affects social behavior and organization. The link between the level of resources and social behavior is twofold: first, differential resources confer differential power; and power has its own social effects. Second, the level of resources affects "social density" or access to social networks that have independent social effects as well as influencing one's social power. In the course of applying his conflict approach to a range of empirical areas of research (e.g., organizations, social change, science, education), Collins developed a multitude of lawlike principles.

One empirical illustration of Collins's conflict theory is his explanation of sexual stratification. He assumes that sexual drives are natural or biologically based and that individuals will use whatever resources are available to achieve sexual gratification. Moreover, men's chief resource is their physical strength, while women use their capacity to withhold sexual favors as their main bargaining advantage. Sexual relations are viewed as a power struggle.

The pattern of sexual stratification depends on two major factors: first, the degree to which the use of force in personal relations is socially regulated and, second, the respective economic status of men and women. To the extent that there are few limits placed on the use of force, men will deploy their superior physical power to dominate women. Thus, in premodern societies where there were few constraints on the use of force in personal relations, men exercised sexual dominance. However, male dominance varied in these societies with women's economic status. As women's economic power increased, their sexual power was enhanced, even if male physical strength secured their dominance. By the nineteenth century, at least in Western societies, the use of force in personal relations lost much of its legitimacy. Men's dominance now lay in their economic authority. However, women's power increased to the extent that the separation of the household and the economy encouraged an ideology of marriage as an individual choice, rather than a family decision. Women's power rested on their capacity to withhold sexual favors and to choose their own spouses. Marriage became a social exchange in which men offered security and status in exchange for women relinquishing to them exclusive sexual rights to their bodies. The rise of a marriage market encouraged men to emphasize their economic and social status assets. Maneuvering to enhance their social value, women developed the ideology of femininity (female purity and virginity) and romantic love, which increased the value of women's chief asset, their sexuality. To the extent that women's economic status has improved over the course of the last two centuries, the exchange system that underlay the marriage market lost social credibility. Economic equalization between the sexes, in the context of the delegitimation of the use of force in personal relations, brings about higher levels of gender equality in intimate matters.

Collins believed that conflict theory would be the vehicle to transport sociological theory into the scientific age. A scientific sociology would reduce the universe to a series of general explanations and universal social laws. Theory has a pivotal role to play: it gives conceptual coherence to the impressive body of empirical research that sociologists have accumulated.

Collins's theoretical justifications for conflict sociology (e.g., epistemological realism or methodological individualism) are, as we have seen, rather weak. In the end, his plea for conflict theory rests on its explanatory and empirical adequacy. But here, too, Collins is on shaky ground. For example, conflict theory is recommended primarily because it "works" or is useful in explaining empirical events. Yet, similar claims regarding explanatory scope are advanced by functional analysis, Marxism, exchange theory, and any number of other theoretical approaches. How do we judge the claims of competing conceptual strategies for superiority on the grounds of explanatory breadth or scope? Collins seems to assume, moreover, that the meaning of the claim that a conceptual approach "works" in explaining empirical events is obvious. However, conceptual strategies can be useful in explaining social phenomena in a variety of potentially conflicting ways. For example, an explanation might be useful because it permits quantification, enhances conceptual economy, maximizes contextual understanding, provides a holistic account, opens up new avenues of research, or makes possible political mobilization. In other words, what we mean by an explanation being useful varies depending on our purposes and point of view. In order to make a credible case for any one conceptual strategy being superior to its rivals on the grounds of its explanatory superiority, it would be necessary to make a plausible case that explanatory goals can be prioritized. Collins would have to make the case that the explanatory values to which he is committed (e.g., scope, propositional formalism, abstractness, or generality) are superior to other explanatory ends (e.g., conceptual economy, quantification, contextual understanding, historical origins, narrative drama). Unfortunately, Collins does not provide arguments that might make credible his assertion of the superiority of conflict theory.

If Collins's claims for conflict sociology are on shaky epistemological grounds, and if the appeal to its explanatory power is no less flimsy, his empirical case hardly compensates. Indeed, the examples that he uses to make the case for conflict sociology are schematic and are not credible on their "evidence" alone. For example, it is not self-evident that individuals are born with a sexual nature or biologically based sexual drives. As we will see in Chapter 12, many contemporary theorists argue that what is "sexual" is a social and historical product. Similarly, Collins simply assumes a natural gender order composed of "men" and "women" that operates uniformly throughout history. Yet, many scholars argue that the gender meanings vary considerably within and between societies and that the very notion of a natural female and male is part of the social construction of gender. Again, while force and economic positioning are important factors in explaining gender patterns, a great deal of recent research highlights the central importance of scientific–medical institutions and discourses, the mass media and popular culture, and the role of the state. Unfortunately, Collins does not entertain the possibility that the premises and concepts of conflict theory may be arbitrary and limiting; he seems unaware that these same premises may gain their credibility as much from their cultural or ideological resonance as from their explanatory value.

Collins's effort to distinguish sociology as a science from sociology as a form of literature, philosophy, or political ideology is not convincing. We need not deny that conflict theory offers useful empirical or conceptual strategies while also maintaining that this sociology projects a moral vision of society. Conflict theory articulates what in the United States is a fairly widespread public ideology: liberal utilitarianism. The languages of individual self-interest, resources, competition, social networks, alliance building, symbol as instrument, and so on are deeply ingrained in American folk culture. Unfortunately, inspired by the spirit of science, Collins remains largely blinded to the moral import of his work.

PETER BLAU

Blau's sociological theory is likewise animated by the spirit of science but also exhibits an undeniable moral vision. Even more than his predecessors and contemporaries, Blau approached sociology as a science. Where Parsons and Berger seem willing to view sociology as part of a liberal humanistic political culture, Blau wishes to establish sociology on strictly scientific grounds. Indeed, his so-called structural sociology is deliberately antihumanistic. Blau admits no role for subjective meanings and cultural symbols. He takes the scientific vision to its logical conclusion: sociology as a formal, logical, quantitative discipline that, in principle, excludes any humanistic residue from its basic premises, concepts, and explanations. Yet, Blau's scientific sociology reveals, centrally, a commitment to a politics of liberal individualism and pluralism.

Like many of his sociological colleagues in the 1970s, Blau reacted against the politicizing of sociology in the 1960s. Perhaps his personal experience of emigrating from Austria to escape Nazism made him feel that the politicization of science and the university would promote social extremism. In any event, Blau embraced a notion of science as a logical and formalistic enterprise. Ideally, science should aspire to become a system of interrelated general propositions hierarchically organized; at the base would be a limited number of "self-evident truths," or axioms, from which are derived theorems that state relationships among abstract concepts which can be empirically tested. In an axiomatic theory, every theorem is logically derived from an axiom, less abstract theorems are derived from more abstract ones, and each theorem is provisionally accepted until empirically falsified. Whether Blau's own theorizing is, strictly speaking, axiomatic, is doubtful, but it is, unquestionably, formalistic. Blau emphasizes developing general propositions that explain empirical reality with the hope that, eventually, propositions will interrelate to form a system of social laws.

Peter Blau's *Inequality and Heterogeneity* is one of the most influential proposals for a scientific sociological theory.[5] Its aim is signaled in its subtitle, *A Primitive Theory of Social Structure*. Departing from standard approaches to social structure that focus on social institutions, cultural constructions, or patterns of individual interaction, Blau defines social structure as the distribution of a population among social positions. Blau's definition abstracts *entirely* from the psychology of individuals, the cultural context of interaction, and the actions of individuals or groups. He excludes any reference to psychology, culture, or history in order to propose a formalistic or, in his own words, a "primitive" theory of social structure. Underscoring the distribution of populations among social positions and its effect on social association signals Blau's intention: to offer a theory of social structure that lends itself to a quantitative analysis. For Peter Blau, it is a Newtonian scientific vision that seems compelling.

Inequality and Heterogeneity aimed to put sociology on the path to science. To make the case for structural sociology, Blau addresses what he considers the basic question of sociology: how to explain social order. Rejecting consensual models (order as a product of moral consensus) and coercive explanations (e.g., order as a

Peter Blau was born in Vienna, Austria, in 1918. He died in 2002. Blau emigrated to the United States in 1939 and was educated at Elmhurst College and Columbia University. He taught at Wayne State, Cornell, the University of Chicago, Columbia, and the University of North Carolina at Chapel Hill. Blau devised a theory that explains social integration in terms of social positions and social associations. According to Blau, higher levels of social integration result from a higher frequency of associations across social positions. Blau was an enthusiastic advocate of a scientific idea of sociology.

product of class domination), Blau introduces an alternative account that emphasizes the centrality of the sheer rate of social association between social positions.

Clarifying the link between social association and social integration requires an outline of Blau's theory of social structure. Social structure is defined as the distribution of people among social positions or what Blau calls "parameters." This refers to those characteristics that a particular society uses to distinguish people from one another. In the United States, gender, age, race, and income (but not eye color or foot size) are parameters. Blau distinguishes two types of parameters. "Nominal parameters" divide people into subgroups with distinct boundaries, e.g., gender, religion, and age. "Graduated parameters" distinguish people by placing them in a rank order, e.g., income or education. Nominal and graduated parameters are respectively linked to two major axes of social differentiation: heterogeneity and inequality. That is, nominal parameters mark out horizontal differentiation (heterogeneity) among social positions or social groups; graduated parameters mark out a social space of vertical differentiation (inequality) between social statuses.

Blau's central thesis is that social differentiation along these two axes – heterogeneity and inequality – is a key determinant of the rate and type of social association which, in turn, directly condition whether society is integrated or divided. Simplifying his position enormously, Blau proposes that the "intersection of parameters" or high levels of heterogeneity produce high frequencies of inter-group association which promote social integration. In other words, as social positions (e.g., racial, religion, gender, class) exhibit minimal correlation, for example, gender not being highly correlated with income, prestige, or education, this condition of social heterogeneity is likely to be correlated with high rates of inter-group association and social mobility which facilitate social integration. Blau's reasoning is that maximizing heterogeneity results in people associating with a large number of small, open, and intersecting groups, which has an integrating effect. If heterogeneity promotes integration, inequality signals a social danger. In Blau's language, the "consolidation of parameters" produces high correlations between social positions; for example, gender predicts income, education, and prestige. This heightens social inequalities which, in turn, minimize inter-group association and results in social division and conflict. In other words, if parameters cluster together, such that Whites have high income, high levels of education, similar occupation, schooling, and residential patterns, while Blacks have low levels of income, low education, similar occupations, schooling, and residences, there will be significantly reduced inter-group association and social mobility and heightened social inequality and conflict.

The promise of structural sociology was its claim to provide a unifying, scientific research program. In this regard, Blau hardly engages rival positions. There is no explicit discussion of the classical tradition,, though Blau does build considerably on the work of Georg Simmel and Emile Durkheim. Similarly, despite his departure from many approaches in theorizing social structure, he does not pause to justify his exclusion of psychology, individual agency, or culture. Blau's primary audience was not sociological theorists but empirical researchers. The value of structural sociology lay solely in its capacity to offer empirical researchers a language and methodology to scientifically explain the social world – anywhere and anytime. Blau's formalistic scientific sociology coincided with the ascendance of a discipline-centered, specialty-focused, quantitatively oriented sociology in the 1970s.

Collins and Blau were troubled by the state of sociological theory. To the extent that theorists were preoccupied with developing grand humanistic theories or with providing justifications for conceptual strategies through textual exegesis, they lost touch with sociological research. Blau and Collins wished to reconnect theory and research. Theory must give up its humanistic legacy in favor of a natural scientific model. Instead of developing elaborate conceptual frameworks that resemble philosophy, scientific theory aims to develop general explanations of empirical reality.

Both Collins's *Conflict Sociology* and Blau's *Inequality and Heterogeneity* proposed literally hundreds of explanatory propositions. It is not at all clear, however, that the mere stipulation of general propositions amounts to science or that, if it does, it achieves what they hoped. Most of the propositions advanced by Blau and Collins are little more than empirical generalizations whose credibility rests on a set of tacit social, philosophical, and ideological meanings. However, whereas a discursive theoretical approach would address these broader meanings, the formalistic approach reduces them to matters of mere empirical status. For example, Blau advanced the following proposition: "Positions of authority over many employees are the source of most authority in contemporary societies."[6] Not only is it seriously doubtful that such a proposition can be tested, given its high level of abstraction and conceptual vagueness, but it gains its coherence only as it is embedded in a broader set of social ideas. The question of social authority – who has power, its source and maintenance – is inseparable from broader conceptual and ideological disputes about the structure of society, social inequality and justice, oppression, and struggles of resistance. In other words, the force of propositional claims would seem to presuppose a discursive context in which narrow empirical statements are part of broader substantive and ideological perspectives. A formalistic theorist such as Blau or Collins is unable to address this broader discursive context; they are confined to reducing discursive disputes to empirical ones.

Collins's *Conflict Sociology* was published in 1975. Curiously, his subsequent work has drawn minimally, if at all, on the hundreds of propositions he formulated in that book.[7] He has made no effort to develop his numerous propositions into anything approaching an axiomatic theory. Indeed, while his conflict theory has had an impact among theorists and researchers as a conceptual strategy, his formalistic, propositional program has had virtually none. Similarly, while Blau and some of his associates have pursued structural sociology as a conceptual and research agenda, there has been little effort to force his theorems into a systematic theoretical structure. In short, few sociologists have seriously pursued their formalistic, strong science program. In part, this may reflect the pull sociologists feel toward a more discursive approach. In part, it may be that a formalistic, propositional approach is believed to be too narrow. If the cost of a scientific sociology is that we must give up a concern with individual psychology, culture, and history – as Blau urges – many sociologists will feel that it is too high a price to pay. If a scientific sociology requires that we focus only on those aspects of social structure that permit an exclusively formal, quantitative precision, sociologists will question the value of such a science. Collins and Blau seem to want a scientific sociology that is driven by the logical dictates of science, without either seriously engaging critics of a natural scientific model or reflecting on what makes such knowledge valuable.

Whatever the scientific merits of Blau's structural sociology, it does not escape value judgments and a vision of the good society. *Inequality and Heterogeneity* projects a liberal, pluralistic social ideal. Horizontal differentiation or enhanced levels of heterogeneity are socially beneficial because they promote an open, mobile, individualistic society tolerant of social differences. By contrast, the major social evil is social inequality, which promotes a closed, static society in which individuals are tightly controlled by large primary groups whose relation to one another exhibits in-group/out-group hostility. While inequality and heterogeneity might function, at one level, as analytical axes of social differentiation, they also mark major axes of moral and political conflict. Indeed, read against Blau's migration to the United States in the shadow of Nazism, it seems plausible to infer that *Inequality and Heterogeneity* is in part about his moral and ideological coming to terms with this experience. Sociologically speaking, Nazi Germany represented an extreme form of a closed society divided by rigid in-group/out-group tensions; that is, a society characterized by the "consolidation of parameters." Blau's coming of age against the backdrop of Nazism might explain something of his championing of extreme forms of heterogeneity. Blau's ideal seems to be a society composed of so many small intersecting social circles that this edges into a celebration of a pure individualism. Any group coherence and solidity threatens to evolve into in-group/out-group conflict, scapegoating, and political extremism. Like many European-born theorists whose coming of age was marked by Nazism, Blau's thinking reveals an antiutopianism that links science and a liberal, pluralistic social vision.

There is an irony to Blau's scientism. His liberal humanistic values are contradicted by his scientific, structural sociology. In its structural explanations, its exclusion of subjective intentions and history, structural sociology projects an image of society controlled by impersonal, nonrational forces, a social view that, in principle, justifies the kind of authoritarian politics Blau abhorred. Unfortunately, Blau seems unaware of how the spirit of his sociology unwittingly promotes the very illiberal values he so detests.

Suggested Readings

Craig Calhoun, Marshall W. Meyer, and W. Richard Scott, eds., *Structures of Power and Constraint* (Cambridge: Cambridge University Press, 1990).

Randall Collins, *Sociology Since Midcentury* (New York: Academic Press, 1981).

Karen Cooke, ed., *Social Exchange Theory* (Newbury Park, CA: Sage, 1987).

Jonathan Turner, *The Structure of Sociological Theory* (New York: Wadsworth, 2002).

References

1   Randall Collins, *Conflict Sociology: Towards an Explanatory Science* (New York: Academic Press, 1975).

2   Collins, *Conflict Sociology*, p. 2.

3   Collins, *Conflict Sociology*, p. 21.

4   Collins, *Conflict Sociology*, p. 59.
5   Peter Blau, *Inequality and Heterogeneity: A Primitive Theory of Social Structure* (New York: Free Press, 1975).
6   Blau, *Inequality and Heterogeneity*, p. 103.
7   Randall Collins, *Weberian Sociological Theory* (Cambridge: Cambridge University Press, 1985) and *Three Sociological Traditions* (New York: Oxford University Press, 1985).

7

The Moral Sociology of C. Wright Mills and Robert Bellah

Contemporary social thought in the United States has been divided between a university-based social science and social thinking outside of the academy. However, some thinkers have managed to address academics while also speaking to a broader public. These thinkers have often been crucial in challenging the orthodoxies of social science and theory. Approaching knowledge as a moral and political enterprise, these critical social thinkers challenge narrow scientific views of social knowledge. In this chapter, we consider two American thinkers who have been pivotal in developing a critical style of social analysis as an alternative to both the scientific ideal and the grand theory of a Parsons.

C. WRIGHT MILLS

Although some fourteen years younger than Parsons, Mills was in many ways his chief adversary through the 1950s and early 1960s. The contrast of personalities and intellectual identities could hardly be more starkly drawn. The son of a Congregational minister, educated at the finest schools (Amherst, London School of Economics, and Heidelberg), Parsons represented the White, Anglo-Saxon, Protestant elite. By contrast, Mills came from a conventional middle-class Texan household. He was educated at large state universities (Texas and Wisconsin). Mills and Parsons spent most of their respective careers as sociologists in rival departments. Parsons was at Harvard where he eventually founded and dominated the Department of Social Relations. Mills spent the better part of his short and tempestuous career at Columbia, which was known for its strong commitment to empirical social analysis. Perhaps most importantly, while Parsons was forging his grand vision of a synthetic scientific sociology, Mills was crafting a moral vision of a critically engaged "public sociology."

Contested Knowledge: Social Theory Today, Fifth Edition. Steven Seidman.
© 2013 John Wiley & Sons, Ltd. Published 2013 by John Wiley & Sons, Ltd.

Charles Wright Mills (1916–62) was born in Waco, Texas. After his undergraduate studies at the University of Texas, Mills earned his doctorate at the University of Wisconsin. Mills taught at Columbia, where he was associated with the Bureau of Applied Social Research. He was one of the most influential sociologists in the post-World War II period. Academics and ordinary citizens read his books. Mills raised serious questions about the actual functioning of American democracy. He developed a theory of the power elite. According to Mills, in the postwar United States, power had become centralized in the hands of corporate, military, and political leaders. Mills showed that these spheres were interconnected through overlapping memberships and that these leaders came from the same elite social background and shared the same interests. Elite social rule, in other words, is passed down from generation to generation.

In one crucial respect, however, Mills surrendered to the influence of Parsons. Mills appealed to the European classics to legitimate his own vision of sociology. By the 1940s, Parsons' *Structure of Social Action* stimulated a growing interest in the European classics. Of course, Parsons did more than introduce European social thinkers to American sociologists; he interpreted their significance through the lens of his theoretical synthesis. As we have seen, Parsons saw in the European sociologists a convergence towards a general theoretical system that could serve as the unifying basis for the social sciences. Curiously, one of Mills' earliest publications (1946) was *From Max Weber* (co-authored by Hans Gerth), a translation of Weber's essays.[1] In his introduction to the book, Mills described a strikingly different Weber than that presented by Parsons. Rather than the pure theorist interested in a general theory of society, Mills viewed Weber as providing a sociohistorical perspective aimed at clarifying the social, political, and moral meaning of modernity. Weber epitomized an ideal of the sociologist who is politically and morally engaged with the major public issues of the day, *the sociologist as public intellectual.*

While Mills looked to the European tradition to legitimate his vision of sociology, he drew considerably on American pragmatists such as William James, John Dewey, Charles Pierce, and George Herbert Mead.[2] American pragmatism appealed to Mills because it approached ideas with an eye to their social consequences rather than exclusively focusing on their absolute truth. Pragmatism assumed an activist approach to thinking; ideas acquired value in relation to their social utility.

Mills and Parsons represent two strikingly different conceptions of sociology. Parsons envisioned a grand synthetic sociology; theory would furnish the basic premises and categories for a unified science of society. Mills imagined sociology as a publicly engaged discourse. Theory had a modest role: to provide concepts that would guide empirical social analysis. Mills sought to create a public sociology.

It was Parsons, not Mills, who achieved dominance in sociology during the 1950s and early 1960s. Mills was an outsider to the discipline, even if much acclaimed. His vision of a morally and politically engaged critical sociology was at odds with a discipline that seemed intent on settling down into either grand theorizing or problem-solving empiricism. If Mills was marginal in sociology, he was perhaps the most influential public sociologist of the time. Like his famous contemporary, David Riesman, Mills spoke to a broadly educated public.[3] He wrote for the major national liberal and Left magazines and newspapers. Moreover, while Parsons was designing his grand system, Mills was publishing his great trilogy on the shape and meaning of postwar modern America: *The New Men of Power*, *White Collar*, and *The Power Elite*. Parsons' functional scientific sociology may have captured the disciplinary center of sociology, but Mills' public sociology shaped national debates for a decade and beyond.

Motivating Mills' sociology was a wish to shake a weary postwar America out of its false sense of security and arrogance. Americans returned from the war and the long, hard period of national economic depression longing for domestic tranquility and civic harmony. They turned to concerns of self-fulfillment, family, career, and consumerism. Despite a surface appearance of national prosperity and unlimited personal and social opportunities, Mills was convinced that America was drifting into a bureaucratic, elitist society in which self-realization amounted to little more than consumer satisfaction. The underlying social trends threatened liberal democracy but neither ordinary citizens, who were dulled by the false idol of consumerism, nor intellectuals, who had been bought and sold by government grants, plush academic positions, or corporate money, were willing to address these dangers. Mills' writings sought to awaken Americans to current dangers and to instigate a renewal of New Deal type democratic reforms.

The first installment of Mills' trilogy, *The New Men of Power*, was his least substantial.[4] It was a project sponsored by Columbia University's Bureau of Applied Social Research, where Mills was the director of its Labor Research Division. Nevertheless, while the bureau was charged with collecting data on labor leaders, Mills provided an interpretive perspective. Disputing Marxist expectations of the politicization of labor as a revolutionary class, Mills was more troubled by the depoliticization and passivity of organized labor. The rank and file had delegated politics to the labor leaders. Contrary to Marxian hopes, union leaders had abandoned any interest in broad social change. They had become major power brokers in a system that promised some material rewards. Contrary to liberal reformers, moreover, Mills doubted the widespread belief that labor leaders act as a countervailing force to the state and big business, thereby preserving the values of freedom and democracy. Taking issue with a liberal pluralistic social model that was ascendant in the 1940s, as well as European Marxism, Mills argued that the new labor elite acted in concert with state and managerial elites; their aim was to maintain a well-functioning, stable social system that could deliver abundant consumer goods to the great social mass.

Despite the absence of any sustained analysis of the rank and file of blue collar workers, Mills had hit upon one of the great themes of his work: the rise of a depoliticized populace manipulated by consumerism and social elites. The depoliticization of the public, moreover, was being ignored by intellectuals. Whereas Marxists took flight in their dreams of a coming revolution, liberals abandoned a critical impulse by serving up little more than apologies for the West in the era of the Cold War. Mills pinned his hopes on the rise of an independent Left and labor coalition which might form the basis of a third political party inspired by social democratic ideals.

Mills' vision of America as drifting into a bureaucratic mass society in which a debased consumerist culture perpetuates the illusion of freedom and happiness is the chief theme of *White Collar: The American Middle Class*.[5] As we have seen, Mills had concluded that labor unions were controlled by elites who desired little more than better wages and working conditions while preserving the overall status quo. The dramatic appearance in mid-twentieth-century America of a new middle class raised social hopes for many intellectuals. Marxists viewed the enormous expansion of white collar workers as marking a new proletariat. Liberals attributed to the new middle classes a socially and morally stabilizing force in America; as the ranks of the white collar workers swelled, class conflict and ideological extremism would, they hoped, disappear. Moreover, unlike the old property-owning middle class, the professional ethos of the new middle classes would lead them to promote a responsible economic and social agenda. Mills agreed that the character of postwar America would be decisively shaped by the new middle classes. However, he disputed the moral and political hopes that liberals and Marxists attached to them. *White Collar* sounded a warning to America: the new middle classes are driving this nation down the road of a new kind of authoritarianism.

The story of the new middle classes is part of the history of America as a society decisively shaped by a middle-class culture. The absence of a feudal-like aristocratic order in a territory of enormous expanse and rich resources made America the land of the entrepreneur. Before the new middle classes burst onto the scene in the last century, there were the free farmer and independent trader of antebellum years and, more recently, the captains of industry and robber barons of American lore. The small farmer shared with the captain of industry a fiercely guarded independence and a suspicion of any institutional dependence. This democratic spirit was rooted in property ownership; economic self-sufficiency bred social independence and a democratic political culture.

The world of nineteenth-century America was characterized by economic competition, small-town democracy, and Protestant individualism. This era came to an end with the rise of corporate capitalism and the tremendous expansion of the state in the early twentieth century. Spurred by technological innovation, a worldwide market forged through Western colonialism, and the creation of new modes of communication and transportation, the small and midsize business gave way to the giant corporation run by salaried managers and manned by an army of sales, advertising, and public relations persons, receptionists, secretaries, file clerks, accountants, lawyers, and technicians. Although small businesses survived, along with the ideological celebration of economic competition and the self-made individual, real power has shifted into the hands of the managerial and big business elite. The middle class, now transformed into an army of white collar workers, was, for the first time in American history, virtually powerless. Except for the highest level of managers and executives, white collar workers were not corporate owners or institutional decision makers. They merely executed the orders issued by the top echelon of a bureaucracy. Even the professions such as law, medicine, or academia experienced a similar dependence on bureaucratic institutions and a considerable loss of economic autonomy and social power.

The bureaucratic standardization of work was compensated for by the status the new middle class attached to white collar jobs. Where blue collar work is physical, white collar work is mental, and was thought to involve considerable skill and intelligence. White collar workers tried to claim a kind of symbolic authority or status. However, as white collar work turned dull and repetitive, as the differences among white collar jobs blurred, the new middle classes looked to consumption and leisure activities to flag their social status and individuality. Instead of realizing self-fulfillment in consumerism, Mills believed that individuals are manipulated by mass culture. Peddling its false dreams and unrealizable fantasies of satisfaction, the new middle classes find in consumerism only fleeting gratification and the feeling of power, not the real thing.

Instead of the new middle classes serving as carriers of a revitalized agenda of social reform, Mills thought that they would become a depoliticized mass controlled by bureaucratic elites and a profit-driven consumer culture. "Among white-collar people, … the absence of any order of belief has left them morally defenseless as individuals and politically impotent as a group. … This isolated position makes them excellent material for synthetic molding at the hands of popular culture – print, film, radio, and television."[6] Preoccupied with self-fulfillment in their private lives, white collar individuals confuse the freedom to consume and work with genuine autonomy. Mills is especially critical of intellectuals. They have forfeited their critical role by either celebrating the making of a postideological society or by awaiting its self-destruction. White collar America may be our worst nightmare: a society of happy robots unaware that they are tumbling into a social hell.

Mills' social vision is deeply pessimistic. In *The New Men of Power*, Mills concluded that the labor movement aimed for little more than its share of America's growing prosperity. Although Mills did not fully relinquish the utopian hope that labor leaders might coalesce with an independent Left movement, he conceded that presently they are becoming a new elite intent on social accommodation. In *White Collar*, Mills analyzed the formation of a new middle-class culture that abandoned meaningful political action in favor of the quest for self-fulfillment, status, and security. As America drifts into a mass society, political power is concentrated among an elite. In his first two major works, Mills had only a vague notion of a tendency towards the consolidation of an authoritarian political culture. However, in *The Power Elite*, he asserts the existence of an elite that exercises power, not always responsibly, and frequently without social accountability, over a politically powerless social mass.[7]

In *The Power Elite*, Mills crafted a story of political change. In the nineteenth century, the economy consisted of small businesses and farms locked in fierce competition; political power was dispersed among the local, state, and federal levels as well as between various secular and religious institutions; the military establishment lacked a major centralized social presence. The great territorial expanse of America, its rich resources, an underdeveloped system of transportation and communication, a weak federal government, and competition between local religious and secular elites impeded the development of a cohesive power structure.

Political decentralization gave way to consolidation in the twentieth century. The growth of big business greatly stimulated the concentration of wealth; technological advances, colonial expansion, World War I, and the Great Depression promoted the enlargement of the federal government. Additionally, two successive wars and the evolution of a military-industrial complex helped to transform the military into a major social force in the United States. By the postwar years, the concentration of economic wealth in corporate hands, of political power in the national government, and of military power in the Pentagon, had evolved to a point where whoever occupied the top positions in these three institutions exercised enormous power.

Mills' chief thesis was that a power elite ruled postwar America. The elite were mostly men who held power in either the corporate, political, or military sector. "At the top of the economy, among the corporate rich, are the chief executives; at the top of the political order, the members of the political directorate; at the top of the military establishment, the elite of soldier-statesmen clustered in and around the Joint Chiefs of Staff and the upper echelon. ... The leading men in each of the three domains of power – the warlords, the corporation chieftains, the political directorate – tend to come together, to form the power elite of America."[8] Although the power elite do not necessarily act in a deliberate, concerted way, they share similar interests and pursue a common social agenda. In part, the interlocking character of the power elite reflects the interrelatedness of economic, political, and military institutions. Top-level decision makers in any one institutional sphere cannot avoid cooperating with policy makers in other spheres. Moreover, there are personal ties binding elites and separating them from the social masses. Elites stand apart from the mass of blue collar and white collar Americans foremost by their considerable wealth. Of course, wealth translates into a whole series of markers that divide the elite from the masses, e.g., education, residence, and social opportunities. Moreover, elites develop a common identity as a result of attending the same prestigious schools and belonging to the same clubs, churches, and social cliques. Finally, the elite often circulate among the top institutional orders; the high-level corporate executive resigns to become a cabinet officer; the retired general sits on the board of directors of a big corporation. The circulation of elites reinforces their consolidation as a politically effective ruling body.

Mills views the power elite as more of a loosely linked network bound by personal and structural ties and interests than a closed, conflict-free class. Nevertheless, elites share similar social interests; in particular, an interest in maintaining the current unequal distribution of wealth, prestige, and power. Moreover, they act in concert to enforce their social interests. Despite declaring that their interests represent the welfare of all Americans, they are guided by self-interest. What makes the power elite so dangerous, in Mills' view, is that they not only have the power to shape society but they exercise it with minimal accountability. Who holds the corporate executive or the appointed military chief or cabinet officer accountable? With a blue collar and white collar public captivated by the illusory promises of consumer and domestic bliss, the electoral process turns into little more than a process of ratifying elite rule.

Mills imagined America as evolving into a society divided between a nonpolitical social mass sedated by the illusions of consumerism and ruled by a power elite. "The top of modern American society is increasingly unified ... [by] an elite of power. The middle levels are a drifting set of stalemated, balancing forces ... The bottom of this society is politically fragmented and ... powerless: at the bottom there is emerging a mass society."[9] Mills was convinced that the preservation of a democratic society required an educated, politically engaged public. Such a democratic political culture thrived on public debate and critical thinking that translated private troubles into public issues. Unfortunately, in the face of the communist threat, liberals abandoned critical perspectives on the United States in favor of celebrating American democracy. Meanwhile Marxists turned away from current realities as they waited for the imminent crash of capitalism. Mills rejected both liberalism and Marxism as each was blinded to current realities by a narrow ideological vision. What was needed, thought Mills, was a public intellectual discourse that was critical yet addressed complex social realities in terms of the practical possibilities for democratic renewal.

In the early decades of the twentieth century, liberal pragmatists (e.g., William James and John Dewey), muck-raking journalists, and independent cultural critics stepped forward as guardians of a democratic public culture. Today these figures are disappearing as universities become the dominant intellectual centers. However, Mills believed that the classical sociological tradition could serve as a successor to liberal pragmatism. In *The Sociological Imagination*, Mills called on sociologists to take up their calling as public intellectuals committed to safeguarding democratic values.[10]

Sociology has a mission: to be a medium for a critical, publicly engaged social discourse. Sociology was to provide critical perspectives on the present which citizens would draw on to understand their social conditions. Classical European sociology was seen as a model of a public sociology. These theorists provided historical perspectives that clarified the implications of current developments for human freedom and democracy. While the European classics may have embraced the rhetoric of objectivity, Mills interpreted this as little more than a respect for empirical realities. Social analysis can never cleanse itself of political and moral values and commitments. Mills envisioned a sociology that would be simultaneously respectful of empirical realities and passionate in its critical role. His own works were meant to exemplify the ideal of a public sociology.

Inspired by a moral vision of sociology, Mills believed that sociologists had renounced a public critical role. Postwar American sociology was divided between two equally undesirable positions: the grand theory of Parsons and abstracted empiricism. Mills thought that Parsons' effort to outline a comprehensive theory of society was doomed to failure. Such conceptual closure and completeness was impossible, he believed. In place of grand theory, Mills advocated devising "working models" or conceptual empirical sketches that can be used to analyze social dynamics in different societies.

If grand theorists retreated from the empirical world into the realm of the "pure mind," empiricists thought truth would surface by focusing on just facts. Unfortunately, much of this research turns out to be common sense dressed up as science. In reality, empiricists engage in highly specialized, narrowly focused research that may have the trappings of science (e.g., methodological rigor, statistics, the language of science) but lack the unifying theoretical goal of natural science. Mills interpreted empiricism as animated by the American spirit of problem-solving, liberal reform. However, whereas an earlier tradition of sociological problem solving aimed to improve the condition of the socially disadvantaged, postwar empiricism was in the service of the power elite. Sociologists were now routinely hired by administrators – the institutional managers of the power elite – in a variety of bureaucratic settings for the purpose of maximizing social control. Mills pointed to a shift in the social positioning of sociology. Instead of orienting to a democratic public, Mills saw sociology, at least in its empiricist aspects, as responsive to clients, in particular, to lower-level managers of society. Both grand theory and abstracted empiricism have retreated from the inspiration of the classical tradition to be a type of public sociology.

Mills imagined America drifting into a quiet totalitarianism in contrast to the noisy, harsher version in the Soviet Union. Its basic feature is the development of a dependent social mass ruled by an elite through impersonal bureaucracies and the media. A totalitarian society is marked by the absence or enfeeblement of public debate and social movements that influence the direction of society. In the Soviet Union, a state dictatorship undermined the possibility of a democratic society; in the United States, the formation of a mass consumer culture coupled with the consolidation of a power elite threatened the demise of democracy. The illusion of freedom perpetuated by consumerism and electoral politics blinded Americans to their social drift. Mills believed that intellectuals had a key role to play in initiating public awareness and political engagement. Mills spoke of the public role of the intellectual in terms of two goals. "What he ought to do for the individual is to turn personal troubles ... into social issues and problems open to reason – his aim is to help the individual become a self-educating man ... What he ought to do for the society is to combat all those forces which are destroying genuine publics and creating a mass society – or put as a positive goal, his aim is to help build and to strengthen self-cultivating publics."[11] Unfortunately, the two dominant social perspectives – liberalism and Marxism – retreated from current realities into ideological dogma. Mills looked to a moral vision of sociology to defend a democratic public culture. As a public discourse, sociology was to be one critical perspective in the broader conversation of society that might help transform a passive public into a politically engaged one.

Mills' legacy was mixed. In the 1960s, he was embraced as a major ideological hero of the New Left.[12] In academe, younger sociologists coming of age in the 1960s looked to Mills for a critical sociology in opposition to conservative functionalism. He also inspired a tradition of sociology as public discourse. Among his contemporaries who have embraced sociology as a moral enterprise is Robert Bellah.[13]

ROBERT BELLAH

Robert Bellah is one of the few major contemporary thinkers who take religion seriously. As a student at Harvard in the early 1950s, he was deeply influenced by both the sociological vision of Talcott Parsons and the existential religious world view of the great theologian Paul Tillich. Bellah has argued, against the current, that religion is, still, a social force of the first order.

Bellah's writings up until the late 1960s focused on religion as a force of modernization, as a cultural system, and as an aspect of the human condition. He published important studies of religion in Japan, the Far East, and Asia. Inspired by Parsons, Bellah also sketched general theoretical statements on religion and society.

By the end of the 1960s, Bellah's concerns and themes had noticeably altered. His attention passed from the non-West to the United States. Moreover, his interest in

Robert Bellah was born in Altus, Oklahoma, in 1927. He was educated at Harvard University, where he earned his doctorate in 1955. Bellah taught at Harvard from 1957 until he moved to the University of California at Berkeley in 1967. Bellah has roamed widely as a sociologist. Much of his earlier work was on the sociology of religion. His masterful book, *Tokagawa Religion*, explored Weber's Protestant ethic thesis in the context of early modern Japan. His most famous work is *Habits of the Heart*. This best-selling book explores the extent to which a therapeutic ethic focused on self-realization has replaced the Protestant work ethic.

religion expanded into a broadly culture-centered critical sociology. For example, in a widely read essay, "Civil Religion in America," Bellah asserts the existence of a cluster of sacred symbols (e.g., July Fourth and the Lincoln Memorial) and beliefs (e.g., Americans as a chosen people) that give coherence and purpose to America.[14] Events in postwar America (in particular the social protests of the 1960s), are said to signal a crisis in the American civil religion. Bellah goes beyond examining the social impact of religion to offering a vision of America in the 1960s as undergoing a great moral ordeal. The turmoil of the Vietnam war and the protests of the 1960s reveal both America's betrayal of its high ideals and its call for moral renewal. The optimistic liberal vision of Parsons increasingly gives way to a more pessimistic social vision akin to that of C. W. Mills. The change is clearly marked in *The Broken Covenant*, a book that dramatically announces America's lost innocence and spiritual malaise.[15] Henceforth, Bellah sounds an almost prophetic voice alerting Americans to their drift into a spiritless, directionless civilization. In *Habits of the Heart* and *The Good Society*, Bellah took his message of social crisis to the wider American public. He called upon Americans to recover the great promise of America, to realize the moral vision of a nation whose greatness should be measured in terms of its commitment to democracy, social compassion, moral virtue, and tolerance, not by its military might or social affluence.[16]

Bellah's concern with issues of moral coherence, public virtue, and community were indicative of his deeply cultural view of society. Although he is not blind to issues of institutional constraint and power, Bellah imagines society as a realm of shared meanings and symbols. Society is envisioned as an order that weds the individual to higher social goals and moral ends beyond self-interest, material gain, and power.

> It is one of the oldest of sociological generalizations that any coherent and viable society rests on a common set of moral understandings about good and bad, right and wrong … It is almost as widely held that these common moral understandings must also in turn rest upon a common set of religious understandings that provide a picture of the universe in terms of which the moral understandings make sense. Such moral and religious understandings produce both a basic cultural legitimation for a society … and a standard of judgment for the criticism of a society.[17]

Without a culture that inspires individuals to lofty social and moral purpose, society deteriorates into a war of all against all – a profane, debased human condition.

From at least the early 1970s, Bellah viewed America as being in crisis, believing it to lack an abiding sense of moral coherence and direction. In *The Broken Covenant*, he underscores a deepening cultural crisis. "In the eighteenth century ... there was a common set of religious and moral understandings rooted in a conception of a divine order under a Christian, or at least a deist, God. The basic moral norms that were seen as deriving from that divine order were liberty, justice, and charity [and] a concept of personal virtue as the essential basis of a good society."[18] In contemporary America, "the erosion of common moral and religious understandings [has resulted in] a decline of belief in all forms of obligation: to one's occupation, one's family, and one's country. A tendency to rank personal gratification above obligation to others correlates with a deepening cynicism about the established social, economic, and political institutions of society."[19] America has evolved from a nation inspired by the high ideals of community, justice, and democracy to a society celebrating greed, money, and self-interest. The signs of cultural crisis are everywhere: in the materialism of daily life, the colonization of public life by commerce, the celebration of lifestyle in place of commitments to community, and the drift of individuals through jobs, residences, fashions, and therapies. America suffers from a failure of its religious–moral traditions to forge a people into a unified social body.

In many ways, Bellah began his career as a fairly conventional sociologist. His early comparative work on religion and society was framed within a broadly Enlightenment scientific approach. Moreover, as Arthur Vidich and Stanford Lyman have shown, there is a long tradition in America of religiously inspired sociologists.[20] Many American sociologists in the early decades of the twentieth century were deeply influenced by the Protestant social reform movement. However, Bellah did more than draw on his religious convictions to guide his sociology; spurred perhaps by movements for social justice in the postwar period, he gradually blurred the boundaries between religion and sociology. His sociology became a vehicle to express a deeply religious and moral vision, a perspective on the crisis of America and its prospects for redemption. By the mid-1970s, Bellah had turned away from the narrow expert circles of social scientists and academics to speak directly to Americans. In this regard, he has sought to refashion sociology into a public philosophy.

In the course of his evolution from a sociologist of religion to a "religious sociologist," Bellah not only became a critic of society, but a critic of sociology. If the moral unity of America was unraveling, one sign of this erosion was the dominance of scientific technological values in sociology. American sociology reflects the broader utilitarian, individualistic culture of this nation. It has become a specialized, discipline-centered discourse oriented to experts and in the service of a bureaucratic welfare state. Just as it had been difficult to become a critic of the society that he so admired, it was with some anguish that Bellah became a critic of the discipline that had introduced him to a fresh vision of the world. Nevertheless, Bellah has abandoned a narrow scientific vision of sociology, in which the sociologist retreats from an ethical responsibility to address fellow citizens on matters of common concern in order to chase the false idol of objectivity and scientific progress. He has advocated a moral vision of sociology; he maintains that it is the responsibility of the sociologist to acknowledge his or her moral commitments and to give reasons for one's value or normative positions. Bellah envisions a sociology which is continuous with a long tradition of ethically driven social analysis linking Plato, Aristotle, Machiavelli, Durkheim, and John Dewey.

Sociology as public philosophy

Bellah has proposed the idea of sociology serving as a public philosophy as an alternative to the standard view of scientific sociology.[21] In response to America's social crisis, sociology's mission is to awaken Americans to this reality. He urges his colleagues to surrender a narrow scientific vision in favor of a perspective that can address the current crisis. Sociology as public philosophy is an effort to refashion sociology into a more public-centered, interdisciplinary inquiry combining empirical social analysis and moral advocacy.

Bellah conceives of sociology as a type of ethical reflection whose aim is to provide a synthetic, critical view of society. In Bellah's mind, contemporary sociology has largely abandoned holistic views of society. Departing from the classical tradition, many sociologists have pursued a scientific model that emphasizes discipline-centered problems, specialization, narrow social research, and the exclusion of values and politics from its concepts and research. Scientific sociology has contributed to a fragmented view of society; the interconnections, long-term trends, and broad moral and political implications of social events are ignored. Sociology as public philosophy intends to recover the holistic view of society that was integral to the Greeks, the classical sociological tradition, and to Parsons and many neo-Marxists. Bellah recommends approaches to human studies that sketch the relations between the self, society, and history; he values broad narratives of societies that trace their origin, evolution, and possible futures. Of course, such a synthetic, integrative social analysis would be interdisciplinary and combine empirical analysis, philosophical speculation, and ethical reflection.

A central feature of sociology as a public philosophy is that its primary audience shifts from exclusively academics to include the educated public. Bellah observes that Marx and, to a lesser extent, Weber and Durkheim, wrote for a public of educated citizens. Unfortunately, sociology, and the social sciences in general, produce discourses that speak almost exclusively to experts. The language of human studies has become technical, its research specialized, and its work published almost exclusively in professional journals. As sociology has evolved into an insulated academic expert culture, this has had the undesirable effect of weakening the realm of democratic public life. When social scientists claim expert status on social problems, public discussion of social issues by ordinary citizens is devalued as mere opinion. Bellah advocates a sociology that effectively engages the educated public. As we will shortly see, he imagines sociologists to be part of an ongoing conversation about society on matters of common interest, e.g., freedom, justice, poverty, war, and community.

At the heart of Bellah's view of sociology is its explicitly moral purpose. Sociologists have tried to avoid bringing moral commitments into their work in order to defend their claim to objectivity. This purging of values from sociology has not succeeded, and cannot. Despite the rhetoric of objectivity, sociologists have not been able to shield themselves from accusations that they make value judgments and form ideas that carry definite social, moral, and political consequences. The effect of sociology's claim to objectivity is not the avoidance of moral and ideological values, but a corrosive cynicism toward all moral beliefs.

Contrary to conventional disciplinary wisdom, Bellah maintains that sociology is inherently value-committed. Sociology is part of society; its basic premises, categories, and explanatory models express the values and ideas of the society of which the sociologist is a member. And is it not the case that the key ideas of sociology are socially situated and shaped by the class, gender, and nationality of their producers? How can sociologists claim that this is true for everyone but sociologists? Instead of trying to neutralize the value-laden character of our ideas, we should admit the moral aspect of sociology and address questions of social norms and ideals.

Bellah's vision of sociology as a synthetic, public-centered, ethical reflection is anchored in a concept of sociology as part of a public conversation. However, sociologists and citizens speak less as individuals than as members of a tradition. The conversation about society is thought of as a dialogue between traditions that makes claims about the origin, development, and future possibilities of society. Let me explain.

In Bellah's view, social ideas are part of "traditions." This is true for sociologists, as it is for ordinary citizens or politicians. Our ideas are not isolated fragments freely put together by individuals in unique ways. Rather, social ideas are part of networks of beliefs, values, and social norms. We never speak from an "God's-eye" point of view, but from a tradition. The aim of sociology is to enter into dialogue with fellow citizens about matters of common concern. These dialogues may be seen as conversations between traditions or between various ways of interpreting social realities. As sociologists and as citizens, our aim is to clarify the social and moral vision in each tradition and state their implications for our lives, i.e., how specific ideas of self, freedom, and justice, if realized, would shape our lives. For what purpose? To clarify and assess the core beliefs and hopes underlying our institutions, with the intent of possibly advocating social changes.

America's cultural crisis and the task of a moral sociology

The concept of sociology as public conversation is central to *The Broken Covenant*, *Habits of the Heart*, and *The Good Society*. In these books, Bellah engages in an ongoing conversation about America. He imagines his fellow interlocutors – interviewees, commentators, imaginary readers – as representing diverse traditions in speaking of the self, society, freedom, justice, and community. He listens to what his interlocutors have to say and tries to hear in their words their social, moral, and political vision of America. He does not listen simply to understand; his aim is not only to provide a map of social interpretations of America, e.g., religious, Marxist, individualistic, Christian, liberal, and conservative. He engages his interlocutors for the purpose of assessing their ideas. He tries to persuade us of the disadvantages or advantages of their social stories by showing how their images of self and society undermine or promote the moral promise of America. He wants to convert us to his moral vision for America. He appeals to the very core values, beliefs, and aspirations of the American experiment to justify his critical standpoint.

In *Habits of the Heart*, Bellah and his colleagues engage the public in a discussion about the way Americans think of the individual, community, private and public life, freedom, success, and justice. They wish to explore the way that Americans imagine the self as giving purpose and coherence to personal and collective life. Questions of the self, society, and moral life are, in their view, matters of urgent social importance, as evidenced in public debate over abortion, homosexuality, prayer in schools, health-care, social welfare, the role of the state, and the aims of American foreign policy. Bellah wishes to engage Americans in a dialogue about these important social and moral matters. In part, the dialogue is carried on with intellectuals (e.g., professors, writers, social commentators, policy makers) who have made public statements on these issues. In addition, Bellah wishes to let ordinary Americans contribute to this dialogue. Drawing on in-depth interviews, *Habits* is filled with the voices of everyday folk. This book is intended to be a public conversation about matters that go to the heart of the meaning of America. His purpose is to persuade Americans to adopt a particular view of America's current malaise and its social remedy. It is an exercise in sociology as public philosophy.

Habits intends to engage readers in a conversation about America among equal participants, but the reality, make no mistake, is that the terms of the dialogue are fixed by the authors. Bellah has set up the terms of the conversation. Interlocutors (e.g., interviewees, writers, readers) are viewed as representing distinct traditions of constructing self and society. The authors outline four such traditions: biblical, repub-lican, utilitarian, and expressive individualism. Each of these traditions is said to have shaped in powerful ways the culture and institutional life of the United States. These traditions are integral to the way that Americans imagine themselves. They comprise a kind of cultural infrastructure of America, providing the core images of self and nation.

The *biblical tradition* is anchored in our Protestant and more broadly Christian heritage. It views the self as a part of a social community; self-realization is tied to living an ethical and spiritual life or a life fused with social goals. The Puritan John Winthrop exemplifies this tradition. For Winthrop, success means "the creation of a certain kind of ethical community," while freedom suggests doing what is "good, just and honest."[22]

The *republican tradition* is rooted in early modern social thought. The self is viewed as a participating member of a political society. Self-realization is accomplished through democratic participation in the shaping of society. Thomas Jefferson is said to represent this tradition: "The ideal of a self-governing society of relative equals in which all participate is what guided Jefferson all his life."[23] In the republican tradition, freedom combines an emphasis on individual rights with the pursuit of an ethical and good society inspired by a vision of transcendent justice.

Utilitarian individualism stands as a counterpart to the biblical and republican traditions. Whereas the latter underscores the unity of self and society and asserts self-realization through social goals, the former views the self as a separate, self-sufficient agent. In this tradition, the individual creates social institutions for instrumental pur-poses, for example, in order to amass wealth or to secure protection, competitive advantage, and power. Institutions are a means or a barrier to self-realization. Freedom is associated with diminished social control and obligation; success means personal gain; justice refers to the distribution of resources and rewards according to individual merit. With his regime of self-improvement aimed at advancing personal gain and success, Benjamin Franklin embodies the spirit of the utilitarian tradition.

Expressive individualism is also a self-centered, individualistic world view. If utilitarian individualism views the individual as a maximizer of self-interest, as a risk taker in pursuit of material gain and power, expressive individualism imagines the self as motivated to develop his or her distinct human potential. The poet Walt Whitman is exemplary of this tradition. "For Whitman, success had little to do with material acquisition. A life rich in experience, open to all kinds of people, luxuriating in the sensual as well as the intellectual, above all a life of strong feeling, was what he perceived as a successful life."[24] Human freedom is conceived of as a personal struggle to express and fulfill oneself by overcoming internal and external obstacles.

The conversation that Bellah orchestrates is one where the interlocutors stand in for these four traditions. These traditions are assumed to be basic to American society. They shape the character of the self and the social values and institutions of America.

The chief theme of the story of America, according to Bellah and his colleagues, is clear enough. In its founding years, the biblical and republican traditions were dominant. These traditions provided a unifying cultural framework that linked individuals and institutions, personal and social ends, individual self-interest and the general good of the society. The individualism promoted by the utilitarian and expressive traditions was not disruptive of order because of the socially integrating role of the biblical and republican traditions. De Tocqueville's *Democracy in America* depicted this American social ideal – a nation of small communities organized around a culture of entrepreneurial risk-taking and participatory democracy and unified by the solidarities of family, voluntary associations, and the church.[25]

From the mid-nineteenth century through the twentieth century, the rise of corporate capitalism, bureaucratization, the growth of a warfare/welfare state, secularization, and the consumer and therapeutic ethos of American culture have favored the advance of the utilitarian and expressive traditions. The erosion of the biblical and republican traditions has loosened the grip of social communities on the individual. We are becoming a nation that celebrates a type of individualism that associates freedom with diminished social control.

Bellah is not a critic of individualism. The American culture of individualism is to be valued for its great social and economic accomplishments and its defense of personal and political liberties. However, Bellah maintains that it is also responsible for a good deal of the malaise in our lives. Our individualistic culture values social institutions only as a means of self-realization; social obligations and the pursuit of shared or common goals are considered burdensome compared with individual achievements. This individualistic culture has contributed to the weakening of the authority of our key institutions, from the family to the government. It has separated individuals from the very communities (families, neighbors, church, or colleagues) that nurture them; it pits individuals against one another in a fight for survival and dominance. The crisis of moral order prompted by the American culture of individualism is evidenced in high rates of illegitimacy, divorce, illiteracy, a church torn between fundamentalism and secular accommodation, and a passive electorate.

Bellah is not arguing that America has become a mere collection of individuals. Americans continue to be members of groups and institutions and to pursue social goals such as voluntary work or public service. However, as much as their lives are involved in group life, Americans cannot coherently express these social commitments within the language of individualism. This world view does not allow Americans to recognize their shared goals, moral commitments, and social interdependence. Americans cannot make sense of their social involvements and obligations, give reasons for pursuing social goals, grasp institutions as worlds of social solidarity, or articulate their ties to a common public life. The language of individualism does not permit Americans to grasp their ties to generations past, present, and future. Of course, the absence of a language of social connectedness doesn't mean a lack of social bonds. However, it suggests that Americans cannot make sense of this aspect of their lives; they cannot adequately assess their collective lives. A weak language of social connection also weakens such bonds.

This enfeebled culture of communal ties is particularly dangerous today. In *The Good Society*, Bellah and his colleagues argue that we live in a world of corporations, big business, huge government bureaucracies, a global economy, and sprawling media empires.[26] To preserve the democratic individualism that Americans cherish, they need to think in terms of social interdependence, institutional responsibilities, and public participation in decision making. Social processes such as bureaucratization and economic globalization require Americans to understand their lives as interconnected with social institutions and assume responsibility for their shape.

Bellah urges a cultural shift in which the self is viewed as a social creature, institutions are perceived as the chief site of our lives, and personal goals are perceived as fused with social goals. Advancing democracy will require the reestablishment of a common religious–moral framework. In this regard, Bellah urges the critical renewal of the biblical and republican traditions that have lost a great deal of their authority in the last century or so.

There is a sense of high drama in Bellah's sociology. Modern America is in a cultural crisis. The culture of individualism has weakened a language of social obligation, virtue, community, and social interdependence. The cultural crisis of American society is echoed in sociology which is dominated by a problem-solving, individualistic, utilitarian spirit. Bellah counsels a reorganization of sociology and society in which a language of moral solidarity is integrated into a dominant individual-centered vocabulary. To play a role in social renewal, sociology must reorient to focus on public life rather than narrow, specialty area disciplinary problems. Bellah envisions a sociology that at once acknowledges its moral and political role while preserving its empirical and conceptual rigor.

Suggested Readings

Robert Bellah, *Tokagawa Religion* (Glencoe, IL: Free Press, 1957).

Irving Louis Horowitz, *C. Wright Mills* (New York: Free Press, 1983).

Bruce Kuklick, *Rise of American Philosophy* (New Haven, CT: Yale University Press, 1977).

Charles Reynolds and Ralph Norman, eds., *Community in America* (Berkeley: University of California Press, 1988).

References

1   H. H. Gerth and C. W. Mills, eds., *From Max Weber: Essays in Sociology* (New York: Oxford University Press, 1946).
2   C. W. Mills' dissertation was published posthumously under the title *Sociology and Pragmatism* (New York: Paine-Whitman, 1964).
3   David Riesman et al., *The Lonely Crowd* (New Haven, CT: Yale University Press, 1950); Thorstein Veblen, *The Theory of the Leisure Class* (New York: Macmillan, 1899).
4   C. Wright Mills with the assistance of Helen Schneider, *The New Men of Power: America's Labor Leaders* (New York: Harcourt Brace, 1948).
5   C. Wright Mills, *White Collar: The American Middle Class* (New York: Oxford University Press, 1951).
6   Mills, *White Collar*, p. xvi.
7   C. Wright Mills, *The Power Elite* (New York: Oxford University Press, 1959).
8   Mills, *The Power Elite*, pp. 4 and 9.
9   Mills, *The Power Elite*, p. 324.
10 C. Wright Mills, *The Sociological Imagination* (New York: Oxford University Press, 1959).
11 Mills, *The Sociological Imagination*, p. 186.
12 C. Wright Mills, *The Causes of World War III* (New York: Simon & Schuster, 1958) and *Listen Yankee: The Revolution in Cuba* (New York: McGraw-Hill, 1960).
13 For example, Joseph Bensman and Arthur Vidich, *The New American Society* (Chicago: Quadrangle Books, 1971); Alvin Gouldner, *The Future of Intellectuals and the Rise of the New Class* (New York: Oxford University Press, 1979); Todd Gitlin, *The Whole World is Watching* (Berkeley: University of California Press, 1980); Richard Sennett, *The Fall of Public Man* (New York: Vintage, 1978); William Wilson, *The Truly Disadvantaged* (Chicago: University of Chicago Press, 1987); Arlie Hochschild, *Second Shift* (New York: Viking, 1989); Judith Stacey, *Brave New Families* (New York: Basic Books, 1991).
14 Robert Bellah, "Civil Religion in America," in *Beyond Belief: Essays in Religion in a Post-Traditional World* (New York: Harper & Row, 1970).
15 Robert Bellah, *The Broken Covenant: American Civil Religion in Time of Trial* (New York: Seabury Press, 1975).
16 Robert Bellah, Richard Madsen, William M. Sullivan, et al., *Habits of the Heart: Individualism and Commitment in American Life* (Berkeley: University of California Press, 1985) and *The Good Society* (New York: Alfred A. Knopf, 1991).
17 Bellah, *The Broken Covenant*, p. ix.
18 Bellah, *The Broken Covenant*, p. x.
19 Bellah, *The Broken Covenant*, p. x.
20 Arthur Vidich and Stanford Lyman, *American Sociology* (New Haven, CT: Yale University Press, 1985).
21 Bellah et al., "Social Science as Public Philosophy," Appendix to *Habits of the Heart*; Robert Bellah, "The Ethical Aims of Social Inquiry," in Norma Haan, Robert N. Bellah, Paul Rabinow, et al., eds., *Social Science as Moral Inquiry* (New York: Columbia University Press, 1983); Robert Bellah, "Social Science as Practical Reason," in Daniel Callahan and Bruce Jennings, eds., *Ethics, The Social Sciences, and Policy Analysis* (New York: Plenum Press, 1983).
22 Bellah, *Habits of the Heart*, p. 29.
23 Bellah, *Habits of the Heart*, p. 30.
24 Bellah, *Habits of the Heart*, p. 34.
25 Alexis de Tocqueville, *Democracy in America*, ed. J. P. Mayer (New York: Doubleday, 1969).
26 Robert Bellah, *The Good Society* (New York: Alfred A. Knopf, 1991).

Afterword to Part II

European social theory has been deeply shaped by Marxism in at least two ways. First, thinkers such as Durkheim and Weber shared with Marx a view that society cannot be reduced to a collection of individuals. Social forces such as the state, social classes, bureaucracy, and the division of labor play the key role in their stories of the past and present. The individual is often portrayed as dominated by society. For Marx, class almost dictates individual destiny; for Durkheim, the health of the group virtually determines individual well-being; even Weber, who was sympathetic to thinking of society in individualistic terms, ultimately emphasized religious culture and big social structures like bureaucracy as the key forces shaping modern social life. Second, Europeans thinkers were ambivalent about the prospects for freedom and democracy in the modern world. Think of Weber's image of modern individuals trapped in the iron cage of bureaucracy and capitalism.

American social thinkers have, as we've seen, drawn considerably on European social thought. Marx, Weber, and Durkheim were canonized as the founding figures of modern sociology by Americans. Yet, Americans have often been uncomfortable with the social determinism of the Europeans. And European pessimism never really resonated with American's sense of social hope. In this regard, American thinkers have been decidedly more sympathetic to British ideas of individualism and social progress. Much of American social thought from the 1880s through World War I bore the deep imprint of the British world view.

In fact, American popular culture has often championed an extreme version of individualism. Perhaps it was the lack of an established class structure and the absence of a strong state, along with a deeply rooted culture of rugged individualism, that encouraged Americans to champion the cause of individual freedom and self-realization. At times, Americans have viewed social life as little more than a collection of individuals who purposefully create institutions for the sole purpose of promoting the welfare of the individual. If Europeans tend to underscore the way society constrains the individual, Americans have often embraced an imperial self who purposefully fashions a social order.

Contested Knowledge: Social Theory Today, Fifth Edition. Steven Seidman.
© 2013 John Wiley & Sons, Ltd. Published 2013 by John Wiley & Sons, Ltd.

American sociological theory absorbed this individualistic spirit. We've observed it in Parsons' voluntaristic theory of action, which insists on viewing the individual as an active creator of social life. For Berger and Luckmann, social reality isn't a product of natural laws or impersonal social forces but is constructed by real active individuals. Both Mills and Bellah appeal to the potential power of individuals to bring about democratic changes in America. Even those theorists who favor a strictly natural scientific approach believe that the individual is the bedrock of society. Collins views social life as made up of the actions and interactions of individuals. Blau makes individuals the elementary particles of his theory of social structure.

However, despite sharing with ordinary Americans a moral and political commitment to individualism, these theorists have mostly rejected a view of social life as simply a product of individual actions. Perhaps reflecting the influence of European theorists, and perhaps responding to events such as the Great Depression and two World Wars, American social thinkers from Parsons to Bellah and Blau have insisted on the reality of social constraint as much as the reality of individual freedom. Yes, individuals do actively shape their lives but they are, in turn, formed by social forces that are beyond their immediate control. The individual is not the only active producer of social life; the state, social classes, ideologies, and world views are no less the makers of our individual and shared lives.

Social thinkers often make a key distinction between what we might call "moral individualism" and "methodological individualism." The former speaks to our values; we value individual freedom; we believe that society should protect individual rights and encourage self-realization. These statements are expressions of moral individualism. By contrast, methodological individualism holds that focusing on individual action is the key to explaining social life. Most sociological theorists reject this view: most believe that, if we want to understand poverty, gender, or race relations, or a culture that cherishes human rights, we need to consider the role of the state, religion, the family, the economy, and so on. Social theory stands and falls on the premise that in the end social life is more than just individuals, that making sense of social behavior involves using concepts that refer to social realities.

Still, American social thinking is undeniably more individualistic in both its moral and analytical values than European theory. Virtually no American sociological theorist would follow Durkheim and Marx's strict "methodological holism." This is the view that holds that subjective motivations and purposes have virtually no role in social explanations. The closest parallel would be Peter Blau's structuralism but Blau, we recall, was a European immigrant.

And, not surprisingly, American theorists generally do not endorse the currents of pessimism in European social thinking. Weber's dark image of modernity falls on deaf ears in the American context. Few American social thinkers doubt a faith in the power of individualism and social progress. Except for the race problem, which has plagued America, Parsons maintained that this nation was a model of a free, democratic society. If thinkers like Berger and Collins are more cautious, they still describe a modern world that is good and that can be made better. Even Mills and Bellah, who shared some of the European pessimism, never abandoned the idea that a reformed America is in the grasp of its citizens. In much of American social thinking, society is never completely in control of humankind's destiny; the individual is in the end the creator of his or her own fate.

Part III

Rethinking the Classical Tradition: European Theory

Introduction to Part III

By the early decades of the twentieth century, Marxism had become a permanent feature of European political culture. From France to Italy and Britain, the ideas of Marxism shaped labor and socialist political parties and platforms. Marxism also became a key part of academic culture. Marx's ideas were being vigorously debated in the social sciences and philosophy.

By the post-World War II period, Marxism was perhaps *the* major language of social analysis and criticism across a substantial part of Europe. In a way that was not true in the United States, much of contemporary European social theory and social science was shaped by its encounter with Marxism.

But, Marx's intellectual legacy was ambiguous. His successors inherited a body of work rife with tensions and contradictions. In his reaction to German idealism, Marx sometimes advocated a one-sided materialism, while at other times he pressed for a multidimensional social theory. Consider his view of human action. On the one hand, Marx described the individual as driven by biological, materialistic needs; consciousness was sometimes viewed as a secondary effect of bodily drives or material needs. On the other hand, Marx was equally insistent that human behavior is always deliberate, goal oriented, and norm governed. If human behavior is purposeful and rule governed, it may be inconsistent to claim priority for a materialistic perspective.

The tension between materialism and idealism in Marx surfaces in the pivotal concept of his social theory: labor. It is through our productive activity that we make and transform human nature and the social world. However, Marx was not clear as to whether labor referred narrowly to economic activity or to all productive activity. If it was the former, Marx assumed a narrowly conceived economistic world view; if labor was interpreted broadly as practical activity, it would be hard to maintain that economic labor has a kind of priority. But admitting this would upset the whole economically oriented social theory that Marx had developed. From this ambiguity in Marx's basic understanding of human action, a whole series of conceptual strains surface. Marx

Contested Knowledge: Social Theory Today, Fifth Edition. Steven Seidman.

oscillated between a mechanistic base/superstructure model and organic social imagery. In the former, the economic base determines in a one-sided way the rest of society; in the latter, the parts of society are causally interrelated. Similarly, Marx shifted between a mechanistic view of history as governed by invariant laws and a humanistic image of history as produced by human actions.

At the root of classical Marxism is also a tension between a scientific and a moral vision of human studies. To the extent that Marx embraced a mechanistic social model (e.g. base/superstructure) and aimed to uncover the laws of history and society, he embraced a strong scientific vision. Yet Marx also framed his work as a social critique of society and social science. This critical impulse flagged the moral and political character of his work.

These ambiguities in Marx's social ideas were perpetuated by his heirs. The history of Marxism in the twentieth and twenty-first centuries evolved in two opposite directions. In the first half of the twentieth century, a materialist and scientific Marxism achieved dominance in the West and East. Marxism was understood as a science that discovered the laws of society. History was viewed as the linear, progressive unfolding of successive socioeconomic formations propelled by internal contradictions in the prevailing mode of production. Capitalism was conceived as the last contradictory mode of production; its inevitable decline would usher in socialism and a classless communist society. The Russian Revolution made scientific Marxism the official ideology of Communist Parties in Europe and the United States. In the postwar period, less dogmatic versions of scientific Marxism such as Althusser's structural Marxism or Wallerstein's world-systems theory found a secure place in the Western academy.

Reacting against the authority that scientific Marxism had acquired in European culture and politics was a tradition that approached Marxism as a perspective that fell somewhere between science and moral critique. If scientific Marxism highlighted the materialistic and economistic aspects of Marxism, "critical Marxism" appealed to its voluntaristic and activist dimensions. Society was understood as structured by multiple, interacting causative factors and history was viewed as the voluntary creation of human actions. Critical Marxists valued the role of social theory as a force of social change. The original home of critical Marxism was Germany. The so-called Frankfurt school combined the Hegelian idealist emphasis on humankind's self-creation through history with the sophisticated political sociology of Weber and Georg Simmel. As we'll see in the discussion of Habermas, these critical theorists sought to broaden Marxism by connecting its political economic approach to an understanding of culture and politics. They aimed to fashion Marxism into a critical social theory that could grasp the movement of Western industrial societies and its potential for change.

The Frankfurt School encouraged the development of new efforts to rethink Marxism. One of the most important efforts has been the so-called Birmingham School of Cultural Studies. Led by the British sociologist Stuart Hall, the Birmingham school tried to revise Marxism in a way that made it into a rich tradition of critical empirical research and analysis. Building on the work of the German and British critical theorists, two other theorists have produced highly original statements of critical theory: Pierre Bourdieu and Anthony Giddens. In Chapters 8–10 to follow, we will try to follow these brilliantly original European efforts to rethink the classical tradition, often producing general theories of society as profound as those of the classics.

8

The Critical Theory of Jürgen Habermas

One of the most important developments in twentieth-century Marxism has been the critical theory of the Frankfurt school. The Frankfurt school refers to a group of extraordinary philosophers, sociologists, and historians who worked together at the Institute for Social Research at Frankfurt between the late 1920s and 1935. Its chief intellectual leaders were Theodor Adorno, Max Horkheimer, and Herbert Marcuse.[1] Despite migrating to the United States in 1935 to escape Nazism, they reestablished the institute under the auspices of Columbia University.

The Frankfurt school proposed "critical theory" as an alternative to both scientific Marxism and orthodox social science. Critical theory draws from the social sciences to forge a synthetic conception of society. Critical theory aims to not only understand but change society. Repudiating the ideal of value neutrality, the Frankfurt school analyzed the major sites of conflict and social crisis for the purpose of advocating political activity. Critical theory was to be a new type of social study: it would unite philosophy's concern with holistic analysis and the empiricism of the social sciences, animated by the moral intention of making theory into a force for human emancipation.

A history of dramatic, often shocking, changes separates Marx and the Frankfurt school. Marx's ideas were formed against the hopeful background of imminent social revolution, e.g., the working-class revolts of 1848, the Paris Commune of 1870, and the formation of unions and socialist parties in the late nineteenth century. By the 1930s, Marxists were considerably less optimistic. Despite recurring economic and social crises, there were no revolutions in Western capitalist societies. Contrary to Marxist expectations, revolution occurred in the economically underdeveloped nation of Russia. Whatever social hope the Russian Revolution inspired quickly disappeared as communist Russia drifted into a bureaucratic empire. Complete disillusionment swamped the Frankfurt school as Germany embraced fascism, rather than socialism, as a response to the twin threats to capitalism: economic depression and communism.

Contested Knowledge: Social Theory Today, Fifth Edition. Steven Seidman.
© 2013 John Wiley & Sons, Ltd. Published 2013 by John Wiley & Sons, Ltd.

Jürgen Habermas was born in Düsseldorf, Germany, in 1929. Habermas received his doctorate at the University of Marburg in 1961. He has taught at the University of Heidelberg and Frankfurt and was the director of the Max Planck Institute in Frankfurt from 1971 until 1983. Habermas should be considered one of the great social theorists of the twentieth century. He developed an original theory of social knowledge, social evolution, language and social action, and late capitalist societies. As a critical theorist, Habermas believes that social knowledge should contribute to human freedom.

Social hope passed into social pessimism for the critical theorists. The Marxist dream of the coming of a new age of freedom came crashing down with the Nazi and Soviet nightmare of social barbarism and mass terror. As the prospects for progressive change disappeared, the dominant currents of the Frankfurt school gradually abandoned empirical social analysis in favor of philosophical theories which explained the era of darkness enveloping the West. The major thrust of critical theory was to trace the current social hell to some elemental defect in the West, for example, its concept of reason or the dominance of scientific–technological rationality. The shift to a philosophical type of social analysis in the face of the crisis of Western civilization parallels the general theorizing of Talcott Parsons, except that the latter theorized with a hope of ongoing social progress. In the face of social barbarism, the Frankfurt school's only social hope was to keep alive the already enfeebled philosophical and aesthetic traditions of critical reason.

Despite the reestablishment of the Institute for Social Research in postwar Germany, it never regained its former unity of purpose and intellectual importance. Many of its key members – Herbert Marcuse, Leo Lowenthal, Eric Fromm – remained in the United States.[2] Horkheimer retired in 1958, and Adorno died in 1969. Nevertheless, if the institute no longer served as the social center of critical theory, its spirit was preserved in the person of Jürgen Habermas.

Between the early Frankfurt school and Habermas was a generational and historical divide. The founding members of the Frankfurt school came of age in the midst of the Great Depression, the rise of Nazism, and the disillusionment with Soviet communism. Habermas reached adulthood during the democratic reconstruction of postwar Germany and in the context of postwar Western economic prosperity. His intellectual development coincided with the renewal of democratic political activism in the student protests and the new social movements of the 1960s. Although the public disclosure of the shocking atrocities of Nazi Germany and Stalinist Russia introduced a profound caution into Habermas's social hopes, his perspective on Western development was much more optimistic than that of his predecessors. Faced with what they considered to be the irrationality of the modern world, Adorno and Horkheimer abandoned the Enlightenment dream that reason could help to liberate humanity. Habermas aimed to recover the modern utopian faith in the beneficent power of reason.

Habermas wished to return to the original aim of the Frankfurt school to integrate philosophy and empirical science for the purpose of moral critique and social change.

He cautioned against the flight of critical theory from empirical analysis into philosophical and aesthetic analysis. Habermas believed that the prospects for progressive change in the postwar West make possible a renewed unity of theory and practice. Critical theory needed to recover the original Marxian aim of clarifying the sites of social crisis and conflict; the value of social criticism lies ultimately in becoming a force in social change. However, Habermas was convinced that this renewal of social critique required the reconstruction of Marxism.

Habermas gave three reasons for reconstructing Marxism. First, Marxism was too easily dismissed as ideology; accordingly, its social criticisms and political intent lacked public authority. Habermas undertook the daunting task of providing an epistemological justification for critical theory. In other words, he wished to make the case that critical theory is an expression of reason, not ideology. Second, the conceptual foundations of Marxism were flawed. The failure of Marxism to explain the absence of revolution in the West and its occurrence in the East, the rise of fascism and, in the postwar years, the rise of the new social movements indicated defects in its most basic premises and categories. Third, Habermas argued that the general conceptual defects in Marxism, combined with postwar developments, rendered the Marxist theory of capitalism inadequate as a basis for clarifying the major dynamics and prospects for change in today's world. Over the past few decades, Habermas has attempted to furnish a sound conceptual foundation and justification for a critical theory of society.

SOCIAL CRITIQUE AS REASON

Habermas described Marxism as a critical social science. In contrast to the natural scientific ideal of Comte or Durkheim or the ideal of value-neutrality of Weber, Marx viewed social theory as committed to promoting human freedom. Theory aimed to reveal the sites of conflict and the prospects for social transformation; it was to be a force of change by altering the social perspective of agents of change. Societies were to be judged by their own ideals and social promises. For example, in *Capital*, Marx criticized capitalism by claiming that the ideals of liberty, equality, and justice that were invoked to justify this society were contradicted by a reality of exploitation and class rule. In arguing that profit is based on the exploitation of labor or that the accumulation of wealth perpetuates class domination, Marx wished to foster a critical attitude on the part of laborers toward capitalism. Indeed, Marx hoped to contribute to the transformation of a mass of blue collar laborers into a politicized working class whose personal discontentment would be translated into a public struggle against capitalism. Marxism was to provide the theory of change, socialism the political ideology, and the working class was to unite theory and practice.

The Frankfurt school absorbed the Marxian ideal of "immanent critique." The basis of moral criticism was the social ideals that legitimated institutions and political rulership. Immanent critique exposed the contradictions between reality and social ideals for the purpose of stimulating critical consciousness. According to the Frankfurt school, social critique is a force for social change to the extent that it challenges the dominant social ideologies that present the existing society as a natural and morally beneficent order. Critical theorists aimed to clarify the socially constructed character of society, to reveal the existence of ruling social groups whose social world views justify an unequal and unfair social arrangement, and to identify social agents who have an interest in bringing about social change.

The Frankfurt school eventually abandoned the ideal of immanent critique. It perceived that the broadly liberal democratic values of modern civilization were declining in the face of fascism and that the power of reason and the modern ideals of liberty, social equality, and justice were becoming feeble and peripheral to the legitimation of capitalist society. As reason fled the world, as the positive moral values of the modern West lost their public authority, immanent critique gave way to a defense of an abstract philosophical critical reason. The Frankfurt school became protectors of a rationality that was committed to the values of reason, morality, and emancipation in the face of the flight of these values from the world.

Habermas shared the Frankfurt school's perception that immanent critique was no longer an adequate basis for a critical social theory. Although he was not persuaded that Enlightenment values had fled the West, he was convinced that social support for them was precarious. He held that the values of critical reason, autonomy, and democracy needed a justification rooted more centrally in reason than in elite cultural traditions (e.g., art or philosophy). But how was a critical theory of society to be rationally justified? It was no longer credible, thought Habermas, to appeal to some notion of reason that was outside of society and history. The modern tradition, from Marx through Nietzsche and Freud, convinced us that behind reason lie interests and desires. Although conceding that knowledge is structured by social interests, Habermas was unwilling to surrender to relativism. This would render humanity unable to defend itself against the evils of Nazi Germany, Soviet communism, or state capitalist societies.

In *Knowledge and Human Interests*, Habermas conceded that human interests structure knowledge.[3] However, instead of thinking of interests and knowledge as thoroughly relativistic, Habermas asserted the existence of three universal human interests that produce three general forms of knowledge. In other words, Habermas argued that beneath the near-infinite variety of human desires are three universal interests. These human interests give rise to general forms of cognition and knowledge. This renders knowledge, including critical theory, general and necessary, rather than merely historical or arbitrary.

Habermas referred to three types of knowledge that correspond to three cognitive interests, each of which is said to be basic to the ongoing reproduction of human existence. The empirical–analytical sciences, for example, the natural scientific ideal, aims to grasp empirical regularities which make predictability possible. They are governed by a "technical" human interest in enhancing control over nature and society. The empirical–analytical sciences are rooted in the necessity of human reproduction through work or controlling our inner and outer environment. Humans need empirical knowledge relating to the causal sequencing of events in order to exercise some control over their environment and their behavior. The reproduction of human life through exercising mastery over the self and world is made possible by our capacity to cooperate, communicate, and share a common world. It is only because we share language and a world of meaning that communication and therefore human survival are possible. This "practical" cognitive interest gives rise to the historical and cultural sciences, whose aim is to clarify the meaning of texts, actions, and social events in order to promote mutual understanding. Basic to both the technical and practical cognitive interest is a third "emancipatory" interest. The technical cognitive interest reveals a desire to free ourselves from the constraints of nature so that we may be self-directing. Similarly, the practical cognitive interest exhibits a wish to abolish distortions and blockages in interactions in order to render communication open and free, i.e., free to hear the voice of reason over the noise of particular interests. The emancipatory cognitive interest gives rise to the critical sciences, e.g., Marxism and psychoanalysis. These aim to identify unnecessary internal (e.g., psychological) and external (e.g., social or environmental) constraints on human action with the hope that such awareness will promote autonomy.

Habermas wrote *Knowledge and Human Interests* to show that critical theory cannot be dismissed as mere ideology. Just as positivism is rooted in a general human interest in control, and interpretive social science expresses an interest in linguistic communication, critical theory is anchored in a universal human interest in autonomy. Habermas wanted to defend a critical moral standpoint as a form of reason. His strategy was to identify a will to freedom or to be free of unnecessary constraint as embedded in the very structures of everyday life, e.g., in work, communication, or power dynamics. Critical theory is characterized as an expression of a universal drive towards human autonomy.

In response to criticisms surrounding the status of cognitive interests, especially the emancipatory interest, Habermas abandoned the position he had taken in *Knowledge and Human Interests*. He did not repudiate the search for a rational basis for critical theory. Instead of trying to identify an emancipatory cognitive interest, he turned to the structure of language and communication to uncover a generalized human interest in autonomy.

In *The Theory of Communicative Action*, Habermas argued that all human action involves language.[4] Moreover, linguistic communication is impossible without raising what he calls "validity claims." In ordinary conversations, people make claims about the nature of the world (e.g., that it is made up of individuals or that unconscious motives explain behavior) and claims about what social rules are right (e.g., people should stop at a red light or reward achievement). Routine, ongoing social interaction is possible insofar as there is some agreement regarding these validity claims. In order for individuals to share a common social world, to cooperate and coordinate actions, there must be some consensus about what we take to be real and what social norms are appropriate in various situations.

Social consensus is fragile and can easily be disturbed. If validity claims are disputed (e.g., if someone challenges beliefs about what is real or individuals disagree about social norms), individuals may respond by trying to coerce or manipulate a "consensus." However, people may also respond by giving reasons for their beliefs about the nature of reality or which norms are appropriate *with the hope of restoring a noncoerced consensus*. The anticipation of arriving at a "reasoned consensus" implies the possibility that the sheer force of the reasons advanced or the possibility of identifying common beliefs, values, social norms, and interests through reasoned discussion are a powerful force in motivating behavior and structuring interaction. In other words, Habermas maintained that insofar as linguistic communication presupposes an orientation to consensus based on appeals to arguments alone, reason is an integral aspect of daily life.

Habermas took this argument for the foundations of critical theory one step further. At the core of the hope for a rational consensus is a social ideal that is implicit and that Habermas explicitly invoked as justifying the moral standpoint of critical theory. The logic of rational consensus or a consensus shaped by the force of the reasons advanced is unthinkable without assuming a social condition in which discourse is open to all individuals who are not constrained by lack of resources or fear of repercussions in contesting validity claims and therefore power hierarchies. If discourses over what is real and right were not open to all and were not constraint free, we could not avoid the suspicion that consensus was achieved through force or intimidation. Rational consensus presupposes what Habermas called an "ideal speech situation," a social condition in which the parties to public discourse are in a situation of equality and autonomy.

Habermas's intent should not be obscured in the detail of his theory of communicative action. He wished to provide a defense of critical theory as a form of reason. He intended to justify the commitment of critical theory to social justice and democracy as more than a culturally specific value or interest. By identifying an orientation to rational consensus as inherent in everyday life, Habermas thought he had found a rational basis for critical theory. The hope for a society free of constraint, founded on a democratic public culture, is not merely the utopian wish of critical theorists but an ideal built into the very structure of daily life. The values of democracy, justice, equality, and autonomy are not arbitrary or irrational but are the very preconditions of communication, the hidden telos toward which everyday life is directed.

RECONSTRUCTING MARXISM AS GENERAL THEORY AND CRITIQUE

Habermas detected in Marx a certain reluctance to think through the basic concepts and premises of his social theory. Marx never really clarified his moral standpoint. He appealed to the liberal and democratic values of Western capitalist societies to criticize them. But what if the social ideals invoked are morally ambiguous, or democratic values are declining? Moreover, Marx assumed that the working class represented the general interests of humanity and that the truth of his social ideas was guaranteed by their inevitable triumph. But what if Marx was mistaken? Indeed, by the mid-twentieth century, the identification of the working class with humanity's hope for freedom was in doubt. The first generation of the Frankfurt school wedded social critique to a relativistic standpoint. As we have seen, Habermas attempted to secure foundations for a critical theory of society.

Marx never adequately clarified the basic concepts of his social theory. As his ideas developed in polemics against idealists and political economists, and in response to key social developments, Marx's core concepts were only sketchily outlined and defended. In fact, Habermas believed that classical Marxism was conceptually flawed.

At the heart of Marxism is the defense of a materialist social theory. Marx often described materialism as little more than an approach emphasizing economic and political dynamics in contrast to idealism's focus on ideas and cultural development. However, Marx at times presses materialism into an economistic, base–superstructure model that neglects cultural and political dynamics. Habermas believed that the tendency of Marxism to favor one-sided "materialist" social explanations accounted, in part, for its growing obsolescence in Western societies. Habermas wished to revive Marxism as a vehicle of critical social analysis by broadening and refashioning its key concepts.

The Marxian theoretical edifice is built around the concept of labor. It is through labor that humans make and remake themselves, society, and history. Yet the concept of labor is confused in Marx and is often reduced to a one-sided materialistic understanding. In principle, labor refers to our struggle to control social and natural forces as a means of survival. Labor also exhibits an "idealist" dimension in that all behavior is guided by norms and involves shared beliefs and values that make possible social cooperation and regulated social conflict. Marx's multidimensional view of labor should have encouraged him to develop concepts, social models, and explanations that emphasized both materialist dynamics such as technological and organizational development and idealist processes that relate to changing social norms and ideals of justice. Yet Marx's social theory repeatedly edges into a one-sided materialism, either ignoring idealist or cultural dynamics or reducing them to secondary effects of materialist social processes.

Habermas addressed the materialism of Marxism in *The Reconstruction of Historical Materialism* (many of the essays appear in the British edition, *Communication and the Evolution of Society*).[5] Drawing on recent anthropological research, Habermas disputed the Marxian definition of the human species in terms of labor. Labor is not a uniquely human trait since it is characteristic of hominoids. What is distinctive to the earliest stages of human evolution is that labor is organized along kinship lines. Kinship, moreover, is an arrangement defined by language and cultural codes. In other words, Habermas suggested that labor and language, or work and communicative or symbolic action, are basic to humankind. Accordingly, social theory must build into its conceptual strategies a dual concern with materialist processes revolving around work and the struggle for survival and dominance and idealist processes centered on the creation of a symbolic world of meanings, identities, and social solidarities.

Habermas's effort to reconstruct Marxism as a multidimensional social theory led him to challenge the centrality of the concept of mode of production. According to Marx, the mode of production defines the core structure of society. Marx understood the mode of production as being composed of the forces and relations of production. The former includes raw materials, technology, labor power, organizational skills, and knowledge; the latter refers to the social relations of property ownership. Marx held that the property-owning class exercises control over the forces of production (e.g., determines the division of labor) and over laborers. The forces and relations of production form the economic base of society that determines the cultural and political superstructure. History is viewed as the progressive unfolding of the internal contradictions in the mode of production or economic base. The development of the forces of production inevitably comes into conflict with the relations of production or the social framework of the economy. For example, the development of commerce and manufacturing in late feudal Europe contradicted the dominance of agrarian socioeconomic relations and institutions. Class conflict is the mechanism by which a new mode of production is ushered in. Thus, the struggle of the new bourgeois class against the landed nobility in late feudal Europe ended in the triumph of the former and a developing capitalist system. The coming to power of the working class and the advent of socialism will mark the end of history as a story of class conflict.

Habermas argued that a reinvigorated critical theory should abandon this formulation of historical materialism. The latter is unable to grasp the interdependency of economy, state, and culture in late capitalist society. Through the concept of relations of production (i.e., the relation between property owners and laborers), Marx can explain how the actions of individuals – laborers and capitalists – are guided and ordered. He relied heavily on an appeal to the power of legal norms and to the economic and political power of capitalists to account for processes of social regulation and integration. What are lacking in Marx are analyses of nonlegal social norms and ideals regulating action; there is no understanding that identity formation is central to both social regulation and conflict; nowhere in Marx is there an analysis of the creation of solidarity communities among workers or capitalists.

Habermas criticized Marxism for reducing the social base to the economic base. Marx defined the economy as the determining factor in shaping cultural, legal, and political structures. The same reductionism is apparent in the Marxist identification of the relations of production with narrowly economic or property relations of ownership. Marx assumed that, in all societies, legal ownership of the means of production determined the relations of production; that is, property owners controlled labor power, the division of labor, the distribution of wealth, and ultimately the institutional shape of society. Hence, all societies can be described in terms of economically based class relations: institutional dynamics are merely the elaboration of this economic base. Habermas disagreed. He suggested that only in liberal capitalist societies (from roughly the mid-nineteenth to the mid-twentieth centuries) do the relations of production assume a directly economic form or is the economy the base for institutional formation. In other societies, noneconomic domains regulate access to the means of production, determine the distribution of wealth, and define the dominant forms of identity and social integration. For example, in "primitive" societies, kinship structures form the social base or institutional core; their formation and functioning cannot be reduced to property relations but are anchored in complex symbolic systems of classification and codes that govern familial, social, and political roles and relations. Habermas did not discount the importance of economic relations, but objects to the collapse of cultural and political dynamics into economic ones.

Similar concerns motivated Habermas's critical revision of the standard Marxian theory of social change. Classical Marxism explained change as driven by the internal contradictions of the mode of production. At certain critical junctures, the relations of production become an impediment to the development of the forces of production. System imbalance produces a social crisis which is resolved by a "readjustment" of the relations of production to a higher level of development of the forces of production. Habermas argued that the pressure exerted by the forces of production on the relations of production might explain the precipitation of a social crisis; it cannot account for the kinds of institutional and cultural changes that must occur in order for a social revolution to ensue. Major alterations in the "relations of production" involve new social norms, ideals of social justice, institutional arrangements, and altered forms of personal and social identity and integration. Faced with a social crisis that requires innovation in social norms, identities, and social integration, individuals will not be able merely to apply scientific–technical knowledge; rather, a broad institutional shift is unthinkable without an alteration in the character of our moral knowledge; i.e., ideas about social norms, justice, identities, and community. In other words, whereas the evolution of scientific–technical–administrative knowledge can explain the development of the forces of production, only the application of moral knowledge can explain the organization of the relations of production or the institutional framework of society. Social revolution occurs through the application of scientific–technical traditions and moral knowledge as it is embedded in cultural traditions, law, social customs, and social world views.

Whether he was addressing the core Marxian concepts of labor, mode of production, or social evolution, Habermas aimed to reconstruct the very foundations of historical materialism. Central to this effort is the claim that, in order to arrive at a comprehensive understanding of society, our core concepts must be able to grasp not only materialist dynamics centered on economic reproduction but idealist processes concerned with the formation of identities and social solidarities. At the heart of Habermas's social theory is a guiding vision of social action, institutions, and evolution. Humanity is imagined as developing along the dual paths of increased self- and social control through scientific–technological progress and undergoing moral evolution through the progress of ethical traditions.

Habermas conceived of social evolution as occurring at the levels of both scientific–technical–administrative development and ethical advancement. Development at the former level involves processes of economic, technological, and bureaucratic rationalization. Advancement is marked by maximizing efficient, effective control over social and natural processes. With regard to moral or ethical evolution, Habermas drew from the developmental psychology of Piaget and the theory of moral development of Kohlberg to sketch a progressive view of history that parallels individual cognitive and moral development. Just as the child progresses from a state of fusion between the self and the world (the symbiotic phase) to a stage in which the self is clearly differentiated from the world and is capable of critical reflexivity (the universalistic phase), moral evolution, as evidenced in our law and world views, undergoes a parallel progression from mythical thought to universalistic ethics to the current Western critical reflective attitude. The story of human evolution that Habermas related is deeply ambivalent; whereas modernity signals an historic breakthrough, making possible unprecedented levels of social control and autonomy, it also unleashes the forces of bureaucratization and scientific–technological rationality that threaten to trap us in a social nightmare.

FAILED MODERNIZATION: THE TRIUMPH OF INSTRUMENTAL REASON

The Marxist critique of capitalism was losing credibility in the 1960s. The absence of working-class radicalism and the authoritarian turn of Soviet communism precipitated a crisis in Marxism. This was reinforced by the rise of radical social movements among the youth, students, and marginal groups (women, gays, ethnic minorities) whose struggles could not be characterized as class conflicts. In the face of these events, many thinkers sought to revise the Marxian theory of capitalism. Neo-Marxists tried to explain these events and to preserve a focus on economic crisis and class conflict by analyzing the shift from competitive to corporate, state-managed capitalism.

Habermas was convinced, however, that postwar developments pointed to a major reconfiguration of Western capitalist societies. The Marxian theory of capitalism required a fundamental reconstruction. The primary site of social crisis and conflict has changed. Social crises have shifted from the economy to the state and culture; the key axes of conflict are around issues of rights, quality of life, protection of the environment, preservation of the integrity of communities, and control over local decisions around education and health, cultural legitimation, and social democracy; the battle for change is now occurring among a multitude of grass-roots-based groups and communities. A critical understanding of these movements requires an analysis of the dynamic interrelations between the economy, state, and culture. Habermas sought to produce a new perspective on late capitalist societies that could provide oppositional groups with a critical understanding of the potential for political action.

Habermas's first major theory of late capitalism was *Legitimation Crisis*.[6] He claimed that the major site of social crisis has shifted from the economic to the political and cultural spheres. Although capitalism continues to experience cycles of growth and recession, state economic management policies (e.g., monetary policies, price supports, purchasing surplus goods) have succeeded in averting a major socioeconomic crisis. Capitalism remains a contradictory society, but its chief crises have shifted to the political and cultural spheres.

Habermas spoke of a legitimation crisis when the public withdraws support from the government due to perceptions that its policies are unfair. Legitimation problems arise because the state must fulfill the contradictory demands of ensuring capitalist growth while maintaining mass public support. The former imperative requires that the state favors the particular interests of property owners and their managers; the latter imperative demands that the state act as if it represents the interests of all citizens. In other words, the class interests of the state that are revealed in its social policies undermine mass public support which is necessary in a formally democratic society. Legitimation crises are manifested in citizen apathy, mass social discontent, and proposals for social reform, all of which threaten the social status quo. The state responds by increasing material compensations for the broader population in the form of state-funded support services or social welfare programs. However, this strategy has limited impact because it absorbs profit and threatens an economic downturn. A more effective response is for the state to promote a technocratic ideology. If politics is redefined as consisting of technical–administrative problems to be handled by experts, citizens are rendered politically inactive. Democratic politics is reduced to periodic voting, which has the effect of reducing legitimation problems for the ruling powers while conferring legitimacy on the state.

Legitimation problems may recur in late capitalist societies, but only when they are joined to a "motivation crisis" can they provoke a full-blown social crisis. Whereas the concept of legitimation crisis brought the state into focus, the notion of a motivation crisis places the cultural sphere at the center of critical theory. Essentially, a motivation crisis indicates a contradiction between the cultural and economic spheres. Let me explain.

Habermas believed that social institutions function effectively only if individuals have the appropriate set of beliefs, motivations, and values. These behavioral orientations are sustained by cultural traditions that are transmitted to individuals through family, the church, education, and the mass media. In late capitalist societies, our lives are centered around work and family and career, consumerist and family ideals. These values are rooted in Judeo-Christian and secular liberal traditions which are today being undermined by secularization, statism, bureaucratization, and radical democratic movements. The cultural underpinning of late capitalist society is being eroded by its core social structural dynamics.

Habermas alluded to two possible outcomes of a motivational crisis. First, capitalist societies could try to establish an institutional order on a technocratic basis. Individuals would accept social roles and institutional policies in exchange for material rewards (e.g., security, order, status) without requiring that institutional norms and goals be justified by substantive values such as justice or freedom. A second possibility is that Western societies will evolve towards social democracy. In the demands by the new social movements for social equality and participatory democracy, Habermas discerned the possibility of a truly democratic society. To the extent that these movements demand that reasons be given for social decisions and policies, they evidence a "communicative ethic" which, if actualized, would transform capitalism into a democratic socialist society.

In *The Theory of Communicative Action*, Habermas's crisis theory of late capitalism was reformulated as part of a grand theory of social evolution. Central to this theory is a dualistic view of society as "lifeworld" and "system." The former refers to a realm of behavior in which social coordination or regulation occurs by means of shared beliefs and values; in the lifeworld, individuals draw from custom and cultural traditions to construct identities, negotiate situational definitions, coordinate action, and create social solidarity. The lifeworld makes society possible by maintaining the identities and motivations necessary for institutional stability. Social life requires not only shared meanings but also strategies for coordinating resources and controlling natural and social forces. This is the function of the systems level of society. In the course of social development, population pressures, intersocietal contacts, technological innovation, and wars create a need to organize complex activities and resources with the aid of functionally differentiated bureaucratic administrative structures. Whereas, in the lifeworld, action is oriented to mutual understanding, at the systems level, the emphasis is on instrumental control and efficiency.

Social evolution is viewed as a two-sided rationalization process of the social system and lifeworld. The development of social systems or social rationalization can be charted as a process of increasing institutional differentiation, complexity, and growing organizational predictability. For example, the emergence of functionally differentiated institutions and roles (e.g., economy, state, education, family), each having its own function, maximizes social control. The evolution of the lifeworld or cultural rationalization is analyzed in terms of enhanced reflexivity, the universalization of beliefs, and the differentiation of value or knowledge spheres (science, morality, and art). In general, Habermas viewed societal development as progressive. The differentiation of functional systems enhances institutional mastery and makes possible higher levels of autonomy. The rationalization of the lifeworld makes possible higher levels of reflexivity and the expansion of a democratic public realm.

Unfortunately, Western capitalism has impeded the realization of the full beneficial human potential of social and cultural rationalization. In particular, capitalism has promoted social rationalization at the expense of cultural development. For example, the advance of bureaucracy has far outstripped the progress of political democracy; the development of scientific–technological rationality has overshadowed the advance of moral and aesthetic reasoning. Capitalist development has favored the bureaucratization of society and rule by an elite of scientific–technical–administrative experts. Habermas spoke, darkly and with echoes of the Frankfurt school, of the "colonization of the lifeworld." He imagined a dominant scientific–technical–administrative elite seizing control of daily life, translating moral issues into cost/benefit decisions, and redefining political disputes as purely administrative or technical problems. As the "system," with its technological–administrative ways of thinking, penetrates the lifeworld, it disrupts identities, traditional forms of life, forms of social solidarity, and cultural traditions. A traumatized lifeworld threatens the very survival of society. The spirit of Marx reappears in the notion of capitalist society as a contradictory, potentially self-destructive system.

Habermas was not wholly pessimistic. He pinned his hopes on the new social movements. Whereas Marx saw in the working class the hopes of humanity, Habermas looked to the new social movements to resist the colonization of the lifeworld.

> In the past decade or two, conflicts have developed in advanced Western societies that deviate in various ways from the welfare-state pattern of institutionalized conflict over distribution. They no longer flare up in domains of material reproduction; they are no longer channeled through parties and associations; and they can no longer be allayed by compensations. Rather, these new conflicts arise in domains of cultural reproduction, social integration, and socialization; they are carried in subinstitutional – or at least extraparliamentary – forms of protest.[7]

Unlike those of the working class, the concerns of the new social movements are not wages or work conditions, but "have to do with quality of life, equal rights, individual self-realization, participation, and human rights . . . The new politics finds strong support in the new middle classes, among the younger generation, and in groups with more formal education."[8] The new social movements, characteristically grass roots, democratic, and motivated by substantive values and moral visions, aim at reestablishing an appropriate balance between social and cultural rationalization; they are the carriers of a rational society.

Suggested Readings

David Held, *An Introduction to Critical Theory* (Berkeley: University of California Press, 1980).
David Ingram, *Habermas and the Dialectic of Reason* (New Haven, CT: Yale University Press, 1987).
William Outhwaite, *Habermas* (Cambridge: Polity Press, 1994).
Stephen White, ed., *The Cambridge Companion to Habermas* (Cambridge: Cambridge University Press, 1994).

References

1   Max Horkheimer and Theodor Adorno, *The Dialectic of Enlightenment* (New York: Herder & Herder, 1972); Max Horkheimer, *Eclipse of Reason* (New York: Seabury, 1947); Herbert Marcuse, *One-Dimensional Man* (Boston, MA: Beacon Press, 1964).
2   Leo Lowenthal, *Literature, Popular Culture and Society* (Palo Alto, CA: Pacific Books, 1967); Eric Fromm, *Escape from Freedom* (New York: Rinehart, 1941).
3   Jürgen Habermas, *Knowledge and Human Interests* (Boston, MA: Beacon Press, 1971).
4   Jürgen Habermas, *The Theory of Communicative Action*, 2 vols. (Boston, MA: Beacon Press, 1984–7).
5   Jürgen Habermas, *Communication and the Evolution of Society* (Boston, MA: Beacon Press, 1979).
6   Jürgen Habermas, *Legitimation Crisis* (Boston, MA: Beacon Press, 1975).
7   Habermas, *The Theory of Communicative Action*, vol. 2, p. 392.
8   Habermas, *The Theory of Communicative Action*, vol. 2, p. 392.

9

Stuart Hall and British Cultural Studies

There were many efforts to rethink Marxism in the post-World War II period. One reason is that Marxism had become perhaps the most important theoretical perspective for analyzing contemporary societies not only in the Soviet bloc countries but in Germany, France, Italy, Britain, Australia, and elsewhere. By the 1950s a version of Marxist socialism had become the official ideology of Communist Parties across the globe and influential in social democratic and labor parties in Europe. Yet, Marxism was in crisis. Soviet communism raised the question of whether the authoritarianism of that society was intrinsic to Marxism. No working-class revolution occurred in Europe or America – the heartland of capitalism. In fact, the postwar years witnessed a resurgence of capitalist prosperity. The radical social movements of this period were not centered around the politics of class, but of gender, race, sexuality, and ecology.

The postwar period presented a challenge to Marxists: how to rethink Marxism so that it could engage current social developments without abandoning its uniqueness, for example, its analysis of political economy and class dynamics, its holistic, critical, and historical methodology, and its aim to link theory and practice.

The work of Habermas and Stuart Hall offered two important attempts at rethinking Marxism. In part, their differences reflect their varied national environments. Habermas drew on the German Idealist tradition of system building; Hall took over the British suspicion towards grand theory, and this influenced his reckoning with Marxism. Moreover, Habermas's critical theory was decisively shaped by his coming of age in the aftermath of Nazism; Hall came of age as a colonial subject. Born and raised in Jamaica, a colony of Britain, Hall approached questions of knowledge in terms of his "postcolonial" identity. He experienced the oppression of being a colonial subject, and yet adopted many "British" values. One benefit of being a citizen of the British empire was that Hall was educated at Oxford University. There he began his engagement with Marxism as he sought a critical perspective on the present, at once national and global.

Contested Knowledge: Social Theory Today, Fifth Edition. Steven Seidman.
© 2013 John Wiley & Sons, Ltd. Published 2013 by John Wiley & Sons, Ltd.

Stuart Hall was born in the British colony of Jamaica in 1932. As a Rhodes scholar, Hall went to Britain to study at Oxford University in 1951. During the 1970s, he was the director of the Centre for Contemporary Cultural Studies in Birmingham, where he helped establish the field of cultural studies. Hall and his colleagues at the Centre broadened the field of cultural studies so that the definition of culture encompassed more than literary works and other "high-brow" forms of culture. Ordinary beliefs, movies, popular songs, and holiday rituals are all part of the culture of a society. Hall argues that our behavior is shaped by the messages that come from the mass media and popular culture. However, he insists that people are not merely passive recipients of these messages; rather, people actively interpret them. The interpretations people give are based on factors such as their gender, social class, nationality and so forth.

Hall has been the guiding force of the so-called Birmingham school of cultural studies. In 1964, Hall participated in the establishment of the Birmingham Centre for Contemporary Cultural Studies (which he directed for some fifteen years). Because Hall is so closely identified with the work of the Birmingham school, and because many of his most important writings are joint or collective efforts, our discussion will consider him in the context of the Birmingham school's effort to develop a distinctive "cultural studies" approach.[1]

The cultural turn of the Birmingham school is in part related to the decline of the British Empire. As its many colonies, from the Caribbean to Africa, revolted against colonial rule, movements for national independence focused on issues of cultural identity and politics.. Also, the simultaneous eruption of cultural conflict in the 1950s and 1960s by youth, the women's and gay movements, and antiracist movements placed issues of social identity at the center of politics. Popular culture, from dress to movies, art, and music, moved to the center of social conflict. A Marxist perspective that defined culture as superstructural or that focused primarily on political economy seemed out of touch. The Birmingham school made the study of culture integral to its rethinking of Marxism.

But, what is the Birmingham school approach to cultural studies? Hall and associates developed their position against two influential perspectives. On the one hand, there was an elite tradition that defined culture in terms of high-brow literature, art, music, and theater. On the other hand, Marxists and many sociologists reduced culture to ideology and made economic-based class conflict the driving force of history. The Birmingham school wished to defend a view of culture as irreducible to political economy and not reducible to high culture.

Against the elite tradition, the Birmingham school argued that high culture is just one aspect of culture. The study of culture must include popular culture such as mass circulation magazines, newspapers, books, movies, television, and popular music. Moreover, not all culture is institutionalized. "Culture" in its broadest sense refers to the language in use and the meanings, symbols, and interpretations of reality that are a part of social life. Culture is less the sort of thing we associate with museums, galleries, and prize-winning literature than the meanings – norms, values, beliefs, ideals – that make up the stuff of everyday life. Social life is shot through with culture. Whether it is the language we use, our ideologies and religious faiths, or the texts and representations we produce, culture saturates society. As Hall says, the Birmingham school of cultural studies sought to shift "the whole ground of debate from a literary-moral to an anthropological definition of culture. But it defined the latter now as the 'whole process' by means of which meanings and definitions are socially constructed and historically transformed, with literature and art as only one . . . kind of social communication."[2]

Enlarging the concept of culture meant that the appropriate method for studying culture was not exclusively a literary-aesthetic approach but a sociology of culture. For the elite tradition, culture was to be analyzed in terms of general aesthetic evaluative standards. That is, formal standards of beauty were the basis for distinguishing "high" from "low" culture. However, if culture, whether high-brow or popular, institutional or noninstitutional, is an expression of lived experience and rooted in people's shared collective lives, it needs to be studied from a sociological perspective.

The Birmingham school proposed a multifaceted approach to the study of culture. In opposition to some Marxists, culture was to be studied interpretively. That is, a cultural studies approach examines the internal organization of meanings whether they are elaborated political ideologies, high-brow literature, or television programs. This sociological approach aims to understand why objects or actions (words, signs, people or things) acquire certain meanings, how these meanings relate to one another, and their social and political effects. In this regard, many in the Birmingham school were influenced by a tradition of "semiotic" analysis associated with theorists such as Roland Barthes and Umberto Eco.[3] A semiotic perspective holds that the meaning of words or signs (such as the flag, clothing, or cars) is less determined by their relation to an objective reality than by their relation to other words and signs. For example, the meaning of "woman" is less a reflection of the objective reality than determined by its relation to the contrasting term "man." If women are defined as, say, emotional and intuitive, it is, in part, because men are understood as rational and intellectual.

The Birmingham school went beyond an exclusively semiotic approach. Cultural meanings are never fixed only by internal relations of identity and difference. It may, for example, be the case that a television program presents men and women respectively as rational and emotional, but that does not necessarily mean that viewers interpret that program in these terms. Semiotic analysis needs to be supplemented by "reception studies" or an examination of the way audiences consume or interpret texts.

For example, many social researchers aim to identify the core beliefs and values produced by the mass media, and trace their effects on the audience (often measured by attitudinal changes). By contrast, the Birmingham school focuses on the "cultural codes" structuring media texts (e.g., television and radio or news programs), their ideological role, and the ways these texts are interpreted by their consumers.

Hall argues that studying the media is a threefold process.[4] First, we examine the media in terms of the meanings intended by the producers. These meanings are not reducible to discrete beliefs and values, but are organized as "cultural codes." Dichotomies such as majority/minority, normal/abnormal, moral/decadent, mature/immature, and healthy/sick typically structure media texts. This suggests that the media does more than transmit beliefs and values; it communicates ways of defining, classifying, and judging individuals and groups. This brings us to the second aspect of the cultural study of the media. The media classifies individuals and groups by race, gender, nationality, and other identity categories and relates each group to the above dichotomies. Thus, the heterosexual/homosexual or Westerner/Easterner binaries overlap with the majority/minority or superior/inferior classificatory and normative binaries. The media does more than influence individual attitudes. It legitimates an unequal social order; it defines the moral boundaries of a society and thereby specifies what practices are acceptable, healthy, normal, and good. A third focus of media analysis brings in the consumers of media texts. The meaning of media texts are not fixed or univocal. By insisting on studying consumers of the media, Hall is making the point that ordinary individuals are not passively controlled by the media but actively interpret media texts and sometimes in ways that are at odds with the intended meaning of their producers. The mass media, and culture in general, is the site of both domination and resistance.

Meanings are said to have a sort of independent reality. Culture is sometimes likened to a text – made up of words or signs whose meaning is related to their internal relations of similarity and contrast. Yet, meanings are not free-floating and detached from social interests, power relations, and material life. Meanings may have internal relations and have an independent effect on social life, but they are created by real, living, struggling individuals whose lives are enmeshed in social institutions and unequal social relations. Indicative of the Marxism of the Birmingham school, Hall and colleagues argue that only by tracing the connection between cultural meanings and social conditions can we grasp their ideological role. Culture may give purpose and coherence to the lives of individuals and groups, but it is also implicated in power relations. Some meanings legitimate social privilege. Thus, defining women as emotional, intuitive, and maternal is integral to norms that women should be in caregiver roles. Such roles mean that women will have less social power and status than men, who will dominate in roles involving public authority.

Although the Birmingham school made culture crucial to social analysis, it is important that we don't lose sight of the Marxist inspiration of their sociology. Like Habermas and the Frankfurt school, Hall and colleagues (many of whom are sociologists) sought a critical social analysis inspired by Marxism. In this regard, we should note the important influence of the Italian Marxist Antonio Gramsci.[5] He argued that class domination is not sustained exclusively by economic wealth and political power. Ruling groups try to make their own culture into the socially dominant culture in order to give legitimacy to their class rule. The notion of "hegemony" was intended to describe this social process. This concept was important for two reasons. First, culture was seen as integral to class rule and politics. Culture became part of the realm of power and rulership. Second, class rule was viewed as unstable. Even a ruling class needs some level of consent by the public to hold power. In this way, Gramsci viewed the poor and the laboring classes as an active force in shaping society. Gramsci suggested, then, a much more fluid, contingent, agent-centered and culturalist view of social life than was to be found in classical Marxism. His work recommended an approach to social analysis which was in many respects closer to the spirit of classical sociology than Marxism, for example, in its emphasis on empirical critical analysis, the practices of individuals and groups, the importance of culture, and the open-ended character of history.

Although there is no one defining work of Hall and the Birmingham school, *Policing the Crisis: Mugging, the State, and Law and Order* is arguably its signature text.[6] Written as the collective effort of five co-authors in response to the British state's turn in the mid-1970s to repressive governing tactics, *Policing the Crisis* nicely shows the "cultural Marxism" of the Birmingham school.

The setting is Britain in the early 1970s. Despite the absence of reliable statistical data, the authors note a phenomenal growth in news reporting about "muggings" and new activity by the police, courts, and government to curb what is seen as a major social danger. Mugging was perceived as a national problem. The authors wished to explain the extreme imbalance between the public response to mugging and the threat it actually presented.

Policing makes the public response to mugging the focus of study. Without denying that violent criminal acts were perpetrated at this time, the term "mugging" is understood as not merely descriptive but "indexical" or symbolic of broader social developments. Similarly, without denying that aspects of the public response to mugging were appropriate, it is the excess of the response by the media, courts, police, and the state that needs explaining. The thesis of this book is that the mugging phenomenon occurred in the context of a national crisis; it functioned to both obscure the real social sources of the crisis and to justify a conservative turn in the ruling government.

The term "mugging" comes from the United States. For Americans, it refers not only to specific types of (violent) crime, but to the urban social dislocations surrounding the protests by Blacks, youth, and others in the 1960s. In other words, the term "mugging" suggests a network of social meanings linked to racial conflict, urban crisis, and the breakdown of law and order. The fact that this term was adopted by the British media, courts, and state suggests similar anxieties in this nation. This hunch receives empirical support in statements by judges, sentences for "muggers" that are way out of proportion to their crimes, and in the creation of anti-mugging police squads.

The media made mugging into a national danger. Large sections of *Policing* are devoted to analyzing the local and national news media. The media framed mugging in a way that reproduced the dominant ideology of ruling groups. For example, while mugging was defined as a social danger, its origin was linked either to the failings of individuals or to a demoralized social environment, without addressing the role of the economy, family, or schools. In the British media, mugging evoked a general sense of social disorder and moral breakdown. The remedy was thought to be moral education, strengthening families, youth education, discipline, and cleaning the environment – rather than calling for more and better-paying jobs and schools. In the end, the media made muggers into "folk devils," the very antithesis of British values such as respect, discipline, modesty, responsibility, and decency.

Emphasizing the social meaning of mugging raises questions about its status as a crime, and indeed raises a broader question about the very category of crime. Rather than viewing certain acts as unambiguously "criminal," the authors argue that what is defined as a crime is often contested because such classifications are linked to broader social conflicts. Criminalizing certain acts can be a state strategy for controlling rebellious individuals and movements. Similarly, engaging in law-violating behavior can be a political act. Indeed, certain "criminal" practices can become the site of intense political conflict. This is the case with mugging. Not only is the public reaction to mugging viewed as a response to a specific crime, but mugging serves as a sign of the perceived breakdown of law and order. The act of mugging itself becomes a way for individuals to stage a social protest. But what was the social and political context that made mugging a site of social conflict?

Recall Gramsci's notion that class rule involves an economically dominant group becoming a ruling national force. This is accomplished by means of coercive state power (laws, legislation, and police and military force), forging alliances among class fractions into a ruling bloc, and, not least, building a consensus around the legitimacy of the dominant class and its social and political values. The latter is necessary in liberal democratic societies that feature regular elections, a parliamentary government, an open civil society, and require citizen loyalty as a condition of rulership. Class hegemony is achieved only when the consent of the governed is gained. If successful, class rule appears to be democratic rule; class domination is rendered invisible by the foregrounding of the language of rights, rule of law, representation, and civic equality. The chief argument of *Policing* is that the early 1970s experienced a breakdown of consent and a crisis of hegemony. In response, class rule shifted to coercive state measures. The mugging panic was a way to gain citizen support for the use of repressive state measures to ensure class hegemony.

Postwar Britain has managed only a fragile consensus. Citizen loyalty was contingent on the state managing capitalism successfully enough to avoid crises, securing full employment, providing a generous welfare state, and on a spirit of cooperation between capital and labor. However, by the late 1950s, declining profits, slower rates of economic growth, inflation, diminished British competitiveness in a world economy, and the birth of protest politics spelled trouble. The consensus was faltering badly by the 1960s. Continued economic decline, strains between capital and labor, an enlarged welfare system that drained the economy of much-needed capital, and, not least, a series of rebellions from youth, students, immigrants, people of color, women, and gays undermined the terms of consensual rule. Britain was undergoing a political crisis. Instead of trying to regain a national consensus, ruling groups shifted to strategies of state repression. By defining the crisis as fundamentally about the breakdown of law and order, the state was able to expand its coercive measures, broaden its scope of intervention into social affairs, and de-emphasize rights and democratic process while emphasizing administrative control.

The mugging panic was part of this national crisis. By condensing the myriad social protests and conflicts into the notion of social and moral breakdown, epitomized by the figure of the mugger, the state could legitimately – under the banner of law, order, and British virtue – censor and control dissenting groups. Not only would the ruling groups maintain their dominance and legitimacy by masking the deep sources of social crisis (e.g., class conflict, capitalist irrationality, protests by subaltern groups), but citizen loyalty would be forthcoming to the extent that citizens viewed the general breakdown of order as the source of their personal and national troubles. Hence, the mugging "panic" allowed ruling groups to displace the British social crisis from the economy and social structure to a specific event and group, and to justify the enlargement of the coercive measures of the state. Its attacks on labor, Black immigrants, sexual permissiveness, and social protests created the basis for Thatcherism – which aimed to dismantle the welfare state, promote free enterprise, and weaken labor unions and dissenting movements.[7]

Policing was not only a masterful social analysis but a critique of the rightward drift of the British state. Hall and his colleagues aimed to underscore the retreat of the state from social democracy. They insisted that the causes were not based in a general social breakdown of law and order but in the contradictions of capitalism and the myriad protest movements which challenged some key institutions and cultural beliefs and values of British society. In other words, *Policing* was an intervention into British politics whose aim was to shape the outcome of social struggles. Like the public sociology of Mills' and Habermas's critical theory, the Birmingham school sought to develop a tradition of critical social analysis that would be empirical yet politically engaged.

Hall at times referred to Gramsci's concept of the "organic intellectual" to describe an ideal relation between the academic intellectual and public life. Such intellectuals aim to use social knowledge to explain and formulate a response to the key social conflicts of the day. Less the universal intellectual of the Enlightenment who proposed grand theories and made weighty pronouncements about the evolution of humanity, the organic intellectual is connected to specific groups, institutions, or social movements. She or he speaks less from the general standpoint of humanity than from a specific social location (in an institution or movement), engaging conflicts in a specific sociohistorical context. It is precisely the social embeddedness of intellectuals that motivates public engagement and makes effective political interventions possible.

Like Habermas and the Frankfurt school, Hall and the Birmingham school sought to rethink Marxism. In the end, however, they fashioned a social perspective that departed from Marx in significant ways. As cultural analysis moved into the center of social analysis, and as movements around identity replaced or supplemented labor as the chief forces of change, it was less the political, economic, class-based analysis of Marxism than its spirit of critique that was preserved in these reconstructions.

Suggested Readings

Paul Gilroy, L. Grossberg, and A. McRobbie, eds., *Without Guarantees: In Honor of Stuart Hall* (London: Verso, 2000).

David Morley and Kuan-Hsing Chen, eds., *Stuart Hall: Critical Dialogues in Cultural Studies* (New York: Routledge, 1996).

Graeme Turner, *British Cultural Studies* (New York: Routledge, 1992).

References

1 For an overview of the Birmingham school, see Stuart Hall, "Cultural Studies and the Centre: Some Problematics and Problems," in Stuart Hall, Dorothy Hobson, Andrew Lowe, et al., eds., *Culture, Media, Language* (London: Hutchinson, 1980).

2 Hall, "Cultural Studies and the Centre," p. 19.

3 Roland Barthes, *Mythologies* (New York: Hill & Wang, 1972) and *Fashion System* (New York: Hill & Wang, 1983). Umberto Eco, *A Theory of Semiotics* (Bloomington: Indiana University Press, 1975).

4 Stuart Hall, "Encoding/Decoding," in Hall et al., eds., *Culture, Media, Language*, p. 19. Also, "Deviancy, Politics and the Media," in Paul Rock and Mary McIntosh, eds., *Deviance and Social Control* (London: Tavistock, 1974).

5 Antonio Gramsci, *Selections from the Prison Notebooks* (New York: International, 1971). See Stuart Hall, "Gramsci's Relevance for the Study of Race and Ethnicity," in David Morley and Kuan-Hsing Chen, eds., *Stuart Hall: Critical Dialogues in Cultural Studies* (New York: Routledge, 1996).

6 Stuart Hall, Chas Critcher, Tony Jefferson, et al., *Policing the Crisis: Mugging, the State, and Law and Order* (London: Macmillan, 1978).

7 Stuart Hall, *The Hard Road to Renewal: Thatcherism and the Crisis of the Left* (London: Verso, 1987).

10

The Critical Sociology of Anthony Giddens and Pierre Bourdieu

The German critical theorists and British cultural studies scholars proved enormously influential in the development of European social theory. They offered alternatives to the often rigid, dogmatic cast of scientific Marxism. Theorists like Habermas and Hall approached Marx's ideas with an eye to revising them in far-reaching ways. Moreover, they each drew considerably on non-Marxian ideas about society, history, and politics. In particular, Habermas and Hall brought Marxism and the classical sociology of Durkheim and Weber into a very inventive, fruitful dialogue. By the 1970s and 1980s the idea of a new theoretical synthesis that integrated Marxism, sociology, and other currents of social thought was very much in the air. Two of the most compelling and far-reaching efforts at theoretical synthesis were those of Anthony Giddens in Britain and Pierre Bourdieu in France.

ANTHONY GIDDENS

Giddens's first major book, *Capitalism and Modern Social Theory*,[1] was intended to shift the way we think about the classics and about social theory away from Parsonian grand theory to approaches that stressed history, social inequality, and social criticism. And yet by the 1980s Giddens had elaborated, if not a "system of sociology," then a theory as far-reaching and "grand" as Parsons'.[2] This was not just a case of a theorist losing himself in logical problems or seduced by the charms of system building. Giddens was reacting to the fragmentation and divisions within sociology in the 1970s and 1980s. Moreover, Giddens's turn to general theory was a reaction to the empiricism and scientism that had triumphed in American and British sociology. Echoing his nemesis, Parsons, Giddens felt compelled to make the case that there is a level of theoretical reflection, apart from empirical analysis, methodology, or building models and explanatory frameworks, that must be recognized as a pivotal part of sociology.

Contested Knowledge: Social Theory Today, Fifth Edition. Steven Seidman.
© 2013 John Wiley & Sons, Ltd. Published 2013 by John Wiley & Sons, Ltd.

British sociologist **Anthony Giddens** was born in 1938. He received his education at the London School of Economics and at Cambridge University. Giddens is now Director of the London School of Economics and Political Science. Although he began his career as a fierce critic of the grand theory of Parsons, Giddens has ironically become one of the foremost grand theorists of our time. Giddens believes that social science not only tells us about the nature of social reality but helps shape our world. Isn't it true today that many of us read and know the ideas of sociologists or economists, and these sometimes influence how we think and act?

For Giddens, the division that is at the root of sociology and social theory is between agent- and structure-centered approaches to social analysis. The former focuses on the individual and his/her intentions, motivations, beliefs, or values as shaping social life. The latter emphasizes social processes such as organizational or class dynamics in explaining individual and social life. Whereas the former is represented by approaches such as symbolic interactionism and exchange theory, the latter is characteristic of both American and French structuralism (e.g., Blau and Lévi-Strauss), Marxism, and functionalism. In a sense, the division between agency- and structure-centered approaches expresses a long-standing division over whether social life and history are a product of the decisions and creativity of individuals or of social laws and impersonal social processes. Giddens believes that the way sociologists conceive of agency and structure will shape their empirical research and broader sociohistorical perspectives.

Social theorists who avoid a one-dimensional action or structure-centered approach tend to conceptualize the relation between the individual and society as a mutually influencing dynamic. The individual is said to create social institutions and culture, but these structures, in turn, constrain individual behavior. The problem with such a formulation is twofold. First, such approaches easily pass into a one-sided reductionism, as either action or structure is given the primary causal weight (e.g., Marx's and Parsons' slide into structuralism). Second, the individual is always already a social being and society is impossible to conceptualize without assuming individual action. Instead of approaching the relation between the individual (agency) and society (social structure) as interactive, Giddens proposes to view agency and structure as simply different aspects of all social practices. We can distinguish an agentic and structural aspect to human action, but this is an analytic, not a real distinction.

Giddens introduces the concept of the "duality of structure" to grasp this dual aspect of social practice. Social structures are said both to be the medium of action and to make action possible, and are reproduced by social action. This approach involves viewing social structure as a "virtual order" rather than as a social reality apart from the individual. By "virtual order," Giddens means that social structure exists, in a sense, in the minds of individuals as practical knowledge of what rules (taken-for-granted procedures or conventions) and what resources (material and social facilities used to get things done) are necessary and appropriate for social behavior in diverse situations.

For example, players know what rules make a baseball game possible, but it is only in their behavior that the rules enter the flow of social life. Or, consider the way in which language exists in a sense only through individual speech acts, yet also exists as a kind of virtual reality, that is, in the minds of individuals yet apart from them. The duality of structure is in evidence in that our speech practices are made possible by language, but language, in turn, is reproduced through these practices. Moreover, the notion of the duality of structure allows Giddens to argue that the structural properties of human action are not merely constraining but, as the example of language indicates, make possible social behaviors as well. Approaching social life as a "structuration" process does not mean that human affairs are always in a state of flux. Social practices become patterned into social systems and institutions. These social patterns can be analyzed in terms of their specific rules and the organization of resources and power dynamics that make up the key structural properties of all social systems. Giddens elaborates these core categories – duality of structure, rules, resources, social systems – into a general theory of the structural principles of different types of societies and the dynamics of social change in world history.

The key point is that, in Giddens's view, social life is neither a collection of individual actions nor a social structural order. Instead, social life is approached as a process in which the key concept is social practice, which has an "agentic" and "structural" aspect. This processual approach to social life is fundamental to Giddens's whole social theory. Thus, he rejects positivism to the extent that social scientific knowledge, including general principles of social life, can be learned by actors, incorporated into behavior, and thereby alter the conditions of its validity. The reflexivity of ordinary actors is said to undermine positivism to the extent that individuals can decide to act contrary to social scientific principles in part because of their knowledge of them. Similarly, Giddens criticizes functionalism, which explains individual behavior in terms of social system requirements or needs. Systemic social patterns can be explained as outcomes, intended and unintended, of social practices. This avoids the problem of identifying system needs and preserves a view of social life as processual and therefore dependent on the reflexive behavior of individuals. For Giddens, societies are not organic or mechanical systems, but consist of networks of practices, some institutionalized but always made possible through reflexive individual action. In this regard, Giddens criticizes evolutionary approaches to history for assuming an inevitable direction and outcome, thereby rendering individual behavior structurally determined. By insisting that individuals be viewed as reflexive, knowledgeable agents, Giddens suggests an approach to history that emphasizes its open-ended, conflict-based character. Assuming the premises of structuration theory means that social life and history cannot be explained without building into our concepts, explanations, and models a way to get at the ongoing dynamics of social reproduction and change that includes reference to the temporal and spatial aspects of social practice, to reflexive, knowledgeable subjects, and to the role of power in shaping rules and resources. In a sense, Giddens aims to substitute a processual view of social life for the voluntarism and structural determinism of much sociology.

To illustrate the force of Giddens's theoretical approach for social analysis, I want to focus on one key idea in his work: the role of reflexivity and knowledge in modern life. As we've already seen, Giddens is critical of sociological perspectives that explain individual behavior as adapting to structural or system dynamics. He insists that individuals play an active role in shaping social life. Yet, he is also critical of sociological perspectives such as exchange theory or versions of conflict theory, which emphasize primarily the goal-oriented, rationally calculating aspect of individual action. Although the coordination of means and ends is part of social conduct, a more basic and sociologically significant aspect is its self-monitoring character. Individuals aren't merely propelled to act by interests, values, and needs, and individuals do not simply conform to social norms and conventions, but their action involves practical knowledge of their world, an ability to reflect upon the conditions of their action and incorporate this knowledge into their conduct. Individuals are knowledgeable, reflexive, and skillful agents.

While reflexivity is made into a key part of his theory of the human actor and action, and therefore a key component of his formal structuration theory, Giddens makes this reflexivity central to his macro-social analysis.[3] In particular, he argues that reflexivity has become a key feature of modern societies. His thesis, to put it as simply as possible, is as follows. In premodern societies "tradition" often guided everyday conduct. That is, behavior was governed by the authority of past practices. In modern societies, social practices are continuously revised in light of new information. Indeed, in more and more social spheres (from family to education, social welfare, and the government) a process of ongoing reflection or knowledge production about social processes is an institutionalized part of social practice. In other words, a key feature of modern institutions is the inclusion of practices aimed at gaining knowledge of their functioning for the purpose of enhancing institutional performance. From prisons to governmental institutions, the continuous production and incorporation of new knowledge into institutional practice is a driving force of modernity.

Giddens argues that modernity is characterized not only by reflexive processes at the institutional and interpersonal level but by the continuous interaction or feedback between these two levels. The expert knowledges generated by institutions are incorporated not only into institutional practices but also into individual conduct. For example, institutions such as universities and psychiatry produce knowledge of intimate life. As this knowledge circulates throughout the social order through the medium of the mass media, schools, churches, and literary publics, they shape everyday intimate behaviors. Giddens offers the following illustration:

> Anyone in a Western country who embarks upon marriage today . . . knows that divorce rates are high . . . Knowledge of the high rate of divorce might affect the very decision to marry, as well as decisions about related considerations – provisions about property and so forth. Awareness of levels of divorce, moreover, is normally much more than just consciousness of a brute fact. It is theorized by the lay agent in ways pervaded by sociological thinking. Thus virtually everyone contemplating marriage has some idea of how family institutions have been changing, changes in the relative social position and power of men and women, alterations in sexual mores, etc. – all of which enter into processes of further change which they reflexively inform. Marriage and the family wouldn't be what they are today were they not thoroughly "sociologised" and "psychologised."[4]

Does this enhanced level of institutional and individual reflexivity mean that humanity is close to realizing the utopian hope of the Enlightenment – of humankind entering an era where reason will govern human affairs? Is the late twentieth century, a world which, in Giddens's view, is increasingly unified and interconnected, inaugurating a new world order of unprecedented democratization and freedom?

As a successor to the classical tradition of social theory, and witness to many of the atrocities of this century, Giddens is cautious. On the one hand, by characterizing late modernity in terms of unprecedented levels of institutional and interpersonal reflexivity, Giddens joins with the *philosophes* and their sociological heirs such as Marx and Parsons in their belief that reason can be a beneficent social force in the world. Institutionalizing reflexivity suggests that social rules and conventions will be sites of contestation and social conflict, as they are implicated in power relations. This same reflexivity, how-ever, opens the possibility that rational or discursively derived agreements about rules might become the highest principle of social legitimation. Democratization and autonomy are accordingly implicit in conditions of late modernity. On the other hand, heightened levels of institutional reflexivity introduce new social risks and dangers. For example, increased reflexivity means heightened contestation over knowledge claims and therefore, ironically, less certitude. Expert systems – whether medical or scientific knowledge or computer-based or aerodynamic systems – introduce unfore-seen and unforeseeable – and to a degree uncontrollable – consequences and social risks. Medical knowledge and technologies might make the treatment of many ail-ments possible but can have unforeseen, and horrific, consequences – e.g., side effects more dangerous than the original ailment. Nuclear technologies make possible cheap, efficient energy for wide populations but introduce unprecedented levels of environ-mental and social risk.

The world of late modernity is less a world characterized by increasing levels of rationality, democratization, and security than a world driven by expert systems. In this regard, modernity is less the "iron cage" of Weber or the unintended vehicle of human freedom of Marx than a "juggernaut" propelling humanity through time and space – if not directionless, surely not towards a predetermined endpoint. Modernity is likened to "a run-away engine of enormous power . . . The ride is by no means wholly unpleasant or unrewarding; it can often be exhilarating and charged with hopeful anticipation. But, so long as the institutions of modernity endure, we shall never be able to control completely either the path or the pace of the journey."[5] Although the Enlightenment dream of humans rationally controlling history is still very much a dream, Giddens proposes a "realistic utopian" hope that humankind aspire to at least "steer the juggernaut."

PIERRE BOURDIEU

Across the channel, Giddens's somewhat older contemporary Pierre Bourdieu succeeded the great sociologist Raymond Aron at the Collège de France. Unlike Giddens, Bourdieu repeatedly rejected the goal of elaborating a general theory or system of sociology. Bourdieu claimed that his conceptual work has always been

Pierre Bourdieu (1930–2002) was born in Béarn, a southern province of France. He studied at the elite Ecole Normale Supérieure. In 1982, he was elected to a chair in sociology at the Collège de France. Bourdieu was a challenging writer and a brilliant sociologist. He was interested in developing a view that understood individuals as active agents but not fully in charge of their own destiny. With his concept of habitus, a general and unconscious set of interpretive and motivational guidelines that individuals acquire based on their social class position, Bourdieu sought to create a theory that would not reduce individuals to mere products of social structures or neglect the place of social structures in placing constraints on individuals. His great work, *Distinction*, applied this concept via the examination of deep patterns of social stratification.

empirically driven. In fact, in contrast to Giddens, whose major contributions through the 1980s were works of theoretical elaboration, Bourdieu's chief writings were empirical studies of social stratification, culture, the university, schools, and so on.[6] Yet, in his social analyses, Bourdieu stakes out a series of general theoretical positions. Indeed, in many essays and interviews, Bourdieu elaborates a series of foundational concepts and theoretical positions.[7]

Like Giddens, Bourdieu described his chief theoretical interest as wishing to overcome the divisions between subjectivism and objectivism, structuralism and culturalism, micro- and macro-social analysis – divisions that have resulted in the fragmented, conflict-ridden state of current sociology. Bourdieu maintained that it is, above all, the dualism between structure-centered and agent-centered approaches that is the core division among sociologists and modern social thinkers.

Structuralism, exemplified in France by Lévi-Strauss and Althusser's structural Marxism (see Chapter 11), refers to a theoretical position that explains individual behavior by social structural dynamics such as markets, social classes, populations, and organizations. The advantage of structuralism is that it clarifies a social reality beneath individual consciousness and intersubjective meanings (beliefs and values). Yet, by treating social processes as autonomous dynamics, the self-determining aspect of individual action is surrendered. Individuals are viewed as the product of social structures. This is, argues Bourdieu, a sociologically and ethically indefensible position. Accordingly, Bourdieu insists that sociology must approach social life with a focus not only on structure but also on individual actions and intersubjective meanings. Unfortunately, traditions such as phenomenology and interpretive sociology which have approached social reality as intersubjectively accomplished have failed to conceptualize structural constraints. Bourdieu rejects one-sided agent-centered approaches because sociologists must be able to explain the social context of individual actions.

Bourdieu's aim is remarkably similar to that of Giddens: to overcome the dualism of structure and agency through a version of "structural" theory. However, the parallels are almost entirely at the level of general theoretical intent. Bourdieu's core concepts bear little resemblance to those of Giddens. An outline of Bourdieu's basic concepts will be followed by a sketch of *Distinction* which is, if not his major work, surely one that pointedly illustrates his core concepts and displays the power of his theoretical perspective.

Social structure is the starting point of Bourdieu's social analysis. Individuals are always structurally located in a multidimensional social space defined broadly in terms of social class position. The latter refers less exclusively to a strictly Marxian definition of class than to an individual's access to a variety of resources, social ties, and social opportunities related to occupation, but also to age, gender, educational status, and so on. Relating individuals to their social structural position does not necessarily, as we will see, commit Bourdieu to a version of structural determinism. Moreover, his notion of agency is not reducible to viewing the individual as a self-defining agent (e.g., symbolic interactionism), a rationally calculating agent (e.g., exchange theory or rational choice theory), or a rule-governed agent (e.g., enthnomethodology and Parsonian action theory); Bourdieu describes individual action as intuitive, strategizing, and inventive.

To clarify Bourdieu's conceptual strategy, we need to introduce a key term – "habitus." To simplify what is often a difficult or at least an elastic concept, "habitus" refers to interpretive schemas, largely unconscious or tacitly at work, that tell us how the world works, how to evaluate things, and that provide guidelines of action. Bourdieu argues that these interpretive schemas regulate individual conduct. However, habitus is less a set of rigid rules determining practice than a loose set of guidelines allowing individuals to strategize, accommodate to new situations, and invent new practices. Bourdieu avoids idealism by arguing that the habitus is not an original creation of the individual; nor does it free individuals from social structural conditions. Instead, the habitus is a product of an individual's social structural conditions and yet structures his or her social practices in ways that reproduce the agent's objective conditions of social existence. This process of social reproduction, to repeat, does not imply an instrumental, mechanistic view of social practice. To the extent that the habitus refers to very general guidelines, individuals need to apply them in strategically advantageous and sometimes innovative ways. In other words, the relation between social structure, habitus, and social practice is not a simple linear, causal, and mechanistic one. Bourdieu holds something like the following: individuals who share a structural or class position have similar, repetitive experiences that produce a common habitus which, in turn, structures their social practices – sets out guidelines and limits but allows for individual innovation. Hence, individuals are neither totally free agents nor passive products of social structure; social life is neither exclusively subjective nor made up of only meanings and voluntary actions, nor exclusively objective or driven by social structural processes and experienced as constrained or coercive.

The concept of the habitus is the conceptual pivot of Bourdieu's theoretical synthesis. The habitus is both a product of social structure and itself a structure generative of social practices that reproduces social structures; it is both subjective (composed of interpretive schemas) and objective (bearing the imprint of social structure); the habitus is both micro (operating at the individual and interpersonal level) and macro (a product of and producer of social structures). Yet, habitus always operates in relation to "fields" and "capital." A word on these two core concepts is in order.

Bourdieu rejects concepts of society as a collection of individuals or as organic unities or social systems. He speaks instead of social fields. This recalls Weber's image of society as consisting of social spheres (religion, law, economy, polity), each with their own relatively autonomous logic. Fields such as academia, the economy, sports, art, and schools, are not reducible to one another or to some system logic – say, capitalism. Rather, fields are made up of individuals – positioned objectively in a set of social relations – who possess varying resources (different types of capital) and struggle for prestige, wealth, and power. For example, in the academic field there are individuals – positioned in relation to the objective social relations set out by universities, disciplines, and faculties – who compete for authority, power, and prestige by using available resources (e.g., social ties and knowledge). Bourdieu insists that different fields value different types of capital or resources; for example, cultural capital or knowledge and credentials are a key resource in the struggle for dominance in the academic sphere and much less so in competition in the economic field. "Capital" refers to resources or qualities possessed by an individual that have social influence or currency. There are many forms of capital – economic capital (wealth), cultural capital (credentials, knowledges), symbolic capital (honor, prestige), and social capital (social ties, confidence).

If one of Bourdieu's aims is to integrate agent-centered and structure-centered aspects of social life, perhaps the overriding impulse of his work is *to bring culture into the center of sociology for the purpose of analyzing the dynamics of social domination.* Bourdieu insists that culture is integral to the social organization of domination. If culture is today in many societies a key site of politics, if people fight over controlling the production and circulation of meanings, it is because culture is pivotal to dynamics of social inequality. Bourdieu's studies analyzed the role of culture in class-based inequalities.

But how is culture related to domination? In general, Bourdieu argues that culture, by which he means symbols, meanings, and cultural goods (from music and highbrow literature to food and furniture), is always stamped by social class. Moreover, culture reproduces class domination to the extent that the dominating classes can impose their cultural values, standards, and tastes on the whole society, or at least install their cultural preferences as the standard of what is the highest, best, and most legitimate in national culture. Class domination is accomplished insofar as the knowledges, lifestyles, tastes, aesthetic judgments, and social mannerisms of the dominant class become socially legitimate and dominant. Class domination is obscured by the ideology – promoted by the dominating classes – which sees the most desired and valued cultural forms and practices as the product of gifted, talented, even charismatic, individuals. In other words, instead of seeing music, art, decorating, clothes, or food as reflecting class inequality, many people see these things as creations of gifted individuals and their appreciation as reflecting natural differences of individual sensibility.

To illustrate Bourdieu's sociological perspective, let us turn to what is arguably his major work, *Distinction*,[8] which is based on extensive survey data. Bourdieu's general aim is to bring class and cultural analysis together, or, more specifically, to examine the cultural mechanisms of class domination. In this regard, Bourdieu is critical of a model of culture, which assumes that there are forms of cultural expression – the arts, literature, music – whose value or worth can be established apart from social interests and power – as a matter of a pure aesthetic reason. Bourdieu locates all cultural practices squarely in the realm of social conflict and power relations. While he is critical of efforts to remove culture from society, he is also critical of Marxist approaches which reduce culture to a class ideology or which analyze culture as merely a means to naturalize and obscure class-based social inequalities. This is surely part of what culture is about, but such approaches fail to analyze the operation of culture in the reproduction of classes. Bourdieu offered a theory of the class production of culture and the cultural reproduction of class.

Much of *Distinction* records class-based lifestyle differences as manifested in reading, music or food preferences of the French. These cultural practices are viewed as class -structured and reproductive of social class. Bourdieu makes at least three general claims and arguments that are crucial to his political sociology of social stratification.

First, he proposes that there are different classes and class fractions which reflect different combinations of economic and cultural capital. Bourdieu distinguishes the working class, the petty bourgeois, and the middle and upper classes, defined grossly by their occupation. He proceeds to further differentiate fractions within each class that are said to vary by their cultural capital. For example, the bourgeoisie is based on their possession of relatively high levels of economic capital, but divisions within this class between say the business and intellectual (teachers, writers, cultural workers) fractions reflect differences largely in cultural capital. The former in relation to the latter possess more economic but less cultural capital. In other words, teachers or cultural workers (writers, journalists, gallery owners) possess credentials and arcane cultural knowledge typically lacking among the business fraction of the middle classes. These variations in the volume and composition of capital within social classes explain internal class differences and antagonisms. Economic position, then, largely determines social class, while cultural capital, in part conditioned by economic capital, creates class fractions.

Second, Bourdieu claims that while these different classes and class fractions are the basis for different cultural styles, within each class fraction cultural patterns are more or less uniform. This is one of Bourdieu's central and, to my mind, most original and provocative claims. Classes and class fractions produce relatively homogeneous lifestyle patterns in the sense that it is possible to identify common class-based cultural patterns across practices as varied as music, theater, food, and home decorating. Bourdieu explains this by arguing that each class creates its own habitus, which involves ways of interpreting and judging objects and events shared by class members. Each class-based habitus leads to consistent patterns of behavior across cultural spheres. In particular, Bourdieu argues that the degree to which class position makes possible freedom from material necessity shapes a class's habitus and cultural practices. For example, the high level of economic capital characteristic of the middle classes permits them significant freedom from material necessity. Accordingly, the middle classes prefer cultural forms that stress the stylization or aestheticization of objects and life. Thus, the upper strata of the middle classes prefer classical music, abstract art, and avant-garde movies and theater. To put it differently, the middle classes or at least fractions of this class prefer cultural objects and practices whose meanings lie in formal considerations of, say, line, color, and technique. By contrast, the working class, characterized by low economic capital, is pressured by material necessities. Accordingly, laborers develop a habitus which disposes them to approach culture in more functional ways. Working-class individuals prefer cultural objects and practices whose meaning is conveyed by their content. For example, they favor music that emphasizes melody and lyrics, content-driven art, and functional furniture. One example of class-based cultural differences is in food consumption. Bourdieu argues that surveys indicate that working-class men prefer food that is meaty and filling, which confirms their class-specific sense of masculinity. Hence they do not like fish because it is too delicate, feminine, and insufficiently filling. By contrast, middle-class men prefer fish precisely because it is delicate, less filling, healthy, and involves a sophistication in cooking and delicacy in consumption that points to stylization. In a sense, Bourdieu is arguing that the middle class idealize their relative freedom from material necessity by embracing a general commitment to form and stylization, rather than the sensual and functional, in all their cultural patterns. Indeed, the devaluing of materiality and function is a way for the middle class to claim a higher moral status – as if the more abstract, spiritual, and formal a practice or lifestyle, the more morally and aesthetically superior it is and are those who are engaged in such practices.

Third, Bourdieu argues that cultural consumption is a way in which different class fractions distinguish themselves and assert a superior status, and to that extent culture is part of class politics. Specifically, cultural production and consumption is a means by which the dominant class fractions seek to establish and maintain their domination. They aim to make their cultural tastes, preferences, standards, and lifestyles into the most valued, desirable, and dominant. To the extent that their values, aesthetic styles, and judgments become socially dominant, their hegemonic class status is maintained. Moreover, Bourdieu explains how dominated classes come to comply with their subordinate social position. He argues that the dominated classes create a class-specific habitus which results in lifestyles and aesthetic preferences that reproduce their social position. That is, dominated classes choose ways of life that are made possible by their class position but also reproduce it. Moreover, Bourdieu believes that these dynamics of class domination are concealed to the extent that the ideology of individual talent and effort is accepted. That is, by viewing cultural practices as products of individual ability, dominant cultural patterns are seen as reflecting a superior sensibility rather than as class-based impositions integral to social inequality.

Bourdieu applies this perspective in his analysis of schools as a chief institutional mechanism for class reproduction. As in the study of status distinctions, a chief focus is how culture makes possible the reproduction of systems of domination almost without any awareness on the part of agents. Schools reproduce class inequality by transforming social class distinctions into educational ones. Bourdieu claims that the dominant class fractions make their class culture into the dominant school culture. Schools become another field for the socialization of the dominant classes. For example, children from the dominant classes bring to schools the kinds of social and cultural capital (e.g., language skills, social ties, styles of interaction, intellectual skills, and disciplines) that virtually ensure their success. They will experience the school environment as "natural," as they possess all the social and cultural capital (e.g., knowledges, social ties, confidence, interpersonal skills) to do well. By contrast, the working classes experience the school system as socially and culturally challenging or as a somewhat alien social environment. Their class-specific skills, talents, and ways of thinking and interacting will not easily translate into educational success. Because their habitus is not dominant in the schools, the working class will fare poorly and be judged inferior. Two points should be emphasized. First, schools don't just reproduce class domination but multiply class-based inequalities. Second, this reproduction of class inequality through schooling is not recognized, because of the ideology that success reflects individual effort and ability. Failure in schools is interpreted as individual, not class based, and this contributes to sustaining class hierarchy.

Bourdieu offers, then, a thoroughly social analysis of culture. Moreover, cultural analysis is brought into the center of sociology. Against perspectives which aim to separate "culture" from power, Bourdieu holds that cultural goods, preferences, and values have no intrinsic value; there is no rational hierarchy of cultural tastes and values. It is a matter of social power which determines which cultural objects are valued. Culture is a sphere of social conflict precisely because different classes struggle over which cultural values, standards, choices, and lifestyles function as the legitimate standard of culture. Bourdieu describes class dominance through cultural imposition as a kind of symbolic violence – the violence of the forced imposition of particular class-based values on all social classes.

Bourdieu's political sociology of culture raises an interesting question: If culture is a social construction and site of class politics, does this hold true as well for knowledge and science? If classes aim to distinguish themselves through claiming superiority for their particular class-based tastes and values, would not science, at least social science, be equally class structured or at least implicated in class politics? Bourdieu is aware of the implications of his political sociology of culture for discourses which make the claim to knowledge, and which might be viewed as a strategy of class politics. He tries to avoid the contradictory position of both claiming that culture is part of the realm of politics while asserting a nonpolitical status for his own cultural production of sociology. His solution is to propose a "reflexive sociology."[9]

Of course, Bourdieu is not the first sociologist to recommend a reflexive strategy as a way to avoid social prejudice undermining claims to scientific knowledge. Against positivists who refuse to acknowledge the nonrational influences on research, many sociologists have argued for a type of reflexivity that encourages the scientist to become aware of how personal values or gender or class interests influence decisions about intellectual problems, categories, themes, and explanations. Bourdieu believes that this is a limited strategy since it is not primarily personal prejudice that is most worrisome, but the impact of our institutional disciplinary position. Academics, Bourdieu argues, approach social inquiry from the structural standpoint of belonging to a particular discipline in an academic institutional milieu. It is the habitus of an individual's particular disciplinary location that must be analyzed in order to avoid imposing a particular disciplinary habitus on the very people we study, and thereby implicating our own practices in symbolic violence.

For example, Bourdieu remarks that the habitus of sociology promotes an intellectualist bias. That is, many sociologists assume that their own focus on understanding and explaining social events is also the logic of social practice of the people studied. In other words, sociologists often uncritically assume that nonacademic social practices are organized around the same emphasis on mutual understanding, intellectual clarification, and systematization. A reflexive sociology aims to expose the structural conditions that produce this intellectualist bias, thereby freeing sociologists from it. Sociologists would then recognize that the logic of social practice is governed less by a motivation to understand and explain than to adapt, satisfy needs, gain power, etc. By objectifying the academic habitus, Bourdieu thinks that we can avoid the mistake of interpreting ordinary social practices in the terms of the habitus of academe. In fact, objectifying the academic habitus permits the analyst to grasp the distinctive features of the logic of social practice, which is more intuitive, strategizing than rule-governed, rationally calculating, and so on. A reflexive sociology that is aware of the institutional structuring of social science makes possible, Bourdieu thinks, a genuine scientific sociology.

Suggested Readings

Pierre Bourdieu and Loic Wacquant, *An Invitation to Reflexive Sociology* (Chicago: University of Chicago Press, 1992).
Craig Calhoun, ed., *Bourdieu* (Chicago: University of Chicago Press, 1993).
Ian Craib, *Anthony Giddens* (New York: Routledge, 1992)
Ken Tucker, *Anthony Giddens and Modern Social Theory* (Newbury Park, CA: Sage, 1998).

References

1   Anthony Giddens, *Capitalism and Modern Social Theory* (Cambridge: Cambridge University Press, 1971).
2   Anthony Giddens, *Central Problems in Social Theory: Action, Structure and Contradiction in Social Analysis* (Berkeley: University of California Press, 1979); *The Constitution of Society: Outline of the Theory of Structuration* (Berkeley: University of California Press, 1984).
3   Anthony Giddens, *A Contemporary Critique of Historical Materialism*, vols. 1 and 2 (Berkeley: University of California Press, 1981 and 1985).
4   Anthony Giddens, *The Consequences of Modernity* (Stanford, CA: Stanford University Press, 1990), pp. 42–3.
5   Giddens, *The Consequences of Modernity*, p. 139.
6   Pierre Bourdieu, *Homo Academicus* (Stanford, CA: Stanford University Press, 1984); *The Field of Cultural Production: Essays on Art and Leisure* (New York: Columbia University Press, 1993); (with Jean-Claude Passeron) *Reproduction in Education, Society, and Culture* (London: Sage, 1990).
7   Pierre Bourdieu, *Outline of a Theory of Practice* (Cambridge: Cambridge University Press, 1977) and *The Logic of Social Practice* (Stanford, CA: Stanford University Press, 1990).
8   Pierre Bourdieu, *Distinction: A Social Critique of the Judgement of Taste* (Cambridge, MA: Harvard University Press, 1984).
9   See Pierre Bourdieu and Loic Wacquant, eds., *An Invitation to Reflexive Sociology* (Chicago: University of Chicago Press, 1992).

Afterword to Part III

European and American theorists look to Marx, Durkheim, and Weber, among others, as founding figures of modern social thought. However, there have been important differences that have led Europeans to develop a more philosophical and moral approach to social science and theory.

As we've seen, European thinkers were much more friendly towards Marxism. Marxism was not a significant force in American political culture. Indeed, anticommunism and anti-Marxism have been a powerful force in American culture. Parsons and Berger, for example, were harsh critics of Marxism. Much of American social thinking either ignored Marxism or was shaped by its rejection of Marxism.

By contrast, Marxism was a major political force in Europe. Mainstream political parties such as labor parties or socialist parties embraced the ideology of Marxian socialism. European thinkers really had no choice but to define their social and political ideas in relation to Marx. Many Europeans rejected Marx, especially after the rise of Soviet communism. However, many major social thinkers were positively influenced by Marxism. Indeed, Marx's ideas were accepted as the starting point or basis for social and political theory by many Europeans.

Habermas, Hall, Giddens, and Bourdieu viewed Marx as a great social thinker. Marx's class theory of society was understood as the starting point for grasping social inequality. His theory of capitalism, which exposed a reality of exploitation and alienation, was understood as marking a major advance over liberal approaches that celebrated market economies as promoting freedom and social progress. Above all, these theorists accepted the Marxian idea of a critical theory of society; its aim was not only to explain reality but to bring about social change that benefited the poor and disadvantaged.

But, by the post-World War II period, critical theorists were also convinced that Marxism needed considerable revision. Its theory of capitalism, its class theory of society, its anticipation of working-class revolution, and its idea of a coming era of

Contested Knowledge: Social Theory Today, Fifth Edition. Steven Seidman.
© 2013 John Wiley & Sons, Ltd. Published 2013 by John Wiley & Sons, Ltd.

communism seemed decidedly dated and in some cases wrong. As we've seen, many European theorists sought to combine Marx, classical sociology, and other intellectual perspectives to create a new critical theory of society.

There is another important difference between Europe and America that shaped social thought. In general, European intellectuals are held in higher esteem. They are expected to take positions on the major moral and social issues of the day, to speak out in public forums, and are often seriously considered by leading public officials and politicians. It is not unusual to find leading intellectuals on television and the radio, and writing regular newspaper and magazine essays.

Also, European social thinkers approach social thinking in much broader terms than is typical of Americans. Europeans are, after all, part of a great philosophical tradition extending from Plato and Aristotle through Descartes, Kant, Hegel, Wittgenstein, and Heidegger. Students in the Humanities and Social Sciences are regularly exposed to philosophy. In contrast to American social theorists, especially sociological theorists, who often draw sharp boundaries between philosophy and science, this is not the case for European theorists. To think hard about social questions of inequality, social order, and change is inevitably to be pushed into a kind of philosophical thinking.

Accordingly, it is not surprising to find that European thinkers often embrace a notion of social science and theory that blends philosophy, empirical analysis, and moral criticism. Even for great social scientists like Durkheim and Weber, social science was never only about revealing facts and proposing explanations of social patterns; the science always involved exposing the social dangers to freedom and democracy or social order and community. Social analysis was to be part of the fight for a rational, good society. This tradition was carried forward by contemporary European theorists. Even someone like Bourdieu, who took seriously the notion of a science of society, spent considerable effort in clarifying the philosophical basis of his social perspective; and Bourdieu, no less than Habermas, Giddens, and Hall, thought of social theory and analysis as a critical practice; its aim was ultimately to promote justice and freedom.

In some ways, Habermas is the exemplary European theorist. Although respectful of empirical research, his great ambition has been to outline a general theory of society and history that would include a theory of modernity and a philosophical account of the moral and epistemological foundations of social science. No other theorist, not Hall, Giddens or Bourdieu, and certainly no American theorist, has taken up the challenge of thinking through the meaning of social science as deliberately and logically as Habermas. But, even for Habermas, theory always, ultimately, proves its worth by what it tells us about the world and how it contributes to creating a better social world.

Part IV

Revisions and Revolts:
The Postmodern Turn

Introduction to Part IV

As we've seen, over the course of the eighteenth and early nineteenth centuries, a new set of social and political ideas gained prominence. Thinkers such as Voltaire, Diderot, Montesquieu, Franklin, David Hume, and Adam Smith rallied around a few powerful ideas such as the objectivity of science, the coupling of scientific and social progress, the unity of humankind, the evolution of humanity from East to West, and from oppression to freedom. These social ideas became woven into the political and cultural history of the modern West. At the root of these ideas was a deep, abiding faith: with the aid of science and democratic institutions, humans could create a world of freedom and justice for all. This belief became a sort of creed for the successive generations of the nineteenth, twentieth, and twenty-first centuries. Even social critics such as Marx, Habermas, and C. Wright Mills were strong believers in Enlightenment idea of progress.

Many of these ideas were challenged from the 1950s onward. As we'll see in Part V, the revolts against Western colonialism in Africa and elsewhere and rebellions by women, gays, non-Whites, and the disabled exposed a history of cruelty, exploitation, exclusion, and genocide. The Enlightenment, these critics said, did not in fact mean growing freedom and justice for all. But this is a story we'll pick up shortly.

After the dust of World War II had settled, many social thinkers began to comment on the huge changes in social and political life that were sweeping through Western societies. A manufacturing-based industrial economy was losing ground to a service-oriented postindustrial economy; a culture that emphasized hard work and the accumulation of wealth was now championing consumption, pleasure, and self-expression; democracy and rights were advancing but real individual freedom seemed to be diminishing; the state was growing larger but also weaker as forces such as globalization, multinational corporations, and international movements were gaining power; the media and new information systems were refashioning our daily lives

Contested Knowledge: Social Theory Today, Fifth Edition. Steven Seidman.
© 2013 John Wiley & Sons, Ltd. Published 2013 by John Wiley & Sons, Ltd.

in unexpected ways; the lines between science and politics were blurring. A debate ensued about the present and future state of contemporary societies.

Some thinkers proposed that social thought needed to be considerably revised in light of the transformation of the world that was presently occurring. These thinkers claimed developments such as a postindustrial economy, a world society, a media-saturated culture, and multiculturalism suggested an epochal shift. Key notions of modern social theory such as the primacy of the nation, the individual, the superiority of the West, and the very idea of modern life as a story of progress, no longer had the ring of truth. The world had changed and social theory needed to change as dramatically. A new world order was in the making, a world at once modern and postmodern.

As we'll see in the chapters to follow, contemporary thinkers have proposed original interpretations of the present social condition. For some theorists (such as Lyotard), it is the end of the idea of scientific and social progress that is definitive; for others (e.g., Baudrillard) it is the unprecedented power of the media in shaping daily life, or the new prominence of nonlegal, nongovernmental ruling powers (Foucault and Bauman) that is refashioning our social worlds.

11

The Postmodern World of Jacques Derrida, Jean-François Lyotard, and Jean Baudrillard

It is instructive to contrast US and French intellectual culture. The separation between academic and public intellectuals that has been characteristic of postwar America is less defined in France. Since at least the 1950s, the spirit of science and professionalism has governed American universities; academic intellectuals are expected to produce scientific or scholarly studies intended to be read primarily by members of their discipline. Although some American academics have assumed the role of public intellectuals, this is neither expected nor does it necessarily confer academic prestige. In France, academics are expected to be general intellectuals; they aspire to produce original perspectives that will address a broad public beyond academia.

The French cultural ideal is that of the general intellectual. Typically, this person has academic affiliations, preferably with the Sorbonne or the Collège de France. It is not, however, this academic status or any purely scholarly virtuosity that confers prestige on the intellectual. Rather, status accrues to those who fashion a singular style of writing and a distinctive perspective on the human condition which elicits interest across academic disciplines and social publics. The public intellectual draws on scholarly learning in order to engage current social developments in an original, provocative way. To be a socially engaged intellectual is to be political.

The tradition of academics as public intellectuals is crucial to grasping postwar French social thought. It explains, for example, why many of its major social thinkers, figures such as Jean-Paul Sartre, Simone de Beauvoir, Albert Camus, Louis Althusser, Roland Barthes, Michel Foucault, Julia Kristeva, and Jean-François Lyotard were not sociologists or social scientists. In turn, many major current sociologists, figures such as Jean Baudrillard or Pierre Bourdieu, can hardly be described as sociologists in the American sense. They are public intellectuals whose thinking is at once scholarly and ethical and political.

In France, we look less to the narrow academic disciplines of the social sciences to locate the major breakthroughs in social thinking than to broader movements of

Contested Knowledge: Social Theory Today, Fifth Edition. Steven Seidman.
© 2013 John Wiley & Sons, Ltd. Published 2013 by John Wiley & Sons, Ltd.

thought that have an interdisciplinary, public character. And while the tradition of French sociology from Durkheim to the present is an admirable one, the defining shape of postwar French social thought was produced, above all, by two powerful theoretical movements: structuralism and poststructuralism.

STRUCTURALISM: A VISION OF A SCIENTIFIC HUMAN STUDIES

Modern French intellectual culture reveals a long-standing division between a humanistic and scientific world view. This cultural conflict was pivotal at the juncture of the institutionalization of the human studies disciplines at the turn of the twentieth century. For example, the major opponents to Durkheim's sociological vision were scholars for whom society was the sum of individual decisions. Reflecting a humanistic world view, they opposed sociology, because its emphasis on social forces was believed to deny individual freedom and moral responsibility.

The tradition of a scientific structural sociology, which connects Montesquieu, Comte, and Durkheim, did not fare well in the French academe. By the end of World War II, Durkheimian sociology was in decline. These years saw the ageing and death of many leading Durkheimians. In addition, the Resistance movement in World War II encouraged a more individualistic and heroic ethos that received a powerful expression in an existentialist philosophy. The marginalization of Durkheimian sociology was further encouraged by the growing importance of Marxism. This reflected, in part, the rise of the French Communist Party to a position of political power. Despite the decline of Durkheimian sociology in the postwar years, its sociological vision did not disappear from French intellectual culture. Its image of society as an autonomous realm of social relations flourished in the 1950s as a program of structuralist social analysis.

French structuralism was a reaction to the tradition of humanistic philosophy, particularly existentialism.[1] At the core of humanistic philosophy is a view of the individual as a self-directing, creative force. Humanism celebrates the individual as a creative force in society and history. In contrast, structuralism looks to forces beyond the individual to grasp social life and history. Indeed, the individual is explained as an effect of impersonal forces. Structuralists hold the view that beneath the surface appearance of a world populated only by individuals in seemingly random interactions are structural patterns. Structuralism aimed to uncover the deep structures that give coherence and order to the human universe.

As is typical of French intellectual culture, structuralism was less an innovation in method than a philosophical movement. Structuralism viewed the human world as ordered by unconscious, rule-bound, principles. Although we can trace its intellectual roots to Marxism, Freudian thought, and the sociology of Comte and Durkheim, the most profound source of structuralism lay in developments in linguistics.

Ferdinand de Saussure (1857–1913), a Swiss linguist, is credited with playing a major role in altering the way Europeans think of language.[2] The conventional view at the time approached language as a neutral medium for representing the world.

Words or signifiers were said to acquire meaning by the concept or reality they summon up in our mind. A relation of identity was assumed between word and concept or word and world. For example, the meaning of "man" would involve a relation of identity between the word, the concept of man, and the existence of real men.

Saussure challenged this view by conceptualizing language as a system of signs whose meanings take shape in relations of difference. Saussure claimed that the relation between a signifier and the signified or between word and world is arbitrary. If there is no natural, intrinsic link between word and world, how do signs get their meaning? Saussure proposed that the meaning of signs is derived from their relations of difference. Words and concepts get their meaning in the particular ways they differ from other words and concepts in a specific language system. Relations of difference between signifier and signified in a particular language fix meaning. Saussure appeals to the oppositional or binary relation of signs to understand how the signs get meaning. The word "man" takes on meaning not because there is a human reality that has the corresponding properties associated with the signifier "man." Rather, "man" takes on meaning because it contrasts to the signifier "woman." Pursuing this further, the structural linguist could relate the man/woman opposition to a more general human/nonhuman animal binary which, in turn, could be linked to an opposition between animals and nonanimal living things, and so on. The meaning of signs lies in their relations of difference, particularly in their binary oppositions, in a specific language system.

Saussure abandoned the standard view of language as a neutral medium through which the mind mirrors the world. This view held that, between word and concept and between concept and world, there were relations of identity that fixed meanings. In contrast, Saussure argued for a notion of language as a system of signs whose meanings were generated by their relations of difference. Saussure thought of language as an active, dynamic social force that shaped both the mind and the world. As a self-sufficient system, language can be studied as it is organized and functions in the present.

Structural linguistics was translated into a program of social science by the great anthropologist Claude Lévi-Strauss. Born in Belgium in 1908, as a child Lévi-Strauss immigrated to France, where he eventually held a chair at the prestigious Collège de France. He authored a series of pioneering works – *The Elementary Structures of Kinship, Structural Anthropology, The Savage Mind, The Raw and the Cooked* – that initiated what some have called "the structural revolution."[3]

Lévi-Strauss aimed to model social thinking after structural linguistics. He assumed that language was the prototype of all social phenomena. Accordingly, the assumptions and methods that guide the study of language can be applied to any social fact. Lévi-Strauss analyzed kinship, myth, ceremonies, marriage, cooking, and totemic systems as systems composed of elementary units (akin to words or phonemes) whose meanings derive from patterns of difference, particularly binary opposition and correlation. Lévi-Strauss invoked language not only as a model of particular social institutions (e.g., marriage, kinship, or religion) but as a paradigm for conceiving any social order. Considered in its cultural or symbolic aspect, society is a kind of superlanguage.

Structural social inquiry examines the relations of difference and correlation among the elementary units of social phenomena. It aims to discover the universal laws that govern the functioning of social forms. Lévi-Strauss imagines that these general laws are, at bottom, unconscious mental structures. In effect, he argues that beneath the apparent randomness of social life are universal structures that create order and social coherence. The real organizing forces of the social world are these structural codes, not the individual.

In the 1950s and 1960s, the "structural revolution" provided an alternative to the humanism of existentialism and the sociologism of Marxism. Many intellectuals who sympathized with Lévi-Strauss's structuralism did not, however, follow his rather literal program to model human studies after structural linguistics. For example, Louis Althusser wished to rethink Marxism in light of structuralism without reducing society to language.[4] In his early writings, Michel Foucault employed a broadly structural approach to the study of madness and the birth of the human sciences but avoided a rigid application of the linguistic model.[5] Nevertheless, even in Althusser and the early works of Foucault, we can detect the structuralist preference for synchronic over diachronic relations, internal system dynamics over narrative succession, and structural analysis of a present system over the historical analysis of events. In the structuralist approach, contingent social events and history move into the background as the analysis of elementary forms, general laws, and static structures prevails.

JACQUES DERRIDA

The popularity of structuralism coincided with efforts to rebuild France in the aftermath of a devastating war. World War II was fought on French soil. The end of the war left an economy and society in shambles. Furthermore, it was a war that produced a divided nation. Long-standing hostilities between France and Germany were greatly magnified during the German occupation. Many French people believed that it was their national duty to resist German occupation. Divisions surfaced between a powerful Resistance movement and those who capitulated to German occupation. Under the leadership of General de Gaulle, postwar France sought to heal these divisions and reassert its national pride.

Jacques Derrida was born in Algeria in 1930. He received his training in philosophy at the Ecole Normale Supérieure in Paris (where he later taught) and at Harvard. Derrida also taught at the Sorbonne, as well as holding visiting professorships at Yale, Johns Hopkins, New York University, and the University of California at Irvine. Derrida is a major theorist of poststructuralism. At the root of this perspective is the idea that the world we experience and know is dependent on the shifting and fragile foundation of language and discourse. Derrida explores the way language creates meanings and shapes social life, including social inequality.

The immediate postwar years saw the rise to prominence of existentialism, a philosophy that expressed the heroic ethos of the Resistance. However, as the memory of the war faded, and a new national and world order began to take shape, structuralism triumphed. Perhaps structuralism gave expression to a particular French view of the current world. This was a world where little dramatic change was expected, and, for many war-weary Frenchmen, desired. General de Gaulle promised neither reform nor revolution but a stable, growth-oriented society. In addition, the rise to superpower status of the United States and the Soviet Union left France a second-rate power. To many Frenchmen, the emerging national and world order seemed to offer few possibilities beyond maneuvering within a fixed structural framework.

The 1950s was a sobering decade for the French. In place of visions of change and aspirations of national grandeur, they were saddled with the humdrum task of rebuilding an economy and national culture in a world order where France was a sideshow. With the heroic spirit of existentialism dimming and with the revelations of the horrors of Stalinism dampening the ideological vigor of the French Communist Party, structuralism took center stage. With its high-minded intellectualism, structuralism seemed an attractive alternative to a depoliticized intelligentsia. If France had to cede world political dominance to the United States and the Soviet Union, at least it could still claim an intellectual dominance by the sheer brilliance of its ideas.

Postwar social calm came to an end dramatically in May 1968. Student revolts ignited a national crisis. Unlike in the United States, French student discontent assumed a radical edge. The agenda of the students involved more than democratizing a state-controlled, elitist university system. They wished to revolutionize society: citizen control, self-government, and sweeping cultural change were at the heart of their rebellion. Their battles shifted from the campus to control over the key social institutions of the French Fifth Republic. Clashes with the police involving thousands of students took place on the streets of Paris. For example, on May 10, some twenty thousand students marched to free imprisoned students and comrades; a clash ensued with the police, injuring hundreds of students. Yet, the students did not retreat; barricades were erected in the heart of Paris as students occupied large sections of the Latin Quarter.

In the United States, the student protests gained mass public support only as an antiwar movement. The radical wing of the student movement, for example, Students for a Democratic Society (SDS), remained isolated. In France, the broad ideological agenda of the student movement was shared by substantial segments of blue collar workers, professionals, and the cultural elite. As one after another campus fell to the students or was closed, blue collar workers went on strike and occupied factories. In alliance with the students, trade unions and the teachers' federation called a general strike on May 13. Within a few days, an estimated six to ten million workers were on strike, bringing France to a virtual standstill. Reinforcing a growing sense of national crisis, some physicians, lawyers, journalists, actors, and musicians joined the students and workers by taking over the cultural apparatus of television, radio, cinema, and publishing companies. What began as incidents of student unrest escalated into a broad-based revolt against French capitalism, Catholicism, and consumerism.

Through concessions to the students and unions, military and police force, counter-demonstrations, cabinet shifts, and legislative elections, de Gaulle triumphed.

By the end of May, the revolt was, to all intents and purposes, over. Yet France was not the same. In its reluctance to support the students, the Communist Party lost a good deal of its credibility among the Left. De Gaulle's cosmetic concessions and attacks on the students and workers did little to shore up widespread public discontent with the Fifth Republic. Perhaps less perceptible was a growing feeling that the key institutions of France lacked legitimacy. Moreover, the revolts threw into relief the importance of the structures of personal and social life beyond the state and capitalism. Radicals turned their attention to those social institutions that produce knowledge, shape personal desires and identities, and form our ideas and ideals (e.g., universities, research centers, advertising, consumerism, and popular culture). They developed critical perspectives on consumerism, the culture of everyday life, prisons, mental health institutions, sexuality, gender, and the family.

The revolts of May 1968 did not occur in a social vacuum. France was changing in important ways. Major population shifts to cities beyond Paris shook up the country; small, family-owned businesses, traditionally the backbone of the French economy and society, were rapidly disappearing, throwing large segments of the population into turmoil. Under the impact of mass consumerism and popular culture, the shape of daily life was dramatically altered. May 1968 was as much the effect as the cause of deep divisions and changes that were shaping France as it began to evolve beyond the task of rebuilding a war-torn nation.

France after 1968 was not a very hospitable environment for structuralism. The renewal of social activism and the experience of social life as fluid and changeable made structuralism, with its scientific formalism, seem irrelevant. Nor were French Left-wing intellectuals prepared to renew their romance with existentialism, which lacked a compelling social theory. Although Althusser's structural Marxism remained attractive to many on the Left, others were disturbed by the contempt of the Communist Party toward the student revolts. Moreover, Althusser's Marxism neglected to seriously analyze the malaise of everyday life.

With existentialism, Marxism, and structuralism losing their grip on the Left, a new intellectual movement took form: poststructuralism.[6] It combined the rebellious spirit of existentialism, the high-minded seriousness of structuralism, and the political engagement of Marxism. It is not too much of an exaggeration to describe poststructuralism as a theoretical expression of the generalized revolt against authority signaled by May 1968. Like the protesters and rebels, poststructuralists emphasized deconstruction rather than social reconstruction. Like their activist counterparts on the barricades of the streets of Paris, these Parisian intellectuals offered few proposals for a good society beyond slogans. Nevertheless, it would be a mistake not to take this theoretical development seriously. Poststructuralism signaled the rise of a post-Marxian critical theory.

Poststructuralism shares with structuralism its antihumanism: the autonomous self is replaced by discursive or linguistic structures as the elementary unit of social life. Poststructuralists underscore the role of language in forming individual subjectivity and social institutions. Language is the place where meanings are lodged; linguistic meanings play a major role in organizing the self, social institutions, and the political landscape. Hence, language is a principal site for the production of social realities and political conflict. Poststructuralists approach language as a system whose meanings derive from relations of difference and contrast. However, whereas structuralists aimed to uncover uniform linguistic patterns, poststructuralists highlight the inherently unstable patterns of linguistic and social order. If structuralism was a "constructive" project intent on identifying a linguistic and social order, poststructuralism had a "deconstructive" aim: to demonstrate that all claims to identify or justify an order to society, knowledge, or morality in something beyond traditions or communities failed; behind the will to knowledge was a will to power.

The chief figure of poststructuralism is Jacques Derrida.[7] Derrida agreed with Saussure that the meaning of the sign lies in its relations of difference. However, structuralists wrongly assume that meanings are fixed once these contrary relations are established. Derrida held that the meaning of the sign is multivocal and changing. For example, the man/woman binary may seem universal, but it carries diverse meanings depending on national context and considerations of class, race, age, and gender. One perspective may view women as maternal, emotional, passive, and asexual; another discourse constructs women as erotic and powerful. In short, the meanings of signs are never fixed; they are a focus of conflict because meanings have social and political significance.

In this regard, Derrida's break from structuralism is more than a matter of amending its view of signs; it is about the politics of language and knowledge. The structuralist aimed to uncover general linguistic and social patterns organized around binary oppositions. The political meaning of this linguistic and social order was not examined. Indeed, Lévi-Strauss thought of the binary structuring of language and society as revealing fixed mental structures, ultimately lodged in the brain. In contrast, Derrida interpreted the meaning of signifiers – words and sounds – as in a state of flux and contestation. He held that, whenever a linguistic and social order is said to be fixed or meanings are assumed to be unambiguous and stable, this should be understood as an act of power or as reflecting the capacity of a social group to impose its will on others by freezing meanings. Poststructuralists opposed efforts at linguistic, social, and political closure. Poststructuralism is a kind of permanent rebellion against authority; that of science and philosophy but also of the church and the state. Its strategy of linguistic and political subversion is called "deconstruction."

Derrida thought that he had discovered a hidden logic in Western thought. He called it "logocentrism." The logocentrism of Western culture lies in its quest for an authoritative language that can reveal truth, moral rightness, and beauty. From Plato to Bertrand Russell, Western thinkers charged philosophy with the task of establishing a universal language that could disclose what is real, true, right, and beautiful. Social thinkers, from Rousseau to Lévi-Strauss, aimed to disclose the order of society – how it is and how it ought to be. Furthermore, Derrida pointed to a series of binary oppositions in Western thought that he thought were crucial in efforts to establish an order of truth. Dualisms such as speech/writing, presence/absence, meaning/form, soul/body, masculine/feminine, man/woman, literal/metaphorical, nature/culture, positive/negative, transcendental/empirical, and cause/effect reappear time and again and lie at the core of Western culture. Moreover, the two terms in these oppositions do not represent equal values. The first term is considered superior; the second is derivative and subordinate. For example, the assumption that speech is superior to writing is basic to Western philosophy. Whereas speech is thought to be an immediate and clear vehicle for the mind's ideas, writing clouds our vision by entangling the mind in the rhetorical and metaphorical aspects of language. Relying on such hierarchical oppositions, Western thinkers have sought to identify an order of truth and reality that could function as an authoritative basis for judging truth/ falsity, knowledge/ideology, reality/illusion, or right/wrong.

Instead of proposing his own system of truth, Derrida turned against the very idea of trying to uncover an order of truth. Beginning with his breakthrough book, *Of Grammatology*, and elaborating further in *Writing and Difference* and *Positions*, Derrida attempted to show that claims to intellectual authority cannot withstand serious scrutiny.[8] He assumed the unstable, multivocal, and changing meaning of signs. If signifiers (words) carry ambiguous, conflicting meanings, if their sense is always contested, the search to identify a fixed order of meanings is thrown into doubt. In particular, Derrida exerted his considerable critical energies toward undermining the hierarchical dualities that occupy a supreme place in Western culture.

The subversion of the hierarchical discursive oppositions for the purpose of questioning their authority is the core of the deconstructive critical strategy. Its aim is less to oppose the hierarchy or reverse its values than to weaken its force and contribute to its displacement or marginalization. A key strategy is to show that the first and superior sign can be explained as a special case of the second and subordinate sign.

For example, Freudian thought is rich in deconstructive moves. Freud interpreted the "normal" in relation to the pathological. He reversed hierarchies such as conscious/unconscious, sane/insane, real/imaginary, and experience/dream. Freud's thought can also be the object of deconstruction; for example, man/woman and masculine/feminine are pivotal oppositions in Freudian psychoanalysis. Feminists have made a persuasive case that masculinity functions in Freud as the superior sign. For example, Freud repeatedly made the penis the norm of sexuality. Women's sexuality is defined by its lacking a penis and therefore as incomplete and inferior. In Freud's theory of psychosexual development, the superiority of masculinity is registered by the centrality of the castration complex for the boy and penis envy for the girl. Whereas the threat of losing his penis signals the loss of the father's power for the boy, the girl's awareness of lacking a penis generates a self-definition as inferior. The masculine/feminine hierarchy in Freud is unstable. In order to make women's sexuality derivative and subordinate, Freud assumed that women originally combined both the masculine (clitoris) and the feminine (vagina) aspects. Women are said to mature by giving up their masculine aspect in favor of a vaginal-centered sexuality. A healthy feminine self is achieved at the cost of repressing a clitoral-centered sexuality. However, since it is women who were originally bisexual, Freudian texts allow the conclusion that they are the general model of sexuality, while men are merely the particular, derivative expression of her phallic aspect. Reversing the hierarchy shifts women from the derivative to the foundation, from the periphery to the center, and from the subordinate to the superior term.

The point of deconstruction, however, is not to reverse the value of the signs, for example, to celebrate women's sexuality as superior. This is a limited strategy since it leaves the hierarchy intact and open to reasserting its original form. Deconstruction aims to displace the hierarchy, to render it less authoritative in the linguistic organization of subjectivity and society. Subverting hierarchical oppositions allows marginal or excluded signifiers and forms of subjective and social life to gain a public voice and presence.

Deconstruction is not conceived only as a philosophical or literary critical strategy; it involves a politics of subversion. It challenges the institutions and public authorities that sustain linguistic, social, and political hierarchies. Linguistic meanings, be they about gender, sexuality, politics, or nationalism, are not innocent of political significance. Constructions of masculinity/femininity or Occidental/Oriental shape Western political life. Thus, imagining femininity as signaling the natural, nonrational, and maternal positions women as socially subordinate or as naturally positioned to assume the wife, mother, and caretaker roles. Linguistic meanings and discourses, however, do not in themselves produce subjectivity and the social world. They are embedded in institutional frameworks and political hierarchies. It is important to trace how signifying and discursive practices empower and give privilege to certain individuals, groups, and forms of social life. Derrida envisioned the deconstructive subversion of signifying hierarchical oppositions as part of a broad critical, social, and political project.

Unfortunately, Derrida never clarified the social and moral vision that guides the deconstructive project. As in the days of rage in May 1968, the deconstructive opposition is poised as a relentless revolt against authority, *any authority*. Derrida seems to have been reluctant to go beyond a vague hope that deconstructive criticism can somehow open social space to a wider expression of human life. Derrida's poststructuralism is animated by a vision of a society that celebrates the proliferation of different individual and social forms of life. It is as if poststructuralism wishes to be a kind of general voice for all the oppressed differences (e.g., women, ethnic minorities, gays). Although Derrida did not elaborate the social implications of poststructuralism, his colleagues did. In the writings of Jean-François Lyotard and Jean Baudrillard, the critical spirit of poststructuralism is taken in a social direction.

JEAN-FRANÇOIS LYOTARD

Like many French intellectuals, Jean-François Lyotard (1924–98) was involved in Left-wing politics. Lyotard's activism preceded his intellectual coming of age. He was active in trade unionism, the radical Marxist group Socialisme ou Barbarie, and the May 1968 events. He took his doctorate in philosophy in 1971. In a quick succession of books – *Discours, Figure, Dérive à partir de Marx et Freud, Economie libidinale* – he developed sketches for a "postmodern" social theory.[9] Lyotard rejected key aspects of the modern Enlightenment. Its quest for truth was said to be allied with the establishment of social hierarchy and oppression. Lyotard appeals to a critical postmodern inquiry that seeks to dismantle foundations, disrupt hierarchy, and speaks on behalf of oppressed peoples. The distinction between modern and postmodern knowledge is central to the book for which Lyotard is most famous, *The Postmodern Condition*.[10] Lyotard sketched a series of broad changes in the character of knowledge. In premodern societies, narrative types

Jean-François Lyotard (1924–98) was born in Versailles, France. He received his training in Paris at the Lycée Louis le Grand and the University of Paris. He taught at Nanterre, the university where the events of May 1968 are generally said to have started. Lyotard also taught at various branches of the University of Paris and at Emory University in Atlanta, in the United States. In addition to his academic work, Lyotard served on the editorial committee for the socialist journal *Socialisme ou Barbarie* and the socialist newspaper *Pouvoir Ouvrier*. Lyotard is known as a postmodernist. According to Lyotard, we can no longer rely on grand narratives or stories that aim to reveal the deep meaning and purpose of world history. Whether it's Marxism's belief in the coming of communism through revolution or the liberal Enlightenment narrative of progress through scientific reason, such grand stories are less credible today. Lyotard sees history as contingent or as a series of accidental events which might have unexpected consequences, rather than as a progressive march toward some utopia.

of knowledge prevailed. Narratives tell a story; they are organized around a plot, a linear, sequencing of events, a beginning and end, and a tale of good and evil intended to shape social behavior. Lyotard reasoned that, in premodern societies, narratives were considered knowledge not because they corresponded to facts but because they conformed to social rules that fixed who has the right to speak, to whom, and when. As long as these social conventions were followed, the stories told, as well as the story-teller, carried authority. Moreover, to the extent that narratives both presuppose and reinforce social conventions, they are said to directly promote social unity.

Modernity is characterized by an assault on narrative knowledge. The Enlightenment dismissed the grand stories in the Judeo-Christian tradition and in the great world mythologies as ignorance and superstition. In place of storytelling and myth making, which is poetic and evocative, modernity substituted science, which is said to yield objective truths. However, whereas premodern narrative is self-legitimating so long as the story and storyteller conform to social custom, science requires an external source of legitimation. This is so because there is no direct link between science and social cohesion. Thus, the question arises: What is the social and moral meaning of science?

Lyotard suggested that modern science must in the end appeal to narratives for legitimation. This is paradoxical because science claims superiority precisely in abandoning narrative. However, science relies on a different type of narrative than premodern ones. Lyotard called them "master-" or "metanarratives" because they synthesize stories that give coherence and meaning to smaller or "local" stories and practices. For example, the Enlightenment story of human progress driven by the advancement of scientific knowledge justifies the practices of the natural and social sciences. Social scientists appeal to the idea that science promotes human freedom by eliminating ignorance and prejudice in order to justify their research. Lyotard viewed the Marxist story of the coming of socialism through class conflict and proletarian revolution as a metanarrative. Local accounts of economic recessions or trade union activity can be interpreted in light of the grand Marxian narrative. Master narratives legitimate social and political practices as well. For example, sex education policies may appeal to an Enlightenment narrative (knowledge liberates); a union strike may gain coherence within a Marxian narrative (class conflict). Grand narratives have been an essential feature of modernity.

The defining feature of the postmodern condition is the decline of the legitimating power of grand narratives: "I define postmodern as incredulity towards metanarratives."[11] By metanarrative, Lyotard referred to "making an appeal to some grand narrative, such as the . . . emancipation of the rational or working subject, or the creation of wealth."[12] Faced with the paradoxical condition of relying on narratives for its legitimacy, science gradually abandons the master narrative. Lacking an integrating story or foundation, science is fragmented into a multiplicity of heterogeneous disciplines, area specialties, and paradigms.

What value does science have in the face of the decline of the legitimating power of metanarratives? Lyotard sketched two possible meanings of science in a postmodern condition. First, science is justified by its social utility. Lyotard spoke of the possible formation of a technocratic society that uses science to enhance bureaucratic, capitalist state control over natural and social forces. At odds with this technocratic vision is an evolving postmodern science. As evidenced in Einsteinian relativity theory, quantum mechanics, Godel's incompleteness theorem, and Heisenberg's uncertainty principle, postmodern science envisions the universe as unstable and unpredictable; knowledge is always provisional, incomplete, and perspectival.

Postmodern science abandons absolute standards, universal categories, and grand theories in favor of local, contextualized, and pragmatic conceptual strategies. Thus, instead of pursuing a moral theory that appeals to universal standards or axioms (e.g., the utilitarian pleasure/pain calculus or the Kantian categorical imperative which enjoins us to treat humans as ends in themselves), Lyotard favors a local pragmatic ethical approach. This underscores the specificity of the situation and the ability of the parties involved to develop agreed-upon, tentative, nongeneralizable social norms. Or, instead of aiming to unify knowledge, postmodern science is oriented towards conceptual innovation, disrupting unifying conceptual schemes, and proliferating paradigms, research programs, and conceptual strategies. Its value lies in producing neither liberating truths nor socially useful knowledge. The value of postmodern science consists in making people more aware and tolerant of differences, ambiguity, uncertainty, and conflict. "Postmodern knowledge . . . refines our sensitivity to differences and reinforces our ability to tolerate the incommensurable."[13] Postmodern science is antisystematic and subversive; it trades on a vision of knowledge as permanent revolution.

Lyotard linked postmodern science to a democratic pluralistic social ideal. Let me explain. Modern scientists believe that scientific foundations were necessary for human progress. In Lyotard's view, this was a well-intentioned but misguided hope. He argued that the quest for a general theory that would permit us to legislate truth, moral rightness, and beauty is not only impossible but undesirable. It is impossible because no one standard, common language, or set of concepts can speak to the irreducible heterogeneity in the ways that people think and speak about reality. The quest for systematic order is undesirable insofar as general theories create hierarchies that marginalize and repress social differences. For example, despite Marx's good intentions to think of the working class as the hope of humanity, his privileging of class conflict as the key site of social change devalues gender, sexual, racial, religious, ethnic, and national conflicts.

Lyotard drew a parallel between the fracturing of knowledge into heterogeneous discourses resistant to unification and the decentering of society. No longer unified by a common culture or institutional core (e.g., economy, religion, the state, kinship), the postmodern society resembles an incredibly complex labyrinth of crosscutting discourses. Lyotard views social life in terms of "language games." This refers to a set of linguistic practices, each marked by their unique rules, conventions, and aims. For example, science is a language game whose aim is truth; its rules enjoin conformity to specific methodological and conceptual conventions; its standards of justification are centered on issues of evidence and logic. In contrast, aesthetics entails different aims (judgments of beauty, not truth) and different standards of justification (considerations of spatial form, color, and dimension, not evidence or logic). Society is conceived of as a multiplicity of language games; individuals function as conduits or junctures in these diverse, conflicting circuits of discursive practice.

Social conflicts in a postmodern society are dispersed and local. Lyotard is not denying the continuing importance of the state and the economy as sites of political conflict. He is challenging the idea that these institutions are today the primary sites of conflict and that the diversity of social conflicts in current Western societies can be reduced to a unifying logic, for example, class struggle or the struggle against patriarchy. Educational institutions, hospitals, psychiatric clinics, prisons, and the mass media are major sites of conflict. Moreover, the struggles that take place in these institutional spheres are heterogeneous. Thus, the struggles around sexuality, gender, ethnicity, class, nationality, and cultural status are irreducible to each other; they cannot be subsumed under some unifying conflict. Lyotard imagines postmodern society as manifesting a kind of generalized revolt against centralizing authorities by marginalized and excluded groups. Though reluctant to spell out a social ideal, Lyotard affirms the awakening of differences and renewed opposition that he attributes to the postmodern condition.

The deconstructive assault on textual authority is applied by Lyotard to the sphere of knowledge and society. The quest for intellectual foundations, objectivity, certainty, and universal truths is abandoned. In place of grand theories, Lyotard described and advocated a postmodern condition featuring the proliferation of multiple, conflicting discourses. Whereas Lyotard detected a shift from modern to postmodern forms of knowledge, Baudrillard describes a similar development, but in more global social and historical terms. In often breathtaking and chilling language, Baudrillard outlines the social contours of a postmodern world.

JEAN BAUDRILLARD

Reaching intellectual maturity in the 1960s, Baudrillard absorbed the critical spirit of May 1968. Indeed, the University of Nanterre, where he held a chair of sociology until 1987, was a key site in the student revolts. Like Lyotard, Baudrillard's writings

Jean Baudrillard was born in Reims, France, in 1929. He completed his studies in sociology at Nanterre in 1966, and taught at the University of Paris. Baudrillard is one of those rare, fabulously interesting academic figures, a sort of academic celebrity. But his celebrated status should not be taken to mean any slight towards his formidable scholarly achievements. From his early efforts to rethink Marxism to his enormously creative years as a theorist of our hyperreal popular culture, including a book on Las Vegas, Baudrillard is indeed a serious and provocative theorist.

in the 1960s and early 1970s aimed to think through the intellectual and political implications of May 1968. He fashioned a post-Marxian critical theory that sought to reveal the contours of a new postmodern world.

In a series of powerful books, *The System of Objects, Consumer Society*, and *The Mirror of Production*, Baudrillard intended to revise Marxism but ultimately turned against it.[14] He argued that, despite Marx's revolutionary aims, the premises and concepts that guide his social ideas mirror and reinforce Western liberal capitalist society. At the center of Marxism was a utilitarian, productivist ideology that reduced society to labor as an instrument of productivity and economic growth. Unwittingly taking over the utilitarian spirit of capitalism, Marxism failed to grasp the cultural or symbolic structuring of society. For example, whereas Marx viewed commodities as part of the economic division of labor, Baudrillard analyzed commodities as a system of signs that organize the social universe by assigning to people and things a social identity and location (e.g., a gender, class, or regional identity). In effect, Baudrillard inverted Marxism. Instead of conceiving of history as driven by natural human need and labor, Baudrillard insisted on the structuring of society by symbolic or linguistic meanings.

Baudrillard sketched a post-Marxian perspective on history. Whereas Marxism outlines stages of successive socioeconomic formations, Baudrillard proposed a history of the "political economy of the sign." He offered an explanation of the changing structure and social role of the sign. In premodern societies, the sign had a clear referent and context-specific meaning. Such societies were organized around what Baudrillard called "symbolic exchange." In these exchanges, communication is immediate, direct, and reciprocal; lacking mediating structures such as the market or mass media, symbolic exchanges are not defined by their instrumental purpose. In acts such as gift giving, religious rituals, and festivities, exchange directly affirms social status and social order.

From the early modern to the postmodern period, the role of the sign changes in two key ways. First, the relation between sign and referent or reality is disturbed. Second, the sign forms a "code" that standardizes meanings and social responses. From roughly the sixteenth through the mid-twentieth century, a modern culture was formed; signs (words, sounds, images) were considered to have a more or less clear relation to reality. Modern culture was organized around a series of distinctions between word and world, concept and precept, mind and reality, truth and falsity, essence and appearance, reality and illusion, and so on. By World War II, these binary oppositions began to collapse. In particular, the line was blurred between sign and reality or word and world. In a postmodern culture, signs, words, and codes create their own universe of meaning without any clear relation to a real world of objects and events.

The somewhat nostalgic, obscure notion of symbolic exchange served as a critical ideal for Baudrillard. In the revolts of 1968, he imagined a renewal of symbolic exchange with its directedness, spontaneity, and reciprocity of communication. May 1968 signaled a break from the alienating codes of high-tech capitalism. The appearance of symbolic exchange among disenfranchised groups held out the possibility of political resistance and change. As the hopes of 1968 were dashed, Baudrillard's thinking became decidedly more pessimistic and obscure. History seemed to come to an end as current realities were overwhelmed by a sign system that virtually destroyed any semblance of order, truth, reality, and, for all practical purposes, political resistance.

In a series of books he wrote in the 1980s, most importantly, *Simulations, In the Shadow of the Silent Majorities*, and *The Fatal Strategies*, Baudrillard conceives of contemporary Western societies as inundated by an excess of meanings and cultural representations.[15] Driven by high-tech information systems, linguistic signs and meanings proliferate, multiplying relentlessly to the point where it is no longer possible to fix the meaning of signs, to relate word and object, and to differentiate truth and error, reality and illusion. The social world comes to resemble a flattened, monotone mass leveled by the spiraling weight of signs, meanings, and information.

We have entered, says Baudrillard, the age of the "simulacrum." Simulacra are signs that function as copies or models of real objects or events. In the postmodern era, simulacra no longer present a copy of the world nor do they produce replicas of reality. Today, simulations no longer refer to any reality; they create the idea of a reality, which they simultaneously claim to represent. Simulations have no referent or ground in any reality outside themselves. Postmodernity is organized around such simulations. From model homes to models of urban planning, good sex, masculinity, fashion, and personal identity, social reality is structured by codes and models that produce the reality they claim to merely represent.

In the age of the simulacrum, we enter a "hyperreal" space. The simulated representations of the real are taken as more real than the reality they are supposed to refer to. Isn't the actor who plays the lawyer, doctor, or homosexual often taken as really a lawyer, doctor, or homosexual? Television viewers take the persona of the actor as his or her true identity. We assume, moreover, that the model (e.g., the representation of the lawyer, the doctor, or the homosexual) defines a reality. Indeed, actors themselves confuse their personal identity with their theatrical role. The actor who takes over the persona of his or her theatrical role or who can no longer distinguish acting from reality has moved into a hyperreal space. In a postmodern hyperreal condition, the quest for reality, for experiences that unambiguously mark reality, is intensified, a marker ironically of our very inability to distinguish the real from the unreal.

According to Baudrillard, modernity has been characterized by the explosion of new divisions (e.g., science is marked off from literature and philosophy), new forms of differentiation (e.g., sociology is differentiated from anthropology and within each discipline area specialties are further differentiated), and by new cultural distinctions (e.g., between popular and high-brow culture). In contrast, postmodernity features a process of "implosion." Boundaries collapse. Does it make sense to distinguish news from entertainment or to differentiate politics and science or politics and business? The proliferation of interdisciplinary studies, for example, gender, urban, gay, and African studies, suggests the implosion of disciplinary boundaries. Institutional borders blur. Is it meaningful to separate mass and high culture? Is the "social" distinguishable from the "cultural" sphere? As media images, advertising representations, and information flows saturate the social space, as a neutralizing stream of signs and meanings engulf experience, the elementary distinctions of the modern era lose credibility.

As a late capitalist technocracy ushers in the age of simulacra, the modern politics of oppression and revolt give way to a postmodern politics of seduction and surrender. In the modern era, power was lodged in a specific class or in the institutions of capitalism and the state. In the postmodern world, power is isomorphic with the circulation of signs and meanings. Hence, power is today diffuse and saturates the social field. Social dominance operates not through coercion or rationalized power but through the seduction of the individual by mass media imagery and meanings. Indeed, Baudrillard contends, perhaps somewhat tongue in cheek, that the social field has been leveled into one great mass. He speaks, without much precision, of the "end of the social." He means that the view of society as composed of social classes, ethnic, gender, or racial identities, and interlocking institutions is today becoming irrelevant. In place of "the social" are "the masses," a manipulated by-product of the age of the simulacrum. In place of modern social theory, Baudrillard urges "fatal theory." The modern politics of revolt is feeble in the face of a system of social domination that operates through the seductive, pacifying capacity of the sign, media image, and simulation. Today, says Baudrillard, resistance must take the form of a deliberate passivity, a refusal to be absorbed into the imploded universe of signs and meanings. Baudrillard seems to believe that our surrender to the "object" or our indifference to the steady eruption of signs and meanings emanating from a cybernetic informational society will somehow lead to the collapse of the system under its own dead symbolic discharge.

Lyotard and Baudrillard take poststructuralism in a social theoretical direction. The aim of deconstructing textual order is directed to the social field. Thus, Lyotard offers a sketch of the rise of postmodern cultural legitimations of knowledge and authority. Baudrillard proposes a sweeping outline of the passing of an era of Western modernity. Nevertheless, neither Lyotard nor Baudrillard anchor their social ideas in an institutional analysis; neither do they frame their ideas in a detailed historical or sociological way. There is a sketchy, sweeping, closed, and authoritative quality to their work that is somewhat inconsistent with their repudiation of the modern aspiration to grand, generalizing theories. The most impressive effort to frame poststructuralism as a form of human studies has been the work of Michel Foucault.

Suggested Readings

Andrew Benjamin, ed., *The Lyotard Reader* (Oxford: Blackwell Publishers, 1989).
Steven Best and Douglas Kellner, *Postmodern Theory* (New York: Guilford Press, 1991).
Jonathan Culler, *On Deconstruction* (Ithaca, NY: Cornell University Press, 1982).
Mike Gane, *Baudrillard Live: Selected Interviews* (London: Routledge, 1993).
Charles Lemert, *Sociology and the Twilight of Man* (Carbondale: Southern Illinois University Press, 1979).

References

1   A fine overview of French structuralism that emphasizes its sociological aspects is provided by Edith Kurzweil, *Age of Structuralism* (New York: Columbia University Press, 1980); also, Jean Marie Benoist, *Structural Revolution* (New York: St. Martin's Press, 1978).
2   Ferdinand de Saussure, *Course in General Linguistics* (New York: McGraw-Hill, 1966).
3   Claude Lévi-Strauss, *The Elementary Structures of Kinship* (Boston, MA: Beacon Press, 1969); *Structural Anthropology*, vol. 1 (Garden City, NY: Anchor, 1967); *The Savage Mind* (Chicago: University of Chicago Press, 1970); *The Raw and the Cooked* (New York: Harper & Row, 1969).
4   Louis Althusser, *For Marx* (New York: Pantheon Books, 1969) and (with Etienne Balibar), *Reading Capital* (New York: Pantheon, 1970).
5   Michel Foucault, *Madness and Civilization: A History of Insanity in the Age of Reason* (New York: Vintage, 1965).
6   For a useful overview of poststructuralism, see Jonathan Culler, *On Deconstruction* (Ithaca, NY: Cornell University Press, 1982).
7   Jacques Derrida, *Of Grammatology* (Baltimore, MD: Johns Hopkins University Press, 1976).
8   Jacques Derrida, *Writing and Difference* (Chicago: University of Chicago Press, 1978) and *Positions* (Chicago: University of Chicago Press, 1981).
9   Jean-François Lyotard, *Discours, Figure* (Paris: Klincksieck, 1971); *The Libidinal Economy* (Bloomington: Indiana University Press, 1993); *Dérive à partir de Marx et Freud* (Paris: Union générale éditions, 1973).
10 Jean-François Lyotard, *The Postmodern Condition: A Report on Knowledge* (Minneapolis: University of Minnesota Press, 1984).
11 Lyotard, *The Postmodern Condition*, p. xxiv.
12 Lyotard, *The Postmodern Condition*, p. xxiii.
13 Lyotard, *The Postmodern Condition*, p. xxv.
14 Jean Baudrillard, *Le Système des objets* (Paris: Denoël-Gonthier, 1968); *La Société de consommation* (Paris: Gallimard, 1970); *For a Critique of the Political Economy of the Sign* (St. Louis: Telos Press, 1981); *The Mirror of Production* (St. Louis: Telos Press, 1975).
15 Jean Baudrillard, *Simulations* (New York: Semiotext(e), 1983); *In the Shadow of the Silent Majorities* (New York: Semiotext(e), 1983); *The Fatal Strategies* (New York: Semiotext(e), 1990).

12

Michel Foucault's Disciplinary Society

If Jean-Paul Sartre was the dominant intellectual force in the 1940s and early 1950s in France, succeeded by the short reign of Claude Lévi-Strauss, Michel Foucault assumed this lofty status in the early 1970s. Foucault was an unlikely successor to the throne of philosopher king. Foucault was mostly nonpolitical through the 1960s. The son of a surgeon he graduated from the elite Ecole Normale Supérieure, and his early interests were psychological and philosophical. In the 1960s, Foucault began to make his intellectual mark through a series of books, *Madness and Civilization*, *The Birth of the Clinic*, and *The Order of Things*.[1] These books did not significantly depart from the structuralist program of sketching the internal rules and systematic order governing social phenomena. Through the 1960s, Foucault spoke the language of structuralism, even as he stretched it in a more historical and political direction.

Although he was only minimally engaged in the revolts of 1968, Foucault thought of May 1968 as a turning point in French political and intellectual culture. His own work and life seem to have been dramatically altered by the social upheavals of the time. Subsequently, Foucault's writings took a political turn; the question of power moved to the center of his thinking. Moreover, from the early 1970s until his death in 1984, Foucault became a truly political man, joining mass demonstrations and protests, writing petitions and lobby reports, making political statements, and traveling across the country and the world to lend his name to various causes for social justice.

The revolts of 1968 did not succeed in bringing about lasting institutional change. Foucault believed, though, that May 1968 marked an important shift among the French Left. Prior to 1968, the Communist Party was a principal political player in French national life. The revolts of 1968 challenged the dominance of Marxism, and the Communist-Party-controlled French Left. The movements of political opposition were not organized around class politics. Revolts surfaced around sexuality, gender, and education, in universities, families, cultural institutions, and prisons, and were initiated by prisoners, students, gays, women, professionals, and laborers.

Contested Knowledge: Social Theory Today, Fifth Edition. Steven Seidman.
© 2013 John Wiley & Sons, Ltd. Published 2013 by John Wiley & Sons, Ltd.

Michel Foucault (1926–84) was born in Poitiers, France. He studied philosophy at the Ecole Normale Supérieure. In 1970, Foucault was elected Chair of the History of Systems of Thought at the Collège de France, the highest-ranking academic institution in France. Foucault was a poststructuralist who focused on the ways in which knowledge and power are mutually constitutive. Knowing is as much about asserting power as about gaining truth; and truth is as much about projecting power as about a will to know. Foucault provocatively stated that the idea of sexuality made possible the reality of sex. Now, you must figure out exactly what this means!

Foucault interpreted these disparate struggles as marking the emergence of a post-Marxian culture. Left politics could no longer be reduced to economic and class conflict; the working class could no longer be assumed to be *the* agent of social change; the Communist Party could no longer claim to be the sole legitimate vehicle for political opposition; Marxism could no longer claim to be *the* ideology of the Left providing *the* understanding of history and modernity.

The character of social revolt was shifting. Intellectuals were pressed to rethink their role. If political opposition was dispersed throughout the body politic, what form should social criticism assume? In a word, how would this new political culture alter the role of critical knowledge?

Central to the Western Enlightenment tradition has been the idea that scientific reason can contribute to human freedom. By revealing the essential dynamics of society, social theory could propose a rational political agenda. This critical spirit has guided liberal and Left culture. In this regard, Marxism remains heir to the Enlightenment tradition. Marxism aspired to reveal the laws of history and society, to disclose the chief site of change (the economy), the principal drama of social conflict (class conflict), the agent of change (the working class), and the future of humanity (communism).

Foucault abandoned much of this Enlightenment historical vision: the quest to liberate humanity through uncovering the laws of social order and change and the appeal to theory as providing a standpoint from which to prescribe a program of social reform. Departing from theorists such as Habermas who attempt to reconstruct Marxism in light of postwar social developments, Foucault questioned the Enlightenment premises of Marxism. He objected to the view that the ultimate aim of social theory is to grasp the essential structure and evolution of history. He was suspicious of a view of theory as synthetic and prescriptive. Foucault did not discount the utility of general theories such as Marxism as critical perspectives. He was, however, critical of the aspirations of these conceptual strategies to be unifying theories. His objections are both intellectual and practical: totalizing theories are reductionistic and exclusionary. Such theories arbitrarily privilege particular social dynamics and political agendas while excluding or marginalizing others. For example, Marxism renders gender, sexual, racial, or nationalistic conflicts secondary, if not entirely marginal, by insisting that political economy and class are the organizing principle behind all societies. In the aspiration to uncover order in social existence and to guide politics, general theories create a false and repressive sense of closure. Foucault's critique of general theory calls to mind Derrida's critique of logocentrism and Lyotard's critique of grand narratives: the longing for intellectual foundations and conceptual closure is purchased at the cost of social repression; the will to truth is entangled with the will to power.

In the revolts of May 1968, Foucault saw the surfacing of a multitude of oppositional social groups. Whether it was movements for prison reform, opposition to the psychiatric control of the self, women's or gay liberation, these revolts exhibited a varied social and political character. They cannot be subsumed under a unifying concept such as anticapitalist or antiliberal. They cannot be described as originating from the same social source, for example, the crisis of capitalism or patriarchy. The dynamics of domination and resistance vary considerably in these revolts. Although it might be desirable to analyze the interrelations between social movements, Foucault objected to efforts to explain these varied social revolts from the standpoint of a general theory such as Marxism. These social conflicts need to be understood in terms of their unique social patterns and history. He believed that if social theory wished to play a critical role in post-1960s Left politics, it must abandon its unifying and totalizing strategies in favor of local, flexible, and provisional critical understandings whose value is proven by their political engagement. "The role for theory today seems to me to be just this: not to formulate the global systematic theory which holds everything in place, but to analyze the specificity of mechanisms of power, to locate the connections and extensions, to build little by little a strategic knowledge."[2] Foucault called his alternative to a scientific vision of human studies "genealogy."

Foucault once referred to genealogy as "anti-science."[3] Genealogy gives up the search for secure intellectual foundations, essences, deep unifying patterns, and grand theories that try to comprehend the origin and endpoint of history. Genealogy does not claim to promote the progress of science or humanity. Indeed, in opposition to the Enlightenment scientific culture, genealogy does not offer a positive agenda of social reconstruction; it lacks a utopian vision. In the spirit of poststructuralism, genealogy aims to disrupt social conventions and norms. Its value lies in imagining the human world as thoroughly social and susceptible to immense social variation and change.

Compared with the Enlightenment scientific vision, the social hopes of genealogy are modest. It intends to show that the dominant discourses defining the social universe as natural conceal social interests and power relations. Although genealogy assumes that there is a close tie between institutions and discourses, its aim is primarily to disturb the "normalizing" role of dominant discourses. It reveals how dominant knowledges shape human life by naturalizing and normalizing the construction of social identities and norms. Discourses that carry public authority shape identities and regulate bodies, desires, selves, and populations. Additionally, genealogy aims to show that these knowledges are entangled in a history of social conflict. Central to this history is the exclusion or marginalization of discourses that give voice to oppressed groups. Foucault intended genealogy to recover those submerged and denigrated knowledges and the lives of their creators, for the purpose of contributing to their political reactivation.

Foucault's studies focused on one particular type of discourse, the human sciences. Even in his pre-1970s writings, which he designated by the term "archaeology," Foucault's concern was with psychiatry and the human sciences. For example, in *The Order of Things: An Archaeology of the Human Sciences*, he challenged the Enlightenment idea that the social sciences had discovered the unity of humanity and had detailed its unfolding as social progress. On the contrary, Foucault proposed that the human sciences constructed the concept of humanity as an essentially unitary, common essence. The idea of "Man" as the basis and active force producing knowledge, society, and history is the creation of the human sciences. As the theoretical object of the human sciences, "Man" has been made into the very subject (original source and active force) of science. Foucault maintained that it is language and discourse that are the agents of knowledge and history. Foucault's early archaeological investigations were important because they advanced a social and historical understanding of knowledge. They did not, however, go much beyond a structuralist analysis of linguistic or discursive order. Absent was any attention to the institutional contexts of discourse – the interconnection of knowledge and power.

As Foucault turned his attention to the interaction between institutions and discourses in genealogical analysis, his focus remained the human sciences. Foucault's major studies, *Madness and Civilization*, *The Archaeology of Knowledge*, *Discipline and Punish*, and *The History of Sexuality*, examined the human or social sciences, for example, psychiatry, criminology, penology, demography, sexology, economics, and sociology.[4] However, his purpose was not to determine whether these disciplines are true or to uncover a path of scientific progress. Rather, Foucault investigated the *social effects* of these knowledges. He asserted that discourses that aim to reveal the truth of the abnormal personality or of human sexuality or the criminal help to create and control the very objects they claim to know. Scientific knowledge functions as a major social power: through the state, the family, hospitals, and therapeutic institutions, scientific disciplines shape the dominant ideas about who we are and what can be said and by whom. It is this power/knowledge configuration, masked by the Enlightenment scientific vision, that is the focus of genealogy.

The genius of Foucault is that he did what he proposed. The great body of his work consists of critical historical studies. Without doubt, his master work, left unfinished at his untimely death, was his multivolume history of sexuality. I illustrate Foucault's idea of genealogical social analysis by outlining the social context, purpose, logic, and political implications of this project.

RETHINKING SEXUAL LIBERATION: FOUCAULT'S GENEALOGY OF SEXUALITY

It is not accidental that Foucault came to devote his greatest efforts to the study of sexuality. As a young man, Foucault was deeply troubled by his homosexuality. French society tolerated homosexuality provided that it was kept private. Even enlightened French citizens were resistant to making homosexuality the basis of personal identity. Homosexuality never became the basis of a community and politics in postwar France as it did in America. As Foucault traveled to American universities in the 1970s, he encountered a very different sexual culture. Homosexuality was made into an identity; a lesbian and gay community flourished, based upon the idea of a common sexual identity; and a liberation movement developed that was inspired by an affirmative homosexual identity ("gay is good" became its battle hymn) and demanded the normalization of homosexuality.

Foucault was ambivalent towards this American culture. He valued the sexual freedom and inventiveness of gay life in America. He particularly admired the creation of new ways of experiencing the body as a medium of pleasure and the creation of new forms of group life. Foucault was troubled, though, by the anchoring of this culture in a notion of sexual and social identity. Didn't the affirmation of a lesbian or gay identity reinforce a culture that assigned individuals mutually exclusive sexual identities? Didn't such identities function to control our behavior? Foucault was suspicious of a sexual liberation movement that was wedded to a rhetoric of authenticity and self-realization. Does normalizing gay identities amount to sexual liberation or the consolidation of a social order that regulates individuals by assigning them a sexual identity? He was uneasy with a gay movement that seemed determined to become a sort of ethnic community. Foucault imagined that such a community would institutionalize a regime of sexual control in the name of a bland assimilationist social ideal.

Foucault's concerns about the direction of the gay movement motivated him to investigate what he took to be the root assumptions of a modern Western culture of sexuality. How did it come about that modern societies developed the notion of a human sexual nature? How is it that sexuality is understood as revealing the truth of humanity? What social forces led people to think of sexual desire as a marker of self-identity? What gives the sexualization of self its power in our lives?

Despite the harmony of voices – sexual liberationists, sexologists, psychiatrists, social scientists – declaring the naturalness of human sexuality and its organization into an order of normal and pathological desires, acts, and identities, Foucault dissented. He relied on two strategies of argument. First, he hoped to make us aware of the historically unique character of the modern sexual culture. Second, he offered an alternative perspective on the history of sexuality. He proposed a radical rethinking of the origins and meaning of the modern culture of sexuality for the purpose, ultimately, of imagining an order of bodies and pleasures beyond "sexuality."

Foucault argued that not all societies assume that humans have a sexual nature, that sexual desires can be isolated and assigned a status as normal or abnormal, and that heterosexual and homosexual desires mark off two, mutually exclusive, self-identities. In his *History of Sexuality*, Foucault intended to undermine the presumption of the universality of the modern system of sexuality.

Perhaps because the Greek city-states are often invoked as the cradle of Western civilization, and perhaps because Foucault wished to challenge a story of the linear evolution of Western humanity, this is the starting point for his historical sketch. He argued that ancient Greek intimate culture was *not* organized around a regime of separate sexual desires and acts, some of which, being dangerous or unnatural, were prohibited. Gender preference was not the basis of a dichotomous heterosexual or homosexual identity. The Greek city-states represented a different universe of sexual meaning from the Anglo-European present.

Instead of a culture organized around "sexuality" (i.e., discrete desires, acts, and identities), Greek culture was centered around "pleasures" and an ethic of self-mastery. Pleasures included not only or primarily sex but also eating, exercise, and marriage. Moreover, moral judgment was not attached to specific sexual acts but to the overall shape of a life, in particular, to an individual's capacity to exercise self-mastery. This did not entail self-denial but involved enjoying pleasures with moderation and assuming an "active" or "passive" role as was appropriate to an individual's social status. For example, adult free men were expected to be active in sexual exchanges, while the subordinate social status of women, slaves, and boys required them to be sexually passive. Disapproval was not attached to particular sex acts or to a particular gender preference but to individuals who were immoderate in their pleasures or abandoned their appropriate role. "For a [free adult] man, excess and passivity were the two main forms of immorality in the practice of the aphrodisia [pleasures]."[5]

Nowhere is the difference between the Greek and the modern culture more evident than in the meaning of homosexuality. Some scholars, gay activists, and sexual liberationists have interpreted the Greek practice of love between adult males and boys as a moral lesson of tolerance and liberated sexuality. Foucault insisted, however, that love between an older and younger man in Greek culture has little, if any, resemblance to modern homosexuality. The Greeks did not view sexual desires as naturally divided between hetero- and-homosexuality. Adult free men were expected to have young male lovers and to be married. Older/younger male love was not a lifelong alternative to marriage; there was no separate, deviant culture of homosexuals and there was no stigma attached to same-sex love. This was not because the Greeks were enlightened, but because gender preference was not a category of sexual and social classification. Far more central to the Greeks was whether individuals were appropriately active or passive and whether they were moderate in their actions. Love between adult free men and boys was simply one domain of pleasure, no different in its moral aspect from that of eating, exercise, or marriage. It was no less regulated; only free adult males could take young men as their lovers. These relations were limited in time as young men became free adults, for whom it would be inappropriate to assume a passive sexual role. The relations between male lovers had to exhibit the appropriate forms of moderation, role playing (i.e., active/passive), and self-mastery in order to retain legitimacy.

An important shift in sexual meanings occurred in the passing of the Greek city-states into the imperial Roman era. Heterosexual intimacy and love assumed a central place in Western culture. In ancient Greece, marriage was organized around a series of social obligations, for example, the maintenance of an orderly and prosperous household. Ideal love was restricted to the love of young men by free adult men. In Hellenistic Rome, marriage took the place of same-sex love as the sphere of true love. Foucault spoke of the emergence of a new ideal of an equal, intimate, and sexual conjugal bond. This narrowing of intimate culture was part of a broader change to a culture preoccupied with "the care of the self" or with the shaping of subjectivity.[6]

Foucault related the centering on personal life and the conjugal bond in the first two centuries to the bureaucratization of imperial Rome.

Foucault interpreted the shift to a self- and marriage-centered culture as a turning point in the evolution of Western society. Sex was emerging as a domain around which prohibitions and formal rules were being formed; in particular, nonmarital sex was becoming the target of explicit prohibitions.

Christianity marked a break in Western civilization. In the Christian epoch, we can observe the beginnings of a modern sexual culture, with its focus on sexual desires and acts, its ideal of virginity and marriage, its prohibitions against nonmarital sex, and its fashioning of a formal, universalistic code to regulate sexual behavior. Perhaps the most far-reaching change initiated by Christianity was the coupling of truth and sex. In the Christian practice of confession, which encouraged the individual to reveal his or her sexual thoughts and behaviors as an act of purification, Foucault found the origins of the modern compulsion to imagine sex as the hidden truth of the self. In the confessional practice, sex is framed as a domain of discrete desires and acts whose power to sin demands vigilant monitoring. Foucault believed that there was a direct connection between the Christian confessional and modern discourses – e.g., sexology, psychiatry, and psychoanalysis – that approach sex as an autonomous psychic and social force. Foucault's death prevented him from writing the volumes linking Christianity and modernity. In the introductory volume to *The History of Sexuality*, he did, however, outline a story of the modern construction of "sexuality."[7]

The practice of confession was confined to the Catholic monastery during the Middle Ages. By the seventeenth century, confessional practices included all Christians. Moreover, the Christian was enjoined to speak frankly and in detail about the far-reaching effects of transgressive sexual desires and acts. The secularization of European societies in the eighteenth and nineteenth centuries did not put an end to the process of making sex a site of knowledge about the self. Confession was replaced by the practice of "examination" by physicians, psychiatrists, sexologists, and scientists; the religious language of sin and salvation gave way to a secular medical–scientific language and a vocabulary of the normal and the pathological.

It was in the Victorian period that the making of sex into a sphere of truth was mainstreamed. In contrast to the stereotype of the nineteenth century as the age of sexual repression, Foucault underscores the proliferation of public talk about sex in this period. A spate of sex-advice manuals, and psychiatric, medical, scientific, demo-graphic, and legal texts on sex exploded into the public realm. Did this profusion of Victorian discourses have the effect of drawing a curtain of silence and shame around sex? On the contrary, Foucault suggests that Victorian discourses created the very idea of a natural sexuality, of an order of desires and acts built into the body and obeying its own logic of natural and normal development. Foucault reverses conventional wisdom. Instead of speaking of sex as a sort of natural fact that science discovered, Foucault argues that medical–scientific discourses produced the idea of sexuality as a natural instinct that has its own laws of development. The idea of sexuality has contributed to producing "sex," i.e., a range of sexual thoughts, desires, acts, and relations.

Sexuality is not a natural fact; it is not built into the genetic or physiological structure of our body. It is, so to speak, an idea, a conception of who we are that has powerfully shaped the experience of our bodies, desires and identities. The power of sexuality does not lie solely in the sheer power of a discourse of truth authorized by science. Foucault insisted that the social force of medical–scientific discourses is related to the fact that they are part of social institutions such as hospitals, clinics, schools, and the state. Through medical and therapeutic practices, and the enforcement of legal statutes, the idea of sexuality is given a material reality in our lives.

Inspired by an Enlightenment vision of unveiling the truth of humanity, an army of sexologists, physicians, psychiatrists, psychoanalysts, and demographers sought to reveal a hidden, often camouflaged, order of sexuality. In search of humankind's sexual nature, the sciences unwittingly helped to create a population of new sexual selves. In a modern culture of sexuality, all individuals acquire a sexual identity; bodily and genital desires stamp us as a sexual type. For example, prior to the mid-nineteenth century, "homosexual" behavior may have been subject to disapproval, but it was the act, not the person, that was punished. Lacking a notion that same-sex behavior revealed a distinct sexual identity, such behavior was treated in the same way that any criminal offense was handled. By interpreting same-sex desire as indicative of personal identity, medical–scientific discourses gave birth to a new human type, "the homosexual." Henceforth, homosexual behavior was not merely a violation of social norms or laws but marked a deviant human type. Social control aimed at punishing the person and suppressing homosexuality. The regime of sexuality creates a new world of deviant and normal sexual and social identities – homosexuals, heterosexuals, fetishists, pedophiles, masochists, and sadists. The modern self is a sexual self.

Sexual liberationists might celebrate the making of sexual identities as a vehicle for liberating desire and creating a sexually free and open society. Foucault was more ambivalent. The modern regime of sexuality simultaneously creates sexual subjects and subjects them to forms of social control. Foucault proposed, however, that social control operates less effectively by a legal–administrative–social system of prohibitions and censorship. He emphasized a mode of social control that was built into the very regime of sexuality – its system of normal/abnormal identities and its norm of a healthy, fulfilled sexual life.

To the extent that individuals are defined as sexual subjects, people are inserted into a social order that fixes how we relate to our bodies and desires; this order regulates our behavior. For example, if we think of our sexual preference for members of the same sex as making us homosexual, regardless of whether we celebrate or lament our homosexuality, this self-identity will regulate our desires, behaviors, and social relations. Sexuality is not really an individual choice. The system of sexuality is built into the fabric of our institutions (e.g., state, law, medial clinics, hospitals, and family), cultural apparatus (e.g., mass media, advertising, educational system, and church), and into the very texture of everyday life (e.g., customs, norms, language, and lifestyle ideals). Thus, individuals whose sexual preference is for members of the same sex do not choose whether they wish to identify as homosexuals. If desire is socially framed in terms of a mutually exclusive identity system of gender preference, if the regime of sexuality is enforced by the dominant practices of a society, individuals will be labeled as heterosexual or homosexual persons, whether they want this to happen or not.

Foucault described a system of social control that operates less by repression than by the very cultural meanings and self-identities that it produces. The regime of sexuality exerts a kind of pervasive, invisible power over us to the extent that we are inserted within it and absorb its cultural definitions, social norms, and self-images. Every time that we look to define ourselves by our sexuality, consult an expert to discover our true sexuality, aspire to liberate our sexuality, seek self-realization through orgasmic fulfillment, or true gay love, we are placing ourselves under the control of "sexuality." We are not liberating our sexuality but putting ourselves under the control of a regime of sexuality. We are reinforcing this regime: the apparatus of cultural definitions, experts, and institutional practices. Thus, the affirmation of gay identity, its celebration and elaboration in the form of a gay culture, does not, in Foucault's view, signal the liberation of sexuality; rather, it reinforces a regime that has produced the very idea that we have a sexuality, that sexuality is our essence, and that gender preferences define our sexual identity.

Did Foucault view modern sexual culture as simply a form of social domination? Are sexual liberation movements only reinforcing a system of domination? At times, Foucault seems to have believed this to be the case. However, he never gave up social hope. He was attentive to the ironies of modern sexual culture and its possibilities for freedom. For example, Foucault observed that the construction of the homosexual as an abnormal, dangerous individual ironically gave birth to an affirmative lesbian and gay identity demanding legitimation on precisely the grounds for which it was initially scandalized, namely its claims to being natural and normal. Similarly, despite the apparent aim of the medical–scientific discourse to contain homosexual desire, its consequence has been to amplify and multiply homoeroticism. The homosexual has had no other choice but to attend to those desires which are self-defining. If the homosexual was compelled to focus on same-sex desires, the lesbian or the gay man deliberately fashions a life around those desires, producing a dense culture of homoeroticism. In the development of new forms of eroticism and in the elaboration of sexual desires into new social relations, Foucault saw much to value in modern sexual culture.

Foucault remained, however, a critic of the regime of sexuality. Although he did not trivialize the significance of reversing social stigma or the creation of movements of sexual affirmation, these developments were said to reinforce the regime of sexuality. Foucault's case against the regime was that it reduced sexuality to narrow sexual pleasures, rigidly forced individuals into restrictive, mutually exclusive identities, created stigmatized, deviant populations, and facilitated an efficient system of social control. Unfortunately, Foucault never spelled out his vision of an alternative intimate culture. It seems clear, though, that he favored replacing a regime that defined sex in terms of identities and authenticity with a culture that recognized "sex" as the basis for pleasures and forms of cultural and social innovation. No doubt his attraction to ancient Greece lies in its repudiation of a regime of sexuality in favor of a regime of pleasures and an ethics of everyday life that gave the individual wide latitude for self-regulation. Always siding with the anarchistic strain of French culture, Foucault, like his poststructuralist brethren, favored a society that permitted the widest possible latitude to self-expression and cultural innovation. Unfortunately, he never addressed the question of what normative and institutional regulation would look like in a freer culture.

THE IDEA OF A DISCIPLINARY ORDER

Some questions remain unaddressed in the preceding sketch: what social forces produced the regime of sexuality? And what social ends are served by a construction of a natural sexuality? What kind of society makes individuals into sexual subjects and objects of social control? In short, what was Foucault's image of modernity?

Foucault's perspective on modern societies can be highlighted by contrasting it to a liberal and Marxist view. Central to liberalism has been the belief in the progress of humanity driven by the advance of human reason. Was it not enlightened reason that substituted imprisonment with an eye to rehabilitation for the brutal torture of criminal offenders? Did not the science of psychiatry put an end to the confinement of mad persons by substituting humane treatment? Although Marxists criticize liberalism and the ideology that associates progress with a market society, Marxism falls squarely within the Enlightenment tradition. In addition, liberalism and Marxism share a basic sociological understanding. Modern society is viewed as a triple-layered order: the state, civil society (economic, educational, religious institutions), and the family. Moreover, the main driving force of society is said to be the dynamics of civil society, in particular, the economic realm. Disagreement between liberals and Marxists centers on their respective moral and political values. Liberals defend modern capitalism as the height of social evolution; the chief danger to social progress lies in excessive state intervention into civil society and the family. Marxists criticize the class-based character of capitalism as inhibiting the progressive potential of modernity; they anticipate a better society with the end of social classes.

Writing in the aftermath of two world wars and a worldwide Depression followed by Nazism, fascism, Stalinism, and Hiroshima, the Enlightenment story of social progress lacked credibility for Foucault. In his investigations into sexuality, prisons, madness, and psychiatry, Foucault stepped forward as a critic of aspects of the Enlightenment. For example, contrary to the Enlightenment story of the liberation of sexuality from the tight grip of repression, Foucault related a tale of the making of a sexual subject who is also an object of social control; the very medical-scientific discourses that were supposed to free our natural sexuality actually create and regulate individuals as sexual selves. Similarly, Foucault disagreed with the Enlightenment account of criminal reform. This view described how the advance of the humanitarian spirit swept away barbaric practices of torture in favor of a humanistic program of rehabilitation. In *Discipline and Punish*, Foucault interpreted the prison reform movement as establishing a new, more efficient, system of control.[8] Contrary to its ideology of rehabilitation, its chief aim is to depoliticize socially discontented populations by incarcerating and regulating them by means of an apparatus of surveillance and psychological management. Foucault was no less critical of the view that psychiatry marks the beginnings of the humane treatment of the insane. Substituting treatment and therapy for banishment or imprisonment, the new sciences of the mind are said to epitomize the humanitarian spirit of the Enlightenment. On the contrary, Foucault underscored the growing authority of mental health experts whose therapeutic discourses and practices created new psychological subjects – e.g., the neurotic, the narcissist, hysteric, schizophrenic, the anal-compulsive, the frigid personality – who are objects of psychiatric and state social control.

Foucault departed from liberal and Marxist images of modern society as a social system that has a center and unifying dynamic, such as capitalism or the idea of progress. He imagined modern societies as fractured and lacking a sense of unity. Neither the state nor the economy is the core of modern societies; and no one drama of social conflict, not class conflict and not gender, sexual, ethnic, or religious conflict, dictates social life and change. No one social group or ideology rules society, nor is society organized around the logic of capitalism, patriarchy, bureaucracy, secularization, postindustrialization, or democratization. In short, Foucault rejected the image of society as an organism or system that has been endorsed by both the liberal and Marxist traditions. Foucault viewed the social field as consisting of heterogeneous forces, institutional orders, processes, and conflicts.

Liberal and Marxist social thinkers have focused on the economy and the state and have aimed to delineate global processes such as capitalism (Marx), bureaucratization (Weber), social differentiation (Durkheim and Parsons), or democratization (Tocqueville). Foucault highlighted the importance of smaller, discrete social units such as hospitals, mental asylums, schools, the military, prisons, and universities. His intent was less to subsume these social units under some unifying global process (e.g., capitalism or bureaucratization) than to analyze their specific social logic and consequences. Foucault did not abandon all efforts at describing general social processes. He did, however, abandon efforts to infer local social processes (e.g., the making of sexual subjects or prison dynamics) from global processes (e.g., capitalism, bureaucratization, or social differentiation). He shifted our attention to heterogeneous local social dynamics precisely because they are important sites of social conflict today; our totalizing theories (e.g., liberalism and Marxism) have failed to understand their specificity because they have reduced them to a global social logic.

Foucault approached contemporary societies as being composed of heterogeneous social dynamics that cannot be said to have a central organizing principle. Although Foucault did not propose a general theory of modernity in the mode of Parsons or Habermas, in his various social sketches of sexuality, prisons, madness, and the human sciences, there emerges the outlines of what we might call a disciplinary social order.

Disciplinary-based societies are contrasted to early modern societies, which were organized around the centralization of authority in a sovereign ruler. In these societies, social order is maintained by the power of a sovereign to take or give life and to demand obedience; power is organized around repression – the capacity to silence, censor, or deny. For example, in early modern Europe, the law was viewed as an expression of sovereign rule. Its violation was a challenge and offense to the sovereign. The offender was punished by torture to demonstrate that the sovereign was omnipotent. Torturing the body of the offender was a way to manifest publicly the repressive, absolute power of the sovereign.

In a disciplinary society, order is maintained through technologies of control such as spatial separation, time management, confinement, surveillance, and a system of examinations that classifies and ranks individuals. If the exemplary institution of sovereign-based societies is the king, it is the military, factory, hospital, and prison in the disciplinary society. Order is maintained less through a hierarchy of ruler and ruled than through an apparatus of disciplinary techniques and discourses. Power in a disciplinary order is manifested less in the form of repression than in the production of subjects or social selves who are also objects of social control. For example, in modern criminological practice, the aim is not to punish the body through torture. Instead the body is observed and managed by a sprawling apparatus of surveillance (e.g., guards, television monitors, prison timetables, and regimented activities). Moreover, it is the psyche of the offender that is the real object of social control. Foucault spoke of criminological discourses and practices as producing a "criminal subject," a personal identity whose essential psychological and social nature is driven to commit crimes. The construction of a criminal subject justifies the creation of a series of technologies of control (e.g., incarceration, surveillance, and strategies of rehabilitation) and experts (judges, wardens, social workers, parole officers, psychiatrists) whose aim is to control the behavior of the offender.

Foucault did not deny the social importance of the repressive power of the state or ruling social strata (e.g., an economic elite or the power of men). He insisted, however, that the disciplinary-based production of social order in prisons, hospitals, factories, the military, and schools is central to contemporary Western societies. It is not the power to enforce obedience that makes possible these social structures; rather, social order is produced by a series of disciplining strategies – from confinement to systems of examinations – whose aim is to regulate behavior by imposing norms of normality, health, intelligence, and fitness.

Foucault offered the most elaborate social historical articulation of poststructural-ism. Whereas Lyotard and Baudrillard rarely go beyond schematic statements about social knowledge and society, Foucault offered historically rich, empirically dense social analyses. His studies of sexuality, prisons, madness, psychiatry, and the human sciences offer a serious alternative to the dominant liberal and Marxist approaches to human studies.

In contrast to many Enlightenment theoretical traditions, Foucault abandoned images of society as a totality, system, or organic whole in favor of a decentered, radically pluralistic concept of social process. In place of the grand evolutionary theories of the Enlightenment that purport to trace humankind's continuous pro-gressive development, Foucault analyzed the making of a plurality of human subjects, and underscored historical continuities and discontinuities, processes of order and conflict, without reducing these to a tale of progress or regress. Liberalism and Marxism aim to uncover a global social logic such as capitalism, bureaucratization, social differentiation, democratization, or individualism. Foucault gave up the search for a unifying social logic in favor of investigating heterogeneous social dynamics. Yet, in the rise of a regime of sexuality, a prison system, the human sciences, asylums, and psychiatric regimes of personal reformation, Foucault sensed the contours of a new disciplinary-based social order. Social control operates less through a system of legal, state, or economic repression than through the application of technologies of discipline that spread from the military to prisons, factories, schools, hospitals, asylums, and virtually all organizations. These technologies of control are interlaced with medical–scientific discourses; the latter control the movement of bodies, desires, identities, and behaviors by contributing to their very formation and by imposing on them normalizing rules or norms.

If power pervades the social field, if it is woven into the very texture of everyday life, social conflict and resistance cannot be centralized. Movements of political opposition cannot be subsumed under the banner of antistatism, anticapitalism, or antipatriarchy. Social resistance must be heterogeneous; oppositional practices must be local, diverse, and specific to the social logic of their particular social field (e.g., prisons, schools, sexuality). In further contrast to the politics of liberation that characterize liberalism and Marxism, the politics of resistance in disciplinary-based societies abandons the illusory dreams of a society free of domination and control. Personal and social existence can never be free of constraint and regulation; every society produces its own configuration of bodies, pleasures, identities, and social norms. Oppositional politics struggles against the disciplines (both the human sciences and the technologies of control) for the purpose of expanding possibilities for individualism, social relations, and producing just, democratic forms of life. Unfortunately, Foucault had little to say about the social hopes of political resistance, beyond making clear his opposition to the reign of a disciplinary order. He was clear, though, that the role of the intellectual in the politics of a disciplinary order shifts from confronting reality with universal truths to producing detailed analyses of the social formation of specific social fields, e.g., sexuality, prisons, and psychiatry. Foucault considered genealogy as one possible form that human studies could assume as part of an antidisciplinary politics.

Suggested Readings

David Couzens Hoy, ed. *Foucault* (Oxford: Blackwell Publishers, 1986).
Michel Foucault, *Politics, Philosophy, Culture: Interviews and Other Writings, 1977–1984*, ed. Lawrence Kritzman (New York: Routledge, 1988).
David Macey, *Michel Foucault* (New York: Pantheon, 1993).
Mark Poster, *Foucault, Marxism and History* (Cambridge: Polity Press, 1984).

References

1   Michel Foucault, *Madness and Civilization: The Archaeology of Knowledge and the Discourse on Language* (New York: Harper Colophon, 1969); *The Birth of the Clinic: An Archaeology of Medical Perception* (New York: Vintage, 1975); *The Order of Things: An Archaeology of the Human Sciences* (New York: Vintage, 1966).
2   Michel Foucault, "Two Lectures," *Power/Knowledge: Selected Writings and Other Interviews* (New York: Pantheon, 1980), p. 83.
3   Michel Foucault, "Power and Strategies," in *Power/Knowledge*, p. 145.
4   Michel Foucault, *Discipline and Punish: The Birth of the Prison* (New York: Vintage, 1979); *The History of Sexuality*, vol. 1: *An Introduction* (New York: Vintage, 1980).
5   Foucault, *The History of Sexuality*, vol. 2: *The Use of Pleasure* (New York: Vintage, 1985), p. 47.
6   Foucault, *The History of Sexuality*, vol. 3: *The Care of the Self* (New York: Vintage, 1986).
7   Foucault, *The History of Sexuality*, vol. 1: *An Introduction*.
8   Foucault, *Discipline and Punish*.

13

Zygmunt Bauman's Sociology of Postmodernity

Zygmunt Bauman (born in 1925) grew up in Poland, a nation that lost its independence first to Nazism and then to communism. Bauman emigrated to Great Britain in 1955, where he eventually became a sociology professor at the University of Leeds. Thoroughly European in his social thinking, Bauman draws considerably on French poststructuralism and the Frankfurt school of critical theory to develop a sociology of postmodernity.

Bauman's Jewish birthright and his coming of age under communist rule were crucial in shaping his social ideas. Poland lost its independence in 1939 as a result of the German invasion. Poland was subsequently freed from German dominion only to surrender to Soviet rule. Though subject to a Soviet military threat, Poland was not a Stalinist state, in the way, say, of Hungary or Romania. For example, an independent Marxist tradition flourished among academic intellectuals. The experience, however, of Nazism, antisemitism, and communism disposed Bauman to distrust claims of reason to fashion a social order or remake humanity in its image. Indeed, as we will see, Bauman came to reject the conventional view of Nazism and communism as accidents of modern history. Instead, he argued that these efforts to design a perfect, controlled order revealed the true spirit of modernity. The defeat of Nazism and the subsequent collapse of communism signaled the failure of modernity and its grandiose aspirations to fashion an ideal world order.

Unlike many European intellectuals who emigrated to Europe or the United States to escape Nazism or communism, Bauman did not abandon a left-wing critical perspective. Perhaps the survival of a tradition of independent Marxism in communist Poland allowed Bauman to preserve a socialist-inspired critical theory. Marxism was, however, abandoned on the grounds that its rationalist utopian impulse was emblematic of the increasingly tattered dreams of modernity. In place of Marxism, Bauman drew heavily on poststructuralism and critical theory in an effort to refashion sociology into a critical tool responsive to the movements of global transformation.

Contested Knowledge: Social Theory Today, Fifth Edition. Steven Seidman.
© 2013 John Wiley & Sons, Ltd. Published 2013 by John Wiley & Sons, Ltd.

Zygmunt Bauman was born in Poland in 1925. He was educated at the University of Warsaw but emigrated to Great Britain in 1955. Bauman has taught at the University of Warsaw, the University of Tel-Aviv, and, from 1972 until his retirement in 1990, at the University of Leeds in England. Bauman is a social theorist who narrates the history of premodernity, modernity, and postmodernity in terms of the relations among cultural norms, the state, and intellectuals. Bauman characterizes premodernity as a plurality of local traditions and decentralized authority. Modernity is marked by the emergence of the centralized state that relies on intellectuals to legitimate its authority and to impose standard cultural norms on local cultures. In postmodernity, the state no longer needs intellectuals for legitimation or to dictate a common culture as these functions are taken over by the market. The role of intellectuals in postmodernity shifts from imposing a common culture to the more modest but noble goal of facilitating communication between different communities.

FROM MODERNITY TO POSTMODERNITY

Bauman sketches a sweeping narrative of Western history. Departing from the Enlightenment stories of the progress of reason and freedom, Bauman relates a tale of social control and the advance of reason as domination. Moreover, whereas classical and contemporary sociological theorists assert that the division between capitalism and socialism is the principal site of social conflict and hope, Bauman substitutes the division between modernity and postmodernity. From this perspective, capitalism and socialism represent social variations in the dynamics of modernity. Despite his desire to break away from much of established sociology, Bauman's social narrative has a decidedly Enlightenment cast: it is a story of humankind's struggle for freedom and the still-lingering hope that reason can make a difference.

Bauman outlines a typology of premodern, modern, and postmodern societies. His perspective begins with premodernity. Furnishing only the barest sketch, Bauman characterizes premodernity as a decentralized, fragmented type of society. Premodern societies were composed of a plurality of self-sufficient communities, each with their own traditions and ways of life. These societies were highly stratified and were stabilized by a dominant religious culture and a well-established social hierarchy. Notwithstanding their social inequalities, Bauman underscores a premodern world that respected , local traditions and social diversity.

Between the collapse of premodernity and the consolidation of modernity in the seventeenth century, there was a brief period of social freedom. European societies were tolerant of social differences and, most importantly, accepted the uncertainty and contingency of existence. A social life evolved without the authority of God or a secular sovereign to impose order, certainty, and purpose. "It was in that brief interlude . . . that diversity was . . . lovingly embraced and hailed as the sign and condition of true humanity. Openness, readiness to refrain from condemnation of the other

and . . . settling for the credible instead of chasing the absolute – were all conspicuous marks of the humanist culture."[1] Unfortunately, the humanist celebration of
difference and ambivalence did not last.

Faced with a growing population of vagrants, the poor, the mad, and the discontented, Western societies responded with new forms of social control. Premodern
local communities were unable to respond effectively to the heightened social chaos
and the escalating administrative requirements of the time. Vast resources, human and
nonhuman, had to be administered: detailed, specialized information on labor, health,
fertility, and national and international developments was needed for national growth
and survival in an emerging era of industrial colonialism, and a system of transportation and communication that spanned huge stretches of territory was a pressing need
as commerce spread. In short, a new modern social order arose in response to the
failure of premodern social controls.

Modernity is characterized by a multilevel system of control which includes law,
disciplinary strategies, and ideological control. At the center of modernity is the state.
Bauman believes that the centralized bureaucratic state, with its concentration of
resources, its monopoly over the use of violence, and its army of civil service workers,
police and military might, is the foundation of modernity. With its mission to control
the social and natural environment, the state expresses the essential spirit of modernity.

The modern state did not simply evolve in response to a functional need for new
forms of social control. It consolidated power at the expense of local authorities, traditions, and ways of life. The modernization of governmental authority entailed the
transfer of power from local agencies and communities to the state. In effect, the
centralization of state authority involved a war on local communities and an effort to
wrestle power away from them. This was paralleled by a cultural war. In order for the
state to administer society in an orderly and efficient manner, it tried to impose a certain cultural uniformity. The state waged a cultural war against local, diverse cultural
traditions. In the name of progress, secularism, science, democracy, freedom, individualism, and public health, the modern state uprooted local cultures and destroyed
particular traditions and unique regional, ethnic, and cultural communities. The birth
of modernity was accomplished by means of a relentless assault on local traditions,
social pluralism, ambiguity, and uncertainty. It is this demand for order and the desire
to classify and control everything that is at the heart of modernity.

The modern state represents a new concept of governing. It is not simply that
powers, previously dispersed, are now centralized; the very character of the modern
state is historically unique. It was born of the wish to create and maintain order; its
mission is to mold society and its citizens to reflect a rational social design. The
modern state is not merely intent on maintaining order; it aims to fashion humanity
to mirror an ideal. Bauman describes the modern state as a "gardening state." It
aspires not merely to rule, protect its citizens, or ensure prosperity, but to tame and
domesticate the disorder of human existence.

The modern state is inconceivable without intellectuals. To run the bureaucratic
apparatus of modern institutions requires information about the dynamics of populations, institutions, and whole societies. Expert knowledges are required for the management of schools, factories, welfare institutions, prisons, hospitals, and local and

national governments. Additionally, the modern state requires legitimation; its war against local traditions, authorities, and communities, its desire to concentrate power, and its social goals must be justified. The modern state and Enlightenment social science emerged simultaneously and exhibit an affinity of interest and spirit.

Bauman disputes the conventional view of the Enlightenment. This perspective assumes that modernization marks a giant step towards freedom, tolerance, and social progress. The social sciences, born in the age of Enlightenment, are said to be a humanitarian force struggling against bigotry, fanaticism, and the evils of the excessive power of the church and the state. Bauman argues that the true spirit of the Enlightenment revolves around the quest for control and certitude. The triumph of the Enlightenment has meant the victory of what he calls "legislative reason." This type of reason is hostile to genuine forms of individuality and pluralism and intolerant of ambiguity and uncertainty. Legislative reason strives to fashion the world in accordance with general principles, laws, rules, or norms. The Enlightenment may, in principle, celebrate individualism and diversity; in practice, it is repressive. For example, the ideology of social progress has been used to justify the destruction of local traditions and communities or to colonize non-Western peoples who are defined as backward or primitive. The claim of science to objective truth has silenced nonscientific knowledges and the communities that they express. In short, the chief ideas of the Enlightenment, the malleability of humans, the doctrine of social progress, the unity of humanity, and the truth of science, are viewed as contributing to a type of society that aims to legislate order, control the unruly, and label deviant those who deviate from conventional norms of health, fitness, beauty, and virtue.

Bauman has no love for modernity. Reversing conventional wisdom that sees modernity as marking the breakthrough for all of humanity towards a freer, more rational society, Bauman views modern culture as driven to eradicate chaos, ambiguity, ambivalence, difference, and uncertainty. "The typically modern practice, the substance of modern politics, of modern intellect, of modern life, is the effort to exterminate ambivalence: an effort to define precisely – and to suppress or eliminate everything that could not or would not be precisely defined."[2] This spirit of control and intolerance characterizes the modern state, social institutions, and the social sciences. Western history is framed as a history of the progressive advancement of social controls inspired by the illusion of a life free of ambiguity and ambivalence.

The modern era has not abruptly come to an end. Nevertheless, Bauman believes that its failure is evident in the recent history of Nazism, the collapse of communism, and the growing crisis of Enlightenment culture in the West. The end of modernity is signaled, moreover, in the changing social role of intellectuals. Indeed, the theory of postmodernity is the product of the changing social position of intellectuals. Let's consider what Bauman has to say about the link between postmodernity and intellectuals.

Bauman maintains that intellectuals fashion ideologies that justify the policies and goals of the state. In postmodern conditions, the state no longer needs intellectuals for legitimation. Why? Social control in postmodernity is less dependent on repressive state measures or on shared cultural values than on "seduction." In the modern era,

individual loyalty to social and governmental institutions is tied to strategies of pun-
ishment and deterrence, disciplinary strategies of normalization, and appeals to
common beliefs and values, e.g., individualism, progress, and political democracy. In
a postmodern era, citizens are socially integrated and their institutional loyalty secured
through the power of the market. Individual needs, identities, and lifestyles are
wedded to consumption. Postmodern selves fashion identities and social lives through
patterns of consumption. They are seduced into social conformity by the fantasies and
lifestyle dreams that commodities are designed to evoke. Disciplinary strategies of
social control, from surveillance to the medicalization of social behavior, have shifted
their focus from mainstream populations to those marginalized groups outside the
reach of the market, e.g., the poor and the deviant.

Intellectuals in postmodernity are politically dispossessed. The state has less need
for expert knowledges and for discursive legitimation. Moreover, their role as arbiters
of culture is significantly diminished. As the cultural domain is increasingly commercialized and merges with the world of entertainment and popular consumption, a new
cultural elite of gallery owners, managers of the mass media, publishers, and mass
cultural entrepreneurs have squeezed out intellectuals. Lacking political or cultural
authority, intellectuals rethink knowledge and power. No longer called upon to
legislate standards of truth, goodness, and beauty, intellectuals now emphasize the
plurality of cultural standards and their rootedness in particular traditions or communities. As intellectuals lose social authority in their legislative role, they adopt an
"interpretive" role. Their aim is less to dictate standards or laws than to facilitate
communication between diverse traditions and communities. This interpretive role
gives to intellectuals a new social value; their advocacy of postmodernity is tied to
their own aspirations for social power.

Postmodernity does not mark a complete break from modernity. Bauman conceives of the former as the development of submerged or marginal aspects of modernity. The values of choice, diversity, criticalness, reflexivity, and agency are modern
ones and are preserved in postmodernity. Yet, there is a profound antagonism between
modernity and postmodernity. The guiding spirit of modernity revolves around creating order, boundaries, classifications, aspiring to certitude and transparency; it is an
epoch celebrating formal reason, laws, typologies, classifications, strict boundary
maintenance, uniformity, and universality. Postmodernity is said to embrace plurality,
ambiguity, ambivalence, uncertainty, and the contingent and transitory; it is disruptive, relentlessly critical, and oppositional.

The postmodern, above all, stands in opposition to the modern ideal of a uniform,
standardized culture composed of individuals who are, ultimately, seen as sharing a
common humanity. It is the assumption of shared humanity that makes the idea of
deducing a universal human interest, truth, or standard of value plausible. In contrast,
postmodernity celebrates the irreducibly pluralistic character of humanity and
culture. Humankind proliferates a multiplicity of traditions, communities, and cultures. In place of the modern notion of the identity of humanity, the postmodern era
substitutes the idea of irreducible human differences. Humanity reveals an immense
social variation; the idea of the unity and identity of humanity is seen as a repressive
normative claim.

Central to postmodernity is the abandonment of any secure basis for claiming certainty or for appealing to universal standards of truth, goodness, and beauty:

> The main feature ascribed to "postmodernity" is thus the permanent and irreducible pluralism of cultures, communal traditions, ideologies. . . . Things which are plural in the postmodern world cannot be arranged in an evolutionary sequence, or seen as each other's inferior or superior stages; neither can they be classified as "right" or "wrong" solutions to common problems. No knowledge can be assessed outside the context of the culture, tradition, language game, etc. which makes it possible and endows it with meaning. Hence no criteria of validation are available which could be themselves justified "out of context." Without universal standards, the problem of the postmodern world is not how to globalize superior culture, but how to secure communication and mutual understanding between cultures.[3]

As Bauman suggests, in a postmodern world, there is no authoritative standpoint from which to know the world. Human knowledge is always situated; we know from a particular standpoint, tradition, or cultural community. Knowledge is always pluralistic, as are values, social norms, and aesthetic styles. Claims to truth have value or credibility in relation to a specific tradition or perspective. The realms of knowledge, morality, and aesthetics are major sites of social conflict and contestation. In the face of endemic conflict and pluralization, the postmodern individual doubts the credibility of appealing to a neutral, Archimedean standpoint from which to resolve cultural clashes. Instead, a postmodern standpoint proposes a case-by-case, local strategy of negotiation that does not aim to abolish ambiguity, ambivalence, and uncertainty. Postmodernity affirms a decentered, fragmented social order that, ideally, creates institutional spaces for continuous discourse, contestation, and negotiation in the face of endemic sociopolitical conflicts.

POSTMODERNITY AND SOCIOLOGY

Bauman assumes that the nature of sociology is closely tied to the social role of the intellectual. In the modern era, there is an alliance between the state and intellectuals. Accordingly, sociology took on a "legislative role," i.e., its aim was to discover the principles of social organization and evolution. Although modern sociology claimed legitimacy on the basis of its assertion of truth and general social utility, it was integrated into the grand aim of the modern state to create and administer a rational society. The preoccupation of modern sociology with principles of social organization and "social problems" reflects the "legislative" spirit of modernity.

The social transition to postmodernity has altered the relation between the state and intellectuals. As we have seen, the state has less need for intellectuals; their legitimating role diminishes as the market replaces the state as an integrating social force. The disempowerment of intellectuals renders their legislative role obsolete. If sociologists are no longer called upon to legislate social order and cultural norms, what is their social role?

Unfortunately, Bauman says, some sociologists will deny a shift to postmodernity. This is a grave mistake. As sociology is needed less by the state and its role as a cultural arbiter diminishes, it will become obsolete if it does not refashion its premises and aims. The appeal to knowledge for knowledge's sake to justify a scientific sociology is increasingly viewed as implausible in a postmodern culture. Sociology ignores the conditions of postmodernity at the risk of its own social relevance.

Bauman notes that many sociologists understand the rise of postmodernism as signaling a crisis of modernity. The focus by postmodern thinkers on decentering identity and culture, and on instability, fragmentation, and change is interpreted as symptomatic of a cultural crisis of modernity. The postmodern championing of radical pluralism and decentered identities is criticized for reinforcing the disintegrative and pathological currents of Western modernity. In other words, postmodernism is interpreted as a symptom of social malaise. Bauman is sharply critical of this perspective: "I suggest . . . that the phenomena described collectively as 'postmodernity' are not symptoms of systematic deficiency or disease; neither are they a temporary aberration with a life-span limited by the time required to rebuild the structure of cultural authority. I suggest instead that postmodernity . . . is an aspect of a fully-fledged, viable social system which has come to replace the 'classical' modern, capitalist society and thus needs to be theorized according to its own logic."[4]

Bauman's perspective on postmodernity suggests a major reorientation of sociology from a legislative to an interpretive role. Surrendering the search for foundations, universal laws or a closed intellectual system, sociology should take up the task of facilitating the mutual understanding of diverse communities. Valuing the plurality of cultural traditions, subcultures, and communities, the sociologist defines his or her goal as making coherent and intelligible these social differences. "A postmodern sociologist is one who, securely embedded in his own, 'native' tradition, penetrates deeply into successive layers of meanings upheld by the relatively alien tradition to be investigated. . . . In the person of the sociologist, two or more traditions are brought into communicative contact. . . . The postmodern sociologist aims at 'giving voice' to cultures which without his help would remain numb or stay inaudible to the partner in communication."[5] The value of a postmodern sociology is in rendering social differences less threatening, fostering tolerance for diversity, making the unfamiliar familiar, and giving voice to submerged or marginal experiences and communities. In a postmodern world, where diverse communities clash, the interpretive sociologist has a role to play in facilitating mutual understanding and suggesting local, case-by-case, strategies for conflict resolution. A postmodern culture underscores a parallel shift to interpretive and ethnographic types of sociology.

Bauman endorses a critical postmodern sociology. Sociology as social criticism has been a key part of its history. However, social critique, from Marx to Habermas, has typically appealed to universal standpoints and foundations, and to a strong program of science, to wrap it in an aura of legitimacy. A postmodern social critique would preserve the emancipatory hopes of the modern era but without the anchor of certitude. The postmodern critic would acknowledge the situated and contingent – merely historical – basis of the interests and values that ground social criticism. The rationalist language of modern criticism, for example, appeals to objective foundations and social laws, which would give way to a more historical and situated language of interests, purposes, and hopes. Postmodern social critics abandon, moreover, the dangerously redemptive vision of social change that has proven so seductive and destructive. "The faith in a historical agent waiting in the wings to take over and to complete the promise of modernity using the levers of the political state . . . has all but vanished."[6] Postmodern critics imagine change as less dramatic and utopian; they look less to the state as an agency of change. Bauman imagines a postmodern criticism whose aim is to enlighten citizens, to alert them to the social forces (e.g., the state, market, and consumerism) that threaten to diminish freedom and democracy.

There is one final possibility for sociology today. Bauman proposes a sociology of postmodernity. Sociologists would strive to understand the origin and social organization of postmodernity in a way similar to classical and contemporary efforts to fashion a sociology of modernization. However, just as a sociology of modernity required sociologists to adopt assumptions and ideas that reflected modern Western societies, a sociology of postmodernity would pressure sociologists to replace modern premises, concepts, models, and explanatory schemes with postmodern ones.

What would a postmodern conceptual reorientation of sociology look like? Sociology would abandon many of the key ideas that have guided classical and contemporary theory, for example, the view of society as a system, organism, or mechanism, the idea of the individual as a natural agent of action, a centering on the categories of labor, production, the division of labor, values, and ideologies, a focus on the nation-state as the unit of analysis, and assumptions of continuous, linear development and progress. In place of these premises, a postmodern sociology would emphasize the fluid, multiple character of social realities, the local or situationally produced character of social institutions, the interpretive efforts of individuals in shaping social reality, and the individual as a socially produced identity. There would be a shift in the axial categories of sociology to center on consumerism, the market, disciplinary technologies relating to the body, self and identity formation; a deliberately international horizon and approaches to social change that address discontinuous, unpredictable, and contradictory social trends.

Sociologists have been slow and often resistant to acknowledge the great transformation from a modern to a postmodern era that has transpired in postwar Europe and America. To the extent that they remain wedded to modern premises and approaches, sociologists will continue their current drift into social insularity. Bauman offers possibilities for renewal. Sociology must shift to a postmodern axis. It should abandon its legislative role (e.g., providing foundations, general principles, laws, overarching theories, systems of sociology) in favor of a critical, interpretive role. Sociologists would aim to enhance mutual understanding among different communities or to clarify and criticize the emerging postmodern epoch. The world has changed, and sociology, Bauman insists, must also reinvent itself to preserve its social role. We must give up an Enlightenment paradigm of knowledge and society; only a shift in the culture of sociology to a post-Enlightenment paradigm of knowledge and society can save it from its growing obsolescence.

Suggested Readings

Peter Beilharz, *Zygmunt Bauman* (London: Sage, 2000).

David Smith, *Zygmunt Bauman* (Cambridge: Polity Press, 2000).

I. Varcoe and R. Kilminster, eds. *Culture, Modernity and Revolution* (London: Routledge, 1996).

References

1 Zygmunt Bauman, *Intimations of Postmodernity* (New York: Routledge, 1992), p. xiii.

2 Zygmunt Bauman, *Modernity and Ambivalence* (Ithaca, NY: Cornell University Press, 1991), pp. 7–8; *Modernity and the Holocaust* (Ithaca, NY: Cornell University Press, 1989); and *Legislators and Interpreters: On Modernity, Post-Modernity and Intellectuals* (Ithaca, NY: Cornell University Press, 1987).

3 Bauman, *Intimations of Postmodernity*, p. 102.

4 Bauman, *Intimations of Postmodernity*, p. 52.

5 Bauman, *Intimations of Postmodernity*, p. 42.

6 Bauman, *Intimations of Postmodernity*, p. 109.

Afterword to Part IV

Key Enlightenment ideas such as the objectivity of science, the coupling of scientific and social progress, the unity and underlying sameness of humanity, the evolution of humanity from East to West, and from a state of oppression to freedom, are not just the beliefs of intellectuals. They are woven into the political and cultural fabric and history of the so-called modern West. These ideas are at the root of a secular creed – a faith in the ultimate value of the individual, reason, freedom, and progress.

Postmodern perspectives do not reject Enlightenment values such as freedom, tolerance, democracy, critical thinking, and social justice. Postmodern ideas are not antimodern; postmodernists are not against freedom or the rule of law or rational argumentation. Postmodern thinkers argue that the way these Enlightenment values have been expressed as a social and political theory or put into practice need to be re-examined and sometimes challenged.

In particular, Enlightenment traditions of social thinking have unintentionally con-tributed to reinforcing the dominance of the West over the East, the middle classes over laborers, European culture over non-White cultures, a society of experts over the masses, and men over women. Think of one of the great champions of freedom, Marx. He criticized capitalism because it created a class-divided society that left the great majority of individuals poor, culturally backward, politically disempowered; in short, unfree. But Marx and most Marxists never doubted that Europe is the seedbed and the future of humanity; they rarely acknowledge that these same societies instill regimes of male dominance, white supremacy, heteronormativity, narrow norms of human "ableness," and so on. Marxist's class view of society render social and political conflicts around gender, race, or sexuality as, at best, secondary or derivative of class. Despite championing human freedom, Marxism has often reinforced a narrowly Eurocentric and male-dominated social order. This is hardly unique to Marx. A quick glance at the sociology of Durkheim, Weber, Parsons, and Habermas reveals similar unexamined views.

Contested Knowledge: Social Theory Today, Fifth Edition. Steven Seidman.
© 2013 John Wiley & Sons, Ltd. Published 2013 by John Wiley & Sons, Ltd.

For many of us in the West it is a great relief that this culture of Enlightenment is under scrutiny. We are not rejecting its values or social hopes but questioning its social and historical vision. And, it is not only intellectuals who are re-examining the Enlightenment cultural heritage. For example, the postwar generation has come of age at a time when science seems to have lost a great deal of its aura of truth and progress. As science is integrated into commerce and the military, as it is used to sell toothpaste and build bombs, Enlightenment views of science as pure knowledge and as a unqualified force of social good seems naïve today. The postwar generation is aware of the dark side of science: Nazism, Stalinism, Hiroshima, scientific torture, genocide, mental asylums, medical dehumanization, and the role of science in pathologizing homosexuals, Blacks, and women. Science and the broader culture of the Enlightenment have lost their innocence.

Postmodern perspectives would not merit serious attention if they were simply against the Enlightenment. Postmodern thinkers are heirs to the Enlightenment, but critical heirs. Their aim is to preserve the core ethical convictions or values of the Enlightenment and its hope for a better world but to offer different understandings of knowledge, self, social life, politics, and history. For example, Lyotard and Foucault reject the grand theoretical and liberationist hopes attached to the idea of social science; they are not, however, against empirical knowledge or rigorous thinking. Instead, they question the absolute privileging of science as truth on both epistemological and political grounds. For example, they argue that the absolutist view of science devalues and socially marginalizes all nonscientific thinking and the communities that support such thinking. If science alone yields truth, nonscientific ideas (e.g., religion, literature, art, and folk knowledges) lack credibility when it comes to understanding human life. Science creates an intellectual and social hierarchy, with the institution of science, and scientists, at the apex. Lyotard and Foucault wish to hold on to the empirical and theoretical rigor of science, but abandon its imperial claims. Both thinkers, and this is true of many who we might think of as postmodern, favor a pluralistic approach that recognizes and values varied forms of knowledge. Is this relativism? Not exactly, since a postmodernist does appeal to empirical-analytical standards to make judgments about knowledge. However, postmodernists would in general recognize that these standards are subject to debate, and never free of the suspicion that they may mask a power dynamic.

As some of the social and historical beliefs of Enlightenment thinkers lose resonance, as it becomes harder for us to think of history as a movement of progress and the West as the lead society, as processes such as globalization, multiculturalism, and the rise of diasporic communities redesign our social landscape, some thinkers have proposed new social and historical perspectives. For example, departing from much of classical and contemporary thinking which has focused on the economy, the state, organizational dynamics, and cultural values, some postmodern perspectives have highlighted the importance of processes relating to the body, sexuality, identity, consumerism, mass media, medical-scientific discourses, the social role of the social sciences, and disciplinary technologies of control. Baudrillard's analysis of the cultural processes of simulation, hyperreality, and implosion; Foucault's outline of the rise of a disciplinary order that creates new identities and imposes normalizing controls (from surveillance to therapies) asks us to shift our conceptual strategies in ways no less dramatic than the "revolution" in social thinking associated with classical sociology.

While postmodern perspectives are sometimes pessimistic, there is also an abiding social hope that comes through. In their most hopeful moments, thinkers such as Lyotard, Foucault, and Bauman seem to be saying that, if we wish to continue to dream of freedom and collective well-being, we need new ways of looking at knowledge, society, history and the very idea of freedom. For many such thinkers, the postmodern vision assumes socially produced selves whose identities are multiple and unstable, an awareness of the coupling of power and knowledge, a new moral responsibility attached to the production of knowledge, and an image of society as fractured order, deeply divided, multicultural, and organized around a myriad of specific struggles. There is a keen sense that power works through repression (e.g., the law, state, class rule) *and* through the production and normalization of bodies, populations, and identities (sexual, gender, ethnic). A permanent struggle for gains in pleasure, choice, self-expression, social bonding, and justice is offered in place of the older dream of bringing unfreedom to a final ending.

Part V

Revisions and Revolts: Identity Politics and Theory

Introduction to Part V

May 1968 ignited a national crisis in France. Students, laborers, professionals, and cultural workers (e.g., editors, actors, writers) united to change France. They opposed the bureaucratization of society, corporate capitalism, the power of the Catholic Church, excessive state control over private life, mass consumerism, and the commercialization of the national culture. The revolts of 1968 aimed at social revolution.

There was no May 1968 in the United States. There were student revolts. However, a coalition between students, blue collar workers, and professionals never materialized. Moreover, student protests received broad public support only as they addressed university reform or were aligned with the protests against US involvement in the Vietnamese war. As students pursued a radical political agenda, they lost much of their mainstream support. Indeed, the withdrawal of the United States from Vietnam sounded the death knell to the student movement.

Social conflict in postwar America surfaced, as well, around issues of race, gender, and sexuality. These conflicts generated two types of social movements: civil rights and liberation movements. The civil rights movements were sparked by the Black campaign against Southern segregation. The sit-ins, boycotts, nonviolent protests, and political lobbying for equal racial rights became a model for struggles by women and homosexuals. These civil rights movements created private and public discord in the United States; they disturbed established racial, gender, and sexual inequalities. Nevertheless, their aim was less to challenge the legitimacy of liberal institutions than to demand that America live up to its ideals of equal rights and opportunities for all individuals.

Paralleling the civil rights campaigns were liberationist social movements. In the North, a Black power movement cohered around an ideology of Black nationalism. Liberal feminists were challenged by radical feminists for whom changing the law was simply part of a broader agenda of dismantling male domination. The struggle for civil rights by lesbians and gay men was overshadowed in the early 1970s by militants

Contested Knowledge: Social Theory Today, Fifth Edition. Steven Seidman.
© 2013 John Wiley & Sons, Ltd. Published 2013 by John Wiley & Sons, Ltd.

who demanded an end to sexual and gender roles. Inspired by ideas of participatory democracy, sexual and gender freedom, and ethnic nationalism, the liberationist movements challenged the legitimacy of liberal America. Although the heyday of the liberation movements had passed by the mid-1970s, they continued to influence the contours of American political and intellectual culture.

Despite some parallels between French and American social rebellions in the 1960s, there is a striking difference in their political culture. Whereas French rebels were more or less united in their opposition to the social status quo, American radicals lacked a unity of purpose. The American rebellions were fragmented into a multiplicity of movements, each organized around an imagined common identity. These identity-based movements created their own cultures, organizations, political strategies, and social visions. For example, the Black liberation movement was unified by the assumption of a common Black identity based on the shared experience of racism and resistance; Black liberation spoke for all, and only, Black people.

Postwar United States saw the rise of a new type of politics: identity politics. Appealing to the idea that all members of the same oppressed group share a common identity, Blacks, women, and gays organized into ethnic-like political communities and movements.

These social movements created new subjects of knowledge (African-Americans, women, lesbians, and gay men) and new knowledges. Socially positioned as oppressed, Blacks, gays, women, lesbians, and Latinos developed new perspectives on knowledge, society, and politics. The dominant knowledges in American public culture were criticized as narrowly expressing the standpoint and interests of White Europeans, men, and heterosexuals. Black nationalists, feminists, gay liberationists, and lesbian feminists produced new social perspectives: Afrocentrism, feminism, lesbian and gay or queer theory. These new knowledges exhibited an ambivalent relation to Enlightenment traditions of social thought. For example, as feminists analyzed the role of science in creating and perpetuating oppressive cultural stereotypes, they criticized the idea of a rigid separation of scientific knowledge and values; science was viewed as entangled in politics.

These new social movements gave birth to social knowledges that have had considerable impact on the shape of social theory and social science. Part V examines these critical knowledges with an eye to the ways they challenge and revise our notions of social thought and analysis.

14

Feminist Theory/Masculinity Studies

The contemporary women's movement developed in response to the contradictions of postwar America. On the one hand, women were pursuing college degrees and careers; they no longer automatically associated self-realization with becoming a wife and mother. On the other hand, women were still expected to assume most of the child-rearing and household duties, and sacrifice their personal and career interests for the sake of their husbands; they were also subject to sexual harassment and at times violence. Inspired by the Black civil rights and liberationist movements, and encouraged by a social atmosphere of idealism associated with the Kennedy and Johnson administrations, a late-twentieth-century women's movement was born.

If the women's movement was the political vehicle for women's quest for social justice, feminism was its ideology. Feminism interprets women's personal troubles as social and political in origin. If women are unhappy in marriage, perhaps this reflects socially imposed roles as wife and mother or a norm of heterosexuality that is at odds with their true selves. If women feel displeased with their appearance, it is male-imposed ideals of feminine beauty, not themselves, that needs changing. Women's discontents were interpreted as social in origin, requiring political action, not personal problems requiring therapy or marriage. Feminists believe that women are men's social and political equals but that is not yet the reality.

Feminism refers to the ideas produced primarily by women for the purpose of changing their self-awareness and changing society. Feminists offer perspectives on social life from the standpoint of viewing women as a socially disadvantaged group. They assume that men and women are *socially formed* and that *social explanations* can be given for why men are dominant. Feminists assert that the relations between men and women in the spheres of work, politics, family, and sex exhibit patterns of gender inequality.

From a feminist perspective, the social world is gendered: feelings, desires, behaviors, social roles, occupations, and whole institutions are defined as masculine or feminine or appropriate for men or women. For example, I would guess that most Americans, even

Contested Knowledge: Social Theory Today, Fifth Edition. Steven Seidman.
© 2013 John Wiley & Sons, Ltd. Published 2013 by John Wiley & Sons, Ltd.

in the year 2012, define nurturing, caring, and empathetic feelings as feminine and view nursing, secretarial, or childcare work as women's work. Would I be far off the mark in assuming that most Americans consider the military and public office as appropriately masculine? If women are expected to assume caretaking roles (e.g., wife, mother, nurse, secretary), while men are expected to aspire to leadership roles (e.g., military officer, mayor, business executive), it is not, say feminists, a result of nature but of social factors.

Gender differences between men and women are socially produced for a reason: to maintain male dominance. The gender order is a hierarchical one. Men are in positions of dominance. If women are expected to be wives and mothers, will they have the time to develop the skills to be corporate executives and political leaders? If women are socialized to be nurturing and responsive to the needs of others, will they have the psychological capacities (e.g., aggressiveness or decisiveness) to assume leadership roles? If women are expected to seek the approval of men, will they be able to demand equal satisfaction in their intimate lives? In short, gender differences sustain male dominance.

In most, if not all, societies, men have power over women. Often male dominance is obvious. For example, in the United States, men occupy the highest positions of power in economic, political, military, educational, and cultural institutions. Men are corporate executives; men are governors and senators; men control the media empires, the military, and the police force. Male dominance is revealed, more subtly, in our intimate lives. For example, men are expected to initiate and more or less control the sex act. Men's dominance is evidenced in the multibillion-dollar cosmetic industry, which promotes an ideal of slim, adolescent-like sexualized beauty that women aspire to in order to feel attractive; men's dominance is revealed in the obscene rates of rape and domestic violence, in the proliferation of households headed by single women who raise children with little or no financial or social support from the biological father.

Like any group that benefits from being in power, men have an interest in maintaining their dominance. As the realities of rape and woman-beating indicate, men use violence if necessary to keep power. They resist the movement of women into positions of institutional power. A more subtle, and perhaps more effective, strategy of male dominance is to control the public images of gender. If the dominant cultural ideas define the "normal woman" as destined by nature to be a wife and mother, men will not need to use coercion to keep women subordinate. Men have used science, medicine, and popular culture to perpetuate the illusion that nature dictates gender difference and hierarchy; defining women's self-realization in terms of the roles of wife and mother reinforces men's social dominance. At the core of feminism is a reversal of conventional wisdom. Feminists view the idea of natural gender difference as an ideology intended to conceal the social and political forces that create an unequal, male-dominated order.

Feminism describes the world of men and women as deeply political. Individuals learn to become men and women. Moreover, women are socialized and coerced into subordinate roles. They have, however, rebelled against male control throughout history. However, the ideology of natural difference and social norms pressuring women to conform to caregiving roles, along with men's superior political, economic, and cultural resources, have perpetuated male dominance. Although feminists agree that gender is a social and political phenomenon, they are divided about the nature of gender, the dynamics of male dominance, and the aim of the women's movement. In this chapter, we consider three approaches to feminist theory: gynocentric feminism, difference feminism, and postmodern feminism. We conclude with a glance at the exciting field of masculinity studies.

GYNOCENTRIC FEMINISM: DOROTHY SMITH

From the early days of second-wave feminism in the late 1960s to the present, many feminists have agreed with antifeminists in one crucial respect: men and women are understood to be different in basic ways. Men and women are said to think, feel, and want different things and to relate to others and to the social world in essentially different, even opposing, ways. And, despite variation among men and among women, there is an essential sameness or identity among men and among women. Some feminists argue, in this regard, that women, all women, share a common biological, psychological, or social reality. Or, they hold that women share similar values, and interests by virtue of being oppressed by men and wanting to be free of this domination. This appeal to women's fundamental common identity and subordination has been at the root of what has come to be called gynocentric feminism. One of its theorists is the sociologist Dorothy Smith.

Smith aimed to craft a social theory from the standpoint of women's experiences. A feminist sociology would aim to enhance women's understanding of the social forces that shape their lives, which both oppress them and make possible social change.

Smith takes gender as a master category of social analysis. Gender structures selves, institutions, culture, and the politics of a society. In contemporary Western societies, human feelings, desires, identities, conduct, occupations, institutions, and ideas are gendered as masculine or feminine. The gendered character of the self and society extends to knowledge, including the sciences. Asserting the gendered imprint of

> **Dorothy Smith** was born in Britain in 1926. She did her undergraduate studies at the University of London and later emigrated to the United States where she completed her doctorate in sociology at the University of California at Berkeley in the early 1960s. She has taught at the University of Toronto for many years. Smith is known for her feminist theory, which takes the position of women as the starting point in the development of knowledge. She argues that most sociological concepts reflect and reinforce a masculine position and world view. As a woman and as a sociologist, Smith claims to experience a bifurcated consciousness; that is, as a sociologist she is familiar with abstract sociological concepts. However, these concepts do not adequately address the concrete, local social world that, as a woman, Smith occupies. Thus, she advocates an approach to social knowledge that begins from the standpoint of women which is, for many women, the world of intimate relations, the body, and the household.

knowledge means that there is no universal, Archimedean standpoint from which to know the social world. "There can be no theory, no method, and no knowledge … that is not made by men and women and made from a definite standpoint in the society and in the interests of those who make it."[1]

In contemporary Western societies, men and women are socially positioned differently and unequally. Smith is aware that both men and women differ by class and race and in many other ways. These differences suggest variations in women's knowledges. Yet, despite such social variation, Smith holds that women share a common gender experience. Women continue to be primarily responsible for household duties and for the care of the physical, material conditions of society, e.g., cooking, cleaning, caring for the bodies of children and men, and the routine material care of selves in sickness and in health. Accordingly, women's lives have been centered around domestic and caregiving tasks.

To the extent that women's lives are focused on household and family care, their lives are anchored in particular localities and social relations, for example, in their homes, neighborhoods, and relations to children and other women. Smith suggests, moreover, that women's values and views of the world express their unique social experiences. In other words, women have their own unique ways of knowing. When women think about social life they emphasize the concrete specificity of time, place, and social relations. For example, instead of speaking about human behavior in general, women might talk about the behavior of specific individuals or groups; instead of speaking about society in general, women will speak about social life as lived by actual people in specific places and times.

Smith argues that women's experiences, values, and ways of thinking have been, until recently, conspicuously absent from what passes as the dominant knowledges. For example, sociology may aspire to be the science of society, but it has not been the science of everyone. "Its method, conceptual schemes and theories [have] been based on and built up within the male social universe."[2] Sociology has been produced by and for men. From classical to contemporary sociology, men are treated as the chief actors, the movers and shakers of social life. Women have largely been excluded from its key perspectives; women's contributions to the making of society have been ignored. The chief topics of sociology reflect men's values and experiences, namely, the world of paid labor, politics, and formal organizations. Women's world of the household, children, sexual reproduction, affective ties, and voluntary work has been either neglected or marginalized. By making men's experiences and world view into the very nature of social experience and knowledge, sociology has contributed to erasing or devaluing women's distinctive experiences. By making a masculine sociology into general sociology, the discipline of sociology has served, perhaps unwittingly, as a vehicle for alienating women from their own lives.

Smith believes that sociology reflects the fact that men's lives have been centered in the public world of work and politics. Despite men's increased involvement in household tasks, the center of their lives in contemporary Western societies is the public world of big business, government, sports, and the military. Men hold the positions of power and privilege in the key institutions of society or what Smith calls the "relations of ruling."

It follows that men's values and social perspectives will be shaped by their public lives. And the public world, at least in Western societies, is organized around the importance of "objectified knowledges" associated with medical, psychiatric, demographic, or penal science. In contrast to everyday understandings of human behavior that speak of actual individuals in specific situations, objectified knowledges, from psychiatry to census and coroners' reports, abstract from the specifics of real living individuals to construct general identities and classifications of individuals and groups (e.g., by age, income, race, and gender). Men have taken over this abstract, impersonal way of thinking about the world; moreover, they have assumed that this type of abstract, impersonal reasoning is the very essence of rationality.

Since men have dominated sociology and the social sciences, their conceptual values – abstract ideas, generalization, objectivity, impersonality – have become dominant. Despite the fact that many sociologists see themselves as reformers, sociology has been part of a ruling order that benefits men as well as the propertied class and White Europeans. Like all ruling ideologies, sociology does not see its own ideological role. It fancies that its own ideas are rational. It considers the topics, problems, and conceptual strategies it prefers to be simply objective, as reflecting the structure of the social world. Sociology masks its gendered character by speaking abstractly of humanity, the individual, society, and moral agency, rather than of gendered selves, behaviors, and experiences. To acknowledge the deeply gendered organization of social life would reveal sociology's patriarchal character.

Smith wishes to expose sociology as a political enterprise. She wants a critical sociology that benefits women. Her feminist sociology aims to liberate women from male-dominated social orders.

What would a sociology look like that was produced by and for women? In contrast to a male-centered sociology that aspires to map abstract processes, a feminist sociology would begin with women as they find themselves in their actual lives. Women's particular local settings, social relations, and daily activities would be the starting point for social knowledge. Smith conceives of a feminist sociology modeled after the social realism of Marx. Marxism begins with real individuals with actual needs, located in specific times and places, and engaged in specific social relations. Social consciousness emerges in relation to actual social relations. For Smith, as for Marx, ideology describes a way of thinking in which ideas are separated from their social origins in the actions of real individuals. An ideological social view makes abstractions such as freedom, values, reason, mind, and attitudes the driving forces of society and history, while real individuals disappear. A human drama is acted out in which the movement of these abstract fictitious entities (e.g., reason, freedom, values) replace the daily, local, specific struggles of real living individuals.

Inspired by Marx's historical realism, Smith's starting point is women's actual lives:

Inquiry starts with the knower who is actually located; she is active; she is at work; she is connected with particular other people in various ways; she thinks, laughs, desires, sorrows, sings, curses, loves just here; she reads here; she watches television. Activities, feelings, experiences, hook her into extended social relations linking her activities to those of other people and in ways beyond her knowing ... The standpoint of women never leaves the actual. The knowing subject is always located in a particular spatial and temporal site, a particular configuration of the everyday/everynight world. Inquiry is directed towards exploring and explicating what she does not know – the social relations and organization pervading her world but invisible in it.[3]

A feminist sociology aims to recover the integrity of women's lives and to give them a critical voice.

Smith rejects the idea that feminist theory or sociology is mere political partisanship. The fact that all knowledge, including feminist sociology, is socially situated, does not mean that valid knowledge is impossible. Smith wishes to steer a middle course between objectivism and relativism. She refuses the idea of one true, comprehensive language of social reality. She is equally critical of the position that assumes that there is a near-infinite number of possible theories. Smith asserts that knowledge is both situational and objective. We can know society because we have created it. Sociology is always an "insider" sociology. Our categories of knowledge are expressive of the actual social organization of our lives. If sociology cannot produce a comprehensive theory, it can at least yield reliable knowledge of "how things work," which may prove useful for women in understanding the social conditions that shape and constrain their lives.

Smith's project is clear: a women-centered, feminist sociology. Her aim is to analyze how configurations of power shape women for the purpose of promoting a critical political awareness and practice. Smith imagines a feminist sociology that contributes to transforming women into social agents who purposefully make their own lives.

A feminist sociology underscores the centrality of gender inequality and women's oppression in society. Smith departs from other feminist theorists, for whom the source of women's oppression is a sex-role system, the family, the norm of heterosexuality, or a patriarchal state. Smith underscores a neglected but central mechanism of social domination: objectified knowledges and discourses.

Smith speaks very broadly of relations of ruling as including the government, big business, the professions, scientific, medical, and mass-media discourses, and the personnel involved in administering these institutions. Relations of ruling exhibit the intersection of male dominance, racism, and capitalism. It is not Smith's purpose to provide an institutional analysis of the interlocking dynamics of racism, sexism, and capitalism. Rather, she focuses on an underlying, common, and central feature of the relations of ruling in contemporary Western capitalist societies: the role of knowledge as a social force of domination.

In modern Western societies, social domination operates through texts, e.g., medical records, census reports, hospital records, psychiatric case studies, marriage records, and employment files. These texts facilitate social control. They create a world of individual and social types and impersonal processes that can be manipulated and controlled. Individuals appear as instances of a group or social type (e.g., the sick, mentally ill, unemployed, married, White, criminal, or disabled); social realities are framed as governed by impersonal processes (e.g., as an expression of "values," "attitudes," "illness," or "poverty"). The texts of rulership are characterized by their abstraction from real acting individuals in their particular social settings. Objectified knowledges translate real-life experiences into a language that is anonymous, impersonal, general, and objectifying.

By way of illustrating the substitution of "virtual realities" for actual realities, and the link between objectified knowledges and domination, Smith refers to the psychiatric discourse on "mental illness." Psychiatric discourses deploy a medical model of mental illness. This model asserts that, for reasons of nature or environment, some individuals become mentally ill. Illness is manifested in psychological or behavioral symptoms (e.g., depression, sadness, phobias) that impede "normal" functioning. The "mentally ill" find their way to a mental health practitioner and are diagnosed. This means inferring from symptoms (e.g., nervousness, anxiety, impotence, failures at work or love) an underlying mental disorder and prescribing a treatment. In the medical model, mental illness is discovered by the expert, appropriately labeled, and treated. Smith notes that many sociologists who analyze variations in mental illness by gender, race, or class rely on this model. Sociologists who depend upon the data provided by mental health practitioners routinely assume a correspondence between psychiatric categories of mental illness and reality.

Smith has grave doubts about this model. For example, she observes a bias towards associating mental illness with women. Many categories of "emotional distress" that are predominant among men are excluded from the category of mental illnesses, e.g., alcoholism or drug abuse. This has the social and political effect of viewing women as more unstable and vulnerable to mental illness and as more in need of medical and social supervision than men; it also follows that women are perceived as less able to fulfill social roles involving power, stress, and social responsibilities. In a word, psychiatric discourses position women as psychologically and socially inferior to men.

Smith raises doubts about the scientific status of the medical model. Psychiatric interventions do more than discover and treat a preexisting mental illness; they create it as a social identity and place the individual under institutional control. Smith doesn't deny that there are individuals who suffer from emotional distress; she challenges the validity of medicalizing distress and criticizes its social consequences. Smith underscores its stigmatizing and disempowering effects. Psychiatry takes away moral agency and responsibility from the individual and transforms the psychiatric self into an object of control. Let me explain.

An individual who is troubled experiences distress in specific ways. Personal distress may be linked to particular situations and persons, and is always experienced in the context of an individual's actual history. Personal distress does not necessarily define that individual's primary relation to the world. However, defining an individual as mentally ill may transform an individual's experience of self and world. The individual's actual life, his or her social bonds and history, are marginalized in psychiatric discourse and practice. Only the individual's symptomatic behavior is considered important and is interpreted in relation to an impersonal schema of normality and abnormality. The individual's actions are seen as symptomatic of a psychological abnormality or illness; the person loses the experience of herself as a responsible, knowledgeable social actor.

The psychiatric order marginalizes the individual's actual history and complex social life; he or she becomes a case history, psychological type, a cluster of symptoms, and an object of varied treatment strategies. In other words, the individual is lifted out of the actual context and meanings of his or her life, erasing agency, locality, specificity, and history. The person is placed in a different set of social relations – a world of patients, case histories, diagnoses, nurses, psychiatrists, insurance companies, and the state. Smith interprets psychiatry as an agency of social control aimed at defining and managing socially inappropriate behavior that cannot be managed by other agencies of control, e.g., prisons, hospitals, schools, and families.

To the extent that sociology relies on the texts of the relations of ruling (e.g., psychiatric discourses, census records, and crime statistics) for its social knowledge, it is part of this hegemonic order. Its subject matter and topics are those of the ruling powers. "Mental illness, crimes, riots, violence, work satisfaction, neighbors and neighborhoods, motivation, and so on – these are the constructs of the practice of government."[4] Sociology speaks the language of rulership. Its concepts and schemas are extralocal, general, and impersonal; its guiding concepts substitute abstract entities and processes (e.g., mind, values, attitudes, roles, and interests) for the actualities of lived experience. Sociological knowledge receives its shape less from the concerns and dilemmas of real individuals in their actual social relations than from the interests in control of the welfare state, professional associations, and bureaucracies.

Smith envisions an alternative sociology whose purpose is to challenge the relations of ruling. In particular, she imagines a feminist sociology that can transform society. Hers is a vision of sociology as a moral or critical inquiry into the everyday conditions of domination for the purpose of changing them.

DIFFERENCE FEMINISM: THE INTERSECTION OF GENDER, RACE, SEXUALITY, AND CLASS

From the vantage point of the mid-1970s, American feminists had good reason to be confident. Between 1972 and 1974, Congress passed the equal rights amendment as well as women's rights legislation covering employment, education, property, and marriage rights. The 1973 *Roe* v. *Wade* Supreme Court decision guaranteed women their reproductive rights. As mainstream feminism absorbed radical feminist concerns with issues of sexuality, healthcare, and violence towards women, the women's movement assumed an ideological unity that has since eluded it.

An antifeminist backlash had swung into full gear by the late 1970s. The New Right mounted a campaign against abortion rights which was translated into legislative successes. For example, the Hyde amendment, which cut off Medicaid funds for abortion, was passed in 1977. The equal rights amendment failed to attain the 38 state ratifications needed for its passage. Key parts of the feminist agenda, for example, national childcare, healthcare reform, and equal pay were stalled by the conservative gender politics of the New Right and the Reagan administration.

To make matters worse, in the face of a well-organized antifeminist campaign, the bonds of sisterhood were strained from within. Internal divisions over issues of lesbianism and race, dissent around whether to ally with the gay movement or the New

Left, and conflicts around political strategy and goals threatened to unravel the fragile bonds of feminist solidarity.

As the women's movement was threatened by internal discord and a rising tide of social backlash, there was a shift in feminist thinking in the late 1970s, a kind of hardening of gynocentric feminism. Many feminists rallied around a theory and politics that emphasized the sameness and goodness of women and the dangers associated with masculinity. Feminist perspectives highlighted the victimization of women by pornography, sex, rape, and physical violence. Men, rather than gender roles, were taken as the source of women's oppression. In Susan Griffin's *Rape*, Andrea Dworkin's *Our Blood*, and Susan Brownmiller's *Against Our Will*, women are viewed as victimized by a violent, uncontrollable male desire to dominate women.[5] Some feminists encouraged women to build their own community to protect and nourish a women's-centered culture against male values and violence.

This ideological celebration of the commonality and goodness of women and the dubious moral character of men found expression in feminist theory. Two of the most important feminist statements of the late 1970s and early 1980s were Nancy Chodorow's *The Reproduction of Mothering* and Carol Gilligan's *In a Different Voice*.[6] They underscored the psychological and moral differences between men and women. Moreover, Chodorow and Gilligan clearly championed women's empathetic, nurturing, and caring ways of relating over men's supposedly more impersonal, instrumental, and controlling patterns.

By the close of the 1970s, feminist theory increasingly emphasized gender difference and women's victimization. The appeal to the identity of women no longer meant invoking a shared state of oppression and resistance. Womanhood now referred to common psychological dispositions, social values, and ways of thinking and being.

This hardening of gynocentric feminism was eventually met with a critical response. As the claims to a common unified female identity grew louder, so too did the critics who underscored differences among women. By the early 1980s, dissenting voices could be heard by working-class women, Jewish women, postcolonial women, and differently abled women. Perhaps the most compelling criticisms of gynocentrism came from nonWhite women and sex rebels.

The leadership of the women's movement had been in the hands of White, middle-class, often university-educated women since the late 1960s. Questions of race and class had bothered feminists through the 1970s. Yet it was not until the early 1980s that women of color coalesced into an organized force to speak with a public voice that could no longer be silenced.

A new "radical women of color" perspective made its way into feminist public culture. These women criticized the women's movement for reflecting the experiences, values, and interests of White, middle-class women.[7] Gynocentric feminism was attacked for not speaking to the lives of women of color. For example, gender oppression for Black women was said to be inseparable from racial and class oppression. These interlocking systems of identity and oppression could not be separated. As the Combahee River Collective states: "We ... find it difficult to separate race from class from sex oppression because in our lives they are most often experienced simultaneously."[8]

Women of color insisted that gender cannot be isolated from racial or class identity. Women are always of a particular race and class. The social positioning of women of color is different in important ways from that of White, middle-class women. For example, only feminists who enjoy the privileges of (White) race and (middle-) class status could afford, economically and politically, to pursue a separatist agenda. Women of color experience not only gender, but racial and often class oppression; they need to forge bonds of solidarity with men to fight racism and classism.

Gynocentric feminism excluded or marginalized the lives of women who were not White or middle class. Women of color did not find their experience reflected in the images of women and in the vision of women's liberation that were dominant in the women's movement. Women of color found themselves oppressed by the very movement that claimed to promote their emancipation! As Audre Lorde, a leading voice of Black feminism, observed: "As white women ignore their built-in privilege of whiteness and redefine women in terms of their own experience alone, then Women of Color become 'other,' the outsider whose experience and tradition is too 'alien' to comprehend."[9] Feminists of color aimed to expand the category of woman to include them by viewing gender, race, and class as interconnected.

Gynocentric feminism received a second major challenge from sex radicals. The 1980s witnessed what some feminists have called the "sex wars." Lesbianism had long been an issue of feminist contention. The women's movement was frequently attacked for its presumed hidden lesbian agenda. Many feminists were uncomfortable with lesbianism. And feminists were divided over whether the women's movement was a sexual liberation movement.

The gynocentric feminism of the late 1970s assumed the essential sameness of women's experience to justify a particular concept of female sexuality. Gynocentric feminists asserted that men's and women's sexuality is essentially different. Appealing variously to nature, socialization, women's oppression or unique culture, women's sexuality was portrayed as person-centered, diffusely erotic, nurturing, loving, and monogamous. Male sexuality was described as body- and genital-centered, driven by pleasure and power, performance-oriented and promiscuous. Gynocentric feminists may have proposed this sexual theory to account for what they perceived as an epidemic of violence against women and as a way to energize the women's movement in the face of internal divisions and external backlash. Yet, this sexual theory policed women by establishing supposedly correct sexual values and norms. Women for whom sex was body- and pleasure-centered or involved role playing or pornography or included multiple partners, were stigmatized as deviant or as male-identified, and were viewed as alienated from their true female nature.

A gynocentric feminist sexual ethic and politics met with stiff opposition. For many feminists, the women's movement stood for sexual choice, diversity, and the affirmation of the body as a site of pleasure. Gynocentric feminists were accused of imposing upon women a prudish sexual ethic. Women whose sexual desires, values, and behaviors didn't conform were stigmatized. By the early 1980s, gynocentric feminists were on the defensive. Books such as *Powers of Desire*, *Pleasure and Danger*, and *Women Against Censorship*, defended erotic choice and variation.[10] The intent of these feminists was to bring sexual choice and diversity squarely under the umbrella of feminism.

Women of color did not intend to undermine the foundational status of the category of women. They wished to expand the range of legitimate identities that women could claim. They insisted that a common female identity varied along the axes of race and class. Thus, there would emerge a diversity of feminist standpoints (e.g., Black feminism or Latina feminism), each reflecting a distinctive racial and class positioning of women. While the intent of many women of color was to multiply the possible articulations of women's identities and politics, this strategy raised doubts about the very idea of a common female identity. If women differ by class or race, in what sense, if any, can we speak of the unity of women? Similarly, sex radicals intended to expand the range of legitimate sexual expression for women. However, if women's sexual experiences and values vary widely, does it make sense to speak of a common female sexuality?

POSTMODERN FEMINISM: JUDITH BUTLER

By the mid-1980s, feminism was becoming very messy. Gynocentric feminists asserting a common female identity and politics remained a forceful presence. But, new feminist identities had surfaced: women of color, working-class women, sadomasochistic lesbians, and postcolonial women. They attacked gynocentric feminists for their Eurocentric, middle-class, straight, White perspective. And, by the early 1990s, a new intellectual voice was being heard: postmodern feminism.

Postmodern feminists posed a broad challenge to the core premise of the women's movement: the idea that "women" refers to a shared essence or common identity that forms the necessary basis of feminist knowledge and politics. They raise doubts about appealing to "women" as the foundation of the women's movement on the grounds that such a concept is incoherent, excludes certain women, and creates norms of the good woman.

Postmodern feminists assert that gender identity is not fixed, either by nature or by society. There is no core gender identity based on common psychological dispositions, cultural values, or social positioning that neatly marks off women from men. Gender always bears multiple, conflicting, and shifting meanings; it is a site of ongoing social conflict. In place of appealing to a pure idea of women or female gender identity to organize knowledge and politics, postmodern feminists favor using multiple categories of identification such as White, middle-class, heterosexual, twenty-first-century women; ultimately, it is practical, intellectual, or political reasons that determine

Judith Butler was born in Cleveland, Ohio, in 1957. She received her doctorate in philosophy from Yale in 1984. Butler has taught at the Wesleyan and Johns Hopkins Universities. She is currently at the University of California at Berkeley where she is Maxine Eliot Professor of Comparative Literature and Rhetoric. Butler's key idea is that we are not born men or women (or male or female). nor is it merely a matter of learning to become men or women. Rather, we learn how to act as if we are men or women. Gender identity is performed.

which categories of identity will be included and excluded. Accordingly, postmodern feminists argue that there is no escaping the multiplicity and instability of feminist knowledges and politics.

Postmodern feminism often draws on poststructural approaches to language as a system of signs whose coherence rests upon internal relations of difference. From this perspective, "women" acquires meaning only in its contrasting relation to "men" in a particular language system. The meanings of signs, including those of women and men, are unstable, multivocal, and subject to contestation. Since individuals are positioned differently with respect to the multiple axes (gender, class, race, sexuality) of social hierarchy, the meaning of gender will vary and signs will exhibit a surplus of meanings. Moreover, the signs, women and men, will serve as a site of social conflict to the extent that gender is an axis of social stratification. For example, defining women as intuitive, nurturing, and maternal in contrast to men who are described as rational, ego- and goal-oriented positions the former in socially subordinate roles, e.g., caretaker, support and service functions. From a poststructural standpoint, gender identity is an unstable and shifting site of meaning and contestation. Efforts to fix gender identity once and for all are seen as political.

Postmodern feminists do not claim that gender is an illusion. Instead, paralleling Foucault's reversal of the relation between sexuality and sex, some postmodern feminists assert that gender is an effect of a discourse of dichotomous gender identities. Discourses (e.g., science and popular culture) and social practices (e.g., law, acts of violence, and the institution of heterosexuality) that imagine humans as opposing gendered types – women or men – do not mirror an objective reality, nor do they create mutually exclusive masculine and feminine selves. They do, however, produce cultural codes and social norms that carry public authority. To the extent that these gender norms are enforced in families, churches, the mass media and the social sciences, they shape our lives. We imagine ourselves in their images; if they do not serve as mirrors of ourselves, they function as templates that guide our behavior. We project our gender identity through our actions, thereby reinforcing conventional gender norms.

A postmodern turn didn't occur simply because it was intellectually compelling. Feminist politics in the 1990s seemed at an impasse. Gynocentric feminism may indeed have promoted internal solidarity but at the cost of silencing differences and creating divisions. With its notions of multiple, composite identities, postmodern feminists hope to encourage alliances among women and between feminists and other movements. They wish to break down the insularity of identity-based communities in order to facilitate the building of broad-based, politically effective coalitions.

The most original and compelling statement of postmodern feminism is that of Judith Butler. In *Gender Trouble*, Butler intends to undermine the credibility of the appeal to women as a secure basis of feminist theory and politics.[11] She maintains that the idea of women sharing a common gender identity may be enabling for feminism but it also misrepresents women's lives and constrains the possibilities of gender politics. Indeed, Butler calls attention to the ways in which feminism has unintentionally reinforced the binary gender order that it has often criticized. In place of the feminist project of forging a general theory of women's oppression and liberation, Butler imagines a "critical genealogy of gender." Its aim is to analyze the social production of gender and its entanglement in a system of male dominance and heterosexuality. She wishes to challenge the idea of a unitary gender identity for the purpose of opening up new possibilities for sexual and gender politics.

Despite the variations in women's lives, feminists have assumed that a coherent gender identity exists. Invoking women as the subject of history and knowledge has seemed necessary, moreover, to promote the political empowerment of women. Butler does not deny the political value of deploying the category of women in light of a history of women's invisibility and disempowerment. Feminism seems to be caught in a dilemma. On the one hand, there is the apparent necessity to invoke the category of women to resist male dominance. On the other hand, every appeal to "women" and every effort to specify the meaning of female gender identity has the effect of excluding and disempowering some women.

Feminists have reacted to this dilemma by urging a variety of strategies, for example, multiplying gender identities but assuming an overarching commonality, or acknowledging the fiction of the category of women but deploying it for political reasons. Butler urges that feminism abandon a strong claim of gender identity as a basis for feminist theory and politics. Many feminists have already concluded that there is no way to state what a woman is without excluding and stigmatizing some women. Butler asks: what political possibilities are denied in the appeal to women as the foundation for feminism? What would feminism look like if it surrendered the foundational status of women without giving up the category of women?

The idea of a core gender identity is basic to modern Western societies. It has been assumed not only by feminists but by men and women who defend the notion of a binary feminine and masculine identity. The view of men and women as two distinct, opposite human types is so vigorously enforced by custom and law that this belief suggests an unconscious political force at work. Is there some social power operating, seemingly behind our backs, which compels us to think of our bodies and behaviors in terms of a grid of fixed, antithetical gender identities? Butler interprets the unconscious compulsion enforcing the production of a binary gender order to be a system of compulsory heterosexuality. Making humans into two opposite gender types, each with its own unique physical, psychic, and social nature, and each imagined as incomplete without the other, naturalizes and normalizes a system of heterosexuality. The pressure to claim a unitary gender identity driven by the taboo against homosexuality is suggested by the compulsion we all feel to exhibit heterosexual desire as proof of a normal gender identity. Linking a binary gender order to a regime of male-dominated heterosexuality provides Butler with a critical standpoint towards gender and sexual politics.

A system of heterosexuality may underpin the making of binary gender identities, but it does not explain the everyday dynamics of gender. In this regard, Butler proposes a performative theory of gender. I will review this theory in the broader context of feminist discussions of gender.

Butler advances a general claim about gender as a social fact. Of course, virtually all feminists believe that gender is social, not natural. However, most feminists propose a fairly limited social explanation of gender. They assume that humans are, by nature, born either female or male, an assumption shared by many nonfeminists. Through a social process, females and males become women and men. Feminists depart from nonfeminists, first, in the claim that society, not nature, explains the shape of women's and men's lives. Second, feminists claim that gender identities are formed in a manner that illegitimately gives men power over women. However, at least some feminists have not questioned the assumption, commonplace in Western cultures, that there exist two, antithetical sexed (female and male) and gendered selves (women and men). These feminists have not challenged the idea that gender identity is an essential defining core of the self that can explain behavior, including male dominance and women's resistance.

Feminists and nonfeminists alike may dispute the relative importance of social and natural forces in producing gender and disagree over the legitimacy of gender hierarchy, but until recently there has been little discord around the belief that humanity divides into two opposing human types: women and men. Feminists have sought to explain how females and males become women and men in a way that perpetuates men's dominance. Despite its critical politics, feminism is entangled in the maintenance of the very binary gender order that it wishes to alter or abolish.

Butler believes that feminism must give up the notion of a core gender identity. Appeals to women's unitary identity are not only incoherent but unintentionally contribute to reproducing the binary gender order and a system of compulsory heterosexuality. Instead of charting the social production of "women" and "men" as unitary gendered selves, Butler proposes that we imagine gender as a performance which is susceptible to subversion and disruption. Let me explain.

Feminists have viewed gender as a social accomplishment. Individuals are born female and male but become women and men. Becoming a woman means adopting a core feminine identity which, in turn, forms the basis for women's actions. For example, feminists might refer to women's unique psychology or social status to explain their specific approach to sex and love. An influential feminist account of behavior that appeals to gender identity is Nancy Chodorow's *The Reproduction of Mothering*. Chodorow wishes to explain how mothering is reproduced over generations. She assumes that the decision to become a mother cannot be entirely explained by social learning or coercion. Her explanation is that females acquire a feminine gender identity that functions as a kind of psychological force driving them to become mothers. Chodorow uses an object relations psychoanalytical model. Girls identify with their mothers; they internalize their mothers as ideals of who they want to be. Girls become mothers because, in a sense, their mothers are lodged within their psyche. To be a mother is part of who they are as feminine selves. In other words, mothering behavior is viewed as an expression of a socially acquired feminine gender identity.

A critique of Chodorow from the standpoint of Butler's performative theory is instructive. Butler challenges Chodorow's story of gender identity. The meaning of identification and internalization is considered. In this regard, Butler argues that children do not identify with actual persons but with fantasies or idealizations of them. Children's identifications, moreover, are multiple, often conflicting. Girls might identify with their mothers but also with their older sisters or an aunt or best friend. Children identify with both men and women and absorb these idealized gendered figures in contradictory ways. Furthermore, Butler has doubts about the idea of internalization. Do we really internalize our idealized images of others, as if these significant others get lodged in some deep psychic space within us? Butler argues that, if our idealized gender images are "absorbed," it is the surface of our bodies, not some imagined inner psychic terrain, which is the arena of gender enactment. Rather than characterize gender as an inner core of the self that drives behavior, Butler reverses this imagery: gender is a learned, situational performance whose dramatic effect is the illusion of an inner gendered self.

Butler proposes a performative theory of gender. Neither nature nor society produces core gendered selves, if by that we mean an organizing psychic center of women's and men's lives. The idea of women and men as unitary contrasting selves is an illusion created by our repeated gender performances. Just as we learn to use language situationally, we learn how to "act" as if we are women or men. Through imitation, a system of rewards and sanctions, and our command of cultural and linguistic conventions, we learn to stylize our bodies and gestures, dress, walk, and talk, and use grooming and grammar to project ourselves as women or men. If the surface of our bodies exhibits the stereotyped traits of masculinity and femininity, our behavior is seen as expressing our authentic gendered selves. There is, though, no true self that guides our behavior. Our gender performances are modeled after idealizations or fantasies of what it means to be a woman or man that are embodied in dominant cultural representations. In other words, gender is in the realm of symbol and power. Representations of gender identity may be fictitious but they are not socially and politically innocent. The illusion of a core feminine and masculine gender identity conceals the social and political forces that fashion humans into sexed, gendered, and sexualized selves; it conceals the role of gender identity in the regulation of our sexuality, in particular, in the perpetuation of the institution of reproductive heterosexuality.

Approaching gender as a performance has far-reaching implications for feminist theory and politics. Butler marks off her own project of "critical genealogy" from the gynocentric project. The latter aims to develop theories of the formation of gender identity, sexism, and male dominance. Critical genealogy aspires to reveal the illusion of gender as an inner truth of the self, and to identify the social forces that produce this illusion. Postmodern feminist analyses of discourses and social practices aim to show how they produce naturalistic images of the body, sex, gender identity, and sexuality that conceal the link of gender to a male-dominated regime of reproductive heterosexuality. Subverting constructions of gender identity becomes the task of a critical feminist genealogy. Butler envisions parody as a key strategy of gender subversion. She refers to "drag" as exemplary of its subversive potential since cross-dressing spotlights disjunctions between anatomical sex and gender identity and, Butler believes, reveals the social, imitative character of gender. Gender subversion aims to denaturalize the body, sex, gender, and sexuality for the purpose of exposing their social and political construction. Echoing the poststructural celebration of play and resistance as subversion, Butler imagines gender subversion as creating alternative ways of being embodied, sexed, gendered, and sexualized.

Butler is not proposing to replace a feminist politics of social equality with a politics of identity subversion. Her performative theory of gender aims to displace "women" as the foundation of feminist politics. If the self is produced in the very act of doing, if there is no "doer behind the deed," feminism cannot assert a unitary identity, "women," in whose name it speaks and acts. Deconstructing women as a category of identity does not mean doing away with "women," but making this category permanently open to contestation and to new social and political deployments:

> I would argue that ... "identity" as a point of departure can never hold as the solidifying ground of a feminist political movement. Identity categories are ... always normative, and as such, exclusionary. This is not to say that the term "women" ought not to be used ... On the contrary, if feminism presupposes that "women" designates an undesignatable field of differences, one that cannot be ... summarized by a descriptive identity category, then the very term becomes a site of permanent openness ... To deconstruct the subject of feminism is not then to censure its usage, but, on the contrary, to release the term into a future of multiple significations, ... to give it play as a site where unanticipated meanings might come to bear.[12]

Making women the site of conflicting meanings creates new possibilities for politics. For example, Butler's own provocative disjoining of sex and gender, and bridging of sexuality and gender, creates potentially new social alliances, for example, between feminists, lesbians and gay men, between feminists and sex radicals or minorities struggling around body norms.

The postmodern subversion of gender identity has been troubling to many feminists. If feminists abandon the idea of a common bond of womanhood, what will be the basis for gender politics? Doesn't feminism need a unitary image of women to create solidarity? Don't women need affirmative, even celebratory, images of themselves to offset their devaluation in the male-dominated cultural mainstream? What social vision of liberation will mobilize women to make social changes? Granted, postmodernists may speak of affinities of interest or coalitional subjects, but this talk is maddeningly vague and abstract, say critics of postmodern feminists. Moreover, is it not suspicious that, at the moment when women find a public and empowering voice, they are, once again, being denied their identity? Is not the idea of women as a fiction, a normative political category, precisely the claim made by critics of feminism?

Many feminists are reluctant to surrender an identity-based politic. The appeal to "women" has functioned as the cornerstone for fashioning an affirmative identity, community, and politics for nearly three decades. Many feminists have built their lives around women's communities and the symbolism of sisterhood. Feminists are not alone in resisting the postmodern turn. African-American intellectuals have been resistant to relinquishing racial identity as the basis of knowledge and politics. It is noteworthy, in this regard, that many African-American feminists have been decidedly cool toward postmodernism or at least toward the abandonment of identity categories as the foundation of their theorizing and politics. African-American intellectuals have, in the main, rejected the postmodern subversion of identity in favor of a variety of Afrocentric social perspectives. However, the instability of the category of "African-American" has given rise to African-American theory that moves on a postmodern terrain.

THEORIZING MASCULINITY

Men were not a focus of theorizing outside of feminism. They may have been, as feminists argue, the rulers of most societies; it may also have been true that they were written as the main actors in the drama of history and society; and, it may also have been the case, as feminists claim, that many of us understood human behavior and social life from a masculine perspective. Still, until the second wave of feminism in the 1960s and after, there was not a deliberate effort to theorize men and masculinity. The study of how individuals become men, how men become rulers, and how norms of masculinity are created and enforced was absent in modern social thinking. if you read the history of European and American sociology from the classics to the 1960s, except for a few feminists, there is no sociology of masculinity; indeed, there is little by way of a sociology of gender.

This changed with the rise of feminism and its impact in contemporary social thought. Feminism not only had a theory that explained women, but feminists provided a social account of the making of men. Feminism inaugurated the social study of men and masculinity.

What exactly did feminists have to say about men? Speaking in broad terms, feminists made several key claims.

Men are not born but socially created. Individuals may be born male but they learn and are pressured, sometimes coerced, into assuming a masculine self-identity. Males learn what behaviors and social roles are appropriate for men. Boys learn to be men by being taught and rewarded for gender appropriate behavior – and criticized for gender deviant behavior.

Learning to become a man means learning to exercise power. Men are socialized to adopt personality traits, values, and behaviors that motivate and enable them to assume power; boys grow up with a sense of entitlement and aspire to be in roles of authority. Boys learn, and this is repeatedly reinforced as adults, that a man must be decisive, in

Australian sociologist **Raewyn Connell** was born in 1944 and was educated at the University of Melbourne and the University of Sydney, where she received her doctorate. She has taught at universities in Australia and the United States. She currently teaches at the University of Sydney, Australia. Influenced by feminist theories of gender, Connell focuses on masculinity. She argues that ideas about what constitutes masculinity are culturally specific. Masculinities are always understood in relation to notions of femininity. If women are seen as weak, passive, and emotional, then men are supposed to be strong, aggressive, and rational. Moreover, ideas about masculinity interact with other important markers of social identity such as race, class, and sexuality, producing different masculinities. Some masculinities are privileged over others so that even among men there is a gender hierarchy.

control, goal directed, aggressive and successful, where success is defined in terms of wealth and social power. In short, men are psychologically shaped to be rulers.

But also, and equally important, men become rulers because social roles involving power are associated with masculinity. Feminists argue that the notion of gender helps us to understand not only the shape of our personal lives but also social roles and organizations. Certain occupations and social positions are defined as masculine or feminine or as appropriate for either men or women. And, considerable authority and prestige are attached to masculine roles. Think, for example, of roles that carry social authority: President, Senator, CEO, General, media executive, or surgeon. While there may be some women executives or CEOs (not many, according to the research), these roles are most definitely associated with masculinity (decisiveness, control, aggressiveness, toughness, performance, or goal orientation). Men are expected to occupy these positions and, in fact, overwhelmingly do. The masculine gendering of roles of power and prestige partly accounts for why men are socially dominant.

Men rule and, like all powerful groups, they resort to various strategies to maintain power. They use coercion, violence, and harassment, as the reality of rape and violence sadly reveals. Men will try to maintain strict boundaries between men and women by restricting masculine behavior and roles to men. Women are pressured to adopt feminine behaviors and roles; men are under considerable pressure to avoid feminine social roles and behaviors. Individuals who violate these gender norms and boundaries will suffer disapproval and worse. For example, women who are too masculine, too career oriented or socially aggressive, and men who are too feminine or occupy feminine typed roles may be labeled homosexual. Homophobia is a chief way in which men preserve the privileges of masculinity. There are, however, costs to men, say feminists. Masculinity may give a clear edge to men in the competition for public success but often this comes at the cost of being alienated from emotionally rich intimate ties that are the stuff of personal happiness.

Feminism made the social explanation of men and masculinity into a focus of study. In the 1970s and 1980s, social scientists, historians, and social theorists turned to the analysis of men as well. These scholars took over the key features of the feminist view, in particular, a social explanation of men's roles, an approach that emphasized masculinity as both an individual identity and a feature of social organizations (e.g. the state, bureaucracies, the workplace, schools), and an emphasis on men's social dominance. However, the new masculinity studies took issue with feminist views of men as ahistorical, essentialist (the idea that men's nature is more or less fixed), and stereotypical.

Let me try to summarize some of the key ideas of recent views of men and masculinity.

First, feminists are criticized to the extent that they are nonhistorical. For example, some feminists view men and the meaning of masculinity as essentially the same throughout history. Thus, feminists often understand men as hypersexual and pleasure-driven or fundamentally motivated to exercise power over women. By contrast, the new masculinity studies point to changes in men's character and social roles. For example, there is a big difference between the masculine styles of middle-class nineteenth-century agrarian America and those of twenty-first-century urban industrial life. In the former, the self-made man whose success was achieved through physical toil and frugality served as a kind of icon of masculinity. In the latter, the industrial tycoon exemplified an ideal of a man's man. And the tycoon was a man who relied on financial deal making and flagged his success through conspicuous consumption. Or, consider changes in men's social roles. Scholars have documented that the male breadwinner role was not part of American culture until the midto-late nineteenth century. Prior to that time, women often played a key economic role either inside or outside the household. And aren't we now witnessing a weakening of that role in the United States or Britain? Men are still career oriented but women are also expected to be wage earners, and it is hardly unusual for a woman to be the higher earner in a household.

Second, feminists are taken to task to the extent that they speak of men as if they all share basically the same mentality and motivations. By contrast, the new scholars underscore the diversity among men. There isn't one norm of being a man or one ideal of masculinity. Ideas of masculinity vary depending on social class, race, ethnicity, sexual identity, religion, and so on. For example, upper-income white collar men may emphasize educational credentials, intellectual work, and participation in high culture as markers of masculinity. By contrast, whereas lower-income, blue collar men lean on physical strength and labor or their breadwinner role in order to signal their manhood. For these men, managerial or professional men whose work is primarily intellectual or social are low on the scale of masculinity. Or, to take another example, American men are today divided regarding the place of parenting in their concept of manhood. For a very long time in Europe and America, caregiving, parenting roles were squarely women's work. But today some men are claiming parenting as a core part of being a man. If parenting were to become a defining gender practice for men, this would be a dramatic change, for caregiving forms of parenting involve traits such as nurturing, patience, emotional play, and empathy, which have been considered appropriate only for women.

Third, feminists crafted social perspectives that pitted men against women as a conflict between the powerful and the powerless. Recent scholars, however, underscore divisions and conflicts among men. As Raewyn Connell, a leading gender theorist, says: "To recognize diversity in masculinities is not enough. We must also recognize the relations between the different kinds of masculinity: relations of alliance, dominance and subordination … This is a gender politics within masculinity."[13]

As Connell goes on to say, every society has a dominant or a "hegemonic" type of masculinity. Those men and their masculine styles associated with roles of power exercise social dominance. That is, men who occupy positions of power and possess great wealth and prestige play a dominant role in relation to both women and other men. Moreover, the masculine traits or behaviors that are associated with these men of power are also hegemonic. For example, a certain look or style of talk, dress, and consumption may be considered the most valued or respected form of masculinity. Men who exhibit these traits or styles, even if they do not themselves occupy positions of power, gain respect and authority as men – in relation to women and to other men. These masculine styles, perhaps a certain type of suit or style of grooming or cultural taste, are idealized in the media, and these individual men of power are championed as popular icons or heroes.

In the context of World War II and subsequently the Cold War in the 1950s, America looked to men who exhibited martial traits. Men who were strong, decisive, action-oriented, fiercely loyal, dependable, and certain of their beliefs and values stepped forward as heroic figures. Think of the iconic status of President Eisenhower, General Patton, or John Wayne.

Fourth, the notion of hegemonic masculinity assumes that there are hierarchies among men. Being a man does not automatically make one a social ruler. True, men, all men, may be in positions of dominance in relation to women by virtue of the higher social prestige and authority attached to masculinity, but even here, lower-income men or men whose masculine styles are devalued may not necessarily be in a position of dominance over all women. Think of the status of an effeminate gay man in relation to a professional, gender-conventional woman. Who has more power or prestige? And, men who do not occupy positions of power and prestige or do not exhibit the behaviors or styles of hegemonic masculinity are dominated by men who do. For example, a man may be a blue collar low-income earner, yet if he exhibits stereotypically hegemonic masculine behaviors he may still claim the respect and status of hegemonic men. That is, he may gain respect among men and exercise authority over women and over men who do not exhibit hegemonic masculine styles. At the lower end of the masculine hierarchy are men who occupy low-income jobs or low-status roles, men who are disabled and effeminate. Stereotypically, gay men have represented a debased masculine status. They are said to deviate from the masculine norm of heterosexuality and they are stereotypically associated with femininity. Despite the considerable weakening of these stereotypes in the United States and elsewhere, hegemonic forms of masculinity are still closely tied to heterosexuality. Think for a moment of political, military, or corporate leaders. How many of them are openly gay?

Finally, the new scholars of masculinity theorize gender, both feminine and masculine, as a social practice. Instead of approaching gender as a fixed status or condition or as something one is (for example, an identity one has internalized growing up), it is viewed in more processual, performative terms, as something one does. Connell writes: "Gender is not fixed in advance of social interaction but is constructed in interaction . . . Rather than treat these pre-existing [gender] norms which are passively internalized in interaction, the new research explores the making and remaking of [gender] conventions in social practice itself."[14] Approaching gender as a social practice suggests viewing gender meanings, norms, and identities as somewhat unstable or open and fluid; fixity, stability, and coherence are achieved in the context of actions, social reactions, sometimes conflict. For example, when boys start to play baseball they must learn the rules and skills to play the game. They also learn which behavioral styles (language, dress, posture, facial expression) gain them respect as a boy. A boy's masculine style is fashioned by watching others, by observing which boys are popular or are leaders and by the way others react to their own behavior. There is then a convergence between men's studies and current feminist theory which emphasizes the performative character of gender.

Suggested Readings

Estelle Freedman, *No Turning Back* (New York: Ballantine, 2002)
Beverly Guy-Sheftall, ed., *Words of Fire: An Anthology of African-American Feminist Thought* (New York: New Press, 1995)
bell hooks, *Feminist Theory* (Boston, MA: South End Press, 2000)
Rosemarie Tong, *Feminist Thought* (Boulder, CO: Westview, 1998)

References

1 Dorothy Smith, *The Conceptual Practices of Power: A Feminist Sociology of Knowledge* (Boston, MA: Northeastern University Press, 1990), p. 32. See also Dorothy Smith, *The Everyday World as Problematic: A Feminist Sociology* (Boston, MA: Northeastern University Press, 1987), and Dorothy Smith, *Texts, Facts, and Femininity: Exploring the Relations of Ruling* (New York: Routledge, 1990).

2 Smith, *The Conceptual Practices of Power*, p. 23.

3 Dorothy Smith, "Sociology from Women's Experience: a Reaffirmation," *Sociological Theory* 10 (Spring 1992), p. 91.

4 Smith, *The Conceptual Practices of Power*, p. 15.

5 Susan Griffin, *Rape* (New York: Harper & Row, 1979); Andrea Dworkin, *Our Blood* (New York: Harper & Row, 1976); Susan Brownmiller, *Against Our Will* (New York: Bantam, 1976).

6 Nancy Chodorow, *The Reproduction of Mothering* (Berkeley, CA: University of California Press 1987); Carol Gilligan, *In a Different Voice* (Cambridge, MA: Harvard University Press, 1982).

7 See Audre Lorde, *Sister Outsider*, (Freedom CA: Crossing Press, 1984); Angela Davis, *Women, Race, and Class* (New York: Random House, 1981); Cherrie Moraga, *Loving in the War Years* (Boston, MA: South End Press, 1983); Gloria Anzaldua and Cherrie Moraga, eds., *This Bridge Called My Back* (New York: Kitchen Table Press, 1981).

8 Combahee River Collective, "A Black Feminist Statement," in Zillah Eisenstein, ed., *Capitalist Patriarchy and the Case for Socialist Feminism* (New York: Monthly Review Press, 1978).

9 Lorde, *Sister Outsider*.

10 Ann Snitow, Christine Stansell, and Sharon Thompson, eds., *Powers of Desire* (New York: Monthly Review Press, 1983); Carole Vance, ed., *Pleasure and Danger* (Boston, MA: Routledge & Kegan Paul, 1984); Varda Burstyn, ed., *Women Against Censorship* (Toronto: Douglas & McIntyre, 1985); Feminist Anti-Censorship Task Force, *Caught Looking* (Seattle, WA: The Real Comet Press, 1986).

11 Judith Butler, *Gender Trouble: Feminism and the Subversion of Identity* (New York: Routledge, 1989).

12 Judith Butler, "Contingent Foundations: Feminism and the Question of Postmodernism," in *Feminists Theorize the Political*, ed. Judith Butler and Joan Scott (New York: Routledge, 1992), pp. 15–16.

13 Raewyn Connell, *Masculinities* (Berkeley: University of California Press, 1995), p. 37.

14 Connell, *Masculinities*, p. 35.

15

Critical Race Theory/White Studies

AFRICAN-AMERICAN SOCIAL THOUGHT: BETWEEN AFROCENTRISM AND POSTMODERNISM

Postwar Black politics, like the women's movement, was a response to the failed promise of autonomy and equality among Blacks in postwar America. Rising expectations for the good life and social justice were dampened by the reality of racism and sexism. Between the two movements, however, there were major differences. The women's movement was primarily driven by White, middle-class women who were responding to the contradictions between their growing social, educational, and economic opportunities and their sustained political subordination and cultural positioning as inferior. The Black movement was a movement by the poor, the working class, and an aspiring, but still marginal, stratum of educated Blacks who were inspired by promises and hope, with little reality of social progress.

The Black movement was divided. In the South, the movement took the form of a struggle to tear down a state-enforced, racially based caste system. Fighting laws and social customs that sustained racial segregation and that denied them equal rights and opportunities, Blacks struggled for civil rights and social equality. There wasn't a rigid racial caste system in the North. However, Blacks encountered a system of segregation enforced by racism and political economic powerlessness. They faced the devastation of Black institutions and traditions that followed their northern migration and their "ghettoization" in America's cities. Northern Blacks generated a distinctive movement: Black power. Where the civil rights movement emphasized equal rights, opportunities, and integration, the Black power movement was nationalistic and radical. Leaders such as Huey Newton, Eldridge Cleaver, Imamu Amiri Baraka, Angela Davis, and Stokey Carmichael emphasized racial pride and unity; they held that racism was institutionalized and not merely a matter of attitudes or laws, and they appealed

Contested Knowledge: Social Theory Today, Fifth Edition. Steven Seidman.
© 2013 John Wiley & Sons, Ltd. Published 2013 by John Wiley & Sons, Ltd.

to a history of racism and to shared African-American traditions to assert their racial unity. The assertion of an affirmative African-American identity would form the foundation for an ethnic nationalist community and politics.

Feminism and Black power are, despite their differences, both identity-based political movements. They invoke a shared social identity as the basis of community and politics. However, their fate as identity political movements has varied. Gynocentric feminism came under severe criticism for its exclusionary politics; contemporary feminism has placed the issue of differences among women at the center of its theory and politics. There has been decidedly less dissatisfaction over a unitary race-based foundation in the African-American movement. Indeed, by the mid-1980s, the ethnic nationalism of Black power had passed into an Afrocentric philosophy that celebrated a common African-American identity. Yet, Afrocentrism, like gynocentrism, has created splits and divisions among race theorists. And, just as the politics of difference in feminism were played out in postmodernism, there have been efforts to bring postmodern themes into an Afrocentric paradigm. I take Molefi Asante as representing a standpoint of Afrocentrism that is critical of the Eurocentrism of the Enlightenment tradition while in other respects remaining within it. I interpret Patricia Hill Collins as intending an Afrocentrism that absorbs the politics of difference without surrendering identity as the foundation. In the recent work of bell hooks, Cornell West and Kwame Anthony Appiah, I see a movement towards a postmodern race theory.[1] In the concluding section, I introduce the rise of a new focus of race theory: White studies.

AFROCENTRISM: MOLEFI KETE ASANTE

By the late 1970s, the African-American struggles for social justice were stymied. Indeed, from affirmative action programs to Head Start and minority scholarships, the gains of the preceding two decades were under attack. Many Blacks perceived a resurgence of public racism in cities and campuses across the country. With the growing public authority of the New Right and neoconservatism, Blacks were, once again, being blamed for their own oppression as family instability, drug use, and welfare dependency were said to be the chief sources of their plight. As the White and Black middle classes fled the inner city, along with government and private aid, many Black communities were left devastated. The election of Ronald Reagan, whose administration was frankly hostile to civil rights legislation, reinforced the perception of the period as one of retreat for Black Americans.

In this social context of anti-Black backlash, some African-Americans called for an ethic of self-reliance and individualism; others redoubled their political efforts to publicize Black victimization through racism; still others sought to emphasize the creation of a culture of ethnic nationalist pride and community building. The latter response was advocated by a Black middle class that had achieved a level of socioeconomic security without the commensurate cultural status. Middle-class Black Americans continued to be culturally devalued despite their class position. The message of Black ethnic pride was also well received in poor Black communities that were devastated by drugs, unemployment, violence, and a sense of hopelessness. Paralleling the popular movement to

Molefi Kete Asante was born in Valdosa, Georgia, in 1942. He was educated at Pepperdine University and the University of California at Los Angeles, where he received his doctorate in 1968. He has taught at the State University of New York at Buffalo and at Temple University. Asante is perhaps the leading theorist of Afrocentrism. This perspective holds that the African experience has produced its own unique values and social perspectives. Eurocentrism and Afrocentrism are considered two distinct and contrasting but equally valid world views. But, questions have been raised about whether it is legitimate to speak of "Africa" or "Europe" as if they represent one coherent idea. France and Germany may be part of the continent of Europe, but in what sense should they be understood as expressions of the same civilization?

redefine Blacks as African-Americans, a people with their own history and culture, some academics were advancing an African-centered philosophy. Afrocentrism may be understood as part of a broader movement to counter the perception of Black inferiority by affirming a sense of racial and ethnic national pride.

Molefi Kete Asante has been a key figure in the fashioning of an Afrocentric social theory. In *Afrocentricity*, he sketched Afrocentrism as a broad philosophy and program of community building and activism.[2] *The Afrocentric Idea* explores Afrocentrism as a critique of the social sciences and as an alternative paradigm of social knowledge.[3]

Afrocentrism approaches knowledge from the standpoint of African traditions. Social perspectives that express African values have been excluded or marginalized in the popular and academic culture of the West. In the scientific disciplines in American and European societies, "Eurocentric" paradigms of knowledge are dominant and often imposed as universal. Eurocentrism pervades the popular culture of the West, which reinforces the public invisibility and devaluation of African-centered ideas and experiences. Asante describes the Eurocentrism of American culture as a form of cultural colonization of African-Americans. Indeed, "symbolic imperialism, rather than institutional racism, is said to be the major social problem facing multicultural societies".[4] Symbolic imperialism alienates African-Americans from their own community; it aims to minimize their social discontent by assimilating African-Americans into White, European culture. Afrocentrism provides Africans with perspectives and traditions that are self-empowering because they reflect their true cultural heritage.

Asante contrasts Eurocentrism and Afrocentrism as distinct, equally valid, cultural traditions. Eurocentrism is said to express an Anglo-European civilization. Eurocentrism is central to Western knowledge from ancient Greek thought to the era of the modern sciences. Eurocentrism is characterized as dualistic (e.g., mind/body, reason/emotion, culture/nature), linear (e.g., evolutionism), and materialistic. By contrast, Afrocentrism is anchored in early African civilizations. Afrocentrism places African experience at the center of its view of the world. Asante argues that, despite the diversity of African cultures, there is a core African identity. It is apparent in Africa and in the African diaspora. Afrocentrism emphasizes holistic approaches to knowledge and society; it values harmony, unity, and spiritualism.

Asante does not deny the value of Eurocentrism in its Western context. He objects to its claims to be valid in all societies and to the imposition of European-based values and perspectives on non-Western peoples. At times, Western cultural ethnocentrism is obvious, as in the case of European societies transplanting their culture, along with their economic or military might, in foreign lands. More often, Eurocentric cultural colonization is more subtle. For example, to the extent that the dominant paradigms of knowledge in the West (e.g., social sciences, philosophy, or literary theory) assume that Western culture and institutions are superior, non-Western ways of knowing are ignored or interpreted as socially backward or "primitive." Eurocentric arrogance obliterates African traditions or renders them inferior. As Eurocentrism pervades the social sciences, they unwittingly perpetuate the oppression of non-Western peoples. An Afrocentric perspective challenges Western symbolic imperialism and aims to give a critical voice to African people.

Asante's Afrocentrism appeals to a unitary African identity as its foundation. Although he acknowledges that there are diverse African traditions, he believes that a core set of values and traditions underlies an African identity. Repudiating biological notions of race as the basis of African identity, Asante emphasizes a cultural and historical concept of African identity. He asserts a unique African view of reality. "African society is essentially a society of harmonies, inasmuch as the coherence or compatibility of persons, things, and modalities is at the root of traditional African philosophy."[5] For example, whereas Western law seeks to establish guilt in order to punish, African law aims to restore "communal balance, therefore, peace." Or, instead of the separation between a speaker and the public characteristic of Western oratory, in African culture, public speaking is seen as a collective experience in which speaker and audience are expected to participate, as is indicated in the prominence of improvisation and the use of call and response between the speaker and public.

Asante connects the African cultural centering on harmony and spiritual unity with the special role of "the word" as a dynamic expressive force generative of reality and community. In a series of provocative and challenging observations on the unique culture of communication and public discourse among African-Americans, Asante makes a compelling case for Afrocentrism. For example, he refers to the importance of "rhythm" and "styling" in African-American communication. This involves regulating the flow of words by using pauses, altering cadences and pronunciation, shifting verbal tone and accent, and visible gesturing. He writes:

> In an education meeting at a university, where a young [Black] speaker gave his view of education, he began by saying Education is for C-O-M-M-U-N-I-T-Y. I mean com-mu-ni-ty. He was styling, and every person familiar with the "tradition" knew that the speaker had seized upon this stylistic device to have an impact. Between the speaker and the audience was an authentic bond, created by the spoken word.[6]

In rhythm and styling, as in the emphasis on improvisation, lyricism, and call and response, Asante observes the traditional African reverence for the generative, transcendent power of the word. Through a series of deft analyses highlighting the differences in communication and public speaking between Afrocentric and

Eurocentric cultures, Asante tries to make credible his belief that there is a unity or unique essence to African identity.

PATRICIA HILL COLLINS: MULTIPLE STANDPOINTS

Asante wished to challenge the imperialism of Eurocentrism; he also wanted to legitimate the idea that African cultures require their own African-based forms of knowledge. Yet in making a plausible case against the Eurocentric bias of Western knowledge, Asante proposed an overdrawn duality between Europe and Africa and between Eurocentrism and Afrcoentrism. The problem is that this conceptual division obliterates differences within the "European" tradition and within the "African" experience. For example, Enlightenment views of knowledge tend to be dualistic (mind/body, science/philosophy) but Anglo-European Romantic traditions associated with German thinking or the poetry of Wordsworth or Whitman favor organic metaphors that look a lot like what Asante describes as Afrocentrism. Also, don't class and gender, among other factors, shape the European and African experience and identity? For example, aren't there gender differences among Africans that shape knowledge and culture? Indeed, as feminists have argued, gender serves as a site of identity and politics that sometimes involves African women aligning with European women against both African and European men. In this regard, Patricia Hill Collins offers one attempt to rethink Afrocentrism in light of this criticism.

In *Black Feminist Thought*, Collins responds to the blindness to gender in Afrocentrism and the marginalization of race in feminism.[7] She proposes an "Afrocentric feminist" social theory whose roots are in a unique intellectual tradition forged by Black women such as bell hooks, Audre Lorde, and Alice Walker. Collins believes that Afrocentric feminism is ultimately anchored in the unique experiences and struggles of ordinary African-American women.[8]

Black feminism exhibits contradictory strains reflecting the different social positioning of Black women along the axis of class, sexuality, nationality, and so on. Collins likens Black thought to a "shifting mosaic of competing ideas and interests."[9] Yet African-American women share a history of racism and sexism that is often interconnected with class oppression to mark out a distinctive social standpoint. If this common history is not expressed in a uniformly coherent world view, Black women's social thought does exhibit some underlying common themes. For example, Collins underscores the emphasis in Black feminism on the interlocking of gender, race, class, and sexuality as sites of identity, social formation, and politics. A key theme of Black feminism has been the suppression of Black critical thinking in the social mainstream, including the university, as one strategy for maintaining White, male, middle-class social dominance. Black women's voices have been excluded or marginalized in public life. Accordingly, Black feminism has found its chief social location outside the dominant institutions of knowledge and cultural production, e.g., in churches, families, political networks, or among poets, writers, and musicians.

Collins maintains that Black thought in America has its roots in African culture. As Africans were enslaved, their Afrocentric values and world view found nourishment in

Patricia Hill Collins was born in 1948. She earned her PhD at Brandeis in 1984 and is currently a professor of sociology at the University of Maryland. In her book *Black Feminist Thought*, Collins develops an Afrocentric, feminist social theory. She believes that gender cannot and should not be thought of as separate from race. Men and women are always men and women of a particular race, class, sexuality, and nationality. Difference is at the heart of social identities. But, critics ask, which differences matter? And, do we surrender a coherent idea of identity if differences are multiplied indefinitely?

American soil. Drawing on Afrocentric theorists, Collins conceives of Afrocentrism as a unique paradigm of knowledge. However, Black women are not only positioned by their history as Africans, but share with White women a history of sexism and certain core experiences relating to female biology, sexuality, motherhood, and roles in the household and workplace. Rather than emphasize the potential differences and conflicts between Afrocentrism and feminism that stem from their divergent social experiences, Collins highlights their similarities.

Collins describes a unique Afrocentric feminist type of social knowledge. In contrast to the Enlightenment paradigm of knowledge that is dominant in the social sciences and mainstream feminism, Afrocentric feminism asserts that knowledge is socially anchored in the experiences of particular groups; the multiple social standpoints of agents of knowledge (e.g., Black women, Latino men, White middle-class lesbians, working-class women) produce a plurality of ways of knowing, each viewed as partial. Furthermore, in contrast to the Western scientific tradition, social knowledge involves the feelings, personal values, and interests of its producers and therefore carries broad social and political implications. For example, Collins highlights the role of concrete personal experience and feelings as a standard by which to assess knowledge claims. Being subjected to multiple oppressions and distrusting the dominant paradigms of knowledge, Black women rely on their own experience to survive and to determine what is real and true.

KWAME ANTHONY APPIAH: DECONSTRUCTING AFRICAN IDENTITY

Despite the diversity of Black women's experiences in the United States, Collins asserts a common experience and identity. She rejects, however, efforts to provide a biological basis for Afrocentric feminism. She conceives of Afrocentricity as a social and historical reality. It reflects a history of resistance to racism and shared African values and beliefs. The foundational assumption of a socially produced core African identity, which is at the root of work by both Collins and Asante, is questioned by Kwame Anthony Appiah.

Appiah challenges the idea of a unitary African or Black identity and its basis in a biological, social, or historical reality.[10] His comments on the great African-American social theorist and leader W. E. B. Du Bois are instructive. Du Bois embraced the

Kwame Anthony Appiah was born in London in 1954 but grew up in Ghana. He was educated at Cambridge University. He has taught at Cambridge, Cornell, Yale, Duke, and Harvard. He currently teaches at Princeton where he is a professor of philosophy and African-American studies. Appiah does not believe that an African identity is real. What is real is that there are Nigerians, Rwandans, South Africans, and so on. However, it is useful and politically wise for those living on the African continent to think of themselves as African. Do you see the difference?

concept of race and assigned to the Negro race a unique social and moral role to play in history. Yet he wished to avoid a biological concept of race by associating race with a shared heritage and history. Appiah raises doubts about whether Du Bois succeeded in uncoupling race from biology. He observes that Du Bois himself, though a Negro, was the descendant of Dutch ancestors. Is it coherent to say that he shared a common history with Africans, with whom he had no known descendants, but not with the Dutch? If Du Bois is united with Africans, it is not because they share a common history, but because he assumes that they are all members of the same race by virtue of their skin color. The idea of defining race by a common history is credible only if the various peoples who are said to share this history (e.g., Africans, American Blacks, Caribbean Blacks) are already assumed to be an identifiable group by virtue of their skin color. Du Bois' social account of race, in the end, relies on a biological concept.

Is there any compelling evidence for biological accounts of race? Appiah sums up conventional wisdom among contemporary biologists:

> Every reputable biologist will agree that human genetic variability between the populations of Africa or Europe or Asia is not much greater than that within those populations . . . Apart from the visible morphological characteristics of skin, hair, and bone, by which we are now inclined to assign people to the broadest racial categories – Black, White, Yellow – there are few genetic characteristics to be found in the population of Britain that are not found in similar proportions in Zaire or in China. . . .
>
> A more familiar part of the consensus is that the differences between peoples in language, moral affections, aesthetic attitudes, or political ideology . . . are not to any significant degree biologically determined.[11]

If biology or common history cannot justify the assertion of an African identity, what about shared culture? Asante and Collins assert a common African cultural sensibility, e.g., the power of the word and the orientation towards harmony and holistic thinking. Appiah raises doubts about this view of race as well. Appealing to the diversity of precolonial, colonial, and postcolonial experiences across the African continent, Appiah finds little credibility in the notion of a common African cultural identity. Compare, he says:

> [the] Asante monarchy, a confederation in which the king is [guided by] . . . his elders and paramount chiefs, with the more absolute power of Mutesa the First in nineteenth-century

Buganda; or the enclosed horizons of a traditional Hausa wife, forever barred from contact with men other than her husband, with the open spaces of the women traders of southern Nigeria; or the art of Benin – its massive bronzes – with the tiny elegant goldweight figures of the Akan. Face the warrior horsemen of the Fulani jihads with Shaka's Zulu impis . . . Surely differences in religious ontology and ritual, in the organization of politics and the family, in relations between the sexes and in art, in styles of warfare and cuisine, in language – surely all these are fundamental kinds of difference?[12]

Some thinkers believe that a shared racial identity is based on a common experience of social disadvantage. Do not Blacks share a history of racial oppression that unites all Africans and Black Americans? Appiah has doubts about this social perspective as well. If Black Americans share an experience of racial oppression with Africans, do they not share this same oppression with Asians? Moreover, Appiah observes that racially based oppression is not a seamless, uniform experience. The system of racial slavery in the American South was very different from the racism of Northeastern urban centers in postwar America; these are hardly comparable to the experience of colonial subjection in British Ghana or to the system of apartheid in South Africa. Racism can be experienced, for example, as more or less personal or systematic and as susceptible to diverse forms of resistance. Finally, the struggle against racism is not exclusive to racially oppressed peoples. To the extent that Whites put themselves in the place of Blacks as imagined victims, they can, and do, identify with antiracist struggles.

Appiah sums up the preceding points as follows:

Whatever Africans share, we do not have a common traditional culture, common language, a common religious or conceptual vocabulary [and] . . . we do not even belong to a common race.[13]

Despite the failure on the part of various thinkers to base a notion of Black solidarity on the idea of a unitary or common African identity, Appiah does not wish to completely give up this idea. African unity remains a compelling cultural and political aim, in part due to commonalities in African history and social struggles. Invoking African identity, moreover, is useful in order to bring about political mobilization, to negotiate civic peace within and between African nations, to build alliances across Africa and the globe, and to focus international attention on Africa and the African diaspora. And, finally, the term "African" is already an integral part of the public culture of many nations and is enforced by social organizations such as the African Development Bank or the Olympics. Appiah aims to defend the appeal to African identity without the strong, and misleading, claims to unity. He proposes that African identity be viewed as chosen, changeable, permanently contestable, and partial. While the practical needs of politics and social organization compel the assertion of an African identity, we – intellectuals and citizens – should not forget that identities are multiple: familial, tribal, national, gender-based, or religious. Appiah opts to combine a strategy of disrupting fixed unitary images of the African while defending a pragmatic appeal to African identity.

THEORIZING WHITENESS

Consider the following: since at least Tocqueville in the 1830s, many social thinkers believe that America's chief challenge is race. Whether the focus is on native Americans, Blacks, the Chinese and Japanese, or Mexicans, race is to America what class is to Britain or Italy or France. It is what divides America as a nation and it is what troubles the conscience of its citizens. Books and articles on race, on Black Americans alone, could fill up a university library. In American sociology, for example, there is no topic written about more than race, in particular the place of Blacks in America. Yet, curiously, until recently sociologists and social scientists have had very little to say about Whites and Whiteness.

Well, to be fair, there is a great deal of research and social thinking by sociologists and others on White racism in daily life and in institutions from work to schools and the church. We have studies of Whites' attitudes towards non-Whites; research on how race prejudice is learned; studies of where Whites live, go to school, and work. In short, we know a great deal about how Whites become racist and how their racial privilege and power is sustained. And, we know an awful lot about the effects of White racism, e.g., on non-Whites' jobs, health, housing, and self-esteem. But, until recently, few scholars researched Whiteness as a distinct social and historical racial identity; few social thinkers analyzed how Whiteness itself shapes social life.

To be completely accurate, not all scholars and thinkers have neglected Whiteness. Non-Whites could not afford to neglect the ways of White people. In order to accommodate to or challenge White privilege, native Americans, Blacks, Latinos, and Asians became keen observers of Whiteness. In particular, from the writings of W. E. B. Du Bois to Malcolm X, non-Whites have tried to expose Whiteness as a particular racial identity and culture. Still, the perspectives of non-Whites have been limited. Whites were often viewed stereotypically and the differences among them ignored. Moreover, Whiteness, like Blackness or being Asian or native American, was often viewed ahistorically, as if these racial markers were a more or less fixed part of being human.

The academic study of Whiteness arose in the 1980s and 1990s, no doubt as a response to a new multicultural reality that made respecting group differences into a core part of the American national identity. As Blacks, Latinos, or Native Americans publicly championed their unique identity and culture, the status of Whiteness became something to be examined. White studies offers a social and historical account of Whiteness. Although the field is relatively new, there are some themes that stand out in the literature.

Invisibility/visibility

The notion of Whiteness as both visible and invisible is commented on by Richard Dyer in *White*:

> Research – into books, museums, the press, advertising, films, television, software – repeatedly shows that in Western representation Whites are overwhelmingly and

disproportionately predominant . . . precisely because of this and their placing as norm they seem not to be represented to themselves *as* Whites but as people . . . At the level of racial representation . . . Whites are not of a certain race, they're just of the human race.[14]

On the one hand, in nations such as the United States, Britain, Germany, and Denmark, Whites are all too visible. Go into an office, hospital, or restaurant in the United States and it's Whites who are seen – as managers, physicians, nurses, and waiters; non-Whites are present but often unseen; they are the busboys, the kitchen help, and the janitors. Think of hotels. Whites are immediately visible; they are at the check-in counter and are the concierges and the managers; non-Whites are the housekeepers or the kitchen staff who are in the background, barely noticeable, at least to Whites.

On the other hand, Whiteness is not necessarily seen. What does it mean to say that Whites are seen but not Whiteness? White people are visible but Whiteness as the basis of a particular racial identity and culture is often invisible. Race or "color" is associated with being non-White. Blacks, Asians, Latinos, and Native Americans are distinct races. White is assumed to be beyond race. That is, many Whites don't think of Whiteness as like being "black" or "red" or "yellow", as a particular racial difference which is associated with a specific culture and history. Instead, Whiteness is often approached, especially by Whites, as "colorless." Whites are "just people" or just human. Nations like America or Sweden or Italy are organized around a dualism: Whites are just people, non-Whites are particular races.

Here's an example of the invisibility of Whiteness. In the United States, journalists will typically refer to the "Black thief" the "Hispanic politician" or the "Asian author." When was the last time you heard a journalist or media commentator refer to a "White bank robber" or a "White Senatorial candidate" or to Norman Mailer, the "White author?" Whiteness is assumed; it doesn't need to be marked or spoken of; it is the default condition in the absence of specifying color. The deracialization of Whiteness conceals that it has a particular history and expresses a specific social standpoint.

The making of White people

Whiteness has simply been assumed, as if there have always been people who are White or as if it's the natural state of humanity. Historians have recently raised some doubts. Whiteness is as much an historical event as being Black or African. Odd as it may sound to some, there have not always been White people or people thought of as White, as belonging to a specifically White social group.

There have always been people with pale skin, many of whom may also have distinctive facial features (e.g., a certain shape of nose, or hair texture), but they have not always been identified as members of a White race. For example, one of the leading scholars of Whiteness, David Roediger, has commented on the fact that many western and southern European immigrants who arrived in the United States in the early twentieth century were not thought of as White by Protestant Americans.

Immigrants could be Irish, Italian, Hungarian, and Jewish, for example, without being White. Many groups now commonly termed part of the "White" or "White ethnic" populations were in fact historically regarded as non-White . . . by the host American citizenry. In the mid-nineteenth century, the racial status of Catholic Irish incomers became the object of fierce, extended debate. The "simian" and "savage" Irish only gradually fought, worked, and voted their ways into the White race in the United States. Well into the twentieth century, Blacks were counted as "smoked Irishmen" in racist and anti-Irish United States slang. Later, sometimes darker, migrants from southern and eastern Europe were similarly cast as non-White . . . Factory managers spoke of employees distinctly as Jews and as "White men," though the "good Jew" was sometimes counted as White. Poorer Jews were slurred as Black.[15]

European ethnics were oppressed not only because they were not of British heritage but because they were not viewed as White. To the extent that Whiteness was associated with being a good, respectable American citizen, European immigrants struggled to gain a status as White. The Irish, Italians, Poles, and Jews were assimilated or became first-class Americans only when they were recognized as White. But, as they became White their sense of European ethnicity weakened. Again, Roediger comments:

> As groups made the transition from Irish in America or Poles in America to Irish Americans or Polish Americans, they also became White Americans. In doing so they became White ethnics but also became less specifically ethnic, not only because they sought to assimilate into the broad category of American but also because they sought to be accepted as White rather than as Irish or Polish.[16]

White studies underscore an important theoretical point regarding the character of race and ethnicity. Race or ethnicity is about establishing boundaries through acts of exclusion or acts of contrast and opposition. Whiteness originates only in a context of contrast to non-Whites, as a way to differentiate human types. Whites exist only because there are categories of people who are not White. Racial identities take shape as part of establishing racial hierarchies; they are always political. White, Black, red or native American, and Asian are not just different racial identities but stand in relations of inequality to one another. And being White is not just a particular racial identity but a privileged one.

White privilege

Whiteness has historically granted privilege. In part, the privilege is obvious and the very visibility of Whites signals their dominant status. Whites occupy positions of power in the government, media, military, schools, corporations, and so on. Whites rule the institutions of many Western nations. Whites are very definitely seen. It is their visibility as managers, CEOs, public officials, military leaders, and so on that announces, loud and clear, White privilege.

But part of White privilege is the invisibility of Whites as a particular culture. Whites purport to speak for all people, not just for a particular race or cultural tradition. The interests and values of Whites are claimed to express broadly human concerns. In that sense, Whiteness claims to speak with the voice of reason; Whiteness serves as a standard, a baseline of what is considered natural and normal. As the culture critic and film studies scholar Richard Dyer says:

> White people have power and believe that they think, feel and act like and for all people; White people, unable to see their particularity, cannot take account of other peoples; White people create the dominant image of the world and don't quite see that they thus construct the world in their own image; White people set standards of humanity by which they are bound to succeed and others bound to fail. Most of this is not done deliberately and maliciously; . . . White power none the less reproduces itself regardless of intention . . . because it is not seen as Whiteness, but as normal. White people need to learn to see themselves as White, to see their particularity.[17]

White rule is somehow made to seem almost natural and expected; after all, it's Whites, and only Whites, who claim to rise above the narrow interests and world views of particular racial groups. It's Whites who are seemingly in touch with what is rational or of interest to all people. There is a kind of entitlement to rule that has been associated with Whiteness.

Whiteness confers a generalized social privilege. Everyone who can successfully claim Whiteness can claim something of its benefits and social advantages. These are privileges of opportunity, choice, voice, and respect. But, White privilege is effective only in relation to non-White racial identities. Thus, White women assume a privileged status in relation to Asian women; disabled or gay individuals who are White presume a sense of entitlement in relation to their non-White counterparts.

Within the category of Whiteness there are also differences of power and status. To state the obvious, there are inequalities among Whites based on wealth, political power, cultural status, sexual identity, ethnicity, and ability or disability. Thus, White men who are gay or disabled give up some of the privilege of Whiteness; they are dominated by Whites who are straight and abled. Whiteness is stratified.

Paralleling the discussion of masculinity, it seems useful to speak of hegemonic forms of Whiteness. Particular nations or societies champion specific ideals of Whiteness, for example, of the White citizen. Certain physical attributes or ways of dressing and talking or particular values and behaviors are associated with ideals of Whiteness or the ideal White citizen. These images and ideals change and are the focus of conflict, as different sectors of the White population strive to have their particular notions of Whiteness become dominant. A quick glance at movies or television reveals iconic images of the White body, face, hair, dress, and lifestyle. Celebrities and movie stars often function as icons of Whiteness. To speak in very rough terms, the ideal White citizen in the United States is straight, enabled, moneyed, married, north European (British, Swede, Scandinavian rather than Italian or Hungarian or Croatian), English-speaking, Christian, and so on.

The founding premise of White studies is that Whiteness is not natural but is part of a socially formed racial system; Whiteness is said to structure the lives of both Whites and non-Whites. Ruth Frankenberg offers a useful summary statement: "First, Whiteness is a location of structural advantage, of race privilege. Second, it is a 'standpoint,' a place from which White people look at ourselves, at others, and at society. Third, 'Whiteness' refers to a set of cultural practices that are usually unmarked and unnamed."[18] The aim of White studies is to expose the social origin of Whiteness and to challenge its privileged status. Richard Dyer writes: "The point of seeing the racing of Whites is to dislodge them/us from the position of power, with all the inequities, oppression, privileges, and suffering in its train, dislodging them/us by undercutting the authority with which they/we speak and act in and on the world."[19]

Suggested Readings

Gloria Anzaldua, *Borderlands/La Frontera* (San Francisco: Spinsters/Aunt Lute Press, 1987).

Beverly Guy-Sheftall, ed., *Words of Fire: An Anthology of African-American Feminist Thought* (New York: New Press, 1995).

bell hooks, *Ain't I a Woman* (Boston, MA: South End Press, 1982).

Jean Stefancic and Richard Delgado, eds., *Critical Race Theory* (New York: New York University Press, 2001).

References

1   bell hooks, *Ain't I a Woman* (Boston, MA: South End Press, 1982); Cornell West, *Prophetic Fragments* (Trenton, NJ: Africa World Press, 1988); Kwame Anthony Appiah, *In My Father's House: Africa in the Philosophy of Culture* (New York: Oxford University Press, 1992).

2   Molefi Kete Asante, *Afrocentricity: The Theory of Social Change* (Buffalo, NY: Amulefi, 1980).

3   Molefi KeteAsante , *The Afrocentric Idea* (Philadelphia: Temple University Press, 1987).

4   Asante, *The Afrocentric Idea*, p. 56.

5   Asante, *The Afrocentric Idea*, p. 79.

6   Asante, *The Afrocentric Idea*, p. 40.

7   Patricia Hill Collins, *Black Feminist Thought: Knowledge, Consciousness, and the Politics of Empowerment* (London: HarperCollins, 1990).

8   bell hooks, *Talking Back* (Boston, MA: South End Press, 1989); Barbara Smith, ed., *Home Girls* (New York: Kitchen Table Press, 1983); Audre Lorde, *Zami, A New Spelling of My Name* (Trumansberg, NY: Crossing Press, 1982); Alice Walker, *The Color Purple* (New York: Washington Square Press, 1982).

9   Collins, *Black Feminist Thought*, p. 10.

10 Appiah, *In My Father's House*.

11 Appiah, *In My Father's House*, p. 35.

12 Appiah, *In My Father's House*, p. 25.

13 Appiah, *In My Father's House*, p. 26.

14 Richard Dyer, *White* (London: Routledge, 1997), p. 3.

15 David Roediger, "Whiteness and Ethnicity in the History of 'White Ethnics' in the United States," in Philomena Essed and David Theo Goldberg, eds., *Race Critical Theories* (Malden, MA: Blackwell, 2002), p. 329. Also see Roediger, *Wages of Whiteness* (London: Verso, 1991).

16 Roediger, "Whiteness and Ethnicity," p. 333.

17 Dyer, *White*, p. 9.

18 Ruth Frankenberg, *The Social Construction of Whiteness: White Women, Race Matters* (London: Routledge, 1993), p. 1.

19 Dyer, *White*, p. 2.

Lesbian, Gay, and Queer Theory/ Heterosexual Studies

Gender and race were categories of identity as early as the founding years of the American republic. Americans understood themselves as men or women or as White or Black (or colored or Negro). The same was not true for sexuality. Historians report that heterosexuality and homosexuality were not a basis for personal identity until the early twentieth century.[1] Previously, same-sex sexuality was viewed as a type of behavior. In fact, historians have documented a middle-class culture accepting of romantic involvements between women, at least as a complement to heterosexual marriage.[2] This came to an end in the first decades of the twentieth century. A medical-scientific discourse announced to the public the existence of a new human identity: the homosexual. Characterized as a gender-confused, sexual deviant, the homosexual was a disreputable figure.

A public culture organized around same-sex behavior initially developed between roughly 1890 and 1930 in the United States. At this time homosexuality was defined primarily as a type of gender confusion. For example, "homosexual" men were said to have male bodies and female souls.

It wasn't until the 1950s that we saw the rise of homosexual organizations, cultures, and politics. Mainstream homosexual groups viewed homosexuality as either normal or at worst a minor psychological deviation that did not justify discrimination against homosexuals. Some activists imagined the homosexual as a new social minority. Homosexual politics at the time aimed at eliminating the legal and attitudinal barriers to social assimilation through public education.

This cautious politics of homosexual assimilation was abandoned by a new generation inspired by the spirit of pride and rebellion in the Black and women's movements. Central to the gay liberation movements of the 1960s and 1970s was an affirmative politics of identity. If it was hard for women and non-Whites to find affirmative images of themselves and a forceful public voice, it was even harder for homosexuals. At least women and Blacks were a visible part of American culture. Blacks had fought in

Contested Knowledge: Social Theory Today, Fifth Edition. Steven Seidman.
© 2013 John Wiley & Sons, Ltd. Published 2013 by John Wiley & Sons, Ltd.

America's wars; there was a Black public culture that could challenge mainstream racist images. Women have been valued in their roles as wives, mothers, and social caretakers; twentieth-century women could draw on women's rich cultural and political history. Homosexuals were invisible. They fought in wars, but no one knew; they were everywhere, but no one saw them. They were "closeted" or hid their identity for fear of losing their jobs and their families. Homosexuals lived through most of the twentieth century with a hidden identity that often imbued their lives with shame and fear. Is it any surprise that the gay movement made the personal and public assertion of an prideful lesbian and gay identity the cornerstone of a movement?

Gay politics of the 1970s was organized around the affirmation of a lesbian and gay self. Positive gay and lesbian perspectives reversed the cultural logic of the social mainstream: homosexuality may have indicated a unique human type, but the homosexual, now redefined as a "lesbian" and "gay man," was the psychological, moral, and social equal to the heterosexual. Although there were disagreements over the degree of commonality between gays and straights, gay perspectives maintained that the lesbian or gay man indicated a distinctive social identity. The experience of heterosexism, the shared reality of being closeted and coming out, the multiple forms of oppression (e.g., law, discrimination, violence, and cultural stereotyping), and the aspiration to social equality and respect produced a common gay identity. As much as the lesbian and gay movement has rallied behind an affirmative personal identity, divisions were never far from the surface. In particular, gender conflicts gave rise to a persisting division. The gay movement split in the early 1970s into a lesbian-feminist and a predominantly gay liberationist culture. These movements generated powerful social perspectives on sexuality and society. However, by the early 1980s, the success of the lesbian and gay movement and its mainstreaming came under attack. Whereas the antigay attack led many gays to embrace a strong naturalistic defense of homosexuality, internal divisions based on gender, class, and race led to novel points of view and politics that sometimes challenged identity politics.

IDENTITY THEORY: ADRIENNE RICH AND JEFFREY WEEKS

A public lesbian and gay culture began to materialize in the 1950s. It centered around bars, informal networks, and political organizing. The development of a postwar gay culture was limited by an atmosphere of homosexual persecution; lesbians and gay men were dismissed from jobs and the military and harassed on the streets; bars were raided and their patrons' names were made public. The power of the state was mobilized to keep homosexuals socially invisible and criminalized.

The broad social liberalization of the 1960s and the appearance of student protests, feminism, Black liberation, and the counterculture encouraged the development of a lesbian and gay movement. In the course of the 1970s, lesbians and gays created their own subcultures anchored in an affirmative self-identity. In major urban centers such as New York, San Francisco, Chicago, Los Angeles, and Houston, lesbians and gay men created their own institutions, cultural apparatus (e.g., newspapers,

Feminist poet and essayist, **Adrienne Rich**, was born in Baltimore, Maryland, in 1929. Rich graduated from Radcliffe College in 1951. In the influential essay "Compulsory Heterosexuality and Lesbian Existence," she argues that masculine dominance is maintained through the imposition of heterosexuality. According to Rich, a range of political, economic, and cultural forces lead women to see heterosexuality as both natural and normal. In other words, we learn to become heterosexual and to see it as the only right way to be sexual. But Rich believes that many women have historically resisted heterosexuality. They have chosen to be celibate, spinsters, or to organize their lives around other women. Provocatively, she calls these women "lesbians."

British sociologist **Jeffrey Weeks** was born in 1945. He was educated at the University of London and the University of Kent at Canterbury, where he received his doctorate in 1983. During the 1970s, Weeks was a member of the London Gay Liberationist Front as well as a founding member of the Gay Left Collective, a group of intellectuals who sought to understand how power has shaped ideas about sexuality from a socialist perspective. Weeks currently teaches at South Bank University in London and is one of the key theorists of "social constructionism." Without denying the biological basis of sex, Weeks argues that the meaning, social organization, and history of sexuality is deeply social. Sex is one of the last places sociologists have looked to find, not nature, but the reality of society.

book publishers, theater, art), and political organizations. By the early 1980s, virtually every mid-sized city in the United States had its own public lesbian and gay community. A central part of this community-building effort was the knowledges produced by lesbians and gay men. In particular, lesbians and gay men developed two new perspectives that placed issues of sexuality at the heart of social analysis: lesbian feminism and gay social constructionism.

Lesbian feminism was a response to the perceived sexism of the gay movement and to the heterosexism of feminism. Lesbian feminists aimed to separate lesbianism from male homosexuality and align with the women's movement. Their strategy involved redefining lesbianism. Rejecting views of lesbianism as a sexual preference or lifestyle, lesbian feminists asserted that a lesbian is a woman who rebels against male dominance by centering her life around other women. Lesbian feminists argued that heterosexuality underpins male dominance. Heterosexuality refers to a constellation of social practices, including norms of sexual and gender behavior, the ideology of heterosexual romance, and the institution of marriage and the family. The system of heterosexuality perpetuates male dominance by centering women's lives around the interests, values, and needs of men. The culture of romance and the institutions of marriage and the family obscure male dominance while positioning women in socially subordinate roles, i.e., wife and mother. To become a lesbian was a political act of rebellion; it challenged the dominance of heterosexuality and men. It defined women as independent, as living for themselves, and highlighted the bonds of solidarity between women. The lesbian stepped forward as the exemplary feminist: independent and women-centered.

Lesbian feminism developed in the early 1970s. Theorists such as Ti-Grace Atkinson, Jill Johnston, Rita Mae Brown, and Charlotte Bunch analyzed the connections between sexuality, gender, and capitalism.[3] These ideas proved to be pivotal not only because they made an alliance between feminism and lesbianism possible but because of their conceptual depth and imagination. However, lesbian feminism generated new tensions within the women's movement. This perspective suggested that only lesbians could be true feminists.

A key statement of lesbian feminism was Adrienne Rich's "Compulsory Heterosexuality and Lesbian Existence."[4] Rich asserts the basic lesbian-feminist thesis: Normative heterosexuality underpins male dominance. She argues that women are not born heterosexual; heterosexuality is neither natural nor normal. Moreover, heterosexuality is not chosen. Women are coerced, sometimes violently, to become heterosexual. Societies marshal an impressive range of resources to shape women's sexuality so that heterosexuality is felt as natural and normal. Compulsory heterosexuality is enforced by a system of laws, economics, public policy, a culture of heterosexual romance and pornography, and the recourse to violence and imprisonment against women who deviate. Central to the making of heterosexual women in recent times is the bringing to bear of a vast cultural apparatus, including the mass media and science, aimed at rendering lesbianism invisible and deviant. As a result, the lives of lesbians have been hidden from history, invisible in academic culture and in public life. Sadly, Rich says, feminism has at times contributed to this public invisibility of lesbian lives by trying to rigidly separate gender from sexual politics.

The "institution" or system of compulsory heterosexuality has been resisted throughout history. Despite the powerful machinery that society enlists to enforce a norm of heterosexuality, "a central fact of women's history [is] that women have always resisted male tyranny."[5] For example, Rich refers to "the refusal of some women to produce children," women's assertion of an "antiphallic sexuality," a commitment to abstinence, or the development of networks of women supporting each other. Women who resist male dominance or who organize their lives in important ways around women are part of what Rich calls the "lesbian continuum." Because all feminists are committed to women's freedom, they can be located on this continuum. But not all feminists live what Rich calls a "lesbian existence." This term refers to women whose primary sexual and intimate lives are organized around women. Rich draws a sharp distinction between lesbian existence and male homosexuality. Whereas men, either straight or gay, retain gender power, women, whether straight or lesbian, are subordinate to men. Their gender power allows gay men to approach their homosexuality as a lifestyle; by contrast, women who become lesbians are making a political statement as they are challenging male dominance.

Rich assumes that heterosexuality is socially imposed. For example, she says that most women marry because they have no choice. They marry for reasons of economic survival, to have children, to avoid social ridicule, or to fulfill male-imposed ideals of feminine self-fulfillment. The institutions of heterosexuality and male dominance leave women little freedom. "Within the institution [of heterosexuality] exist, of course, qualitative differences of experience; but the absence of choice remains the great unacknowledged reality."[6] Women are forced to become heterosexual and accordingly surrender some of their sexual and social autonomy. Choosing a lesbian existence is to choose freedom. Rich assumes that the vast social machinery enlisted to maintain the heterosexual norm suggests the natural force of lesbianism. However, documenting the social forces conspiring to maintain a heterosexual norm does not imply anything about the relative natural force of homosexual or heterosexual impulses. Women may feel a forceful impulse to bond with women, but this need not preclude the existence of an equally impressive desire to bond with men. The assumption that the heterosexual norm will be experienced by all women as necessarily coercive does not follow.

Rich assumed the universality of lesbian existence. She held that there have always been lesbians and that the meaning of lesbian existence is uniform across history. Just as heterosexuality is imagined to be a seamless, uniform order of domination, lesbian existence is assumed to have an essential meaning. This assumption of a universal lesbian continuum and identity that unites women across different histories has been the target of a great deal of criticism. From the mid-1970s through today, scholars have fashioned perspectives that emphasize the socially constructed character of sexuality and variations in the meaning and social roles of homosexuality.

The British historian and social theorist Jeffrey Weeks is a pioneer of social constructionism.[7] Weeks reacted against two major currents of social thought. First, the formation of a lesbian and gay community was accompanied by the claim that "the homosexual" has always existed as a distinct person with a specific identity. Gay activists and scholars produced lists of famous men and women in the past whose true homosexual identity was revealed. Although claiming a noble ancestry may have been useful to legitimate a homosexual identity, it failed, according to the constructionist view, to capture what was unique about homosexual life in the present. Second, although Weeks was influenced by a Marxist critique of an ahistorical approach to homosexuality, he criticized Marxism – and feminism – to the extent that they explained sexuality as an effect of class or gender dynamics. Such arguments in effect assume that there is no need to develop a gay and lesbian theory and politics. Issues of sexuality and homosexuality are surely connected to dynamics of class and gender, but they are not reducible to them. Sexuality has its own history and social patterns, requiring its own theories and politics. Weeks imagines homosexuality, like all forms of sexuality, as a social and historical phenomenon requiring an independent sexual theory.

Declaring the social character of sexuality was hardly news. Freud made sexuality into the driving force behind human behavior and social dynamics; Freudo-Marxists such as Wilhelm Reich and Herbert Marcuse linked sexuality to capitalism. Anthropologists such as Bronislaw Malinowski and Margaret Mead described the social organization of the sexual lives of so-called "primitives." These diverse approaches exhibit, however, a common set of assumptions about sexuality that Weeks calls "essentialism." This approach views sex as a natural instinct built into the biological structure of the individual.

Moreover, an essentialist approach assumes that sex is a powerful force driving the thoughts and behavior of individuals. Although essentialist approaches to sexuality disagree over what is natural or normal and therefore over the appropriate role of society in regulating sex, there is little disagreement that sexuality and society stand in a relation of antagonism. Essentialist perspectives often argue that sex is a natural force pushing from deep within the self for public release; society represses and regulates sex.

Instead of assuming the opposition of sex and society, Weeks proposes a social constructionist perspective:

> First, . . . we can no longer set "sex" against "society" as if they were separate domains. Secondly, there is a widespread recognition of the social variability of sexual forms, beliefs, ideologies and behavior. Sexuality has . . . many histories. . . . Thirdly, . . . we must learn to see that sexuality is something which society produces in complex ways. It is a result of diverse social practices that give meaning to human activities, of social definition and self-definition, of struggles between those who have power to define and regulate, and those who resist. Sexuality is not given, it is a product of negotiation, struggle and human agency.[8]

Rather than approach sex as a matter of personal desire and behavior, Weeks views sexuality as social, as involving social meanings, norms, institutions, and conflicts. Sex is not an instinct the nature of which is fixed; it is a site where the personal and the political, the body and society, become a focus of social meanings and struggles.

Weeks's social constructionist approach can be nicely illustrated by outlining his perspective on homosexuality. Conventional wisdom assumes that the human population is divided between individuals who are, by birth, either heterosexual or homosexual. Same-sex sexual desire and behavior are thought to indicate a distinctive homosexual identity. From this perspective, society either tolerates or represses homosexuals. Freedom is living authentically as a homosexual. Gay politics has absorbed this view of homosexuality. For example, gays and lesbians, even today often appeal to the naturalness of homosexuality in order to justify claims for land rights and respect.

In *Coming Out: Homosexual Politics in Britain from the Nineteenth Century to the Present*, Weeks proposes that the idea that homosexual behavior reveals a human identity did not emerge in Western societies until the late nineteenth century.[9] In previous centuries, homosexuality was often subsumed under the broad category of sodomy, which included a range of illegal same-sex and opposite-sex acts. The notion that acts of sodomy indicated a type of person and that sexual desire marks off a distinct homosexual and heterosexual identity was alien to Western societies prior to the late nineteenth century. The sodomite was punished by law and custom for his or her particular behavior, not as a deviant person. The homosexual stepped forward recently, and only in the West, as a unique physical, psychological, and social identity marked in all these ways by his or her sexuality.

Weeks places a great deal of importance on the rise of a science of sexuality in the making of the modern homosexual. Paralleling the rise of economics, sociology, anthropology, and political science, a new science of sexuality – sexology – materialized in Germany and Britain and subsequently in the United States. Sexologists aimed at discovering the sexual nature of humankind. They sought to chart the development of the sexual instinct and document its manifold forms and its normal and pathological evolution. From the twelve volumes on homosexuality published by the German sexologist Karl Heinreich Ulrichs to the thousands of interviews of the sex lives of Americans by Alfred Kinsey, sexology has sought to uncover the hidden truth of the self that was thought to be buried in the lower regions of human sexuality.

Between 1898 and 1908, over 1,000 publications appeared on homosexuality. Sexologists seemed obsessed with charting the development, types, and psychological and behavioral manifestations of homosexuality. Sexologists did not create the homosexual; there were already individuals engaged in same-sex behavior and networks of such individuals. Sexology did, however, contribute to creating the idea that humans have a specific sexual nature and identity, that humans divide naturally into "heterosexuals" and "homosexuals," and that sexual desires, behaviors, and identities can be classified as either normal or abnormal.

The ideas of the sexologists had great social impact. Ideas about the homosexual were taken up by the state, lawyers and judges, psychiatrists and psychoanalysts, and the mass media. Weeks highlights the role of sensational public events in giving social impetus to the circulation of sexologists' ideas. In public events such as the 1890s British trial of Oscar Wilde for his alleged homosexuality, the idea of a homosexual identity became absorbed into popular culture. The language of sexuality and sexual types, the opposition of heterosexual and homosexual, and an ethic of sexual normality and abnormality become part of the language of daily life through such public dramas. By the early decades of the twentieth century, individuals who identified as homosexual became a part of the public sphere. Although the language of homosexual identity stigmatized the individual, Weeks observes that it also stimulated a heightened homosexual awareness. This, in turn, facilitated the creation of networks that have gradually led to the development of movements of gay and lesbian liberation. This did not happen immediately, but, after World War II, a plurality of movements of lesbian and gay affirmation, which often drew on science and sexology for legitimation, had reversed the stigmatizing views of homosexuality. Movements affirming lesbian and gay identities appealed to the very ideas of normality and naturalness that originally scandalized them.

QUEER THEORY: DIANA FUSS AND EVE KOSOFSKY SEDGWICK

Despite his critique of the popular view of the homosexual as a natural, universal type, Weeks's social constructionist theory of homosexuality was very much influenced by the identity-based gay community-building efforts of the period. Weeks may have historicized gay identity, but he did not doubt its positive role. In effect, he endorsed an ethnic model of gay identity, even as he analyzed its historical and social evolution. Weeks was, though, attentive to the tendency of an ethnic model of identity to be exclusionary and to defuse its critical political potential by evolving in a separatist or

Diana Fuss was born in 1960. She received her doctorate from Brown University in 1988. Fuss is a major figure within the field of queer studies. Before the advent of queer theory, lesbian and gay studies traced the ways in which lesbian and gay identities were constructed historically. This work was important because it showed that sex has a history and social basis. Today, it is important to show the instability of categories of sexual identity. In this regard, Fuss shows that the categories, heterosexuality and homosexuality, are inherently unstable since they are mutually exclusive yet at the same time they rely on one another for coherence. For Fuss, then, the aim of lesbian and gay theory becomes not the theorization of lesbian and gay identities but an examination and destabilization of the division of people, identities, and desires into the heterosexual or homosexual. Fuss currently teaches at Princeton University.

liberal assimilationist direction. In this regard, he advocated that lesbian and gay identities be articulated in relation to differences of class, race, and gender. Weeks did not question the importance of the identity framework of contemporary gay life, even if he understood identity as a necessary historical fiction. Indeed, identity politics was enormously successful in community building and political mobilization. Through the 1970s and 1980s, lesbians and gay men created national and international movements that challenged compulsory heterosexuality.

By the early 1980s, the gay movement was challenged from two very different directions. On the one hand, a powerful antigay backlash campaigned to roll back the gains of the preceding decade. On the other hand, the consolidation of what we might call a gay mainstream came under attack by lesbians and gays of color and activists, some of whom turned militant by the AIDS epidemic. Two responses to this crisis of gay life are apparent. First, in response to antigay attacks and the growing internal divisions around sexual politics, some lesbians and gay men retreated into biological essentialism, asserting a natural basis for sexual identity. Others responded to the crisis by rethinking the connection between identity and politics in ways that would depart from lesbian feminism and social constructionism. Paralleling the renewal of radical politics among AIDS activists and Queer Nation groups, there emerged a rethinking of sexual politics that is associated with queer theory. Interestingly, in contrast to earlier generations of sexual theorists who were either independent scholars, historians, or social scientists, the new theorists were mostly professors of English who were deeply influenced by poststructuralism.

Much gay theory in the postwar period has assumed that homosexuality is a condition or identity of a segment of the human population. Despite disagreements between essentialists and constructionists or separatists and assimilationists, gay and lesbian theories have theorized homosexuality as a minority experience based upon a more or less common homosexual identity.

Queer theorists contest the view of homosexuals as a social minority. In place of analyzing the natural or social making of a gay and lesbian minority, with its focus on the acquisition of a gay identity and the building of an ethnic community, queer theorists

Eve Kosofsky Sedgwick was born in Dayton, Ohio, in 1950. She earned her doctorate at Yale. Sedgwick has taught at Hamilton College, Boston University, Amherst College, and Duke University. She currently teaches at The Graduate Center, City College of New York. Sedgwick is a leading figure in queer theory. She argues that instead of focusing narrowly on explaining particular sexual identities (heterosexual or homosexual) we should ask how we've come to think of ourselves as having a sexual identity at all. Would it be a better world if there were no sexual identity labels?

focus on the social impact of the very categories of homosexuality and heterosexuality, for example, the way these categories influence popular culture, laws, and social life in general. Queer theorists aim to broaden gay and lesbian theory into a general critical sexual theory.

The questioning of the notion of a core homosexual identity is at the heart of queer theory. The case against a unitary gay identity is both analytical and political. Every attempt to define what it means to be a lesbian or gay man is incomplete and misrepresents. It is simply not possible to define what it means to be gay or lesbian in general; and every attempt to specify this identity projects a normative model of being gay which excludes the lives of many other lesbians and gay men. Multiplying identities by speaking of Black lesbians or White, working-class gay men doesn't avoid these problems. For example, the category of White, working-class gay men itself contains enormous differences depending on considerations of age, religion, ability or disability, and ethnicity. In addition, multiplying identities has the potential consequence of creating divisions and weakening efforts at political mobilization.

Diana Fuss advances a distinctively queer critique of gay identity theory. She argues that every attempt to define and affirm being gay recreates the division between homosexuality and heterosexuality. Individuals are classified as one or the other; and inevitably one identity will be thought preferable, thereby enforcing a social hierarchy or a condition of inequality. She writes:

> Deconstruction . . . view[s] . . . identity as difference. To the extent that identity always contains the specter of non-identity within it, the subject is always purchased at the price of the exclusion of the Other, the repression or repudiation of non-identity.[10]

Fuss contends that the identity of a person is implicated in its opposite. Heterosexuality has meaning only in relation to its opposite, homosexuality; the coherence that the former is built on depends on the exclusion and repression of the latter. The homosexual must be only and thoroughly homosexual with no trace of heterosexuality – and the same is true for the heterosexual. The logic of identity is, according to Fuss, a logic of boundary maintainance that inevitably creates divisions and hierarchies. Even if gays were to be assigned an equal status to straights, individuals who are bisexual would become the new outsiders. Fuss concludes that the politics of identity is fraught with difficulties; every effort to affirm an identity inevitably produces new outsiders. The good straight produces the bad gay; but the good gay produces the bad gay; and the good gay and straight produce the bad bisexual. Fuss urges a shift from a politics affirming a minority identity to contesting a sexual system that compels us to announce an exclusive sexual identity; she wishes us to shift our theoretical focus from explaining how individuals become homosexual to explaining how a sexual order took shape that produces a parade of rigid sexual identities.

The shift from theorizing homosexuality as a minority experience to theorizing a sexual system that is organized around the hetero/homosexual opposition is central to Eve Sedgwick's *The Epistemology of the Closet*.[11] Instead of approaching homosexuality in terms of questions of identity, Sedgwick analyzes how the hetero/homosexual opposition structures the core modes of thought, culture, and identity in the twentieth century:

> *The Epistemology of the Closet* proposes that many of the major modes of thought and knowledge in twentieth-century Western culture as a whole are structured – indeed, fractured – by a chronic, now endemic crisis of homo/heterosexual definition. . . . The book will argue that an understanding of virtually any aspect of modern Western culture must be, not merely incomplete, but damaged in its central substance to the degree that it does not incorporate a critical analysis of modern homo/heterosexual definition.[12]

The hetero/homosexual definition not only assigns identities to individuals but shapes broad categories of Western thought and culture. For example, the hetero/homosexual definition frames people's experiences, regardless of sexual orientation, in terms of self-disclosure. In other words, the distinctive dynamic associated with homosexuality, "coming out" of the "closet," spreads from the homosexual to his or her friends, family, and co-workers. The relative of a gay person must reiterate the latter's experience of the closet and coming out. Moreover, heterosexuals' experiences entailing secrecy and disclosure might also be framed today as coming out experiences. As the title of Sedgwick's book suggests, the closet and coming out become general categories of knowledge and cultural organization in societies featuring the hetero/homosexual definition.

Sedgwick imagines the hetero/homosexual symbolic figure as a kind of core logic, akin to the masculine/feminine gender code. It structures identities, the basic categories of knowledge and culture, and the normative organization of society. In other words, the issue of homosexuality is no longer simply an issue for a social minority, nor is it an issue exclusively of rights, pride, respect, and equality, but one that touches on the whole of society. Queer theory is no longer a minority theory; it is a general analysis of the social productivity of the hetero/homosexual definition in the service of a heterosexual norm. At one level, the aim of queer theory is to show the pervasive, structuring presence and power of the hetero/homosexual code. At another level, it attempts to underscore the instability of this binary for the purpose of diminishing its force and releasing new possibilities for desire, identity, and social organization.

In Fuss and Sedgwick, we can observe an important effort to shift gay and lesbian theory away from a minority theory to a broadly critical sexual social theory. The focus of analysis should be a sexual system that is organized around the hetero/

homosexual opposition; this system shapes social and cultural life. This implies a version of a poststructural politics of subversion: if not subverting identity, then challenging the naturalness and inevitability of the hetero/homosexual binary code itself. Queer theory envisions a broad cultural politics, struggling against the social and political forces that naturalize and normalize a rigid sexual and gender order.

RETHINKING HETEROSEXUALITY

If I were forced to state the one great insight of gay theory, it would be that homosexuality is a social and historical, not a natural, phenomenon. There have always been individuals who are attracted to persons of the same sex, but they have only rarely been viewed as a distinct human type or identity. Gay theory made a crucial distinction between sexual behavior and identity; same-sex behavior may be universal, but it becomes the basis of a sexual and social identity only in some societies.

But what about heterosexuality? Curiously, heterosexuality has not always been the focus of social analysis. To be sure, historians have studied the history of marriage and the family; sociologists and demographers have analyzed fertility and conducted surveys of heterosexual behavior. However, much of this scholarship assumes that heterosexuality is natural and universal. There has been virtually no socio-historical analysis of the making of heterosexuality and heterosexual identity. Similarly, the normative status of heterosexuality has been assumed to be also natural and normal. Accordingly, heterosexuality as a field of rich social and political research has been, until recently, neglected.

Approaching heterosexuality as a social and historical event goes against the grain of popular and academic thinking. Most of us would, if asked, be likely to say that heterosexuality is natural or a basic human drive that makes life possible. And, of course, this is true in the sense that without heterosexual behavior humans would become extinct, at least before recent technologies such as artificial insemination. What we call heterosexual sexual behavior has always existed. But, have there always been heterosexuals? To raise this question might sound foolish. Doesn't nature produce heterosexuals, just as it produces males and females, or right- and left-handed people, or green- and blue-eyed individuals? Isn't heterosexuality a necessity for human survival and therefore haven't there always been heterosexuals?

Well, some scholars have asked: what does it mean to say that one is a heterosexual today? Most Americans or British people would probably say that it refers to individuals who are attracted to persons of the opposite sex. A heterosexual is a man whose sexual preference is for women or a woman who is attracted to men. We need to be careful and precise. To be heterosexual in contemporary America means simply to exhibit sexual attraction towards the opposite sex. In other words, we don't say that to be heterosexual an individual has to be motivated to marry or have a family. We simply say that heterosexuals are individuals who feel sexual desire for someone of the opposite sex – regardless of whether their aim is pleasure, love, marriage, or creating a family. Moreover, Americans approach heterosexuality today as an identity. Many of us declare ourselves to be straight in the same way we would identify as a woman or a

Latino. In contemporary America or Britain, to be heterosexual means that you are sexually attracted to the opposite sex and that you claim a distinct sexual identity.

Historians tell us that this notion of heterosexuality was not necessarily shared by our ancestors. For example, in nineteenth-century America, individuals were thought of as being born with a sexual instinct. This instinct was like a genetic program to procreate. In other words, the sexual instinct was a reproductive instinct. To be sexually normal meant to be oriented to reproduce in the same way that hunger drives one to eat. I want to underscore a subtle but key point here: heterosexuality indicated a reproductive drive, not simply a sexual attraction; and it was a drive or behavior, not an identity. Accordingly, Americans who sought only sexual pleasure in the opposite sex were sometimes considered abnormal or immoral. In other words, what we today call heterosexuality, a sexual desire for the opposite sex, was in the Victorian era considered a perversion like sodomy or adultery. Moreover, there was no notion of the heterosexual as a type of person or an identity to be contrasted to the homosexual. The concept of the homosexual was not present throughout most of nineteenth-century America. Without that concept, there could be no notion of the heterosexual as a distinct identity.

According to Jonathan Katz, one of the pioneers in rethinking heterosexuality, the term "heterosexual" first appeared in the scientific and medical literature in the 1890s.[13] It was defined in contemporary terms – as an identity based on sexual attraction for the opposite sex. The key point is that heterosexual desire was uncoupled from procreation. Normal sex was defined as heterosexual erotic attraction; abnormal sex was homosexual erotic attraction. In other words, the concept of the heterosexual cohered in relation to that of the homosexual. Both terms indicated a sexual desire that was unrelated to reproduction and that was the basis of personal identity. It was an individual's gender choice, not a reproductive drive, which by the early twentieth century defined sexual identity.

We can see this change in the meaning of heterosexuality in the ideas of Freud. Unlike his nineteenth-century colleagues, Freud, you might recall, viewed the sexual instinct as oriented to pleasure, not reproduction. Furthermore, he held that sexual satisfaction can involve many different acts with varied goals in mind, for example, pleasure, self-expression, love, or procreation. In Freud's writings, the modern heterosexual steps forward: this is a human sexual type defined solely by a general sexual attraction to the opposite gender but whose sexuality is otherwise fluid or flexible.

Why did the meaning of heterosexuality change from a reproductive instinct to a sexual desire and identity?

One perspective holds that there was a crisis of gender identity in the early twentieth century. Throughout much of the nineteenth century, men and women occupied different social roles. Men dominated the public world of work and politics, while women's primary role was to be a housewife and mother. This was thought to reflect essential differences between men and women. Men were viewed as intellectual, rational, aggressive, and goal-oriented while women were defined as emotional, nurturing, empathetic, and maternal. Marriage was based on the complementarity of gender identities and roles. Men supported and protected the family, while women provided a moral and loving environment for the family.

This social arrangement started to break down in the early decades of the twentieth century. Women started to attend college, entered the work force, began organizing for their rights, and were active in social reform movements. At the same time, men's work was gradually shifting from farm and blue collar labor to white collar jobs. Being a white collar worker in a corporation or the government meant that most men had little power and were increasingly reliant on "feminine" skills such as cooperation, communication, and making an agreeable self-presentation. From the perspective of many contemporaries, women were becoming more masculine while men were becoming more feminine. The gender division between men and women, which was thought to be the basis of a stable social order, was collapsing. A sense of crisis was heightened by the fact that many women were choosing to stay single or divorce, or were marrying but remaining childless.

One response to the blurring of gender identities and to the sense of crisis of marriage was a new emphasis on the norm of heterosexuality as a way to reassert the normality of dichotomous gender roles. By emphasizing the naturalness and rightness of heterosexuality, the differences between men and women were also viewed as natural and good. That is, if heterosexuality was natural and essential for a stable social order, men and women should continue to occupy different roles. Asserting a clear heterosexual identity became a way to flag a normal gender identity. Heterosexuality came to be associated with a person's core self-identity and its meaning was centered on being sexually attracted to the opposite sex.

Another result of this emphasis on a heterosexual identity was the creation of a culture of homophobia. As heterosexuality became an important way to assert a normal sexual and gender identity, homosexuality came to represent a deviant status. It was not only sexual attraction to a person of the same sex that was stigmatized, but gender deviance was disapproved of as a sign of homosexuality. The result was that men and women feared exhibiting any gender traits that deviated from norms of masculine men and feminine women. A sexual system that aggressively enforced heterosexuality as a norm aimed to shore up a fragile gender order.

Let's shift our focus somewhat from the history to the sociology of heterosexuality. If establishing a heterosexual identity has become an important way to project a normal, respectable gender identity, how is this accomplished in everyday life? The new scholarship views heterosexual identity, like homosexual identity, as a social accomplishment. How do individuals convince others that they are heterosexual?

Let's keep something in mind that I mentioned previously. Our identities are established in relations of contrast. Fashioning a convincing identity as a woman means not displaying any (or too many) traits associated with men and masculinity. An individual fashions a normal or respectable identity as a woman by rejecting masculine traits such as being overly aggressive, intensely competitive, or sexually assertive. Of course, there are different versions of what it means to be a woman. They may conflict with one another, but all involve contrasts to some notion of manhood. If a woman exhibits certain masculine qualities such as intellectualism or a career orientation, she might still command respect as a "good woman" but she will likely have to be emphatically heterosexual.

Similarly, individuals establish a heterosexual identity in part by distancing themselves from any associations with homosexuality. For example, homophobic conduct not only announces that one is heterosexual but declares that heterosexuality is good while homosexuality is bad.

Some British researchers have studied how high school students used homophobic practices to establish a public heterosexual identity.[14] They found that students, especially boys, were anxious to avoid any suspicion that they might be gay. The high school culture they studied had its own codes for defining sexual identity. For example, good students, hard-working students, boys who were gentle, quiet, or avoided sports were sometimes labeled "gay." Students anxiously interpreted each other's behavior as signs of their sexual identity.

In response to such anxieties, the researchers found that male students disassociated themselves from any homoerotic feelings by creating rigid boundaries in their male friendships that excluded any intimate expression that might be construed as sexual. Boys maintained clear social boundaries separating themselves from students who were suspected of being gay. Moreover, some boys engaged in aggressive public displays of homophobia, for example, verbally demeaning students believed to be gay, ridiculing them in loud, visible ways, and at times resorting to violence. The researchers view homophobia as a means to establish a respected straight identity. Boys distance themselves from their own homoerotic feelings by projecting them onto others and denouncing them as gay. This allows these boys to present themselves as consistently heterosexual and masculine.

Students and others feel compelled to publicly declare a straight identity because heterosexuality is a privileged, respected social status. In this regard, scholars have argued that heterosexuality is not simply a behavior or identity but, in most societies, it is an "institution." Societies impose heterosexuality as a sexual and social preference by means of the power of the state, law, medical-scientific institutions, the family, and gender roles, and a culture that simultaneously celebrates heterosexuality while polluting homosexuality. Some theorists proposed a kind of sociology of heterosexuality as a form of social domination.[15]

In sum, recent critical sexual and gender theory offers a new social perspective not only on homosexuality but on heterosexuality. The shift from sexual behavior to identity requires a social and historical explanation. Similarly, nature may require heterosexual behavior but it does not require that heterosexuality becomes the social norm; nor is it inevitable that heterosexuality becomes an institution or a system of power; these developments are social in origin. At the root of this new thinking is a far-reaching proposition: sex itself is social. The desires, fantasies, acts, identities, and relationships that we view as "sexual" are a product of social factors and dynamics; we may be born with bodies but we become sexual only in society.

Suggested Readings

Vanessa Baird, *The No-Nonsense Guide to Sexual Diversity* (London: Verso, 2001).
Annamarie Jagose, *Queer Theory* (New York: New York Press, 1997).
Steven Seidman, *The Social Construction of Sexuality* (New York: W. W. Norton, 2003).
Michael Warner, ed., *Fear of a Queer Planet* (Minneapolis: University of Minnesota Press, 1993).

References

1 Jonathan Katz, *Gay/Lesbian Almanac* (New York: Harper & Row, 1983); Steven Seidman, *Romantic Longings* (New York: Routledge, 1991); Lillian Faderman, *Odd Girls and Twilight Lovers* (New York: Columbia University Press, 1991).

2 Carroll Smith-Rosenberg, "The Female World of Love and Ritual: Relations between Women in Nineteenth-Century America," in *Disorderly Conduct* (New York: Alfred A. Knopf, 1985); Lillian Faderman, *Surpassing the Love of Men* (New York: William Morrow, 1981); Anthony Rotundo, *American Manhood* (New York: Basic Books, 1993).

3 Ti-Grace Atkinson, "The Institution of Sexual Intercourse," in *Women's Liberation: Notes from the Second Year* (New York: Radical Feminism, 1970); and "Lesbianism and Feminism," in Phyllis Birkby, Bertha Harris, Jill Johnston, Esther Newton, et al., eds., *Amazon Expedition* (Washington, DC: Times Change Press, 1973); Charlotte Bunch, "Lesbians in Revolt," in Nancy Myron and Charlotte Bunch, eds., *Lesbianism and the Women's Movement* (Baltimore, MD: Diana Press, 1975); Jill Johnston, *Lesbian Nation* (New York: Simon & Schuster, 1973); Rita Mae Brown, "The Shape of Things to Come," in Myron and Bunch, eds., *Lesbianism and the Women's Movement*.

4 Adrienne Rich, "Compulsory Heterosexuality and Lesbian Existence," in Ann Snitow, Christine Stansell, and Sharon Thompson, eds., *Powers of Desire* (New York: Monthly Review Press, 1983).

5 Rich, "Compulsory Heterosexuality," p. 195.

6 Rich, "Compulsory Heterosexuality," p. 202.

7 Jeffrey Weeks, *Sexuality and Its Discontents* (London: Routledge, 1985).

8 Jeffrey Weeks, *Sexuality* (New York: Tavistock, 1986), p. 26.

9 Jeffrey Weeks, *Coming Out: Homosexual Politics in Britain from the Nineteenth Century to the Present* (London: Quartet Books, 1977).

10 Diana Fuss, *Essentially Speaking: Feminism, Nature and Difference* (New York: Routledge, 1989), p. 103; also see "Inside/Out," in Diana Fuss, ed., *Inside/Out: Lesbian Theories, Gay Theories* (New York: Routledge, 1991).

11 Eve Kosofsky Sedgwick, *The Epistemology of the Closet* (Berkeley, University of California Press, 1990).

12 Sedgwick, *Epistemology of the Closet*, p. 1.

13 Jonathan Katz, *The Invention of Heterosexuality* (New York: Penguin, 1995).

14 Debbie Epstein and Richard Johnson, *Schooling Sexualities* (Buckingham: Open University Press, 1998).

15 For example, see Chrys Ingraham, *White Weddings: Romancing Heterosexuality in Popular Culture* (New York: Routledge, 1999); Mary Louise Adams, *The Trouble with Normal: Postwar Youth and the Making of Heterosexuality* (Toronto: University of Toronto Press, 1997); and Michael Warner, "Fear of a Queer Planet," Social Text 9 (1991), 3–17.

17

Colonial Discourse Studies

Sociology had its origin in Anglo-European societies. These societies were undergoing dramatic social changes – for example, industrial capitalism, with its factories, wage labor, and commercialization of social life, occurred initially in England, France, Germany, and the United States. These nations became world powers in the course of the nineteenth and twentieth centuries. This was the era of Anglo-European world dominance. England and France ruled the nineteenth century, and the United States and the Soviet Union were the superpowers of the twentieth century. These nations were imperial powers.

In many respects, World War II marked the end of the imperial era. The United Nations declared the principle of universal national sovereignty, underscoring world disapproval of nations colonizing each other. To be sure, the United States and the Soviet Union continued to be imperial powers but they no longer relied on direct military and political power to control other societies. Instead, they relied on their economic power, the threat of their mighty military, and at times limited military interventions, and pervasive covert operations. The postwar period also witnessed a wave of anticolonial nationalist movements across the globe. In Africa and in Southeast Asia, independent movements, animated by the spirit of nationalism and independence, rebelled against their colonial rulers. India struggled to end British rule; African societies ended the European colonization of their continent, and in 1989 Eastern Europe ended the rule of the Soviet Union and inaugurated the unraveling of that empire. The postwar period was, then, a time of great turmoil and hope.

As the global social landscape was being refashioned, a new class of thinkers was nourished in these newly formed national states. These thinkers were situated betweeen colonialism and postcolonialism. They looked at the Anglo-European world through the lens of colonial subjection but were also a part of that world in the sense of being educated in the West and in many cases living there.

Contested Knowledge: Social Theory Today, Fifth Edition. Steven Seidman.
© 2013 John Wiley & Sons, Ltd. Published 2013 by John Wiley & Sons, Ltd.

These intellectuals developed new critical perspectives on Anglo-European history. In particular, they viewed the West from the vantage point of a history of colonialism. They asked new questions: why did America and European nations become imperial powers? How did these imperial nations manage to colonize and rule over foreign territories and peoples? And, what was the relationship between the colonizers and those colonized? How did these powerful nations justify acts of colonial domination while at the same time championing ideas of individual freedom, national sovereignty, and social progress?

FRANTZ FANON

The 1950s and 1960s witnessed movements of decolonization – in Africa, the Caribbean, Central and South America, the Middle East, and Asia. Peoples that had been colonies were declaring their independence – from Jamaica and Kenya to India, Vietnam, and Hungary. A new class of intellectuals came of age in the context of these global changes. They were, at once, intellectuals and activists deeply engaged in these movements of rebellion and national reconstruction.

Thinkers such as Frantz Fanon, C. L. R. James, Aimé Césaire, and Albert Memmi were exemplary of this new type of political intellectual.[1] They lived in two worlds – of the colony and of the empire. For example, Fanon was neither just a native of Martinique nor just a Frenchman, but both. The experience of living in two worlds but not belonging entirely to either gave these intellectuals a distinctive social perspective. Specifically, they insisted that the focus of social analysis should be societies in interaction – in particular, the East/West exchange which was a relation of colony and empire.

Many of the leaders of these anticolonial nationalist movements drew on Marxism to understand and critique Western colonialism. There was a tradition of Marxist analysis of colonialism. Central to this perspective is the notion that imperialism is an extension of capitalism. As a dynamic economic system that must continually expand in order to realize profits and growth, capitalism inevitably drives businesses to expand beyond national borders. In search of new markets, raw materials, cheap labor, and stable social environments, capitalism drives nations to establish and maintain colonies. As the prosperity of Anglo-European nations rests on controlling the resources

Frantz Fanon (1925–61) was born in the French colony of Martinique. He left Martinique during World War II to fight in France against Nazi Germany, and after the war he remained in France to train in psychiatry. Fanon served in an Algerian hospital during the French–Algerian War. He was one of the originators of a theory of colonialism. His psychiatric training proved helpful in exploring the psychology of colonial domination. How do victims of colonial power end up reproducing it? What is the role of physical and psychological violence in maintaining and overthrowing colonial rule?

and peoples of foreign territories, Western governments do the political and military work of establishing and maintaining colonies.

Postcolonial thinkers drew from Marxism but also offered new ways of understanding colonialism. In particular, they emphasized cultural perspectives. Fanon and others underscored the point that colonialism involves more than establishing markets, military outposts, and puppet governments in nonsovereign territories. Colonialism involves a cultural distinction between sovereign nation-states and colonized territories such that the former are viewed as superior to the latter. In other words, before one nation can invade, conquer, and dominate another nation, there is often a cultural context that establishes a moral division between types of societies. Accordingly, territorial conquest may be seen as a legitimate, indeed a necessary, vehicle of social progress.

Frantz Fanon, a native of Martinique, which was a colony of France, was the author of major works that detailed the logic of colonial domination and resistance.[2] He asked: how do colonizing nations justify domination? And, just as importantly, how do previously independent peoples become dominated and accommodate to their colonial status? How does colonization shape the psychology and social lives of the colonized in ways that sustain their condition?

Fanon argued that at the heart of empire is the dehumanization of the native. The colonized are defined as inferior, as a lesser human type. In particular, the colonized are often understood as racially inferior. For example, Fanon analyzed the ideas of "the Black" held by European colonizers in Africa and the Caribbean. In colonial discourse, Blacks are seen as thoroughly sexual and instinctual, and as lacking self-control and discipline. The very nature of the Black is said to impede social progress in Africa and the Caribbean. Curiously, colonialism is often justified in the name of Western humanism. As the presumed carriers of reason and advanced civilization, the peoples of Europe and the United States imagine that they have a duty, indeed a destiny, to spread enlightenment and progress to the rest of humanity. It is the mission of the West to lift humanity out of the darkness of the reign of impulse, superstition, and despotism into the light of reason, democracy, and social progress. Fanon believed that the fact of Western dominance results in the colonial subject taking over the view of the colonizer as superior. This cultural imperialism is partially what makes colonial rule possible. In effect, the colonial subject, faced with a superior power, accommodates by assuming his or her own social inferiority. The colonial subject may become passive and even actively support the civilizing mission of the colonizer. Yet, while colonial domination penetrates into the psyche of the native, there is also rage towards the colonizer's power to destroy, dehumanize, and demoralize the native and her culture. It is this deeply rooted psychological and social rage that fuels the risks and hopes – and sometimes the violence – of movements of national independence.

In Fanon's view, violence is a central feature of colonialism. There is the violence the colonizers perpetrate on the bodies of the colonized, e.g., practices of imprisonment, torture, beatings, rape, starvation, genocide, and the denial of decent housing and healthcare. There is also the violence done to the hearts and minds of the colonized by being denied freedom, integrity, and self-respect. Furthermore, colonial domination perpetrates violence against native culture. The history of the colonized is suppressed or destroyed. Their customs are ridiculed and demeaned. They are pressured to adopt the culture of the rulers; their beliefs and values are dismissed as backward and primitive. Speaking of the African experience, Fanon describes how colonial powers acted to obliterate the diverse tribal and national cultures of Africa by treating them as the expressions of the primitive mind of the Negro:

> Colonialism . . . has never ceased to maintain that the Negro is a savage; and for the colonist, the Negro was neither Angolan nor a Nigerian. For he simply spoke of "the Negro." For colonialism, this vast continent [Africa] was the haunt of savages, a country riddled with superstitions and fanaticism, destined for contempt, weighed down by the curse of God, a country of cannibals – in short, the Negro's country. Colonialism's condemnation is continental in its scope.[3]

Fanon's ideas are important because he insists that colonialism has a deeply cultural and psychological aspect. He understood that as much as colonial domination involves territorial, economic, and military control, it also involves capturing and dominating the very souls of the colonized. The ruthless psychic, cultural, and social violence of colonialism helps to explain two defining features of decolonializing movements. First, they have been anticolonial nationalist movements. Independence movements across Africa and the Caribbean have rallied the masses by appealing to the authenticity and value of their historical cultural traditions. These movements have sought to rehabilitate native culture as the basis of an independent sovereign nation. As nationalist movements, the colonized take over the nationalist framework of the colonizers. A second defining feature of colonial rebellions has been their own violence. Driven by a collective rage, these anticolonial movements have all too often relied on the very practice that was used against them: violence. If the initial targets of violence were the European colonizers, this rage sadly has often been turned against native rivals once the colonizers have been vanquished.

EDWARD SAID

Fanon believed that at the root of Western colonialism is ironically what he called "humanism." Humanism was less a philosophy than a messianic culture. At the core of humanism is the belief that reason and freedom are definitive of humankind. It is the destiny of the West to lift all of humanity from a childlike state of nature to the heights of civilization. As the most advanced sector of humanity, European societies are obligated to bring reason and civilization to all of humankind. This evangelical spirit is what ultimately drove Western imperialism and blinded the peoples of the West to the suffering and chaos they created.

Whereas Fanon was brilliant at imagining the cultural and psychological aspects of colonialism, Edward Said was the master theorist who was to make colonialism central to modernity. A Palestinian who lived most of his adult life in the United States, Said believed that the stark realities of colonialism and imperialism should be at the center of modern history. He wrote:

Edward Said was born in Jerusalem in 1935. He attended schools in Jerusalem, Cairo, and Massachusetts. Said earned his PhD at Harvard University in 1964. He taught at Columbia University until his death in 2003. Said proposed the idea that before there could be Western colonialism there had to be the idea of the "West" in distinction from the "East." Western power could be exercised in the form of territorial conquest only if it was seen as worthy and noble. If the East was viewed as despotic and backward, expanding Western power to this region could be rationalized as a tool in the service of progress.

Consider that in 1800 Western powers claimed 55 percent but actually held approximately 35 percent of the earth's surface, and that by 1878 the proportion was 67 percent . . . By 1914 . . . Europe held a grand total of roughly 85 percent of the earth as colonies, protectorates, dependencies, dominions, and commonwealths. No other associated set of colonies in history was as large, none so totally dominated, none so unequal in power to the Western metropolis . . . And in Europe itself at the end of the nineteenth century, scarcely a corner of life was untouched by the facts of empire.[4]

Notice: Said is saying that the realities of empire shape the worlds of the colonizers and colonized. For colonizing nations such as Britain, Belgium, Holland, or Germany, their economy, government, military, and culture were deeply shaped by the need to acquire and maintain dominance over other lands and peoples; for colonized nations such as India, Egypt, virtually the entire African continent, and large stretches of Southeast Asia, there were, of course, the harsh realities of phyical and social violence and subjugation.

Said argues that the making and sustaining of empire in modern Western history cannot be explained exclusively in political and economic terms. He writes:

At the heart of European culture during the many decades of imperial expansion lay an undeterred and unrelenting Eurocentrism. This accumulated experiences, territories, peoples, histories; it studied them, it classified them, it verified them, and . . . above all, it subordinated them by banishing their identities, except as a lower order of being, from the culture and indeed the very idea of white Christian Europe. This cultural process has to be seen as a vital, informing, and invigorating counterpoint to the economic and political machinery at the material center of imperialism.[5]

In *Orientalism,* Said aims to deliver a cultural account of colonialism that is far more complex than Fanon's bold but overly reductive claim regarding its humanistic origins.

Said argued that before there could be an era of European colonization there had to be an idea of "Europe" or the notion that there is a social and geographical space called the "West" in contrast to the "East." In his view, the ideas of the West and East are not natural geographical–civilizational complexes. The different peoples that make up the so-called Orient are diverse in language, culture, history, and politics. The desert nomads of the Arabian peninsula are as different from the Mandarins who ruled successive Chinese empires as they are from the American industrialist or the

French civil servant. If today the West and East are thought of as two distinct civilizations, each with its own identity or essence, it is because historically we have been led to think this way. Binary notions of West/East and Occident/Orient were present as far back as the ancient Greeks. Yet, it was only between the eighteenth and twentieth centuries in Europe that there developed a network of beliefs that were institutionalized in universities, institutes, governments, and popular culture and that made a sharp division between the Occident and the Orient.

After the eighteenth century, it became conventional wisdom in England, the United States and across Europe that the West is rational, promotes individual freedom and democracy, and is the vehicle that drives social progress. By contrast, Western thinkers agreed that the East is socially backward, despotic, or childlike, and incapable of advancement and progress. Often the inferiority of the Orient was understood in racial and gender terms. The Oriental was imagined as non-White and "primitive" and associated with stereotypical feminine traits such as passivity, indecision, childlikeness, and the ornamental. Said calls the network of discourses, representations, knowledges, and folk beliefs that construct this global symbolic division, "Orientalism":

> [Among the] principal dogmas of Orientalism . . . is the absolute and systematic difference between the West, which is rational, developed, humane, superior, and the Orient, which is aberrant, undeveloped, inferior. Another dogma is that abstractions about the Orient . . . are always preferable to direct evidence drawn from modern Oriental realities. A third dogma is that the Orient is eternal, uniform, and incapable of defining itself; . . . A fourth dogma is that the Orient is at bottom something either to be feared (the Yellow Peril, the Mongol hordes, the brown dominions) or to be controlled (by pacification, research and development, outright occupation whenever possible).[6]

In short, a Eurocentric culture took root in Anglo-American societies that asserted a geographical, civilizational, and moral division between West and East. It was the destiny of the West to bring civilization and progress to the East.

Orientalism was central to Western imperialism. Orientalist ideology motivated colonization: the West was imagined as bringing social progress and freedom to the Orient. Left on their own, societies such as India, China, Saudi Arabia, or Egypt drift into stagnation, endless civil conflict, and despotism. In a sense, Said is arguing that colonization was made possible because colonizing nations never really saw actual Egyptians, Indians, or Palestinians. Western colonial powers only perceived these peoples as examples of "the Oriental," and therefore as childlike, feminine, despotic, and immature – in short, as needing the moral and rational guidance of the West to civilize them.

HOMI BHABHA

It is not too much of an exaggeration to say that the work of Fanon and Said shaped an entire new field of knowledge, colonial discourse studies. While this field is influenced by Marxism and continues to insist on the important role of economic, political, and military forces in explaining the dynamics of colonialism, there is an emphasis on the central role of culture. In particular, the focus is on the way "Western" ideas about the West and the East, about the Occident and the Orient, shaped a history of European colonialism. Initially, colonial discourse studies was the product of thinkers who had roots in colonial societies but also in Western societies. They were intellectuals situated somewhere in the gray space between colonialism and postcolonialism. This ambiguous standpoint made it possible for them to understand the complexities of colonial rule, the subtle complex dynamics between the colonizer and colonized.

The key assumption of colonial discourse studies is the notion that culture and power are connected. Specifically, language, knowledge, the media, popular culture, art, and literature are, whatever else, also forms of power. These cultural forms shape the behavior of powerful elites and popular culture, providing motives and justifications for imperial practices. A Eurocentric culture has created images or ideas of West and East, modernity and tradition, progress and stagnation, that are an indispensable part of colonialism.

If *Orientalism* is the starting point for studies in this field, it is not the final statement. His successors bear the weight of Said's ideas but also the obligation to critique this founding figure. Said's *Orientalism* is criticized for assuming a flat notion of the Orient and Occident. In a way that reproduces Orientalism, Said's view of the Eurocentric discourse of East and West is criticized for ignoring or discounting variations in Western images of the East, some of which were used to critique the West. Critics argue that Said also ignored the images non-Westerners had of themselves and of the West. The peoples who occupied the "Orient" often resisted Eurocentric representations and preserved their own culture or invented new hybrid cultures. In short, the relationship between Western colonizers and the colonized was much more complex than either Fanon or Said imagined.

The literary theorist Homi Bhabha made the complexity and ambiguity of the colonial experience into a central theme. He introduced three concepts that have proven to be influential: ambivalance, mimicry, and hybridity.[7] Where Said argued that Anglo-European societies construct the East as the inferior Other to the West, Bhabha suggests that the West has an ambivalent relationship to the East. As much as Western societies represent the Oriental as different and inferior, Eurocentric discourses also reveal a desire, an attraction, or a longing for the Orient. The Orient

Homi Bhabha was born in India in 1949, was educated in both India and Britain and has held various academic positions in the United States. Currently, he is a professor of English at Harvard. Bhabha's perspective has been shaped by his ambiguous social positioning between a youth and early adulthood in a former colony and life as an adult in the two major imperial powers of the twentieth century, Britain and the United States. His preferred genre is the essay. His major book to date, *The Location of Culture*, is a collection of his essays. At the center of his writing is an attempt to introduce layers of complexity in the understanding of colonial dynamics. Bhabha pushes us to see ambiguity, ambivalence, and fluidity, where both colonizer and colonized want to see only sharp division and opposition.

serves as a possible alternative to the West, an attractive Other to be desired and imitated. But also, and adding to the ambivalence of the West, as much as the West is repulsed by the East, it also identifies with the East. To the extent that the West sees itself in the East, the East has a certain power over the West and it becomes a threat to the West. It threatens to undermine the claim of the West to superiority, which is dependent on its claims of the Otherness and inferiority of the East. Accordingly, the relationship between the West and East, which serves Bhabha as an exemplar of the relationship between colonizer and colonized, is not just opposi-tional but involves identification, a mix of repulsion and attraction, and a standpoint of dominance that is always in danger of reversal.

Bhabha introduces the notion of mimicry to further complicate the dynamic of colonialism. Is power only a linear, one-sided equation? Is it only the West or the colo-nizer who has power? In fact, colonialism, especially nineteenth-century European colonialism, involved "indirect rule." Colonial powers such as Britain or France relied on the colonial subject to maintain their rule. Britain was able to rule India with only a few thousand British officials and a small British army because it relied on the Indians to administer and enforce British rule. Native Indians administered British rule in order to maintain positions of privilege or gain privileges. The British were dependent on the Indians. The colonizer had to bring the colonized into the sphere of colonial rule. Collaboration, mutual dependency between colonizer and colonized, is what made colonial rule possible. But this very condition also empowers the colonized; they have to be educated and trained in the skills of rulership. Ironically, this collabo-ration creates a desire on the part of the colonized to "mimic" the colonizer, that is, a desire to rule, to become self-governing. After all, once the colonized realize that they have the skills and capacities to rule and to be self-governing, the colonizer becomes superfluous. Mimicry threatens to undermine colonial rule. Resistance as much as subjection is an integral part of the colonial dynamic.

With the concept of "hybridity" Bhabha proposes a final challenge to framing the colonial relationship in flattened binary terms (colonizer/colonized, ruler/ruled). The colonial condition of collaboration and mutual dependency, as we have seen, is an unstable or dynamic condition. Power is more fluid than fixed; identification blurs the boundary between colonizer and colonized. Moreover, the condition of collabo-ration which makes indirect rule possible means that the colonized not only takes over the skills of rulership but some of its culture – its language, practices of self-presenta-tion, and the aesthetics and affectations of the ruler. This very deep level of identifica-tion or mimicry undermines the psychic and cultural boundaries separating the colonial power and the colonial subject. Moreover, if the latter appropriates some of the culture of the former, the colonizer takes over something of the culture of the colonized self as a condition of collaboration. In other words, identification and mim-icry occur for both the colonizer and colonized. Colonial selves and cultures are less appropriately understood in binary terms than in the language of hybridity or mixing. Again, Bhabha's conclusion is that colonialism shapes in basic ways the colonized and the colonizer.

Bhabha's theoretical views might seem removed from the historical context, but they offer a rich conceptual approach to the empirical study of colonial dynamics. His perspective compels us to pay close attention to patterns of collaboration, mutual dependency, and cultural innovation in colonial practice. Instead of approaching power as flowing in a linear, one-sided way from the ruler to the ruled, he underscores the two-way directionality of power, even if rulers clearly have more social power. The power of rulers is always limited because they are dependent on colonial subjects to enforce their rule and because they identify with and become attached to, even desire, the colonial subject. This condition of dependency and identification on the part of the colonizer gives to the colonized the skills and the space to potentially resist and subvert the former. At the same time, the identification on the part of the colonized creates an ambivalent relationship to the ruling power. Does the colonized wish to take a position alongside the colonizer or to replace the colonizer? And, perhaps more tellingly, does the identification of the colonized with the colonizer set in motion a dynamic to replace colonial rule only to become new colonial-type rulers in postcolonial conditions? With a glance at the decidedly mixed histories of postcolonial rule in Africa and elswhere, Bhabha offers a theoretical perspective on the sobering political meaning of anticolonial nationalist movements of the twentieth century.

Suggested Readings

Iain Chambers and Lidia Curti, eds., *The Postcolonial Question* (New York: Routledge, 1996).
Patrick Williams and Laura Chrisman, eds., *Colonial Discourse and Post-Colonial Theory* (New York: Columbia University Press, 1994).
Robert Young, *Colonial Desire* (New York: Routledge, 1995).

References

1   Frantz Fanon, *The Wretched of the Earth* (New York: Grove Press, 1968); C. L. R. James, *The Black Jacobins* (New York: Random House, 1963); Aimé Césaire, *Discourse on Colonialism* (New York: Monthly Review Press, 1972); Albert Memmi, *The Colonizer and the Colonized* (Boston, MA: Beacon Press, 1974).
2   Frantz Fanon, *Black Skin, White Masks* (New York: Grove Press, 1968).
3   Fanon, *The Wretched of the Earth*, p. 211.
4   Edward Said, *Culture and Imperialism* (New York: Vintage, 1994), p. 8.
5   Said, *Culture and Imperialism*, p. 222.
6   Edward Said, *Orientalism* (New York: Vintage, 1978), p. 301.
7   Homi Bhabha, *The Location of Culture* (New York: Routledge, 1994).

Afterword to Part V

As we've seen, the Enlightenment was arguably a key turning point in social thought. Human behavior and social institutions were understood as social. Whatever the biological bases of human motivation, the shapes of our lives are, to a considerable degree, a product of social factors.

Much of modern social theory has tried to say exactly which social factors matter – and to understand the shape of human and social life today. Also, modern thinkers wished to comment on the moral and political meaning of modern life. Accordingly, theorists have fashioned different perspectives, each often very compelling. Marx said it was the economy that truly mattered; and modern societies are torn between a world driven forward by technology and ideas of freedom and a world divided by class and social inequality. Other theorists offered their own view. Weber gave more weight to the role of politics and culture in shaping social life; he thought that bureaucracy was our chief threat to freedom and individuality. He was deeply pessimistic about humankind's future. Parsons was perhaps the most optimistic. Propelled by the democratic, industrial, and educational revolutions, freedom, he thought, is advancing steadily in the modern world.

The figures of the Enlightenment, from Montesquieu to Adam Smith, and their nineteenth-century heirs such as Comte, Marx, Weber, and Durkheim created, then, a powerful tradition of social thinking. Anyone thinking about the social world today must wrestle with their social and moral visions of the world. We are all standing on the shoulders of these intellectual giants.

Yet, serious doubts have been raised about some of the key ideas of this tradition of social thinking. We saw the rise of so-called postmodern perspectives that seriously challenged many of the standard ways of thinking about society and modernity. In the work of Foucault, in particular, we can speak of a serious break from the theory canon. Foucault challenged conventional views of social knowledge and the social and

Contested Knowledge: Social Theory Today, Fifth Edition. Steven Seidman.
© 2013 John Wiley & Sons, Ltd. Published 2013 by John Wiley & Sons, Ltd.

moral dynamics of modern life. A similar challenge comes from social thinkers associated with recent social movements for gender, sexual, racial, and international justice.

Feminist, Afrocentric, gay, and postcolonial theorists are highly critical of many aspects of the dominant tradition of social theory.

First, the tradition is criticized for ignoring key aspects of social life. Where, they ask, are the analyses of the body, sexuality, gender, race, empire, and personal identity? Marx speaks of labor, but what about the labor of producing children, and caring for the bodies and minds of adults, which has been mostly the labor of women? Durkheim analyzes the division of labor in society, but nowhere is there an analysis of the making of the divisions between men and women, between races, and between sexual citizens. Weber's brilliant comparisons of civilizations to explain Western modernization oddly fail to consider the role of colonialism and imperialism! It wasn't just that France, Britain, or Holland were "modernizing," but they developed at the expense of societies which were being exploited and conquered.

Second, if this theoretical tradition neglected key aspects of social life, their stories of modernity are also deeply flawed. Marx's analysis of the political economy of capitalism lacks an analysis of the gendered, racial, and sexual aspects of this mode of production. For all the brilliance of Weber's portrait of bureaucracy, the gendered and sexualized aspects of organizational dynamics are completely absent. Similarly, where in Weber or Habermas or Giddens is the story of the making of a norm of heterosexuality? How did heterosexuality become associated with what is natural and right? And, after all, how did so much of social theory, from Comte to Parsons, Habermas, and Collins, end up telling a story of modernity that made the West into the dramatic center, thereby reducing the non-West to bit players in this world of historical human drama?

Third, identity-based thinkers challenge a tradition that has associated objective knowledge with science. From Condorcet through Durkheim, Parsons, and Bourdieu, science, and science alone, was thought to yield social truths. Philosophy, literature, religion, common sense, journalism, and tradition offered subjective or prejudiced social ideas. Such ideas may be helpful for living but they are not solid truths. Only science can rise above prejudice, social interests, and politics to reveal the world "as it is."

But some feminists, gays, critical race thinkers and postcolonial theorists have challenged this view. For example, some feminists described Western science as androcentric, or reflecting the interests and values of men. The masculine coloring of science is revealed in sociology, for example, in its chief problems and topics (e.g., the economy and government rather than gender, sexuality, or families), its basic categories and explanations (e.g., wage labor rather than domestic labor, or class explanations rather than gender-role accounts), and methodology (e.g., quantitative rather than ethnographic). The very criteria of social knowledge are said to be gendered. Thus, the identification of knowledge with objective, value-neutral standards is said to reflect men's abstract formalistic culture. By contrast, women are thought to prefer a personal, experiential, dialogic, and contextual approach to knowledge. If scientific knowledge is identified with men's values, women's ways of knowing are devalued as inferior or pre-scientific.

Identity-oriented thinkers view science as political. For example, psychology and sociology have been central in producing "scientific" perspectives defining women as maternal, emotional, and nurturing. These gender definitions pressure women to assume the roles of wife, mother, and social caretaker (e.g., nurse, secretary, or social worker). Similarly, psychology has been a formative social force in shaping a culture that views heterosexuality as natural and normal while stigmatizing homosexuality as abnormal and deviant. In its discourses of deviance and "the family," sociology has often viewed heterosexuality and nuclear families as natural and good. The social sciences have constructed non-Western societies as backward, primitive, static, and authoritarian. From Marx to Habermas, social science has been a major source of "Orientalism" or the contrast between the presumed superior West and the inferior, subordinate East. These identity theories then view science as entangled in social practices of exclusion, marginalization, and devaluation, from justifying the denial of civil rights to gays to promoting colonialism as a contribution to social progress. This doesn't mean that science is dismissed as evil; science has also been used to combat heterosexism, sexism, and Eurocentrism. The point is that politics is said to shape and be shaped by social knowledge in ways that we have not usually acknowledged.

Part VI

Revisions and Revolts: Theories of World Order

Introduction to Part VI

From Comte to Habermas modern social theory has assumed the sovereign nation-state as the basic unit of modern social life and analysis. It has further been assumed that nation-states change as a result of primarily internal social and cultural dynamics. For example, the crisis of capitalism, according to Habermas, is a result of the internal contradictions between the political, economic, and cultural aspects of a specific society. Weber and Parsons were convinced that Western development was driven by internal cultural developments set in motion by Roman law and Christianity.

However, today many scholars have underscored a telling point: the nation-state has not always existed. Although there is considerable disagreement on the origins of nation-states, most scholars agree that the age of nationalism and the nation-state was in the nineteenth and twentieth centuries. By the end of World War II virtually every society across the globe was organized as a nation-state. For example, between 1870 and 1970, the continent of Africa went from no nation-states in 1870 to a continent made up of only nation-states. Today, the United Nations recognizes some 194 independent nations.

Yet, at the very time when the age of the nation-state seems to be triumphant, scholars are beginning to question their actual sovereignty. Some thinkers are wondering whether the age of nationalism is in fact on the decline. Many social and political thinkers have declared a postnational age characterized by a global order and the dominance of international movements and agencies. And still other social critics highlight the improbable return of imperial practices reminiscent of the nineteenth century. The US invasion of Iraq, the Russian suppression of Chechan aspirations for nationhood, an Israeli policy of promoting colonial settlements in Palestine, or the crushing of Tibetan culture by the Chinese state suggest that it may be too soon to close the book on the era of colonialism.

Contested Knowledge: Social Theory Today, Fifth Edition. Steven Seidman.
© 2013 John Wiley & Sons, Ltd. Published 2013 by John Wiley & Sons, Ltd.

In the next several chapters, we examine some of the most provocative and challenging perspectives on the shape of the nation and world order today. Debates about globalization, the changing nature of capitalism, and the question of the role of imperialism pose a challenge to two of the key principles of the post-World War II world order: the sovereignty of the nation-state and the reliance on international institutions and law to create civil order and peace across the globe.

18

From Nation to Globe
David Held and Mary Kaldor

Many of us are today accustomed to thinking about current affairs from a global perspective. We know, in a manner of speaking, that events in one part of the world can have effects in other regions of the world. But, when it comes to clarifying the concept of globalization, there is considerable disagreement. Generally speaking, in the United States, an economic perspective on globalization is prominent. American thinkers from the Nobel Prize economist Joseph Stiglitz to the *New York Times* columnist Thomas Friedman understand globalization as the making of an economically integrated world.[1] The expansion of markets has tied the different regions of the world into a network of commercial exchanges; goods, money, capital, and labor circulate across national boundaries in dizzying numbers and at mind-boggling speed. Today, these thinkers say, the exemplary enterprise is multinational, the field of capital investment is international, and labor is global. In short, some American thinkers argue that we live in a global order driven by a global economy. This is a powerful perspective and speaks, of course, to America's economic world dominance. It is not, though, the only point of view on globalization.

Across the ocean, the British have fashioned an equally compelling sociological view of globalization. In light of Britain's recent history as a world power, we should not be surprised that the British are more accustomed to viewing nations as part of an international arena. If the Americans underscore the economic aspects, the British emphasize the social and political dimensions of globalization. There is, to speak loosely, a distinctive "school" of sociologists that has staked out a unique and sociologically important perspective on globalization. Centered in the London School of Economics, and with roots in critical Marxist traditions, these sociologists look hopefully but with a keen sense of historical irony at globalizing dynamics.

Contested Knowledge: Social Theory Today, Fifth Edition. Steven Seidman.
© 2013 John Wiley & Sons, Ltd. Published 2013 by John Wiley & Sons, Ltd.

David Held was born in 1951. He is currently the Graham Wallas Professor of Political Science at the London School of Economics. He is the author of *Models of Democracy* (2006), *Global Transformations* (1999), *Cosmopolitanism: A Defence* (2003), and *Global Covenant: The Social Democratic Alternative to the Washington Consensus* (2004). Held aims to provide an alternative to the neo-liberal view of globalization as well as to the antiglobalization perspective of some radical critics. He defends a complicated sociological view of globalization as well as a cosmopolitan approach to global regulation. The latter would rely less on the market or nationalist strategies to resolve international conflicts; instead, Held would encourage the development of institutions such as international law and the International Court of Justice to play a central role in global regulation.

THE PROMISE OF GLOBALIZATION: DAVID HELD

The sociologist and political theorist, David Held, has been a key figure in shaping British globalization studies.[2] Held sketches the broad outlines of a sociology of globalization that is at once a forceful empirical portrait and a compelling ethical–political assessment.

Drawing from recent scholarship on the history of nations, Held argues that from roughly the eighth to the fifteenth centuries the nation-state was not a salient feature of Europe. During this time, Europe was characterized by a decentralized and fragmented system of rule. Its territories were made up of a web of kingdoms, principalities, cities, and other power centers. Power was personal and local. If there was one overarching political power it was Christendom, or the Holy Roman Empire, which extended from Germany to Spain and from northern France to Italy. And while its secular power was limited, the Catholic Church was a major rival to more local feudal powers.

The modern state developed as a challenge to the dominance of the Catholic Church and to the multiple power centers of feudalism, which aspired to concentrate and centralize power. In the course of the sixteenth and seventeenth centuries, new political regimes emerged: the absolutist monarchies in France, Austria, Spain, and Russia, and the constitutional monarchies of Britain and Holland. European monarchs claimed a legitimate right to rule over a territory and a population by virtue of a divine right. These kings proceeded to elaborate a state administrative apparatus, a standing army, a professional bureaucracy, a system of fiscal management, which made possible their social rule over a wide territory. In short, the key elements of the modern state were created by the great monarchies of the sixteenth and seventeenth centuries.

What social factors led to the development of these features of the modern states? First, endemic rivalries and wars between monarchies put a premium upon military power. Developing and sustaining a standing army and navy, and paying for it, required the forging of a centralized political administration. Second, commercial competition between European powers pressured each government to centralize political power in order to enhance economic development. The state was involved in promoting commerce and industry and protecting its national wealth from foreign powers. Third, the development of the modern state was promoted by the increased power of the middle class and a wage labor class. As the state depended on recruiting citizens for the military and encouraging economic development, the government needed the loyalty of the people. In exchange for national loyalty and service the propertied classes were given citizenship rights. Individuals who were "subjects" or dependants under monarchies were becoming "citizens" of a national state. Indeed, in the course of the eighteenth and nineteenth centuries, monarchies were being transformed into something like democratic national states characterized by elections, the rule of law, political parties, and a public sphere. Unlike monarchies, which appealed to tradition or divine right to justify political rule, the new national states appealed to the power of the people and expressed the social ideal of national sovereignty and a self-governing democratic society. The national state was viewed as a sovereign social system and the container for democracy.

The formation of the modern state is distinct from the rise of the nation-state. The modern state refers to a system of political administration that includes centralized political power, a monopoly of control over the means of violence, and clear territorial borders. As we've seen, these features were present in the monarchies of the sixteenth and seventeenth centuries. The idea of a nation involves the idea that members of a society share a common history, culture, and identity. The great European monarchies evolved powerful states but not necessarily nations. Generally speaking, it was only over the nineteenth and twentieth centuries that modern national states developed.

The ideal of national sovereignty gained considerable traction in the nineteenth and early twentieth centuries. Each national state was said to be sovereign and autonomous within its own borders. International law was to recognize the territorial sovereignty of states, their formal equality, and the right of states to establish their own social laws and policies.

The reality, however, contradicted this principle of national sovereignty. From roughly the eighteenth century until after World War II, many European nations were imperial states. World empires such as those of Britain, France, and Germany exercised considerable control across the globe. In fact, colonialism helped create an interconnected global order. The devastation of World War II resulted in the decline of these European empires. The rise of the League of Nations, and subsequently the United Nations, saw the gradual acceptance of peaceful civil forms of international regulation in place of the Realpolitick of imperialism and colonialism. Held believes that a new international order has taken shape, creating the possibility of a civil global order.

The global order today

Despite the principle of national sovereignty and autonomy announced during the last two centuries, national states have been enmeshed in relations of interdependence with other societies and states. In that sense, globalization is not new. Globalization means simply the interconnectedness of societies. What is new, says Held, is the intensity and extent of globalization since World War II. The range and intensity of societal connections and the flows of goods, resources, people, capital, and culture across national borders are historically unique. Today, nations, all nations, are inextricably a part of a global order.

This global order is characterized by the following features:

Global economy. Societies today are part of an international economy and accordingly have less control over their national economies. From the richest nations such as the United States or Japan to the poorest nations in Africa, national economies are dependent on an international division of labor, global financial flows, and the flux of a world market. For example, multinational corporations account for almost one-third of world output, 70 percent of world trade and 80 percent of foreign direct investment. These corporations operate as international firms with global networks; they establish enterprises in multiple territories. Economic production is international in many sectors of the economy, such as automobiles, electronics, and textiles. Similarly, nations have less control over capital and financial transactions. International banks, markets, stock systems, and currencies operate largely outside the control of individual nations. London, Tokyo, and New York today function as global financial centers.

One result of the internationalization of economic life is that national governments find it hard to manage their economies. For example, the oil crisis in the Middle East during the 1970s created an economic crisis across the Western world. As oil-producing nations increase the price of oil, the producer and consumer across the world are affected by paying more for goods, machinery, transportation, and day-to-day living expenses.

The consolidation of a global economy also means a global labor market. Today, more and more workers cross national boundaries seeking jobs or new economic opportunities. Immigrants are streaming into Europe from North Africa and the former Soviet states. In the United States, workers from Mexico and Latin America have become integral to the national economy. India has experienced a "brain drain" as professionals migrate to Britain and the United States for jobs in the high-tech sector.

Global politics. We are living in a time where many social problems transcend national borders, for instance, nuclear proliferation, terrorism, poverty, global warming, and the refugee crisis. In response to these global problems there have developed transnational organizations and movements. For example, in 1909 there were 176 NGOs (nongovernmental organizations); in 1989 there were almost 5,000. NGOs vary from the International Telecommunication Union to world meteorological associations to the World Bank, UNESCO, and Amnesty International. These transnational organizations address concerns that affect nations but cannot be easily managed by them.

Environmental problems, for instance, such as global warming, ozone depletion, threats to specific species, acid rain, and industrial pollution are today global concerns. Individual nations must cooperate to protect the earth's ecosystems. New transnational organizations, treaties, and conventions have been established to facilitate such cooperation. New social movements have been formed in response to global environmental concerns. For example, Greenpeace was founded in 1971; by the mid-1990s it had over 6 million members and revenues of over 100 million dollars.

Greenpeace engages in a range of political actions from media spectacles to lobbying and promoting international policies to hold individual nations accountable. With an elaborate governing council and representatives from dozens of countries, Greenpeace views the threat to environmental sustainability of biodiversity as a world problem requiring a global response.

Or consider the IMF (International Monetary Fund) founded in 1944. Initially created to oversee global currency relations, today the IMF provides technical economic advice and loans to hard-pressed national economies. The IMF can require a nation to alter its economic policies in basic ways in order to get technical and financial support. The sovereignty of nations that depend on the IMF is seriously limited. Along with the World Bank, which is chiefly involved in development policy, the IMF has become a powerful global force shaping the domestic economic and social life of many nations.

The postwar period has also seen the rise of international political organizations that directly impact on nations. For example, the European Union sets policies, passes laws, and issues governance directives that limit the national sovereignty of individual European nations. Members of the EU are directed to avoid certain levels of debt, unemployment, and inflation in order to sustain membership. The European Union has established a European Court of Justice that regulates disputes between nations and considers nations in the European Union to be accountable to the court's decisions.

Global military security. This refers to multilateral and collective defense arrangements and international military coordination that underscore the weakening of national military sovereignty. For example, NATO speaks to the internationalization of security. With its joint military command structure headed by the supreme allied commander in Europe, NATO makes decisions about military security that represent transnational or regional interests, not narrowly national ones. Almost all nations are today part of military networks that transcend and limit national sovereignty.

International law. Although there have been laws regulating the relations between nations since at least the seventeenth century, there has not always been a network of international legal organizations, courts, and laws that also regulate domestic national practices. For example, since World War II, numerous laws have been passed and treaties signed that recognize human rights, not just nation-based civil or political rights. As of 2005, the UN human rights declarations have been signed by 140 out of 190 states. The Organization of African Unity adopted the Charter on Human and People's Rights in 1981 and established a commission to promote and enforce human rights. In 1950, the European Convention for the Protection of Human Rights and Fundamental Freedoms established a new principle that individual citizens can initiate proceedings against their own governments by appealing to international principles of human rights. States cannot just treat their citizens as they see fit. International systems of law hold individual nation-states accountable. Today the individual is a focus of legal moral protection as a citizen of the world.

Global culture. Central to the notion of a nation-state is a distinct national culture and identity. Every nation claims that its citizens share a common history and culture that bind them together as a unique community. Today, this idea has been challenged by the formation of a global culture. For example, despite resistance on the part of many nations, English has become the dominant language throughout the world. And, as the United States has emerged as the sole superpower, its national culture, for example, its television programs, films, music, and art have become global.

The new technologies associated with the telecommunications revolution, along with multimedia conglomerates that operate across national boundaries, have weakened the link between the physical place one lives in and one's cultural experience. Worldwide telecommunications networks give access to information and cultural forms (television, news, the Internet, and websites) no matter where they originate. Cultural products from news documentaries to soap operas to popular music to protests and art circulate across societies. People have access to worlds that they had never encountered before, and likely never will in actual time. To the extent that people are linked to telecommunications networks, we live, no matter where we actually reside, with an acute awareness of being part of a global world.

A global culture does not necessarily mean everyone has the same culture. Local, regional, and national cultural variations remain. Indeed, in many cases local or national cultural traditions and conventions are more deliberately defended, as national citizens resist global cultural dynamics. It does mean, though, that there is a greater awareness that we live in a global cultural environment.

Globalization and democracy

Today, nations are enmeshed in economic, administrative, legal, and cultural networks that limit their independence and sovereignty. We can no longer assume that the sovereign nation-state is the cornerstone of democratic politics in a world that is increasingly shaped by globalizing forces. New questions about the accountability of political authority, representation, and participation are raised in the light of globalization. As power shifts from the nation-state to transnational authorities, or as power is shared between national and global social agencies, we need to reexamine questions of democratic representation and accountability.

Held argues that democracy in a global age requires the establishment of democratic practices at an international level. Just as there are democratic forums of public discussion in national states, for example, parliaments or congress, the same must occur at an international level. In short, we need public deliberative and decision-making bodies that are global. In this regard, Held advocates the notion of a cosmopolitan democracy. Paralleling local and regional political bodies in national states, there must be deliberative global political agencies. Indeed, this notion of a cosmopolitan democracy has already been imagined and partially realized in the UN, the European Union, and in transnational legal agencies. At the heart of these global political institutions is the idea that regulation at the global level is a condition of international order and that such regulation must involve the representation and participation of all the nations of the world.

Held recognizes that establishing democratic practices at a global level will be difficult and will encounter much resistance. However, given a reality of globalizing social and political dynamics which limit national sovereignty, the choice is either rule by the most powerful state or bloc of states, chaos, and war, or the creation of democratic bodies and practices that holds out the possibility of a civil form of global order.

The making of global democracy would require a global civil society, that is, a sphere where social organizations and movements would represent the interests and agendas of varied populations. It would also require a global public political sphere made up of international deliberative and legislative bodies that would do the day-to-day work of global regulation. Organizations like the UN or the International Court of Justice would have to be firmly established and effective, so that decisions by these global organizations would be binding on individual nations. Also, global democratic institutions would require real administrative power to implement laws and policies across the globe. Most importantly, individual states, especially powerful ones, would have to accept political limits to their sovereignty. This would not mean that individual states would lose all of their power but that they would have to learn to share power. These global civic, political, and administrative organizations would complement the nation-state.

GLOBAL CIVIL SOCIETY: MARY KALDOR

As we've seen, Held believes that globalization presents new political opportunities and challenges. In light of the historically unique intensification of exchanges between nations, and the rapid flows of money, people, images, and capital across national borders, a strictly national response to the demands of the day is inadequate. The world of nations must develop transnational social and political organizations and principles to regulate a global order. Still a question lingers: given the weakness of the UN and other international organizations, is the idea of a democratic global order utopian, or are there good reasons to think that it's a real possibility?

A colleague of Held's at the London School of Economics, Mary Kaldor, suggests that the idea of a global democracy is indeed a real historical possibility. Kaldor's *Global Civil Society* is an attempt to sketch the meaning and prospects of a civil democratic order at a global level.[3] In many respects, Kaldor exemplifies the combination of a scholar-activist or, in terms we used in the Introduction to Part VI, a discursive and moral theorist. Her ideas were shaped by social movements in the West and, in particular, the rebellions in Eastern Europe in the late 1980s. Kaldor was both an observer and partisan of these movements for peace and social justice.

Let's begin with the notion of civil society. Generally, scholars think of civil society as indicating a social condition in which individuals can participate in the governance of society through the shaping of public opinion and public policy. At times, the civil sphere is thought of as the social realm between the state and the family, which would include voluntary associations, social movements, the media, and the economy. In that sense, civil society is the social sphere where individuals associate with one another, form groups or organizations, express their needs and desires, engage in

Mary Kaldor was born in 1946. She is a professor at the London School of Economics and Political Science. She also directs the Study of Global Governance, London School of Economics and Political Science. Her books include *The Imaginary War* (1990), *New and Old Wars* (1999), and *Global Civil Society: An Answer to War* (2003). She was a founding member of European Nuclear Disarmament, and founder and Co-Chair of the Helsinki Citizens' Assembly. Kaldor argues that in a global social environment, social regulation must also be global. However, in order for global regulation to be effective, there must be a global civil society. She believes that the elements of a global civil order are already in existence, but whether it will develop the authority to enforce general principles of civic order and justice is an open question.

debate and competition over social policies and norms, and through this collective action shape their own history. In a sense, the civil sphere is the realm where individuals express their sense of ownership of society, and claim an entitlement to shape society in accord with their interests and ideas.[4] A robust civil society at once limits the power of the state over the individual and empowers the latter to make claims on the former.

Although civil societies have existed in Europe for several centuries, Kaldor argues that today civil society is no longer confined to the borders of the territorial state. Since World War II a global civil order has taken shape. It is manifest in the proliferation of international laws, organizations, movements, treaties, and so on. For example, Kaldor underscores the globalization of social movements. "Whether we are talking about isolated dissidents in repressive regimes, landless laborers in Central America or Asia, or even religious fundamentalists and fanatic nationalists, what has changed are the opportunities for linking up with other like-minded groups in different parts of the world, and for addressing demands not just to the state but to global institutions and other states." [5] In this regard, Kaldor argues that the 1989 revolutions in Eastern Europe which played a key role in bringing down the Soviet empire were made possible by a global human rights discourse, international courts of justice, global media, and a transnational peace movement. In short, a global civil society made the revolutions of 1989 possible.

However, if there is no global state or world society, what exactly does a global civil order do? Like a national civil society, it aims to regulate global affairs or the interactions between nations. It is one of Kaldor's chief arguments that a robust global civil society would make possible a significant reduction of violence between nations. Let me explain. Prior to World War II, relations between nations were primarily governed by power, the threat of force, and ultimately military intervention or war. Two world wars and countless regional wars and genocidal episodes testify to a history of uncivil relations between nations. As Kaldor says, we had civil order within nations (at least in the best of cases) while uncivil order prevailed between nations. A global civil society would make possible the extension of civil order into the international realm. Relations between nations would be governed by law and ethical principles such as the respect for human rights, minority rights, and so on. Of course, there will always be rivalries and conflicts between nations, and even "wars without nations," such as the nationalist conflicts in Spain (Basques) or Russia (Chechnya) or the terrorist politics of Al-Qaeda, but a vital global civil society would reduce the likelihood of world wars, which today poses a genuine threat to all humanity.

What are the prospects for a global civil society? Kaldor is hopeful, but cautious. What gives her hope is the proliferation of social movements in the postwar period. Because many social problems and conflicts are today understood as global, whether they be environmental, refugees, or economic inequality, there have developed international organizations and movements to address these concerns. Kaldor underscores the importance of social movements organized around peace, human rights, women's, gay and lesbian, and indigenous rights movements as bringing the voice of disadvantaged peoples into a global public arena.

Kaldor sees in global civic organizations the possibility of controlling repressive and intolerant national governments. To the extent that Amnesty International or Oxfam or Médecins Sans Frontières (Doctors without Borders) can hold national governments accountable to international legal and administrative principles, a global civil sphere is doing the work of expanding human rights and social justice. It was, for example, the worldwide pressure exerted on South Africa (boycotts, mobilization of global human rights organizations, and antiracist movements) that contributed to ending apartheid. In the best of cases, social movements create transnational civic networks that carry on the task of empowering and democratizing a global civil order.

Kaldor is a realist. The potential for expanding civic peace and justice across the globe must be assessed in light of actual realities. The revolutions of 1989 surely contributed to the end of Soviet rule, but instead of a multipolar world order, the United States has tried to assert its unipolar world dominance. Although the growing power of East Asia is a counter-balance, it is not at all clear that these new Asian powers have a strong commitment to ideals of human rights, minority rights, and a civil global order.

Moreover, Kaldor has a mixed opinion on the global impact of democratizing social movements. On the one hand, these movements have been institutionalized in transnational "civic networks" which maintain a grass-roots connection while continuing to work for justice and social change. On the other hand, these movements have been increasingly replaced by NGOs or INGOs (international NGOs). One survey in 2000 counted some 13,000 NGOs with over 250,000 members. These organizations are indispensable to a robust civil society as they give a voice to disadvantaged populations and provide aid, skills, and resources. Yet, they are professional service-oriented rather than advocacy movements. Moreover, NGOs may be easily controlled by national interests and commitments. Also giving pause to Kaldor's hopes for global democracy is the growing power, nationally and globally, of right-wing fundamentalist and nationalist groups which reject a democratic civil society.

Finally, the record of national and international violence in the postwar world is decidedly mixed. On the positive side, Kaldor observes that in the 1990s the world witnessed a turn against war-making states. Arms control treaties, reductions in military spending after the Cold War, and the strengthening of human rights laws point to the promise of extending civil order from the nation to the globe. However, we've also witnessed the spread of new forms of warfare. In weak or failing states such as in the Balkans, Africa, and the Middle East, wars between states have given way to wars involving non-state actors such as terrorist networks, mercenary soldiers, warlords, and paramilitary groups. These wars are often carried out by organized global networks linked by ideology, especially religion and nationalism, in which violence has become a form of politics. These practices, and at times national responses, undermine a global civil order. Tellingly, Kaldor mused: "Will we look back on ... the 'happy Nineties'? Was it an interregnum between global conflicts when utopian ideas like global civil society, human rights, a global rule of law, or global social justice seemed possible? Or was it, on another interpretation, the moment when global civil society came of age? I fear the answer is already pretty clear."[6]

Suggested Readings

Ulrich Beck, *Power in the Global Age* (Cambridge: Polity Press, 2005).

Anthony Giddens, *Runaway World* (New York: Routledge, 2003).

David Held and Anthony McGraw, eds., *The Global Transformations Reader* (London: Polity Press, 2000).

Anthony King, ed. *Culture, Globalization and the World-System* (Minneapolis: University of Minnesota Press, 1997).

Saskia Sassen, *Globalization and its Discontents* (New York: New Press, 1998).

Martin Shaw, *Theory of the Global State* (Cambridge: Cambridge University Press, 2000).

References

1 Joseph Stiglitz, *Globalization and its Discontents* (New York: W. W. Norton, 2002); Thomas Friedman, *The Lexus and the Olive Tree: Understanding Globalization* (New York: Farrar, Straus & Giroux, 1999).

2 David Held, *Democracy and the Global Order* (Stanford, CA: Stanford University Press, 1995).

3 Mary Kaldor, *Global Civil Society: An Answer to War* (Cambridge: Polity Press, 2003).

4 See Jeffrey Alexander, *The Civil Sphere* (Oxford: Oxford University Press, 2006).

5 Kaldor, *Global Civil Society*, p. 2.

6 Kaldor, *Global Civil Society*, p. 149.

19

Global Capitalism
Immanuel Wallerstein and Manuel Castells

From Comte to Habermas, social thinkers have taken the individual society or nation-state (e.g., France, Italy, or Japan) as the focus of social analysis. They have assumed that understanding the internal dynamics of individual societies could provide a basis for comprehending human history. From this perspective, the relationship between nations and the international environment is a minor consideration in understanding the way societies are organized and change. Even Marx, we recall, explained the development of capitalism as a product of a society's internal dynamics, in particular, the drive for profit and the conflict between capital and labor. To be sure, Marx understood that in its drive for profits capitalism would ignore national borders and create international markets. However, this internationalization of capitalism is explained as a product of the growth of national economies. Similarly, Durkheim assumed that the division of labor would eventually connect nations and territories across the globe. Yet, such an international order would be composed, Durkheim thought, of individual national states, which would remain the central actors in history. The work of Wallerstein and Castells challenges a nation-state-centered social theory.

IMMANUEL WALLERSTEIN

Wallerstein pioneered what has come to be called "world-systems theory."[1] His theoretical perspective may be said to be driven by one overriding idea: nation-states can only be understood as part of a social network of states and economic processes. Wallerstein's early research contributed to his rejection of the conventional assumption that the individual society or nation-state is the basic unit of social analysis. While his colleagues focused their sociological attention almost exclusively on Europe and the United States, Wallerstein was in Africa during the 1950s and 1960s researching the process of decolonization and the formation of postcolonial states: "I went to Africa

Contested Knowledge: Social Theory Today, Fifth Edition. Steven Seidman.
© 2013 John Wiley & Sons, Ltd. Published 2013 by John Wiley & Sons, Ltd.

Immanuel Wallerstein was born in 1930. He taught at the State University of New York at Binghamton, where he was a Distinguished Professor of Sociology and the Director of the Fernand Braudel Center for the Study of Economies, Historical Systems, and Civilizations. He is known for his world-system theory. Wallerstein's theory highlights the interdependence and asymmetrical relations among nations. He divides nations into three categories: the capitalist core, the peripheral nations, and the semiperipheral nations. The capitalist core exercises economic, political, and military dominance in the world system. Peripheral nations, which have weak economies and governments, are controlled by core nations. The semiperipheral nations combine features of the core and periphery. By making the world-system into the basic unit of social analysis, Wallerstein's work has proven immensely useful for researchers and theorists.

first during the colonial era, and I witnessed the process of 'decolonization,' and then the independence of a cascade of sovereign states."[2] Wallerstein's first-hand experience of colonization and decolonization disposed him to viewing individual societies as inextricably linked together or as part of a broader social network. Gradually, Wallerstein imagined these social networks as having their own distinct identities, boundaries, internal dynamics, and histories. He came to call such patterns of societal interconnection "world-systems."

Wallerstein distinguishes two types of world-systems. There are "world-empires," which are networks of societies that are unified by the domination of one state or centralized political authority, for example, imperial Rome, China, and the Ottoman Empire. Wallerstein believes that world-empires declined with the rise of what he calls a "world-economy." There has been but one historically sustaining world-economy: the capitalist one. This is a world-system characterized by a plurality of states or political authorities; its unity is provided by an international division of labor and unequal political economic relations. Wallerstein imagines a third possibility – a socialist world government, which would supersede capitalism. From this perspective, the former Soviet Union and China do not signal the beginnings of a new social formation, but are socialist-controlled states in a capitalist world-economy.

Wallerstein outlines the social logic of the capitalist world-economy. For our purposes, it is less the historical details of the evolution of capitalism that command our attention than the main ideas about the organization and dynamics of the modern world-system.

The modern world-system operates on the principles of capitalism. It is a market economy composed of businesses that are profit- and growth-oriented. Profit involves exploitation or unequal social exchanges. However, instead of focusing on national class divisions, Wallerstein recasts the drama of capitalism on a worldwide scale. From its origin in sixteenth-century Europe, capitalism has been a world-system, and its contradictions (producing immensely wealthy and poor states) have been its driving force.

Wallerstein conceives of the capitalist world-economy as divided between three zones: the core, semiperiphery, and periphery. Societies can be classified roughly as belonging to one of these zones. Each zone has a specific socioeconomic and political character. The way a specific society is situated in the capitalist world economy will define its chief features and possibilities for development. It is, in other words, the patterned relationship between societies that is the primary social force in shaping national development.

At the center of world capitalism are "core" societies. They are economically, politically, militarily, and culturally dominant in the world-system. Core societies are economically diverse, technologically advanced, involve highly capital-intensive economies operated by cadres of skilled, educated laborers, and are centers of manufacturing, commerce, and finance. Core societies have stable and powerful states. States protect economic investment at home and in foreign lands. The former is sustained in part by developing a welfare system that maintains high wages and worker security, thereby integrating labor. The latter is maintained by developing an impressive military, which will protect foreign investments. Core societies are characterized by a strong middle class, an advanced education system, and a cosmopolitan culture.

Wallerstein argues that core states are rivals. They compete with one another to exploit noncore societies. For example, throughout much of the nineteenth century Britain and France were bitter rivals as they competed to gain access to and control over noncore societies. In the twentieth century, the conflicts initially between Germany and Japan for hegemonic status gradually gave way to conflicts between the United States and the Soviet Union. The rise of Islamic societies and economically strong Asian nations in the last few decades presents a challenge to the dominance of Europe and to the hegemonic status of the United States.

At various times, one core state will become hegemonic in the capitalist world system. Establishing hegemony means maintaining economic supremacy in the different sectors of the economy (agriculture, industry, commerce, finance) and sustaining military and political dominance over other core nations. In effect, a hegemonic state is unstable and temporary, as other core nations eventually challenge the dominant state.

It is one of Wallerstein's chief claims that core societies need weaker, subordinate societies to dominate and exploit. These exploited societies belong to the periphery. In contrast to core states, they are economically specialized, even monocultural (specializing in one product), labor-intensive, technologically underdeveloped, and lacking an elaborate financial, commercial, and manufacturing base. Peripheral societies have uneven and underdeveloped economies as a result of their subordination to core nations. Their economies may be reduced in the worldwide division of labor to the role of producing one product or providing raw materials and cheap labor to core nations. For example, prior to decolonization, African nations specialized in providing such cheap labor; Caribbean societies were often reduced to monocultural economies specializing in sugar or cotton production and dependent economically, politically, and militarily on core nations. Such societies also have weak and unstable states. It is not unusual to find authoritarian states propped up or installed by core states. Culturally speaking, peripheral societies experience cultural degradation. Native or indigenous cultures are debased – ridiculed and labeled inferior. Often there is a racialization of the debased native culture which justifies core dominance (as a civilizing mission).

Wallerstein identifies a third zone: the semiperiphery. Societies that belong to the semiperiphery share features of both the core and periphery. Such societies may have an uneven economy, for example, a developed manufacturing sector but underdeveloped financial sector. The key feature of these societies is that they serve as a buffer for the core nations. Wallerstein believes that states in a semiperipheral status become the chief focus of peripheral opposition and in that way protect the core states.

The chief dynamic of the capitalist world-system is the conflict between nations driven by socioeconomic inequalities. Although the conflict among core nations for hegemony is important to understanding social change, the central dynamic is the exploitative relationship between the core and periphery. The core extracts surplus value from the periphery and exercises social and political dominance in order to sustain economic exploitation. This world-system dynamic creates wealthy, powerful nations on the one side and poor, weak nations on the other. In other words, social development in the core is made possible by creating social and economic underdevelopment in wide stretches of the globe. This socioeconomic inequality is sustained by the overwhelming economic advantages of core nations and enforced by political and, if necessary, military means. This can involve installing political rulers in peripheral societies that march to the orders of the dominant core nation, or using overt or covert military intervention to protect foreign investments. Such relations of dominance and exploitation between nations are justified by ideologies of free enterprise, democratization, and social progress.

Much of Wallerstein's *Modern World-System* details the evolution of world capitalism and shifts in the status of nations. His account of the making of the modern world-system moves deftly between an economic and a political level. With regard to the former, he analyzes cycles of economic expansion and contraction (i.e., depressions and recessions), but these occur in 150-year cycles, rather than the 10-year cycles Marx sketched. These long economic periods provide the basis and framework for the chief political conflicts.

I sketch the broad features of Wallerstein's view of the evolution of the capitalist world-system. Briefly, there are four periods: (1) 1400–1640, the origins of the capitalist world-economy in Europe; (2) 1640–1815, the period of its consolidation in Europe; (3) 1815–1917, the beginnings of a true world-economy and social system under the hegemony of Britain; and (4) 1917– the 1960s, the rise of the United States to world hegemonic power in the modern world-system. In the past few decades, the United States has begun to lose its dominant social position; decolonizing movements, the rise of Japan, Brazil, and West Germany to first-rate economic status, along with the rising economic might of Arab and Asian nations, the Soviet military challenge, and the collapse of the New Deal liberal consensus, which unleashed general social discontent, have set the stage for the intensification of national conflict across the globe.

Wallerstein argues that a world capitalist economy emerged from the crisis of feudalism precipitated by the spread of cities, manufacturing, and the rise of a merchant-capitalist class. Additionally, as land was commercialized, peasants became wage-laborers. Thus, by the sixteenth century the conditions of modern capitalism were created – a class of capitalists and wage-laborers.

Between 1600 and the 1750s a capitalist world-economy was established in northern Europe. The core states were Great Britain, Holland, and Belgium. Initially, it was Holland that assumed a hegemonic status by virtue of its advancements in shipbuilding, textiles, the fishing industry, and its impressive naval power. By the end of the nineteenth century, the capitalist economy had expanded beyond northern Europe to wide stretches of the globe. With its industrialization and overwhelming sea power, Great Britain replaced Holland as a hegemonic power. During the nineteenth century, Great Britain, with France as its major rival, was the center of finance, commerce, and shipbuilding, and an unrivaled military and political power. Britain's world hegemony had come to an end by World War II. It was the United States that now assumed the role of the hegemonic core state. US economic, political, and military might was unsurpassed. Moreover, by the end of World War II, global capitalism was a world-economy. In Wallerstein's view, US hegemony came to an end in the 1960s with the rise of the powerhouse Asian economies, the reassertion of Europe as an independent political force, and the resurgence of the Soviet Union as a military equal.

Although Wallerstein acknowledges the rise of movements challenging the capitalist world-economy, he does not anticipate its imminent collapse. There is little likelihood of revolt in core nations. Working-class movements in Western nations are unlikely to experience political radicalization. Rich core nations can afford to raise the standard of living of workers, create elaborate systems of welfare, and provide relative social security for most of their citizens. And where economic stagnation might threaten political radicalization, this is largely avoided by scapegoating racial minorities and the poor. Movements against core nations have, of course, emerged in waves throughout the last century. These movements, however, are often anticolonial struggles intent on establishing national independence. It is, in other words, their opposition to colonial powers, not their opposition to a capitalist world-economy, that defines their struggle. Moreover, their nationalism has often impeded their interest or capacity to form the kind of international organizations and alliances that would make possible an effective challenge to hegemonic nations. Like Marx, Wallerstein in the end pins his hopes on economic cycles and trends to create the conditions for world revolution. Eventually, he thinks – and hopes – world capitalism will produce global movements for a socialist world order.

MANUEL CASTELLS

Wallerstein's theory of a world capitalist economy was developed in the 1970s but has remained extraordinarily influential. In particular, the idea that capitalism is a global order captured the imagination of many social thinkers. One such thinker, the sociologist and urbanist Manuel Castells, developed a highly original theory of global capitalism.[3] In contrast to Wallerstein, who relied on a fairly conventional Marxism, Castells integrated into his theory of capitalism the telecommunications revolution.

In Castells' view, the new telecommunication infrastructure of contemporary capitalism is part of a wider and deeper change in the very social meaning and organization of global capitalism.

Castells agrees with Wallerstein that the current world order is best understood as a global capitalist order. However, Castells argues that there has been a shift in the character of capitalism from a primarily industrial and service oriented economy to a new type of capitalism which he calls "informational capitalism." Informational capitalism is characterized by the following features:

- A telecommunications-based infrastructure. Distinctive to informational capitalism is the continual advancement of knowledge, computerization, and new forms of technology that drive the economy.
- A competitive global economy. Under conditions of informational capitalism, firms or businesses are multinational and global. In order to be competitive, firms must be attuned to shifts in knowledge and technological change. This requires that they be multinational and open to change so that they can incorporate the latest innovations in knowledge and technology, and maintain a highly skilled, specialized labor force. From Castells' perspective, what makes capitalism into a global order is less the internationalization of the market than a telecommunications infrastructure which requires global enterprises attuned to an environment of ever-changing knowledge and technology.
- Flexible and decentralized firms. In a global economy in which knowledge-based technological innovation is ongoing, it is essential for firms to compete in a global economy. Maintaining a competitive edge requires that firms be flexible. That is to say, they must be open to continuous changes in knowledge and technology and be flexible enough to incorporate these changes into their apparatus of production. Such flexibility means that under conditions of informational capitalism firms will be decentralized and loosely linked organizations. It is characteristic of global capitalism for businesses or enterprises to be dispersed across the globe and to appear less as clearly bounded corporations than as networks. In more conventional terms, Castells believes that the organizational structure of capitalism is undergoing a shift from so-called Fordist practices (centralized, hierarchical, rigid division of labor) to "post-Fordist"-type firms, which are global, decentralized, flexible, and organized as loosely linked networks.
- The rise of "reprogrammable labor." Both manufacturing-based and service-based capitalism relied upon a mass of unskilled or "generic" labor. Of course, unskilled labor is still in demand in the manufacturing and service sectors of the economy. However, informational capitalism is accompanied by the need for an educated, technically skilled, but flexible and mobile labor force. In order to service informational global capitalism, with its decentralized, flexible, and change oriented culture, the worker must be flexible and mobile in terms of where she works, the work schedule, and even in the kinds of skills the individual worker brings to the economy. By "reprogrammable," Castells means that a laborer today will need to be capable of retooling and reskilling in order to adapt to an ever-changing work

environment. As reprogrammable labor replaces unskilled generic labor, unions decline. The new worker is self-reliant , mobile, and non-unionized.

- A world organized by informational global capitalism is no longer dominated by America and Europe. In part, the innovations that allowed America and Europe to become the most advanced economies in the mid-twentieth century, such as mass production, scientific production, and big corporations, put these nations at a disadvantage in the context of informational capitalism. As we've seen, flexible, decentralized, and loosely connected network firms are best suited to the conditions of informational capitalism. Accordingly, it is not surprising that in Castells' view the new network enterprise and worker developed more quickly and more effectively in Asian societies. In other words, the economies that are driving informational capitalism have been Japan, South Korea, Taiwan, Hong Kong, and Singapore. One of the reasons for the acceleration of the Asian economies is their close alliance between the state and firms. Informational capitalism seems to require a government that makes considerable investment in a technical informational infrastructure.

Despite these important changes in the structure of capitalism, one feature has remained unchanged: capitalism produces dramatic social and economic inequalities. Still, to the extent that the organization of capitalism has changed, to that extent we can anticipate changes in the dynamics of inequality and social conflict. Castells underscores several axes of social inequality and potential social conflict.

In classic Marxian terms, Castells acknowledges that the division between capitalists and laborers persists into the early twenty-first century. There are still owners and managers of capital, along with their intellectual apologists, who stand opposed to the overwhelming majority of individuals who continue to live from paycheck to paycheck. Yet today class structure is much more complex than that ever imagined by Marx. There are divisions among the various sectors of capitalism, for example between the financial and the technical-managerial sectors, just as there are significant divisions among laborers, in particular, between laborers who have telecommunications knowledge and skills and those who don't. In the extreme case, there is a class of citizens concentrated primarily in the inner cities in the United States and Europe who, lacking education and telecommunications skills, have fallen into what Castells calls "the black hole of informational capitalism." Without the skills to plug into the circuits of informational capitalism, these individuals will either remain at the extreme margins of the economy or will resort to a life of crime or bare existence.

Following Wallerstein's thinking of capitalism as a global order, Castells underscores divisions and conflicts at a global level. However, whereas Wallerstein speaks of global divisions between core and peripheral nations, Castells analyzes global inequality in relation to the dynamics of informational capitalism. Specifically, he distinguishes between social regions or nations that are at the center of informational capitalism and nations and regions that have been left out of the circuits of informational capitalism. Whole nations and continents, such as parts of Central and Southeast Asia, and Africa, are trapped in a spiral of economic stagnation and impoverishment, in large part because they lack the infrastructure and capabilities, both technical and human, to be

Manuel Castells was born in Spain in 1942. He has taught at the University of California, Berkeley, and is currently at the University of Southern California. He is the author of *The Information Age*, which many scholars regard as the most significant attempt to consider the broad social and political implications of the telecommunications revolution. Castells examines the relationship between global informational capitalism, the state, and social movements. The question he raises, in the end, is whether social movements and global institutions can harness the emancipatory potential of the recent telecommunications technology.

part of a global informational capitalist order. In effect, these regions of the world also tumble into the black hole of informational capitalism. Out of this morass of stagnation, impoverishment, and illegality, there has emerged a "fourth world" ruled by tyrants and featuring genocide, endemic violence, and a global criminal underworld economy. The latter revolves around trafficking in drugs, sex, women, immigrants, and labor. In some parts of the world, these criminal cartels and organizations are as powerful as some governments.

Castells argues that under conditions of global capitalism national states surrender some sovereignty but remain centers of power in the world order. As states are compelled to function as part of a world economy, international institutions – from financial institutions which set exchange rates and regulate currency, to the World Bank, which shapes national domestic economic decision making, to multilateral trade agreements such as NAFTA – seriously restrict the independence of individual national states. The intensification of social interdependence, which is a condition of global capitalism, is also a condition of politics today. As a political agent, the state must also operate in a global context of interdependency. For example, governments, both powerful and weak, depend on foreign lenders. Similarly, almost all national states are part of multilateral regional military bodies such as NATO.

In more general terms, Castells argues that, paralleling the flexible, decentralized, network character of firms, states also take the form of networks. He describes the contemporary state, at least in America and in Europe, as a "network state." Political power or authority is less concentrated and centralized at the national level than disbursed between the local, regional, federal, and global levels. In the last several decades, the modern centralized state has surrendered some of its power to local or regional political authorities such as cities, municipalities, state governments, and regional governmental authorities and associations. At the same time, some of the state's authority is now effectively exercised by global institutions and organizations such as the United Nations, various international governmental organizations, and tribunals. This dispersal of political power is what Castells means by the network state.

It is possible to see a democratizing dimension to this dispersal and decentralization of political authority. In principle, one would expect a network state to be more socially accountable and to institutionalize a series of checks on the concentration of power at the national level. If power is dispersed or shared between the local, national, and global levels, it would seem that the excessive monopolization of political power at any one level would be blocked by political authorities at the other levels. And yet, Castells' political outlook is guarded, if not pessimistic.

In countries such as the United States and West European nations, Castells sees a change for the worse in the character of politics. As the mass media assume a central role in national politics, a focus on substantive social issues, social policy, and a culture of elaborated debate and argumentation is marginalized in favor of a premium placed on personality, charisma, media imagery, soundbites, and scandal. In other words, Castells argues that "First World nations" are experiencing a decline in democratic politics and its basis in a robust civil society. This political debasement in the United States and Europe is paralleled by the impoverishment of anything approaching a democratic political culture in large stretches of Africa, Central and Southeast Asia, and Russia, where demagogues or petty tyrants rule with ruthless violence. And where popular political mobilization does occur, such as in parts of Southeast Asia and the Middle East, it is often wedded to a form of religio-nationalist fanaticism that is the enemy of democracy.

Castells is not, however, without some hope for the future. In particular, in the rise of new communities and movements organized around affirmative identities and a life politics concerned with individual, societal, and environmental well-being, he finds social forces promoting liberal and democratic principles. For example, in the women's movements in the United States, Europe, and elsewhere, Castells observes a powerful social force committed to social equality, accountability, and open discussion of the social norms that regulate family and social life. Similarly, the environmental movement, backed by powerful elites with wide popular support in many nations, promises an altered relationship between the world, humans, society, and nature.

Suggested Readings

D. Acemoglu and J. Robinson, *Economic Origins of Dictatorship and Democracy* (Cambridge: Cambridge University Press, 2005).

Jeffrey Frieden, *Global Capitalism* (New York: W. W. Norton, 2007).

William Robinson, *Theory of Global Capitalism* (Baltimore, MD: Johns Hopkins University Press, 2004).

References

1 Immanuel Wallerstein, *The Modern World-System*, vols. 1–3 (New York: Academic Press, 1974–89). Also see *The Essential Wallerstein* (New York: New Press, 2000).

2 Wallerstein, *The Modern World-System*, vol. I, p. 4. See his *Road to Independence* (Paris: Mouton, 1964).

3 Manuel Castells, *The Information Age: Economy, Society, and Culture*, 3 vols. (Oxford: Blackwell Publishers, 1996–8).

20

The Return of Empire?
Michael Hardt and Antonio Negri,
David Harvey and Michael Mann

Sociology was developed in nations that became empires of unprecedented scope and power. As we've seen, modern sociology and social theory have flourished primarily in Great Britain, France, Italy, Germany, and the United States. Since the nineteenth century, these nations also exercised dominion over much of the earth's surface. It is, then, curious, to say the least, that "empire" and the dynamics of colonialism and imperialism have been neglected by classical and contemporary sociologists. To be sure, Weber and Durkheim, or Parsons and Giddens, were aware of imperialism and at times offered insightful observations. However, the dynamics of empire were not incorporated into the basic categories and points of view of their social theory. Accordingly, colonialism and imperialism do not figure in the core sociological perspectives on the formation and structure of the modern world.

This is true with one major exception: the tradition of Marxism. We recall that Marx understood capitalism to be a dynamic type of society. Capitalism is driven by the pursuit of profit and sustained economic growth. Profit is based on exploitation: laborers are paid less than the value of the wealth they produce. Growth occurs by expanding production, which involves both producing more and getting more people to buy more goods. Inevitably, Marx thought, capitalism bursts national borders and becomes an international system. As capitalists search for raw materials, cheap labor, and new markets, they create global economic networks. For example, enterprises are established in poor countries to exploit their cheap labor and plentiful resources; these goods will be sold in rich nations for considerable profit. Or, capitalism promotes trade and the movement of people between nations as a flexible workforce and profits are sought. In short, capitalism creates a global social order.

Moreover, Marx believed that capitalists would enlist the state in the service of promoting free trade, big business, and economic growth. After all, the state has an interest in promoting national economic growth; it expands its tax base and makes possible high levels of employment and well-paid laborers, which encourages a stable, peaceful citizenry. Accordingly, the state makes the success of capitalism into a vital national interest. For example, as capitalists invest heavily abroad, the government will protect their capital investment. Capitalists will pressure the government to create an international environment that is favorable for business. This may mean forging national alliances, supporting friendly rulers, and opposing, sometimes militarily, political regimes that are hostile to the nation's economic interests. In short, Marx thought that imperialism, or the extension of one nation's political power over other societies, inevitably accompanies capitalism.

It might be surprising to learn that Marx was ambivalent towards imperialism: he condemned it for destroying indigenous cultures and bringing about vast human and environmental ruin. He also criticized rich nations for dominating and exploiting poorer ones. But Marx believed that the European economic and political conquest of the non-European world was necessary to advance social progress. European imperialism would bring industry, urban development, and secular culture to what he often considered to be socially backward societies. Marx was no romantic championing tradition and local cultures; he was very much a man of the Enlightenment, and a believer in social progress and Europe as the engine of historical advancement.

Marx's ideas on empire were never systematized. It was left to his heirs to develop a Marxist theory of imperialism. Social thinkers such as Rosa Luxemburg and the Russian revolutionary Lenin filled in the details of a Marxist view of imperialism. The title of Lenin's book *Imperialism: The Highest Stage of Capitalism* says it all. The growth of capitalism inevitably exceeds national boundaries; surplus profits and goods drive capitalist firms to look for new investment opportunities, markets, and resources, and the state paves the way and protects this investment by expanding its control over foreign territories and peoples. All nations, through peaceful or violent means, are brought into the market nexus. Inevitably, rich nations dominate poorer ones; specifically, powerful Western capitalist nations seek economic and political control over vast global territories. Hence, imperialism is seen as an inevitable outgrowth of the dynamism of capitalism.

Marxists distinguish imperialism from colonialism. The former describes the broad political power a nation exercises over other nations; the latter involves the actual physical occupation and control of other people's land. From the vantage point of the early twentieth century, Marxists such as Lenin and Luxemburg thought that colonialism was declining but that an imperialism which operates by means of the market and extending national political power was becoming the ruling principle of the contemporary international order.

With the development of the United Nations and the establishment of the principle of national sovereignty in international conventions, treaties, and declarations of rights, it seemed that the age of imperialism was also at an end. After all, the great world empires of Great Britain, France, and Germany were destroyed after World War II and unraveled with the waves of decolonization that swept across the globe. Of course, the United States emerged as a superpower, but one that declared itself to be against empire-building. The final death-blow to imperialism, it seemed to many observers, was the breakup of the Soviet Union in the 1990s. Yet, just a decade later, theories of empire have reclaimed academic and public attention.

Michael Hardt was born in Washington, DC, in 1960. He spent the 1980s in Guatemala and El Salvador, involved with a movement to provide religious shelter in the United States to refugees who were fleeing from death squads. He completed his doctorate in comparative literature in 1990 at the University of Washington. Italian philosopher and activist **Antonio Negri** was born in 1933. He fled to France in 1983, where he spent 14 years in exile. While in France, he taught political science at several universities. Negri returned to Italy in 1997 to serve a 13-year prison sentence for his alleged involvement with the terrorist group the Red Brigades. *Empire* is a bold effort to rethink the meaning of globalization *as* empire.

GLOBALIZATION AS EMPIRE: MICHAEL HARDT AND ANTONIO NEGRI

Despite their differences, both Marxists and postcolonial thinkers approach the social world as one composed of nations in competition for resources, markets, and national power. The social world is seen as divided between dominant or core nations and subordinate or peripheral nations, or between the developed and underdeveloped world. From this point of view, imperialism is understood as an inevitable part of a world order; dominant nations will seek to control less powerful ones. The major social drama revolves around which nation is dominant and whether it uses force or other means to achieve dominance. For example, France and Britain were said to be the dominant imperial powers in the nineteenth and early twentieth centuries; Germany was said to replace them in the mid-twentieth century, only to give way to the United States in the post-World War II period.

This view of imperialism and the modern world has been challenged in the last few decades. Many thinkers now approach world social dynamics and politics through the idea of globalization. This is a slippery and complex concept. But, generally speaking, it refers to a shift from focusing on particular nation-states to considering the ways that nations are enmeshed in webs of social, economic, and cultural interdependence.

Two views of the global order have been especially influential. The first view is often referred to as "neoliberalism." This perspective sees market capitalism as bringing all parts of the globe into contact with one another. The drive of capitalism is global. All nations, small or large, rich or poor, are brought into the market. In a global order, goods, people, and ideas flow freely, more or less, across national boundaries. Neoliberals believe that globalization is a good or positive development. Bringing nations into contact with one another and creating a more or less open market of goods and ideas weakens dictators, elevates the standard of living of all peoples, and helps create a vital world culture that respects individual rights. From a neoliberal perspective, empire and the dynamics of imperialism are a thing of the past. To be sure, there will still be local skirmishes and national conflicts, but imperialism and empire-building are seen as incompatible with the free movement of things and people in a global order.

The second view of globalization is associated with a variety of critics. For example, some Marxist critics argue that globalization amounts to little more than the expansion of American power. Today, it is not just the power of the government of the United States that reaches across the globe, but its corporations, media conglomerates, and mass culture. And, these critics argue, American expansion is not promoting freedom and democracy in the world; instead, poverty and authoritarian regimes trail in the footsteps of US world dominance. Other critics attack globalization on the grounds that it destroys local native culture and communities. As markets and Western mass culture and consumption penetrate into small villages and towns in all parts of the globe, the preservation of local customs and ways of living is seriously threatened.

The neoliberal celebration of globalization and the Left-wing critique were challenged by two unlikely thinkers, Michael Hardt and Antonio Negri. The former is an English professor in the United States, the latter a political activist and academic who, until recently, resided in an Italian prison after being convicted of terrorism. Still, their book *Empire* proposes an alternative to both neoliberal and Marxist approaches to globalization.[1]

Hardt and Negri agree with neoliberalism in one important way: the current era is a new one. A world order defined by rival nations seeking imperial domination is not definitive of the present. Hardt and Negri share with neoliberals the belief that the internationalization of a market economy has made imperialism outdated. They argue that the guiding principle of a global order is the free flow of goods, people, money, and ideas across national borders. Imperialism, which implies hard and fast national boundaries and the violent interruption of the fluid circulation of people, capital, and goods, goes against the core dynamics of globalization. Imperial ambitions are understood by more and more nations as an unacceptable obstacle to a well-functioning global system. Nations find ways to avoid imperial conquests and wars. But Hardt and Negri take issue with neoliberals to the extent that the latter believe that market forces alone drive globalization and that, at its core, the global order is a system of free trade and movement of peoples and ideas. By contrast, Hardt and Negri view globalization as establishing a new type of "sovereignty," or novel political and social order.

Hardt and Negri call this new world order "Empire." Unlike in the era of imperialism, where there were clearly dominant nations, under the conditions of Empire there is no central power and no one dominant nation. Empire can be likened to the World Wide Web, a sort of network composed of many powers; where power is dispersed, not centralized. Nations share power with transnational corporations, media conglomerates, NGOs, and organizations such as the European Union and the World Bank. "Our basic hypothesis is that sovereignty has taken a new form, composed of a series of national and supranational organisms united under a single logic of rule. This new global form of sovereignty is what we call Empire." Hardt and Negri continue:

> In contrast to imperialism, Empire establishes no territorial center of power and does not rely on fixed boundaries or barriers. It is a *decentered* and *deterritorializing* apparatus of rule that progressively incorporates the entire global realm within its open, expanding

frontiers. Empire manages hybrid identities, flexible hierarchies, and plural exchanges through modulating networks of command. The distinct national colors of the imperialist map of the world have merged and blended in the imperial global rainbow.[2]

Hardt and Negri propose that the shift from the era of imperialism to that of Empire is part of a broader change from a modern to a postmodern society.

The modern world is understood by them as an order of nations, power struggles, relations of domination and subordination; it is regulated by law and social hierarchy. For example, in the realm of political rulership, the principle of the modern world is the rule of law and bureaucratic authority; in the economic sphere, factories, scientific production, and Fordist-style mass production characterize the modern world.

The postmodern era is a global world order composed of many different types of authorities and entities, from nations to international relief agencies. These entities are enmeshed in networks of power relations. There is no center, no controlling force. Top-down order, which characterized modern institutions, has given way to more flexible principles of regulation such as post-Fordist economies; sharply demarcated boundaries have given way to a highly mobile labor force, more open, porous national boundaries, hybrid identities, and multiple citizenship. Social order emerges out of interdependencies, market networks, new forms of cooperation, and agreements between different global entities. Empire evokes less the modern era than the era of the Roman Empire, with its mix of peoples, social principles, circulation of things and people, and its combination of centralized and decentralized forms of political rule.

But is Empire a force of good or evil? Hardt and Negri share neither the Pollyannaish optimism of neoliberals nor the dark fatalism of the Left. They are not blind to the inequalities and injustices that are part of the present global order, and they understand that the United States is a dominant power today, but not an imperial power in the nineteenth-century sense. For Hardt and Negri, Empire is not just a type of social domination. As much as Empire witnesses its share of exploitation and genocide, it is also about rights, freedoms, and democratic movements. Its decentralization, fluid character, and the plurality of entities, including international social movements, that make up the current global order, make positive social change possible. The authors are hopeful about the future. They speak, vaguely, about possibilities of an alternative or "counter Empire." In effect, they believe, like Foucault, that where there is power there is resistance. However, not all forms of opposition are defended. For example, they are not sympathetic to movements that are narrowly against globalization. Moreover, they see acts of political resistance that aim to defend traditions or local forms of life or community as having limited social effect. Ultimately, they favor protests and movements that address a global social level with the aim of promoting further decentralization and democratization. We would expect them to be supportive of recent protests, from the 1999 WTO protests in Seattle and in 2001 in Genoa, to the 2012 protests in Greece against the World Bank and the International Monetary Fund for narrowly focusing on fiscal matters while neglecting issues of political empowerment or social justice concerns.

IMPERIAL AMERICA: DAVID HARVEY AND MICHAEL MANN

Not all theorists of empire, especially in the Marxist tradition, believe that the age of imperialism is over. In response to the United States' interventions in Afghanistan and then Iraq many social thinkers have reconsidered the place of empire in today's world. Specifically, US actions raise the question of whether the United States is an imperialist nation. Two important efforts to theorize empire have been made by David Harvey and Michael Mann.

The title of David Harvey's volume, *The New Imperialism*, speaks of his point of view. America is an imperialist nation but of a sort different than the recent world empires of Great Britain or France.[3] Nineteenth- and twentieth-century imperialism often involved territorial occupation and military conquest. Perhaps the best illustration of this style of imperialism was the European conquest of Africa. Individual European nations carved up this continent into new nations, which they proceeded to control, often after ruthless military conquest. However, through most of these two centuries European imperialism relied less on territorial conquest than on a liberal ideology and the internationalization of the free market. As the economically most powerful and dominant nation, Great Britain was able to become a world power by promoting liberal policies of free enterprise, open markets, and the abolition of tariffs and trade regulations. After World War II, Great Britain's supremacy gave way to that of the United States. The latter nation repudiated colonial conquest but continued to rely on the free market to maintain an imperial status. However, Harvey believes that relying on the market to maintain world dominance proved limiting, as Asia and Europe were able to challenge the economic predominance of the United States. Accordingly, in the late twentieth century the United States gradually shifted to a neoconservative ideology which, under the banner of spreading freedom and democracy, and global order, pursued an aggressive, interventionist and militaristic foreign policy. Neoconservatism represents the ideology of the new imperialism while a politics of territorial control expresses something of its practice. From this perspective, 9/11 did not make this new imperialism possible but made it possible for it to be more open and politically acceptable, just as it made it more acceptable to trade off domestic freedoms for greater world dominance. This is the situation, says Harvey, in America today.

Born in 1948, **David Harvey** is the Distinguished Professor of Anthropology at the City University of New York. He is a geographer by training, but his work integrates this discipline with critical social theory. He is the author of many books, including *The Condition of Postmodernity* (1989), *Paris: The Capital of Modernity* (2003), and *Spaces of Capital* (2001). Harvey's work is notable for addressing the changing character of capitalism and its relationship to postmodernism and globalization.

Unlike many other contemporary social thinkers and observers who also view the United States as an imperial power, Harvey, aims to understand the social structural logic of American imperialism. He speaks of a dual logic of imperialism – political and economic. The political logic of imperialism involves territorial control. Its economic logic is that of capitalist accumulation.

> I here define that special brand of [imperialism] called "capitalist imperialism" as a contradictory fusion of . . . imperialism as a distinctively political project on the part of actors whose power is based in command of a territory . . . and imperialism as a diffuse political–economic process in space and time in which command over and use of capital takes primacy. With the former I want to stress the political, diplomatic, and military strategies invoked and used by a state . . . as it struggles to assert its interests and achieve its goals in the world at large. With the latter, I focus on the ways in which economic power flows across and through continuous space . . . through the daily practices of production, trade, commerce, capital flows.[4]

Harvey aims to show how these territorial and capitalist logics of power operate often in alliance but just as often in tension to shape the contours of the new imperialism.

As a Marxist, Harvey assumes the primacy of the capitalist logic. He argues that capitalism today is characterized by post-Fordist firms engaged in what he calls "flexible modes of capital accumulation." This means that capitalism today must be mobile and flexible in order to survive and flourish in a highly competitive global economy. Capitalism's flexibility and mobility prove well suited to respond to the chief crisis of capitalism today, namely the "crisis of over accumulation." As markets are saturated, and profits soar through financial deal making, capital must find investment outlets or suffer devaluation and spirals of depression and deflationary recession. "If the surpluses of capital . . . cannot be absorbed internally [domestically] . . . then they must be sent elsewhere to find a fresh terrain for their profitable realization if they are not to be devalued."[5] In response to these periodic crises, capital looks to new markets and territories to absorb its capital and realize profits. As huge amounts of capital are invested in foreign economies, often less advanced ones, local people lose control over their own productive property and resources. As multinational capitalist firms take charge of foreign economies, indigenous firms, producers, farmers, and small businesses are displaced or marginalized while new monopolies are created. Harvey calls this "accumulation by dispossession." The era of global and flexible capitalism is also the era of predatory capitalism with its practices of multinational corporate dominance, mergers, rapid property transfers, and financial manipulation of interest rates and currencies. Predatory capitalism creates a world characterized by wide social and economic disparities between nations, regions, and peoples, and uneven development within and between societies, as capital flows move rapidly and ruthlessly across the globe driven by profit and the threat of crisis.

While the logic of capitalism drives global dynamics, it does not explain everything. Alongside the logic of capital is a political logic of territorial expansion and control. The state creates the conditions that make flexible global capitalism possible. It maintains a stable global environment for overseas investments and protects capital as it moves restlessly across the globe. Accordingly, in the centers of global capitalism today, in the United States in particular, the state pursues an aggressive foreign policy. Against neoliberal ideology, the United States government has sought to exercise political control over foreign territories and peoples in order to establish and maintain favorable conditions for global, flexible capitalism. So, in Harvey's view, the new imperialism of America today involves a dual logic of capitalist expansion and political–territorial control.

From this perspective, US intervention in Iraq is not accidental. Rather, it must be understood as part of a decades-long pattern of an increasingly militarized foreign policy (the two Gulf Wars, the Balkans, and Afghanistan) that underscores the prominent role that political–territorial control plays in the American political economy. Iraq is simply a more transparent manifestation of the new imperialism. When all is said and done, the Iraq invasion was one way to secure cheap oil to sustain American global capitalism.

Harvey argues that neoconservatism and its aggressive and militaristic foreign policy may be harmful to capitalist development. Wars drain the economy and interrupt capital development. Harvey views the United States as an imperial power, but an unstable one that is bound to generate discontent and opposition. Its political–military might is inevitably challenged by new forms of war (Vietnam, Iraq, al-Qaeda) and by rising political–military powers in Asia or Southeast Asia. Moreover, Harvey believes, as do many observers, that eventually America's economy will slow down considerably, if not crash, either because of debt, the costs of militarization, or the rise of other emerging economic powers that challenge American economic supremacy.

In the end, Harvey places his hopes for America's future on domestic progressive social and political forces. In public criticism of neoconservatives and predatory global capitalism, Harvey finds the beginning of a spirit of social accountability and social rationality. But, for this opposition to be truly effective, it will have to coalesce into a bloc opposing the considerable power of the social forces supporting militarism and finance and monopolistic capitalism. Harvey's gesturing to such a possibility speaks more to his hope than to a social realism to be found in his analysis.

Despite Harvey's attempt to separate analytically the political and economic dynamics of imperialism, it is, in the end, the logic of capitalism that drives and organizes a pattern of imperialism. As Harvey says, "what sets imperialism of the capitalist sort apart from other conceptions of empire is that it is the capitalistic logic that typically dominates."[6] It might be instructive, then, to place Harvey's work alongside that of Michael Mann, who offers a Weberian-inspired perspective on American empire.

Michael Mann (born 1943) is a professor of sociology at the University of California at Los Angeles. He is the author of, among other books, *The Sources of Social Power*, volumes I and II. Mann emphasizes the role of power in social life. He develops a multidimensional theory of power which is the basis for his historical and comparative analyses of societies across the globe and sweep of history.

Like Harvey, Mann is responding to America's invasion of Afghanistan and Iraq, along with its unilateralist and militaristic foreign policy. And, like Harvey, he argues that the Bush administration did not, and the Obama administration likely does not represent a dramatic shift or departure in American political culture and foreign policy but rather expresses in a more open and clear way a pattern signaling America's imperial ambitions. Unlike Harvey, however, Mann interprets America as a failed empire.[7]

To a considerable degree, the divergent perceptions of American power by Harvey and Mann reflect their different theoretical standpoints. Whereas Harvey leans heavily on an analysis of the political economy of capitalism to understand American imperialism, Mann operates with a multidimensional theory of power. According to this view, power is distributed between the economic, military, political, and cultural spheres. Mann analyzes American power through this fourfold social topology, concluding that America is a faltering, incoherent empire.

Since World War II, America has replaced Great Britain and Germany as the economic powerhouse of the world economy. For a period of time, it could truly be said that the United States exercised economic hegemony across the industrial, manufacturing, financial, and telecommunications sectors. However, Mann argues that this is no longer the case. In the last few decades, Europe and Asia have become economic forces equal to the United States. Indeed, with its growing trade deficit, international debt, and vast military expenditures, Mann anticipates the decline of America's international economic dominance.

There are few thinkers who doubt that the United States is the sole military superpower. This nation has the conventional and nuclear capacity to exercise military dominance across the globe. And indeed, with military bases strategically installed in every region of the world, US military dominance is unquestionable. Yet, to the extent that recent wars have been nonconventional, involving, for example, nonstate actors or terroristic cells stretched across territories, America's military might have proven inadequate. From Vietnam to Afghanistan and Iraq, America's overwhelming military power has not translated into victory in these nonconventional wars.

With its aggressive unilateralism and militaristic foreign policy, America's imperial ambitions moved to the very center of the politics of the George W. Bush administration. Ignoring international conventions and treaties, and engaging in a preemptive war without United Nations Security Council approval, the Bush administration represented America's public assertion of its imperial status. However, nowhere is the failure of American empire more obvious and poignant than in this nation's failure to gain international legitimation for the Iraq invasion and then its inability to secure civic order and peace in that country. In the end, America had to appeal to other nations and the United Nations to salvage this failed military intervention.

It is almost a cliché to identify cultural globalization with Americanization. Popular culture across the globe, whether it is McDonald's, hip-hop, or Nike, is stamped with the signature of America. Yet, as much as American popular culture is globally disseminated, it is also frequently ignored, marginalized, and resisted. Local cultures have not disappeared in the face of Americanization. Indeed, in many cases they have been revitalized, reinvented, and celebrated as symbols of religious, ethnic, or nationalist purity and pride.

Mann does not deny or discount America's imperial ambitions. He does, however, aim to show the limits of American power and its failure to become a coherent empire. In particular, Mann underscores a postwar pattern of the militarization of American national and foreign policy. Confronted with political–economic problems or geopolitical crises or conflicts, the United States is quick to turn to military solutions. Thus, in the face of militant Islam in the Middle East, noncooperation on the part of Iraq, or Serbian aggression in the Balkans, the United States responded militarily. Moreover, lacking the manpower, the national will, and the varied skills required to sustain political–military global dominance, America repeatedly comes up against its own limits and failures. Rather than imagining a successful world empire in its future, Mann anticipates that, with its growing domestic and international deficit and debt that accompanies its expanding militarism, America's challenge may be to avoid economic crisis and political decline. To give the final word to the author:

> We shall see that the new imperialism creates more, not fewer, terrorists, that it creates more determined "rogue states," and that it weakens American leadership in the world. But the enemies of the United States are wrong to see it as the Great Satan or the Evil Empire. It is not that well organized. This is an incoherent Empire whose overconfident, hyperactive militarism will soon destroy it.[8]

Suggested Readings

Craig Calhoun, Frederick Cooper, and Kevin Moore, eds., *Lessons of Empire* (New York: New Press, 2006).

Noam Chomsky, *Hegemony or Survival* (New York: Henry Holt, 2003).

Chalmers Johnson, *The Sorrows of Empire* (New York: Henry Holt, 2004).

References

1 Michael Hardt and Antonio Negri, *Empire*, (Cambridge, MA: Harvard University Press, 2000).

2 Hardt and Negri, *Empire*, p. xii.

3 David Harvey, *The New Imperialism* (New York: Oxford University Press, 2003).

4 Harvey, *The New Imperialism*, p. 26.

5 Harvey, *The New Imperialism*, p. 117.

6 Harvey, *The New Imperialism*, p. 33.

7 Michael Mann, *Incoherent Empire* (London: Verso, 2003).

8 Mann, *Incoherent Empire*, pp. 15–16.

Afterword to Part VI

Classical social theory equated the individual society with the nation-state. From Comte to Weber, it was assumed that the nation-state is the basic unit of social life, at least of modern social life. The classical theorists were aware that societies were not always organized as national states, but historically have been organized as kinship groups, clans, tribes, federations, city-states, or empires. In a sense, they understood that the nation-state is historical, but they never tried to analyze the historical and social construction of nationalism and the nation-state. Interestingly, these theorists, with the possible exception of Weber, believed that in the long term nation-states would either disappear or lose their social power. Marx, for example, anticipated a communist revolution that would spell the end not only of social classes but of distinct national states. And Durkheim imagined a future state of the human condition in which a world society would witness the gradual disappearance of individual national states.

In many respects, the classical theorists had it right. Although scholars today debate whether the nation-state is a distinctively modern development, none of them seriously question the historical prominence of the nation-state in the modern world. Indeed, whatever else can be said about the so-called modern era, nationalism and nation-state formation have been at the center of this historical period. Today, the world is territorially organized as an order of national states. Apart from a few city-states such as Singapore and Hong Kong, it is difficult to identify any internationally recognized society that is not organized as a nation-state.

As much as the nineteenth, and especially the twentieth, century can be characterized as the age of nationalism and the nation-state, the future of the national state is today being reconsidered by social thinkers. We should be clear about what such thinkers are claiming. They're not saying that the nation-state is disappearing or is losing its power in the contemporary world order. All of the thinkers we have discussed in this section believe that the state will remain a powerful social force into the

Contested Knowledge: Social Theory Today, Fifth Edition. Steven Seidman.
© 2013 John Wiley & Sons, Ltd. Published 2013 by John Wiley & Sons, Ltd.

near and not so near future. Although the fall of the Berlin Wall and the heightened awareness of living in a global world have led some social thinkers to imagine the rise of a new world order composed of post-national forms of social life, most social thinkers continue to assume that the nation-state will remain the fundamental social unit across the globe.

However, as we've seen, there is a growing sense that there are social processes and dynamics that cannot be grasped exclusively within a national state framework. For some theorists, such as David Held and Mary Kaldor, the extent of societal interdependence or the ways in which every society is today connected in immensely dense ways with other societies means that we should not analyze societies simply in terms of their internal dynamics. Societies today must be understood as part of socially dense networks. Moreover, globalization means that these societal networks have produced distinctively global processes and institutions such as forms of global inequality and global social movements, and national and international nongovernmental organizations. So, while the nation-state remains in many ways the basic social unit of the world order, from the perspective of globalization contemporary societies are structured and organized as much by their external global environment as by their internal national environment.

Although the idea of globalization has become a powerful point of view from which to understand contemporary social and global life, it does have its critics. As we've seen, Wallerstein and Castells do not dispute the global context of societal dynamics but they claim that what is new or distinctive about the current global environment is the globalization of capitalism. Where capitalism was at one time a nationally based economy, today it is a world economy. And, unlike social thinkers who see in the internationalization of capitalism the spread of individual freedom and political liberty, Wallerstein and Castells argue that, as capitalism goes global, so too do social inequalities. There are unique inequalities between nations and whole regions of the world that reflect the contradictory character of contemporary global capitalism. Their perspective is sharply at odds with the globalization views of Held and Kaldor. For example, where the latter thinkers see the chief problem of a global order as relating to global regulation, the former theorists highlight conditions of global social inequality.

Theorists of globalization and global capitalism agree on one point: the contemporary world order leaves no place for imperialism and empire building. However, this claim has also been recently challenged. Thus Hardt and Negri make the somewhat paradoxical argument that globalization itself is a new and distinctive form of empire: neither an empire of colonies and conquest, nor an empire built on the internationalization of the markets, but rather an empire without a political center but nevertheless controlling the world order. Perhaps an even more radical challenge to globalization perspectives is posed by Harvey and Mann. They dispute the very claim that the imperialism of colonies and conquest is part of the historical past. Despite its self-understanding as the anti-empire, America's aggressive and militaristic foreign policy over the last several decades suggests a society that in fact has not renounced its imperial ambitions. Whether this nation is a successful imperial one or a declining empire, their perspectives have compelled us to reconsider the role of empire in the modern world, including the present one.

Part VII

The Rise of Postdisciplinary Theory

Introduction to Part VII

When Comte or Marx and Durkheim were writing, the disciplines of sociology or anthropology were barely formed. Comte and Marx were independent thinkers; neither held an academic position. It was only towards the very end of the nineteenth century that social science became part of the university. Weber and Durkheim were academics, but they were not trained as sociologists. They were trained in the history of law, economics, and in philosophy and languages; there was no discipline of sociology. In fact, Durkheim was a pivotal figure in making sociology a respectable discipline in French universities. Weber and others played a similar role in Germany.

Between 1890 and the 1920s, sociology was slowly becoming a recognized discipline in universities in the United States, Germany, France, Italy, Britain, and elsewhere. And yet, thinkers such as Durkheim, Weber, or Herbert Spencer in England or W. E. B. Du Bois or Albion Small in the United States were general thinkers who moved comfortably in the realms of history and philosophy, as well as sociology.

Sociology didn't become what we know it to be today until the 1960s and 1970s. At that time, student enrollment in Euro-American universities increased dramatically. In the United States, the number of trained PhDs in sociology soared; state, regional, and national professional associations were formed and membership increased dramatically. In short, the discipline of sociology became a well-established part of the university and American culture.

From the 1970s to the present day, social knowledge has been organized around an academic culture of disciplines. Each discipline has its own subject matter, methods, problems, and theories. While there is some exchange of ideas, each discipline has been more or less insular. For example, sociological theorists have rarely read the canonical figures of political theorists, such as Aristotle, Plato, Machiavelli, Locke, or Hobbes. Similarly, anthropological theory has its own tradition that includes Bronislaw Malinowski, Margaret Mead, Franz Boas, Claude Lévi-Strauss, and Mary Douglas – none of whom is part of the sociological canon. Each discipline, then, has fashioned

Contested Knowledge: Social Theory Today, Fifth Edition. Steven Seidman.
© 2013 John Wiley & Sons, Ltd. Published 2013 by John Wiley & Sons, Ltd.

its own world of canonical figures and texts, key themes and problems, and styles of theorizing and research.

This disciplinary culture is breaking down; the boundaries separating the social science disciplines, and the divide between the humanities and the social sciences, have become porous and fluid; the idea of separate disciplinary islands of theory and research is losing credibility and coherence.

Theory is increasingly postdisciplinary. The problems theorists engage with are not discipline-specific. To be sure, sociological theorists are still preoccupied with distinctive problems such as the link between an individual or micro level and a structural or macro level of analysis. However, many of the key debates in which sociological theorists engage today are decidedly not discipline-specific, for example, debates over civil society, nationalism, social identities, or globalization. Theoretical debate and research today occurs less in narrow disciplinary enclaves than in postdisciplinary clusters or networks. In these clustered debates, participants come from diverse disciplines and are expected to be competent in many theoretical approaches, such as feminism, poststructuralism, classical sociology, and cultural studies.

Instead of established "schools of theory" or a fixed canon of theory figures and texts, theory is today eclectic, decentered, and decidedly "local" in its engagement with specific clustered debates. Something of the postdisciplinary character of theory will be illustrated in the three clustered debates we review in this final part of the book.

21

Theories of "the Other"

Classical and contemporary Anglo-European social theory took shape in no small measure as a theoretical reckoning with industrial capitalism. Whether we consider Marx's critique of political economy, Durkheim's analysis of the social division of labor, or Weber's thesis of the Protestant origins of the disciplining of capital and labor, these thinkers aimed to explain the origins of industrial capitalism and its political economy class system, patterns of solidarity, and link to bureaucratization and state formation. A century later, "capitalism," now understood as an information-based global economy, remains a central focus of social theory and politics.

That said, the theoretical terrain of contemporary Anglo-European academic culture has experienced a sea change. As we have seen, the claim that the analysis of capitalism should be the *foundation* for comprehending contemporary societies has been challenged by the view, roughly speaking, that differences of gender, race, class, sexuality, disability, religion, nationality, and so on structure our social worlds in ways that cannot be explained exclusively or chiefly by the dynamics of capitalism. Across the social sciences and humanities, many scholars and researchers maintain that the analysis of the multiplicity of social differences and their intersection across national and global spaces should be at the core of social analysis. Today, the political economy of capitalism coexists, often uneasily, with a sociology and politics of difference.

In this chapter, I address one aspect of the sociology and politics of difference. If we consider the scholarship associated with feminism, postcolonial studies, queer studies, or cultural studies, which have been the chief sites for the elaboration of a politics of difference, we repeatedly encounter the concept of "the Other." This notion is, however, often used in loose and confusing ways. Often, the Other is said to indicate a non-normative status. For example, women are cited as the Other to men or, in "Western" contexts, the Arab Muslim is the Other to the European Christian. Women and Muslims are assumed to occupy a different and subordinate social position (e.g., possessing fewer rights and social opportunities) in relation to

Contested Knowledge: Social Theory Today, Fifth Edition. Steven Seidman.
© 2013 John Wiley & Sons, Ltd. Published 2013 by John Wiley & Sons, Ltd.

men and Anglo-European Christians; the latter serve as the implicit, sometimes explicit, normative standard. But the concept of the Other is also frequently used to underscore a unique cultural status: the Other as an outsider and as a social threat. I argue that these two senses of the Other should be *analytically* distinguished as they suggest distinct lines of social analysis. The former, the Other as a non-normative, socially subordinate status, is best analyzed as part of a sociology of difference. The latter notion, the Other as a dangerous outsider, points to a social analysis of Otherness.

So, how does the politics of difference diverge from a critical sociology of the Other? The former refers to the social making of a spectrum of social identities or statuses marked by a hierarchical division between those that are socially privileged and normative and those that are non-normative and socially disadvantaged. Not all non-normative statuses should be understood in the analytical language of difference. Only those that exhibit a *pattern of social disadvantage* are relevant to a sociology and politics of difference. For example, gender is an analytically significant axis of differ-ence, to the extent that gender norms and practices produce social patterns of diver-gence and inequality between persons designated as male/female or men/women. By contrast, being left-handed in a normatively right-handed society, or a vegetarian in a meat-eating nation, would lack analytical significance as a status difference in so far as these "irregularities" do not entail patterned sociopolitical disadvantage. In short, only non-normative statuses that evidence an empirical pattern of social structural disadvantage are to be treated as social differences.

However, and this is crucial for understanding the sociology of difference, a disad-vantaged status in one or more social spheres (e.g., family, work, military) does not necessarily mean subordination across all spheres. And, despite suffering structural disadvantage, status differences are still recognized as morally legitimate, or as right-fully claiming inclusion in a normative civil order. For example, American working-class men suffer class subordination in the workplace and social disadvantages in terms of educational opportunities and access to institutionalized offices of political power. Yet, if blue-collar male workers are also White and heterosexual, they would retain gender, racial, and sexual privileges. And, despite structural disadvantages, this class of men, barring other non-normative statuses, would also be enfranchised and respected as American. Furthermore, even a status difference that reproduces subordination across multiple social spheres may still command respect and citizenship status. For example, prior to the 1950s, many native-born White American women lacked equal economic opportunities, equal civil and political rights, and suffered status deflation (in relation to men) due to the tight link between femininity and the roles of wife and mother. Nevertheless, if these women were otherwise gender conventional, their status difference (in relation to a masculine norm) would not position them as Other. To the extent that these women were able to marry and participate in routine familial and civil affairs, they would occupy a respected social status. The social making of pat-terned status differences and hierarchies, and their contestation, is the focus of a sociology and politics of difference.[1]

By contrast, sociology of Otherness aims to understand how non-normative behav-iors and identities acquire a status that positions them outside of a normative familial–civil moral order. Otherness signals, foremost, a condition of *symbolic exclusion* or a state of social disqualification and cultural inferiorization. Moreover, because the Other is also represented as an imminent and grave social threat, symbolic exclusion is typically accompanied by systemic patterns of social marginalization (e.g., ethnic and racial apartheids, Jewish and gay ghettos, and refugee camps).

At a minimum, Otherness assumes a social world that is symbolically divided into two antagonistic orders: a symbolic moral order conferring full personhood and a respected civil status, and its antithesis. Othering is a process in which certain persons and the spaces they occupy are excluded from what is considered to be the legitimate familial–civil life of a community. Moreover, figures of Otherness are surrounded by an aura of danger and may become a site of moral panic and a politics of purification. To inhabit this morally contaminated space is to be denied the range of rights associated with personhood, dignity, and decisional autonomy. Examples of the Other might include the colonized racial subjects of the European imperial era, the Jew of late nineteenth-century Europe and Russia, the Negro in post-civil war America, the homosexual in post-World War II America, and the North African Muslim in contemporary Europe or the Mexican immigrant in the United States.

If Otherness is a distinct theoretical topic, what sort of theories have been proposed to account for this phenomenon? This chapter reviews four major theoretical approaches to the notion of the Other.

However, before reviewing these theories, something of the social and intellectual context needs to be sketched. Interestingly, the theme of Otherness was largely absent from classical European social theory. It's telling that it was Georg Simmel, a colleague of Max Weber's, who perhaps edged closest towards such an account. As a Jew, Simmel experienced cultural marginalization in Germany's academic culture. He apparently modeled his well-known concept of the stranger on the experience of the German Jew. But Simmel's stranger was not so much a menacing outsider as a signature figure of modern urban life. The stranger was arguably a projection of Simmel's wish that European Jews might be tolerated as different but non-threatening. If Simmel's assimilationist hope prevented him from developing a full-blown account of the Jew as an Other, some Jews in Europe and Russia abandoned this aspiration. Zionists such as Theodor Herzl, Max Nordau, and Max Pinsker offered the outlines of such an account in the context of defending the project of establishing a Jewish state beyond the borders of the Euro-Asian continent. However, their nascent sociology of the Jew as an Other was ignored by the chief figures of classical sociology, with the possible exception of the German Jewish émigré Louis Wirth.[2]

Across the Atlantic, some American sociologists and critics were also developing the rudiments of a sociology of Otherness. In particular, W. E. B. Du Bois's notion of the veil and double consciousness, as it applied to American Blacks, highlighted a dynamic of presence/absence and inside/outside that is central to an account of Otherness.[3] It was the combination of decolonizing movements in Africa, Asia, and the Middle East, and the populist rebellions in Anglo-European nations, which provided the immediate context for theorizing Otherness. These movements challenged Anglo-European cultural hegemony as oppressed populations in the metropole and their colonies rebelled. Central to their rebellion was embracing formerly denigrated, stigmatized statuses and traditions. These currents of social and intellectual rebellion shaped a political and intellectual culture that made questions of social difference and Otherness central. Among the many thinkers for whom such issues proved theoretically significant, the work of four social thinkers have proven especially compelling in the current debates: Erving Goffman, Michel Foucault, Edward Said, and Mary Douglas. I offer brief critical overviews of their work as it bears on our theme.

GOFFMAN: THE PRAGMATICS OF STIGMA

Goffman's *Stigma* is one of the earliest sociological accounts of a process of othering.[4] Stigma refers to a labeling process whereby selves acquire a socially disqualifying identity. Goffman explores the way individuals respond to stigma by either managing a discredited identity or managing information that could expose such an identity. Despite efforts to sustain a "normal" life, stigma often forces the self outside of the routine orders of daily life. Some individuals become part of an outsider subculture, finding solidarity but at the cost of considerable social estrangement and personal distress.

Stigmatization, at least in its extreme version, is a process of Othering. Goffman aims to show how labels produce the illusion of selves as fundamentally different from "normals" (Goffman's term). A complex, multidimensional self disappears; one becomes simply a Negro, homosexual, or mentally ill, for example. Stigma renders the self an abstraction, an almost spectral figure or a metaphor for some undesirable condition. The stigmatized self may acquire a "supernatural cast" and be perceived as both powerful and dangerous. She may be feared as much as loathed, and avoided for fear of contamination. The world of normals is protected by circumscribing the lives of the stigmatized, and ultimately by excluding them from the respected civil orders of a community.

Although the Other may try to pass as normal or as an ordinary citizen, such individuals may also withdraw into an alternative, shadowy world. In this way, Goffman drives home the point that stigma creates a split between a world of normals and the stigmatized.

The notion of stigma loses some of its analytical value insofar as Goffman failed to differentiate among the wide range of stigmatized behaviors or statuses. From the examples he cites, the stigmatized fall into three categories. There are stigmas that cause personal distress (the stutterer and the divorced), stigmas that result in patterned social inequalities (women, Asian-Americans, pre-World War II European-Americans), and stigmas that yield social exclusion (Black Americans, pre-Stonewall homosexuals). Selves in the first two categories suffer disadvantages but remain part of the routine civil orders. To the extent that such stigmatized selves are accorded elementary rights and respect, they would appropriately be classified as "status differences." By contrast, stigmas of the last type speak to a condition of Otherness. So, the divorced may suffer personal distress but not job loss; the Italian-American may be denied access to the upper echelons of the business world but is a first-class citizen who can intermarry with Protestant Americans. By contrast, the homosexual or Black American of the 1950s was denied basic rights and respect. By not differentiating among the stigmatized, Goffman failed to consider the way in which varied types of stigma socially position the self in decidedly different ways. And, by focusing exclusively on labels and their behavioral consequences, Goffman did not consider how stigmas vary in their structural implications. In fact, the social significance of stigma rests precisely on whether such a labeling process is institutionally enforced and whether it creates institutional and symbolic patterns of exclusion and social inequality. Goffman's interactionist analytic does not address the formation of norms and their institutionalization, as the condition which makes stigma possible. In short, he lacked a structural account of the conditions of stigmatization.

Although prescient, Goffman's labeling theory of stigma is limited by his exclusive focus on the effect of stigma labels on individuals. By contrast, Foucault sketches a historical–structural explanation of why certain statuses and behaviors are non-normative, and how they are dealt with in culturally and institutionally specific ways. With Foucault, we shift from a labeling/agent-centered approach/the social consequences of stigma labels to a power/knowledge structural analysis.

FOUCAULT: THE MAD AND THE ABNORMAL

In *Madness and Civilization*, the mad are not so much stigmatized as produced by a European culture that claims to represent the progress of reason.[5] In the "classical age," the mad played a key role in establishing the boundaries of reason. They symbolized the point at which reason ends and unreason begins. As Foucault observed, "for classical man, madness . . . was only unreason's empirical form." As the Other to the enlightened man of reason, the mad were excluded from the normative familial–civil orders. Indeed, Foucault argues that over the seventeenth and eighteenth centuries madness occupied a borderland between human and beast as the mad represented an "animal ferocity" and an "unchained animality." By the end of the "age of reason," the mad were to be confined or separated from a rational, civil order. Ironically, the age of confinement was inaugurated in the name of reason.

After *Madness and Civilization*, Foucault shifted his focus from the history of representations to the analysis of power. The notion of Otherness drops out as an explicit category of analysis. Foucault turns to the examination of disciplinary power – its structural dynamics and its spread across Anglo-European societies. Nevertheless, there is an implicit, unstated Foucauldian perspective on Otherness in his account of disciplinary power.

The key text is *Psychiatric Power*, a volume of lectures which Foucault referred to as the successor to *Madness and Civilization*.[6] In these lectures, Foucault argues that the social meaning of madness in Europe changed dramatically between the early and late nineteenth century. In the first half of that century, state and medical authorities promoted the confinement of the mad. The mad lacked rights, decisional autonomy, and were excluded from the familial–civil sphere. They were said to be in the grip of delusion and unreason. Although he does not use the language, Foucault is describing a process of Othering. But this Othering is very different to the conditions that existed for the mad in the pre-classical era. In the nineteenth century, the mad were confined and, most importantly, subject to a new form of power: disciplinary power.

Unlike "sovereign power," in which the body of subjects never escapes the sovereign's personal authority, disciplinary power speaks to the way the impersonal organization of an institution forms and regulates bodies and subjectivities by means of surveillance, supervision, norms of normalization, and maximizing bodily productivity. Foucault contends that psychiatric treatment is built into the disciplinary structure of the asylum or hospital; the relation between the doctor and the mad person is not a psychiatric dynamic, as we know it today, but a relation of power – a battle between the institution and the delusions of the mad.

A sea change in the culture of madness and psychiatry occurred during the nineteenth century. Disciplinary power became entrenched in the medical field but also psychiatry in the modern sense (what Foucault called the PSYCH function), became integral to disciplinarity. The mad were said to suffer from intra-psychic conditions such as hysteria or compulsions. This was the age of psychiatry; the family drama took center stage. Disciplinary power spread across social spheres, for example, in schools, factories, hospitals, and the military. The idiom of normality and abnormality became a meta-language to identify and classify organizational and personnel problems. With its norm of normality (e.g., the normal soldier or student, the normal, productive worker), disciplinary power inevitably produced "irregularities," that is, selves who cannot adjust, cooperate, or be productive. Some of these irregularities were understood as "abnormalities" to be addressed by a secondary tier of organizations, what Foucault calls "recovery systems." Guided by a psychiatric model of psycho-sexual normality, these recovery systems (e.g., clinics, hospitals, asylums, therapies, counseling centers, orphanages, and juvenile homes) sought to re-normalize and reintegrate these failed selves. Abnormalities were seen as signs of disturbed family dynamics requiring psychiatric treatment and normalization. A tight circuit was established between disciplinary-based social institutions and families, both of which identified maladjusted selves to be transferred to the appropriate recovery agency.

Although Foucault does not provide an explicit analysis of Otherness in *Psychiatric Power*, there is an implicit argument worth considering. Contemporary forms of Otherness would come from the class of "irregularities" produced by disciplinary power. Otherness would be understood in the psychiatric idiom as abnormal types, for example, psychopaths, homosexuals, sociopaths, pedophiles, sadists, the learning disabled, the criminal-minded, the juvenile delinquent, and so on. Psychiatric power produces abnormal selves but also channels them into recovery systems, which aim to fashion productive, normal selves.

A disciplinary order projects the ideal of an airtight social machine that routinely produces a space outside this order, an outside, which in turn is subject to disciplinary power. It is though perhaps less airtight than Foucault might have imagined. For selves who spend extended time in recovery systems (prisons, reformatories, asylums, hospitals), or are repeatedly recycled through them, they may very well acquire a status as an Other, e.g. the "hardened criminal," the irredeemably insane, the repeat sex offender, or the drug addict. Also, some irregularities and abnormalities may elude the iron grip of recovery systems (the closeted homosexual or the professional criminal); others may be subject to disciplinary power for only short periods (e.g., sex workers, migrant laborers, inner-city drop-outs). There is still another possibility: selves who resist disciplinarity and opt to live outside its confines, such as illegal immigrants, flamboyant homosexuals, gender queers, the homeless, and Gypsies.

Disciplinarity produces an outside, an exterior to discipline. This outside stands in opposition to disciplinary power. If the latter features surveillance, supervision, uniformity, and normalization, the former is imagined as a zone of disorder, ungovernability, and danger. The space outside of disciplinarity will be inhabited by others, figures feared as agents of disorder and ruin. Foucauldian analysis presupposes an outside to disciplinarity, but does not provide an account of it. The space of the outside is ignored; it may, however, acquire social significance as it is imagined to be populated by menacing and powerful figures.

EDWARD SAID: THE RACIAL OTHER

Both Goffman and Foucault assume that medicalization or the language of normal/ abnormal and healthy/sick is the chief idiom of Othering in contemporary Anglo-European societies. Perhaps, but it is not the only idiom. Race also serves as a meta-language of Othering. It has its own rhetorical strategies, narrative figures, iconic images, and hierarchies. In principle, the conventions of a racial discourse of Otherness would likely apply broadly, as much to the native American of colonial times or the Australian or Taiwanese aboriginal as to the colonized African or Arab of the twentieth century, and the North African immigrant in Europe.

In the wake of national independence movements between the 1940s and 1970s, postcolonial critics such as Fanon, C. L. R. James, and Memmi, among others, provided compelling accounts of racial Othering. No text, however, has proved more influential than Said's *Orientalism*. Moreover, whereas Goffman focused on labels and Foucault on disciplinary power, Said attends to the structure of a discourse of racial Othering. In *Orientalism* and *The Question of Palestine*, Said identifies a series of rhetorical conventions that structure representations of racial otherness.[7] Racial discourses such as Orientalism are often institutionalized (e.g., in universities, learned societies, policy institutes, conferences, publications) and are geopolitically embedded. And while Said sought to analyze the interplay between structural context and discourse in establishing an asymmetrical relation of power between the Occident and Orient, it is Orientalism as a discourse that will command our attention here.

Said underscored the way Orientalism fixes the Oriental as a "subject race." Occidental discourses stipulate the racial unity of the Oriental. However much Orientals vary by language, geography, history, and cultural practice, race is imagined as establishing an elementary and stable identity. The Oriental – the Arab, the Chinese, and the Asian – is represented as an unchanging, unitary racial figure. The biology of race, not its history or sociology, sets in stone the essence of the Oriental. And what this biological background reveals is a history of the Oriental as a "subject race" or a people that has been incapable of governing itself. The Orientalist text "knows" this racial figure as either infantile and submissive, or predatory and despotic. This ontology of deficit and excess has destined the Oriental to recurring patterns of stagnation or cycles of rise and decline. The Oriental is, then, a social threat, as if always teetering on the edge of disorder and ruin.

The Orientalist narrative positions this figure as inferior to the Occidental. The Arab Muslim, for instance, is depicted as an imposter, drenched in an aura of inauthenticity, as if Islam is a false copy of Christianity and Mohammed an insincere rehearsal of Jesus. Indeed, in extreme versions the Oriental "is *first* an Oriental, [and] *second* a human being."[8] In this formulation, the Oriental occupies a moral space between human and nonhuman.

Furthermore, Orientalism assumes that this racial subject cannot progress of its own accord. The Oriental never escapes the eternal present, the endless patterns of stasis, decline, and chaos. Change can only come from the outside, from a force powerful enough to trigger a break from this relentless repetition. According to the Orientalist logic, the Oriental is, then, a racial type for whom governance must be imposed from the outside. The Oriental needs the beneficent governance of the West, just as a child needs the wise guidance of a parent. In this regard, Orientalism can be said to have summoned, as it were, an imperial West that can present itself as an agent of historical progress.

Orientalism may be read as a case study of a discourse of racial Otherness. In this regard, Said identifies a series of general discursive strategies that would potentially be relevant across a range of representations of racial Otherness. For example, the opposition between a normative and inferior race would likely apply to the relationship between the European and the Arab in Zionism, or between the White European-American and the "dark" Arab in postwar American representations. Said also refers to "blocking" and "silencing" as representational strategies. These aim to prevent a subject race from representing itself to publics. This is accomplished either by claims of a hegemonic discourse to have already exposed racial truths, or by denying the voices of a subject race access to the relevant media. Said also refers to the discursive practices of "reductionism," "totalization," and "exemplification." These entail relying on reductionist abstractions to summarize an entire race, for example, the Oriental as "feminine" or "seductive" or "despotic."

As a general approach to Otherness, Said's studies of Orientalism and the Palestinian question have a broad analytical reach. Discursive strategies such as binarism, essentialism, blocking, and reductionism would seem to be relevant to nonracialized others, for example, the homosexual, the immigrant, or sex worker. For example, the racialist notion of an inferior human type seems characteristic of all discourses of otherness. The Other, whether the Oriental, the homosexual, the Jew, or the sex offender, is also unchanging, governed by repetition, spoken for by experts, and so on. Racialism itself might be considered an instance of "essentialism." Whether the idiom is race or medicalization, the Other is a type whose nature is essentially fixed; a type that is unstable, ungovernable, and dangerous.

The scope of Said's account of the Other is limited, however, by an exclusive focus on territorially foreign racial Others. The Oriental occupies a geographical region beyond the territorial borders of the West. It is precisely the exteriority and ungovernability of the Oriental in relation to the normativity of the West that drives the Western Orientalist to a politics of colonial subjugation. In the mythology of the

Enlightenment, the West aims only to liberate the Orient from a vicious pattern of repetition. But the Oriental is not only a figure of exteriority; she also occupies a space inside the West. The Chinese or the Asian in the United States or the North African or Muslim in West Europe is often represented less as a subject race to be civilized and governed than an inferior population threatening to spread disease and disorder. These *defiled* racial Others are to be segregated or exiled in order to avoid contamination. Borderlands are to be established to secure an unpolluted space for White Christian Europeans. If Said had addressed the Oriental inside the West, the theme of defilement would likely have been salient. As it is, this notion is left untheorized by him.

DOUGLAS: THE MICROPOLITICS OF POLLUTION

Goffman introduced the notion of defilement in his account of stigma as a spoiled identity. But the focus on the behavioral consequences of labels prevented him from addressing defilement as a symbolic and ritual drama. Similarly, as Foucault abandoned the "analysis of representations" for a power/knowledge analytic, the category of Otherness became residual. By contrast, the anthropologist Mary Douglas brings the symbolic and ritual process of defilement into the center of an analysis of Othering.[9]

Douglas famously sketched an account of pollution that pivoted on the claim that "dirt is essentially disorder." She argued that imposing order on our experience is fundamental to human collective life. At a micro level, order is established through practices of classifying, arranging, dividing, sorting, and ranking. At a macro level, laws are enacted, gender and sexual norms established, societal borders fixed, institutional norms enforced, lines of social authority clarified, and status classifications mapped out. Inevitably, though, we encounter "anomalies" or things that don't fit or which confound our classifications, arrangements, and rankings. In morphological terms, there are parts of the social structure that are ambiguous, inarticulate, in transition, that blur distinctions and perhaps sites in the social order where laws or norms are only weakly or unevenly enforced. And, there is always an "other side" to the lines and borders that establish internal order and coherence. This exteriority forms a space of foreignness that may unsettle or threaten a normative order. Often, Douglas says, we simply deny, ignore, or discount these anomalies and ambiguities, or we revise our classifications or make new rules to secure order. Sometimes, though, these anomalies and ambiguities cannot be ignored or managed in routine ways. If we also believe that these anomalies are sites of disorder and threaten to bring ruin through contact, and if our social response to these anomalies involves practices of avoidance, for example, enveloping them in a web of taboos and prohibitions, we are engaged in a pollution drama. Its aim is to restore symbolic and social order.

Although Douglas believed that pollution dramas were central to "primitive" cultures, she acknowledged their relevance for "moderns." In the former case, they are part of a unified cosmology and are woven into the fabric of daily life. By contrast, in differentiated, secular cultures pollution dramas are fragmented or local to specific sites in the social structure and have a circumscribed place in our life-world. Additionally, idioms of pollution vary. Magical-supernaturalism informs the pollution beliefs and practices of primitives; hygiene, etiquette, and aesthetics are the idioms of modern pollution beliefs. In Anglo-European societies, we often engage in pollution practices when we speak of something or someone or someplace as being unclean, filthy, and disease-producing, when there is in fact no demonstrated link to pathogenicity. Of course, the language of uncleanliness can also be "rational" but many of our hygiene practices are symbolic, or ways of managing disorder and danger. Despite the logic of her argument, and her polemic against viewing the primitive as a world apart from the modern, at times Douglas seems to have believed that pollution dramas are an insignificant part of modern life. I think she was mistaken, perhaps confusing the rhetoric of modern rationalism with the reality.

Pollution dramas are efforts to secure order by informal means. Specifically, Douglas believed that pollution dramas secure order by enveloping anomalous and dangerous things, people, or spaces in a web of taboos, prohibitions, and avoidance rituals. Order is restored when the defiled are separated, segregated, confined, or expelled from the routine normative orders of daily life in order to avoid contact and its anticipated trail of disorder and ruin. A zone of exclusion is carved out for the polluted.

Persons are no less susceptible to pollution than objects or spaces. Selves associated with structural sites that are anomalous, ambiguous, formless, or weakly regulated; selves who confound categories or classifications; or selves who are marginal or in transitional states may be polluted. As Douglas says, "a polluting person is always in the wrong. He has developed some wrong condition or simply crossed some line which should not have been crossed and this displacement unleashes danger for someone."[10] In Durkheimian fashion, Douglas maintains that the danger associated with the polluted self symbolizes a collective anxiety evoked by structural stresses and tensions.

To be a polluted self is, then, to be emphatically marked as Other – a figure to be feared and avoided. Danger lay in the self standing-in for a generalized anxiety of disorder. In modern idioms, the polluted Other may be represented as diseased, sick, psychopathic, abnormal, mad, degenerate, racially inferior, crude, or ugly; she threatens disease, death, degeneracy, and moral breakdown. In response, taboos, prohibitions, rituals of aversion and avoidance are intended to isolate polluted selves and minimize contact with a normative order of pure selves and spaces. The polluted self represents a condition of defilement -- one that must be ritually managed.

Douglas's notion of pollution is limited in a number of crucial ways. *Purity and Danger* leaves pollution dramas in contemporary societies largely unexamined. Accordingly, Douglas hardly addressed the role of rituals of avoidance and the politics of purification in dynamic, mobile, national cultures. And, characteristic of Durkheimians, power figures very little apart from in its role as a formalized part of the social structure. Contextually specific social inequalities play a minimal role in her account. Yet, if we assume that ambiguities, transgressed borders, and transitionalities evoke unease and perhaps rituals of pollution and purity, we have to explain why *specific* transgressions, ambiguities, and contradictions become sites of collective attention, and why *specific* normativities are protected by pollution beliefs. In short, pollution dramas are enmeshed in contextually specific symbolic and material conflicts over normativities, material resources, and institutional power.

Suggested Readings

Jeff Alexander, *The Civil Sphere* (Oxford: Oxford University Press, 2007).

Julie Kristeva, *The Power of Horror* (New York: Columbia University Press, 1982).

Edward Said, *The Question of Palestine* (New York: Vintage, 1979).

Peter Stallybrass and Allon White, *The Politics and Poetics of Transgression* (Ithaca, NY: Cornell University Press, 1986).

Tzvetan Todorov, *The Conquest of America* (New York: Harper & Row, 1982).

References

1   Iris Marion Young, *Justice and the Politics of Difference* (Princeton, NJ: Princeton University Press, 1989).

2   Louis Wirth, *The Ghetto* (Chicago: University of Chicago Press, 1997).

3   W. E. B. Du Bois, *The Souls of Black Folk* (New York: Simon & Schuster, 2005).

4   Erving Goffman, *Stigma* (Englewood Cliffs, NJ: Prentice Hall, 1963).

5   Michel Foucault, *Madness and Civilization* (New York: Vintage, 1988).

6   Michel Foucault, *Psychiatric Power* (New York: Picador, 2008).

7   Edward Said, *Orientalism* (New York: Vintage, 1979) and *The Question of Palestine* (New York: Random House, 1979).

8   Said, *Orientalism*, p. 102.

9   Mary Douglas, *Purity and Pollution* (New York: Routledge, 1978).

10 Douglas, *Purity and Pollution*, p. 113.

22

Intimate Life in the "West"

In previous chapters, we've seen that the varied traditions of European and American social theory, through at least World War II, were focused on macrosocial transformations and dynamics such as the development of capitalism, bureaucratization, the division of labor, secularization, class conflict, racialization, and urbanization. We've also observed that these powerful cultural traditions have had little to say about the social construction of gender, sexuality, and emotions. This began to change in the 1950s and 1960s, as sociologists turned to the study of microsocial dynamics such as everyday life, self-presentation, stigma, identity, and so on. Erving Goffman and Harold Garfinkel in the United States, and Alfred Schutz, Peter Berger, and Thomas Luckman from a European standpoint, pioneered a sociology of everyday life.

Curiously, emotions and, in particular, romantic love and intimacy, remained more or less neglected until the 1980s and 1990s. If we ask why, the simple answer is that they approached sex, love, gender, and marriage as natural or as a superficial aspect of social life. Not surprisingly, women sociologists, who were deeply influenced by feminism, pioneered a sociology of emotions. Feelings were understood as socially formed and organized by social processes. In particular, emotions were viewed as thickly gendered in their meaning and expression. So, for example, American women were expected to display feelings that were consistent with normative ideas of femininity, such as empathy, nurturance, modesty, and pleasantness; by contrast, stereotypically men were expected to be aggressive, assertive, competitive, and decisive while containing vulnerable, nurturing, and emotionally expressive feelings. Feminist sociologists analyzed the way emotions were gender-structured and organized in various social settings in ways that reproduce gender division and inequality.

Similarly, it was not until the 1990s that intimacy and romantic love surfaced as a sustained focus of social analysis and research. Paralleling the sociology of emotions, it was the women's movement, but also the gay and lesbian movements, which positioned sexuality, intimacy, and love topics worthy of social knowledge. Moreover, in

Contested Knowledge: Social Theory Today, Fifth Edition. Steven Seidman.
© 2013 John Wiley & Sons, Ltd. Published 2013 by John Wiley & Sons, Ltd.

both Europe and the United States, the spread of contraception facilitated by the birth control pill, the growing equality between women and men, the institutionalization of gay and lesbian communities, and more recently a free-wheeling cyberworld have contributed to making sex, love, and intimacy legitimate topics of politics and sociology.

We have already reviewed theories of sexuality and gender. Frankly, the literature on intimacy, especially romantic intimacies, is much thinner than that pertaining to sexuality and gender. In part, this seems to be political. That is, it was the politics of non-heterosexuality and gender that in many ways fueled the immense output of theoretical and research studies on sexuality and gender in the past few decades. These are now well established fields of knowledge, with their own journals, conferences, organizations, and recognized sociological specialties. This is much less true of intimacy; to be sure, there is considerable sociological research on marriage and families; and psychologists and psychoanalysts have written a great deal on the psychological aspects of romantic intimacy. But much of this research is exclusively focused on heterosexuality, often exclusively on marriage; very few studies address the sociohistorical context and changes that have occurred in intimate life. This might have made sense prior to, say, World War II, but it exposes a serious shortcoming from the vantage point of contemporary realities in the United States and much of Europe.

Since World War II, especially during the last few decades, there has been a sea change in "cultures of intimacy" in Europe and America. Marriage is no longer the sole legitimate arrangement for the drama of intimacy. Many heterosexually-identified citizens are choosing to forge intimate lives outside the confines of marriage; they are cohabiting, living apart, and living as single for longer periods of time; and, in dramatic contrast to before World War II, non-heterosexuals are forging intimacies that demand and are receiving (however incompletely) public recognition. Also, and importantly, sex, love, or parenthood are not exclusively tied to marriage. Individuals are choosing how to combine these aspects of personal life in ways that are increasingly reflecting their own preferences rather than rigid institutional norms or fixed social scripts. In short, there has emerged a distinct realm of "intimacy," which includes a wide range of options and arrangements. As I see it, intimacy has become a field of social knowledge as the institution of marriage has weakened sociologically and lost considerable public authority. It is perhaps for that reason that it was only in the 1990s in the United States and Europe that novel theories of intimacy were presented. My aim in this chapter is to review some of the most prominent perspectives, conveying something of the contours of this emerging field of social knowledge.

ANDREW CHERLIN: THE DEINSTITUTIONALIZATION OF MARRIAGE

The shift from a sociology centered on marriage to one that focuses on intimacy is partially explained by the changing meaning and status of marriage in the United States and elsewhere. The American demographer and sociologist, Andrew Cherlin, has sought to chart the transformations of marriage in the United States. In a series of essays and in his most recent book *Marriage-Go-Round*, Cherlin argues that marriage has been "de-institutionalized" in America and parts of Europe.[1] This refers to the weakening of social and normative supports for marriage, and a shift in its status from a social imperative to a choice.

What evidence does Cherlin marshal to support this thesis? He underscores three empirical trends that illustrate a process of the deinstitutionalization of marriage.

First, the increase in cohabitation as an alternative to marriage. This is especially prominent in Europe but also common among younger Americans. In particular, Cherlin makes the telling point that it is not simply that more individuals are choosing to cohabit, but that such households are gaining legitimacy as a respectable alternative to marriage.

Second, the exclusive link between parenthood and marriage is loosening. Cherlin observes that many Americans and Europeans are choosing parenthood outside of marriage, often as single persons. While the American media often portrays this as a "pathology" of young Black women or as a sign of a "disorganized" family and culture, Cherlin shows that it is actually a salient trend among the white middle class. The key point is that, for segments of American society, parenthood is becoming a legitimate choice for single women or unmarried couples. This is a stunning break from "traditional" social norms, which defined a "successful" marriage as one that produces children and that restricts parenthood to within the confines of marriage.

Third, since the 1980s, in the United States and across much of Europe, we have witnessed the evolution of a gay and lesbian movement demanding recognition for same-sex relationships. In just a few short decades, the status of gay and lesbians has shifted from an almost uniform condition of a polluted closeted minority to one that is increasingly public and recognized as having legitimate rights, including the right to relationships and more recently to marriage. This is a truly major change in US history which has great implications for the institution of marriage. Until very recently, marriage was restricted to heterosexuals. The legitimation, still very much contested, of same-sex relationships, including the right to marry, not only expands the population covered by marriage but challenges a cornerstone of marriage, namely, gender-binary norms. Legitimating same-sex marriage implies that this institution no longer is a chief enforcer of gender-binary norms, and marriage will no longer be seen as dependent on such norms. In other words, gender would in principle become much less relevant, if not eventually irrelevant, to marriage.

To summarize, historically, marriage in the United States has been an institution. As such, it was the only legitimate arrangement for romantic, sexualized intimacy; it was also the only legitimate arrangement for family-making and enforced restrictive sexual and gender norms. Today, Cherlin says, marriage is undergoing a process of deinstitutionalization, as illustrated by the spread of cohabitation, parenthood outside marriage, and the public recognition of same-sex relationships.

Marriage may be loosening some of its social authority, but it is not declining. Indeed, Cherlin argues that in the United States rates of marriage remain very high. In other words, Americans continue to marry, divorce, and remarry. If more and more Americans have expanded intimate choices, why are they continuing to marry, especially as this arrangement has lost authority? Cherlin's answer is that, while Americans are today as married-oriented as their grandparents, the meaning of marriage has changed between the early and late twentieth century.

Throughout much of the twentieth century, a "companionate" model of marriage was the norm and ideal. The heterosexual couple were viewed as partners; they were expected to share common values and interests, and their lives were intertwined in complex ways. Companionate marriage assumed a rough equality between husband and wife, even though they continued to assume different social roles. Men were the chief breadwinners while women were responsible for domestic order and child-rearing. Sex was a crucial part of marriage but at its core was romantic love, a gendered division of labor, and shared interests and activities. Between 1900 and 1960, roughly 95 percent of Americans married … and more or less aspired to a companionate ideal.

Beginning in the 1960s and accelerating in subsequent decades, fewer Americans are marrying, more are staying single for longer periods of time, and more are choosing cohabitation, parenthood without marriage, love outside of marriage, childless marriages, or gay and lesbian relationships. These changes point to a new norm and ideal of marriage: "individualized marriage." This refers to the new salience of self-development or individual fulfillment in choosing to marry and stay married. Today, many of us look to marriage not necessarily to raise a family or to fulfill gender identities and roles, but to develop ourselves as individuals, to find a relationship where we can explore our individual wants, needs, and desires while also forging an intimate social bond. Marriage is just one relational option for exploring our individuality and ties of belonging. But why do so many people choose marriage? Because, says Cherlin, while marriage is losing its institutional status, it retains its symbolic value as a way to mark adulthood, as a symbol of commitment, as a sign of personal accomplishment, and a respectable social status.

ULRICH BECK, ELIZABETH BECK-GERNSHEIM, AND ANTHONY GIDDENS: INDIVIDUALIZATION OF INTIMACY

Cherlin wished to explain the puzzling juxtaposition of the deinstitutionalization of marriage and the continued high rates of marriage. He highlighted changes in the meaning of marriage, from a companionate to an individualized marriage, and the increasingly symbolic role that marriage plays in America. But there is another thread in Cherlin's argument that he doesn't develop; namely, the decentering of marriage. That is, marriage is today becoming just one way of forging an intimate relationship. Intimate life is no longer necessarily played out in marriage, but also marriage looks increasingly like nonmarital intimate relationships. We are perhaps living in a post-marital era in the sense that intimate life itself has become a separate sphere with its own conventions, norms, ideals, challenges, conflicts, and politics.

In 1990, the German sociologists Beck and Beck-Gernsheim published *The Normal Chaos of Love*.[2] Tellingly, their focus was not the institution of marriage but a culture of heterosexual romantic love and intimacy. As early as the 1980s, the research suggests that many individuals in Germany and elsewhere seem to focus their intimate lives on romantic love – not necessarily marriage. For these two sociologists, what seems to matter was less whether individuals marry but the intimate arrangement they *chose*. Intimacy, they suggest, has become a site of choice and difference. As they say:

> Women and men are currently compulsively on the search for the right way to love, trying out cohabitation, divorce or contractual marriage, struggling to coordinate family and divorce, love and marriage, "new" motherhood and fatherhood, friendship and acquaintance. This movement is under way, and there is no stopping it.[3]

Although institutions such as the family, the state, the church, and media continue to influence our choices, for example, by promoting heterosexuality or marriage, many of us today feel that in the end it is up to us as individuals to negotiate our intimate arrangements.

It wasn't so long ago that intimate life was played out exclusively in marriage and the family. Intimate arrangements felt imposed by kin or class, and the organization of intimacy was governed by rigid gender roles. Men were breadwinners; women took charge of domestic labor, including child-rearing. Since at least the 1960s, intimacy and love has gradually been "freed" of the imperative to marry and make a family. The inherited scripts that dictated rules of courtship, marriage, gender roles, that made love secondary to security and family well-being, have weakened. While many of us still marry, love has become the focus of our intimate lives, and love has migrated from the narrow confines of marriage. The chief institutional enforcers of a marriage system, the family, church, and the state, have steadily lost their authority to enforce narrow gender, sexual, and intimate norms. These institutions are also less able to give individuals a solid sense of security, belonging, and identity. There has occurred what the authors describe as a process of "individualization":

> Men and women are released from traditional norms and search for a "life of their own." They are driven into seeking happiness in a close relationship because other social bonds seem too tenuous or unreliable. The need to share your inner feelings with someone, ... is not a primary human need [but] ... grows the more individual we all become.[4]

Today, in cultures that promote individualization, many of us pursue a life project that aims at crafting authentic lives. At the center of this life project is the quest for love and intimacy. Authenticity is possible, many of us believe, only if our intimate arrangements (e.g., social roles, work priorities, household duties, childcare responsibility, and aims) are self-creations. Unlike our ancestors, who leaned on tradition or taken-for-granted scripts to enact a personal life around marriage, today we create the conventions and rules that organize our intimate lives. And, given the fluidity and amorphousness of these conventions and norms, and the enormous complexity of our individual lives, it is hardly surprising that "love" sometimes feels like a sphere of chaos.

Two developments in Euro-American societies have contributed significantly to this process of individualization.

First, the evolution of "labor-market freedom." Today, we take this for granted but the job market was not always an open, competitive arena. For centuries, kin and class often allocated work roles. For at least the last century or more, individuals have faced an open labor market. In order to sustain ourselves, we are compelled to enter the labor market and exchange our capacity to labor for a wage. This public freedom, unintentionally and often unacknowledged, structures and restricts our private choices. No matter how much we imagine our personal life to be free, it is organized by our status in the labor market, for example, by our occupation and income, work schedule, the kind of work we do, our colleagues, and economic good and bad times. The labor market serves as an external force impacting on all aspects of our personal lives, including our intimate choices. We must all conform or accommodate to labor market trends, ready to retrain or change jobs and residence as the market shifts. Today, and this is especially significant for intimate matters, the reality is that both men and women are subject to labor market dynamics. So, an open, free labor market has contributed mightily to individualization but has also created a level of complexity and chaos in intimate life as partners now have to negotiate complex work aspirations and demands in relation to equally complex expectations in our intimate lives.

Second, there has occurred a transformation of gender dynamics in postwar Germany and elsewhere. As women pursue college and university degrees in rates equal to men, as they gain legal civil and political equality, and most importantly as they enter the paid labor market and are career-oriented, they claim the right to be autonomous and fulfilled in the public world but also in the home and in their intimate relationships. Women's growing equality and sense of individual entitlement has made possible the individualization of love and romantic intimacy. Whereas men have had less reason to challenge intimate conventions, women have contested "traditional" intimate conventions; asserting a right to equal participation in the public world, women also claim a right to control their bodies and sexualities, to sexual autonomy, to pursue a career that requires sharing domestic duties, to be recognized and loved in ways that parallel the ways men have long expected from women.

In this altered social environment, individualization and social dynamism are ruling principles. "Time-honored norms are fading and their power to determine behavior. ... In search of intimacy the actors turn out to be their own critics, directors, and audience, acting, watching and discussing it, unable to agree on the rules for achievement as fast as they are needed. The rules constantly prove to be wrong, unjust and therefore merely provisional."[5] But more: the intimate sphere is a site of conflict and dislocation, bringing stresses, anxieties, and insecurities that betray its promise of self-fulfillment and romantic well-being.

Gender equality may be the ideal in the culture of individualization, but the reality often tells another story. There has been tremendous pressure on men to yield some of their power and privilege. Many men have resisted. Women's continued second-class status in the workplace and household remains the greatest obstacle to fashioning a rich, egalitarian, satisfying intimate life out of the normal chaos of love. Beck and Beck-Gernsheim speak of a "stalled gender revolution." In the workplace, men resist women's ascendance to the upper reaches of institutions; at home they resist equal domestic labor and sharing fully responsibilities for their relationship, for example, reciprocity in self-disclosing, nurturing, and caregiving practices. The contradiction between an ethos of individualism and egalitarianism and a reality of gender inequality with women continuing to be responsible for stereotypically feminine roles creates pervasive tensions, conflicts, and confusions at the heart of intimate life today.

Even under the best of circumstances, a culture of individualized love is challenging, if not inevitably prone to chaos and anomie. When we have to rely on our own desires, interests, and values to create intimate rules and order there is bound to be conflict, heartbreak, violence, and psychic wounds. Beck and Beck-Gernsheim believe that the sheer practical logistics of organizing intimacy when both adults work, claim a right to pursue their own projects of self-realization, and when every intimate decision (from getting married to having children to mutual erotic and affective satisfaction) must be negotiated without clear social rules, that it is realistic to expect a level of chaos.

At times, the authors seem to suggest that individualization itself is an inadequate basis for establishing and sustaining intimacies. An ethos that declares, "I am, I want, I desire," that anchors intimacy in personal feelings, desires, and aspirations, is a weak, fragile foundation. If "traditional" intimate conventions, scripts, and norms are unsettled and lack binding authority, if relationships can no longer rely upon the authority of marriage to cement affective ties, how are couples to weather the routine storms of intimacies? The sheer weight that intimacy places on individuals, without societies necessarily equipping us with the capacities and skills to effectively navigate difficult emotional terrain, is perhaps too much. It's no wonder that many of us turn to relationship "experts" – therapists, TV and radio talk shows, sex advice and self-help literature, intimacy gurus, and so on.

If individualization is, at best, a shaky foundation for intimacy, intimacy is even more fragile because of our single-minded, seemingly obsessive, search for love. Romantic love has become our new religion – the path to self-redemption and well-being. Beck and Beck-Gernsheim argue that many of us approach love with unrealistic expectations and escalating dreams of realizing ourselves and finding our soulmate. Yet, ultimately, we rely on the good will of partners to steer the stormy seas of love. It's no wonder that separation, breakups, and divorces are a part of the "normal chaos of love." We have freed love from its social moorings, leaving just the sovereign couple to create the social framework that will somehow stabilize and sustain intimacy.

Despite a real sense of freedom and choice, and our anticipation of intimate fulfillment, Beck and Beck-Gernsheim sketch a rather pessimistic portrait of this evolving world. Even hopeful signs, such as a trend toward gender equality, are at war with a culture that seems to have taken individualism too far, leaving shaky grounds for sustaining intimate ties. The normal chaos of love seems fated to leave a trail of broken hearts and wounded, disillusioned souls in its tracks.

In ways that parallels the two German sociologists, the British sociologist, Anthony Giddens (see Chapter 10) also underscores the individualization of intimacy, but offers a more sanguine portrait of the present. Giddens conjectures that a major transformation is occurring in Euro-American intimate life. Marriage, at least the institution of marriage (with its rights, obligations, duties, gender norms, and tight link to family-making) is less and less the dramatic center of intimacy. Today, "relationships" are at the center of our personal lives. Relationships are individualized and primarily about intimacy. That is, individuals choose to enter into relationships with the aim of establishing intimacy. As Giddens says, relationships are "a world of sexual negotiation ... in which new terminologies of 'commitment' and 'intimacy' have come to the fore."[6]

Giddens is making a compelling point that is often lost in these discussions. In the current world of relationships the focus of the partners is not, in the first instance, social respectability, affirming heterosexual and gender normality, or family-making; nor is it protection, economic benefit, or social status, all of which continue to be part of relationships. Relationships are chiefly about intimacy or creating emotional closeness and a sense of personal well-being that is tied to the state of the relationship. In other words, the ideal today is what Giddens calls the "pure relationship":

> It refers to a situation where a social relation is entered into for its own sake, for what can be derived by each person from a sustained association with another; and which is continued only in so far as it is thought by both parties to deliver enough satisfaction for each individual to stay within it.[7]

The pure relationship is about intimacy – mutual self-disclosing, each partner opening up to the other, sharing core threads of identity, and exposing one's true self. In the pure relationship, individuals are committed to the relationship not for its extrinsic benefits (status, protection, economic security) but for its intrinsic value as an intimate social bond. Selves forge social ties that are emotionally rich, that allow each self to unfold its authentic selves not as wholly separate, distinct beings but as interconnected and interrelated.

But are such relationships able to withstand the stormy seas of love? Are critics right that this new world of relationships is fundamentally unstable and dysfunctional because it ultimately relies on the shaky foundation of personal feelings and desires? This is an important question and challenge to Giddens and all theorists of individualized intimacies. I'm not sure that Giddens or Beck and Beck-Gernsheim fully rise to this challenge.

As we saw, Beck and Beck-Gernsheim maintain that a culture that pivots around individualized love is necessarily chaotic and prone to breakups. Giddens is more nuanced and at least proposes the outlines of a culture that can sustain stability and intimate solidarity. It is true, says Giddens, that a pure relationship can only be sustained by personal commitment; there is no institution – for example, the state or the church –that enforces these relationships. Instead, pure relationships gain their coherence from the intimacy created and maintained by the partners. Giddens seems to hold that the dynamic of mutual self-disclosure, the in-depth psychological opening of one to the other, creates an emotional and moral web of trust and commitment, even though each knows that termination is always an option. "In the pure relationship, trust has no external supports, and has to be developed on the basis of intimacy. Trust is a vesting of confidence in the other and also in the capability of the mutual bond to withstand future traumas."[8] In contrast to a language of rights and duties or appeals to gender roles or security that characterizes a marriage-centered culture, in the world of relationships a language of choice, intimacy, authenticity, trust, and commitment becomes the grammar of belonging.

In contrast to the era of marriage, intimacies are no longer exclusive to or necessarily centered on marriage or romantic relationships; they proliferate outside marriage, for example, in same-sex relationships, among friends or between patient and therapist, between siblings or between parents and adult children, or grandparents and grandchildren. This multiplication of intimacies speaks in part to a social world in which more and more of us spend considerable time as single, either never having entered into a romantic relationship or between such relationships. It also suggests that flexible, mobile work lives are fast becoming the rule. Intimacies, like jobs and homes, will likely be more temporary, or to rephrase, more of us will exhibit a multi-layered pattern of intimacies, some short-lived, others long-term, some being more in-depth than others, and so on.

Women, and especially lesbians, are pioneers of this "transformation of intimacy." The former because, as they enter the labor force at rates equal to men, they push for changes in the domestic and intimate sphere. Their growing economic independence, coupled with their sense of entitlement, creates in many women an expansive sense of entitlement and choice in their personal lives. Straight women will press their partners to assume more domestic duties, including child-rearing, and will be able to project similar rights to personal emotional/erotic fulfillment as men. Lesbians, and to a lesser degree gay men, also provide models of relational intimacy. "Freed" from the institution of marriage, and until recently lacking family and societal legitimation and support, lesbians and gays have had the opportunity and need to create the ground and contours of intimacy themselves. In particular, lesbians are positioned to step outside of gender conventions in a way that is not possible for men; accordingly, they may be pioneers of models of intimacy that are genderless or beyond gender.

Although something of the solid sense of security and stability that was present in the era of marriage is lost, there are definite gains, according to Giddens. Today, many of us, at least in Euro-America, have far more choice regarding intimacies, and an egalitarian spirit inspires these relationships. There is also a sense of sharing an ongoing project of self–other making that aspires to unite authenticity, democratization, and belonging. As Giddens concludes, the transformation of intimacy promotes "the democratization of personal life, as a potential, extends in a fundamental way to friendship relations and, crucially, to the relations of parents, children and other kin."[9]

FEMINIST INTERVENTIONS: LYNN JAMIESON AND FRANCESCA CANCIAN

Giddens's notion of a coming era featuring an ideal of the pure relationship has been challenged. In particular, feminists have raised serious doubts, empirical and theoretical.

While agreeing with his claim that relationships and intimacies are moving into the center of personal and relational life in at least Euro-American societies, a British colleague, Lynn Jamieson, disputes the gender account that underpins Giddens's account.[10] Jamieson objects at two levels.

First, despite the proliferation of diverse intimacies, relationships, and families, and the decentering of marriage, the norm of heterosexual marriage and the family persists as ideology and in practice. Individuals may have more choice with regard to partners and intimate arrangements, but heterosexuality is still normative while heterosexual marriage is still given considerable institutional support and privilege through government policies in many countries. Varied intimate arrangements are not equally respected and supported by the state, social institutions, and popular culture. This view suggests, then, that the world of relationships is still hierarchical, and a site of contestation between privileged and disadvantaged, marginalized sexualities.

Second, Giddens assumes a rough egalitarianism in the pure relationship, which makes possible the kind of open communicative negotiation of intimacy. But, drawing on a wide range of research, Jamieson concludes that gender inequality continues to pervade the world of relationships. Whether we are addressing the division of household labor, time spent on domestic tasks, the prioritization of work careers, child-rearing responsibilities, and so on, studies consistently confirm that while men aged under 40 do more domestic labor than older men, they still do considerably less than women. This is true for full-time moms or career women, for those in straight childless relationships, for cohabitating couples, and for women who earn more than men. Jamieson doesn't deny the egalitarian ideal of contemporary intimate relationships, and she concedes that a minority of straight relationships is "postgender," but the reality for the vast majority of heterosexual relationships is gender inequality. Indeed, Jamieson concludes, perhaps overstating her case, that the relationship model featuring men as the main earner and women as the main domestic worker is alive and well.

Jamieson introduces, but doesn't really develop, a third line of criticism, which revolves around gendered patterns of love and intimacy. Giddens, and especially Beck and Beck-Gernsheim, seem to have assumed that while the meaning of love may change historically or vary across a population the variation is not gendered but historical, or ethnic, or class-based. Jamieson disagrees. Drawing on a rich archive of feminist theory and research, she asserts that women associate intimacy with expressions of feeling, caring, and emotional sharing; by contrast, men use their breadwinner and protector role to express their intimate bonding. These suggestive remarks are not developed by Jamieson, but have been elaborated by other feminist sociologists and theorists.

In *Love in America*, Francesca Cancian offers a gendered account of love and intimacy that in many ways crystallizes a powerful feminist view.[11] Drawing on a wide body of research, she suggests that Americans associate romantic love with emotions and practices that are stereotypically feminine. Sharing tender, expressive, nurturing feelings and engaging in caregiving practices are at the heart of American notions of love, but they are also viewed as appropriate for women, indeed as defining of their nature.

From a feminist viewpoint, this feminization of love is doubly problematic. On the one hand, it makes women responsible for matters of the heart. Women are expected to remember birthdays and anniversaries, plan romantic events, and to keep romance alive and well. If love is waning, this may be blamed on women. Although women may claim a certain authority in this sphere, the feminization of love also means that women are taken less seriously in roles that deviate from this cluster of emotions and practices, for example, laborers, engineers, politicians, athletes, policy makers, and so on. On the other hand, the feminization of love means that those ways of enacting love associated with men or masculinity are erased or become invisible. For example, many men demonstrate their love by being good providers, giving practical assistance, by initiating sex, by being a steady presence during times of crisis, by just being together, or by performing household chores such as mowing the lawn or fixing a leaky faucet. If love is feminized, men's loving practices may go unrecognized and undervalued. But as feminists point out, rightly in my view, the other side to this lack of recognition is that men are excused from being responsible for matters of the heart so they may concentrate on the "really important" business of making money and governing nations.

Why has love become gendered? Cancian makes an historical argument. In many respects, Victorian America was a rigidly gender-divided society. Women were responsible for the private sphere; they focused on the roles of wife and mother and their lives were filled with domestic tasks revolving around childcare, food preparation, cleaning, and maintaining a respectable moral family milieu. Whether married or not, women were thickly connected to networks of other women. By contrast, men took charge of the public sphere of paid work, politics, and the military. They provided, protected, and governed. Their lives were absorbed in a male-centered world. The private and public spheres, Cancian argues, demanded different capacities, skills, emotional dispositions, and social practices. The private sphere, with its dense domesticity, put a premium on tender, empathic, caregiving feelings and practices. This cluster of feminized feelings and practices became the kernel of what came to be seen as romantic love. Indeed, Victorian women would often promote this feminized view of love because it gave them authority in the domestic sphere, and allowed them to regulate sexuality and the moral environment of the family. To the extent that the public sphere was associated with a contrasting set of feelings and practices, which were more instrumental, competitive, emotionally contained, and officious, women were seen as inappropriately equipped for public life. By contrast, because men were associated with the public realm they were simultaneously "excused" from primary domestic responsibilities and expected to assume the lion's share of authority in public life.

Even as the private/public divide eroded over the course of the twentieth century, for example, as women work and fully participate in politics and social life, the association of romantic love with femininity or with women persists. Why? Because while the rigid divide has weakened, women are still viewed as ultimately responsible for housework and childcare. To that extent, women are still seen as essentially designed to flourish in the realm of relational intimacy.

Still, gender is changing in America and it is possible, even likely, that this gendered social divide will weaken further in future. Perhaps images of the sensitive man or the metrosexual, which allow men to be masculine but also emotionally expressive, empathetic, and nurturing, indicate a blurring of the gender divide. In fact, Cancian argues that the dominant trend in America is towards a view of love that loses its thick feminine gendered associations. She defends an androgynous culture of romantic love which would mix gender styles; love would be degendered and therefore less of a site of gender politics. Writing in a hopeful register, Cancian imagines an expansive, gender-fluid culture of love and intimacy.

> Love is the responsibility of the man as well as the woman, and it includes "feminine" emotional support and expression as well as "masculine" material assistance. They have a relationship of fairly equal interdependence, instead of reverting to the roles of dependent

woman and independent man; they encourage each other in diverse experiences and ways of relating ... yet they have developed their own rules and expectations to establish trust and security.[12]

Suggested Readings

Lauren Berland, ed., *Intimacy* (Chicago: University of Chicago, 2000).

Eva Illouz, *Cold Intimacies* (London: Polity Press, 2007).

Stephen Mitchell, *Can Love Last?* (New York: Basic, 2002).

Sherry Turkle, *Alone Together* (New York: Basic, 2010).

Jeffrey Weeks, Brian Heaphy and Catherine Donovan, *Same Sex Intimacies* (New York: Routledge, 2001).

References

1   Andrew Cherlin, *The Marriage-Go-Round* (New York: Alfred Knopf, 2009).

2   Ulrich Beck and Elisabeth Beck-Gernsheim, *The Normal Chaos of Love* (London: Polity Press, 1995).

3   Beck and Beck-Gernsheim, *The Normal Chaos of Love*, p. 2.

4   Beck and Beck-Gernsheim, *The Normal Chaos of Love*, p. 24.

5   Beck and Beck-Gernsheim, *The Normal Chaos of Love*, p. 8.

6   Anthony Giddens, *The Transformation of Intimacy* (London: Polity Press, 1992), p. 8.

7   Giddens, *The Transformation of Intimacy*, p. 58.

8   Giddens, *The Transformation of Intimacy*, p. 138.

9   Giddens, *The Transformation of Intimacy*, p. 177.

10 Lynn Jamieson, *Intimacy* (London: Polity Press, 1998).

11 Francesca M. Cancian, *Love in America* (Cambridge: Cambridge University Press, 1987).

12 Cancian, *Love in America*, pp. 149–50.

23

Nationalism and the Crisis of Postcolonial Nations

Modern social theory took shape as nation-states were being formed. As we have seen, the formative period of social theory was, roughly speaking, between the French Revolution of 1789 and World War I. Great Britain, France, Italy, Germany, and the United States became powerful states and truly national states only in the course of the nineteenth century.

Prior to the nineteenth century, neither the European countries nor the United States were nations in the contemporary sense. For centuries the territories of Europe were ruled by kings, nobles, alliances of aristocratic families, and the church. During the eighteenth century the great European imperial states came to the fore – Spain, France, Great Britain, Holland, and Portugal. They aspired to be world empires rivaling the Ottoman Empire. The borders of these empires were unstable and shifted over time; the population under their rule consisted of diverse cultures, mostly local or regional; and there were many centers of political authority in these empires. To the extent that these political entities lacked a sense of a people sharing a common culture and identity within recognized territorial borders, it is difficult to speak of these imperial states as nations. Think of the North American colonies after independence: there were immigrants from diverse European territories, a multiplicity of Native American tribes, slaves from the Caribbean and the African continent, explorers and settlers from France, Spain, and Great Britain; there were Catholics, Protestants of varied denominations; local, regional, and primordial identities ruled the day. Neither southern farmers nor northern textile craftsmen imagined themselves as belonging to a "national community." It was not until the postbellum period that the idea of America began to truly correspond to a shared national identity.

It is curious that the pioneers of social theory, brilliant though they were, more or less ignored the movements of nationalisms that were altering the shape of their lives. Of course, they were aware of the nationalist rivalries between France and Britain and the nationalist revolts in the Americas; they were surely cognizant of the national

Contested Knowledge: Social Theory Today, Fifth Edition. Steven Seidman.
© 2013 John Wiley & Sons, Ltd. Published 2013 by John Wiley & Sons, Ltd.

chauvinisms in Europe that would lead to World War I. Yet, they did not make these varied expressions of nationalism into a clear, definitive object of knowledge; they did not, in other words, try to understand and explain why nationalism was becoming a typically "modern" event. We can only speculate as to the reasons; perhaps they assumed nations were natural and always existed; or that nations were temporary developments destined to give way to empires again; or that new global types of territorial and cultural entities would supersede nations.

If the founding figures of modern social theory failed to theorize nationalism, the post-World War II generation of sociologists and scholars could hardly avoid this phenomenon. From roughly the 1980s through to today, nationalism has been one of the most fertile fields of theory and social analysis. This is not difficult to understand. Since the 1950s, the world has witnessed an explosion of new nations and nationalisms coming primarily from the former colonies of European empires, but also from the more recent revolts against the Soviet Union. Across Africa and much of Asia, the Middle East and the Caribbean, anticolonial rebellions were chiefly national liberation movements. Oppressed peoples were in revolt and they were claiming the status of nations and the right to popular sovereignty. If we keep in mind that in 1860 there were perhaps fewer than a dozen national states across the globe, it is telling that today we live in a world in which there are some 196 nation-states! Truly, the twentieth century was the age of nationalism, and the fires of nationalism continue to rage today in Iraq, Iran, Chechnya, the Basque country, among the Kurds, Puerto Ricans, and Tibetans, and in almost every corner of the globe.

However much globalization manifests a dazzling movement of capital, people, ideas, and culture across national borders, the fundamental core principle of nationalism, the notion of a people bounded together by a shared culture, history, language, and aspiring to public recognition and sovereignty, is still a fundamental force in the world. We turn then to some of the key debates about nationalism.

PERENNIALISTS AND MODERNISTS

Before proceeding, let's define some of the key terms. *States* refer to governing or political–administrative structures that regulate or administer a territorial-based population. States may exert centralized or decentralized political control; they vary by their degree of concentrated power, scope of territorial control, public accountability, and whether they are constitutionally bound or some form of autocracy.

Nations refer to a type of community or group. Specifically, nations are said to share a common heritage, culture, history, and language. Nations include many smaller groups such as families, clans, tribes, and perhaps ethnicities or religions. A nation may provide a shared identity to its citizens despite many local or specific social differences. Nations are different from other groups such as families, religions, fraternities, unions, or political parties; they typically include many or all of these other groups. Nations also differ from empires, which include a multiplicity of cultures and may not share a common history, language, culture, or identity. Despite the many specific differences of its citizens, nations provide, at least as an aspiration, a sense of shared identity and belonging. Like kin or ethnic or religious communities, nations demand the loyalty and sacrifice of its members, but also furnish them with a sense of identity and belonging.

Nationalism is the belief in the nation as a fundamental or core community. Just as there have been social justice movements (civil rights, women's liberation, the gay movement, socialism), nationalism can become the driving force or ideology of a movement; for example, Zionism in the late nineteenth and early twentieth centuries was a nationalist movement of European and Russian Jews which aimed at establishing a Jewish homeland. The Basque movement in Spain, the Kurdish movement in Turkey, and the Tibetan independence movement in China are contemporary examples of nationalist movements.

Nations and states have not always been aligned or linked. Most scholars believe that it was not until the eighteenth and nineteenth centuries that *nation-states* became a featured part of Europe and the Americas. At this time, powerful centralized states with recognizable territorial borders were combined with an emerging sense of collective identity. Something else seems new at this time: the nation was equated with "the people"; in principle, all the people who at least were born into a territorially based political community. And the individual members of this national community were imagined as equal citizens. In effect, the nation-state gave expression to the idea of a society as a self-governing people.

We should highlight two dimensions of the modern nation. First, the idea that the nation meant that the people had a right to exercise popular sovereignty. Second, the nation also aspires to be a culturally unique community, different from all other communities and all other national communities. There is a tension, then, is at the heart of modern nationalism between its democratizing impulse and its chauvinistic disposition (our national interests come before those of all other nations).

Few scholars doubt that the modern condition of a global order of national states is historically unique. Today, almost all of humankind is organized into sovereign nation-states. And new nations are still being created, such as the recent addition of the Republic of South Sudan. Nation-states recognize each other and are recognized by a great variety of international agencies, from the United Nations to the World Bank and the thousands of NGOs and INGOs.

However, there is no agreement as to whether nations are also historically unique or specific to the modern times. For some scholars, so-called perennialists, nations are socially produced but they are not unique to the modern period. The British sociologist, Anthony Smith, has argued that nations have a long history that predates the eighteenth century.[1] Their roots are in ethnic communities and the line separating ethnic and national communities is fuzzy. For example, almost all nations, Smith argues, forge an identity through myths of common ethnic descent. Such world-views appeal to an origin, a golden age, to enemies and heroes, defeats and triumphs, and express hopes for collective renewal or liberation. These myths are powerful. Smith says that nationalist myths confer a transcendent meaning on ordinary life; they imbue the land and its inhabitants, heroic figures, epochal events, battles, places, and documents with a sacred meaning. Think of the way Americans worship George Washington, the Declaration of Independence, the Constitution, Abraham Lincoln, or FDR and Martin Luther King.

In the modern world, nationalist ideologies often play the role that religious faith assumed in the past. The erosion or weakening of religions as public faiths, and the inability of science and ideogical politics to step into that void, has opened the way to nationalism as a powerful modern faith. From this perspective, nations are not unique to modern times, nor is modernity such a dramatic cultural break from the past.

Taking issue with perennialists, scholars claim that ethnic communities are protona-tionalist but are not really nations. Distinctively nationalist movements and ideologies took shape as part of the great transformation from "traditional" to "modern" societies. It is true that nations draw on ethno-religious cultural resources that may be centuries or even millennia old (e.g., Serbia, Israel, Palestine). Yet it was only in the last few centuries, and in the context of centralized sovereign states, that nationalism and nations as inclusive communities were consolidated across the globe. More specifically, nationalisms were responses to, and part of, sweeping changes associated with industrial capitalism, the modern bureaucratic state, mass education, democratization, and secularism. Moreover, modernists view the nation as a culturally integrating force in an increasingly secular, diverse, and mobile social world. The most influential modernist is the anthropologist, Benedict Anderson, whose views generated a wide-ranging and productive debate.[2]

NATION AS IMAGINARY COMMUNITY: BENEDICT ANDERSON AND CRITICS

The question of the nature of a nation has vexed scholars for a very long time, and continues to generate a lot of debate. Given the extraordinary social diversity charac-teristic of most nation-states, how should we think of the nation? Is it the sum of the individuals or citizens who live in a specific territory? Is it made up of all the shared beliefs and values of a society? Is it an illusion produced by the state or a ruling class?

Anderson proposed an ingenious and compelling view: the nation is an imagined community. Imagined does not mean unreal or illusory, but an idea that somehow has the capacity to be a real social force in people's lives since, after all, we make sacrifices, sometimes of our lives, for this idea. Anderson reasons that unlike a family or a frater-nity, we never can know all of the citizens who comprise a nation. Still, we believe, or at least many of us believe, that (say) all Americans share a similar idea and feeling of belonging to the American community.

So, the nation is an idea and a feeling of belonging shared across a range of social differences. The nation is a specific kind of imagined community. It is a "horizontal fellowship"; the members of the nation are considered similar or equal as nationals. There is furthermore the presumption that citizens share a sense of solidarity because they are part of a national community. But this horizontal fellowship is a finite, bounded community. It does not, for example, include all of humanity or even per-sons who live just outside one's national borders. And it may not be the largest or most inclusive imagined community. A church or even an ethnic group may involve more people – think of the Catholic Church or the Muslim community. Finally, the nation, unlike, say, an imagined ethnic community, is sovereign or self-governing. This means that it is in principle not subject to an authority outside itself. Nations aspire to be independent and self-governing.

What social forces help to explain the origin of nations in the modern world? And, why have they become such an integral, defining feature of the current global order?

Let's first address the last question. Anderson offers a straightforward account: nations provide a collective sense of identity and belonging. In many premodern societies, which were often rigidly divided between elites and the masses, kings and the church created a sense of political and cultural community. And both the political and religious community rested on religiously-based world-views, in particular creation myths and genealogies of divine descent. Anderson believes that "modernization" or dynamics associated with industrial capitalism and urbanization shatter the centrality of religious-mythic beliefs and faith which provided a sacred canopy in premodern societies. The disruption of these communities led to a search for new grounds of collective identity and solidarity. The imagined community of the nation, with its utopianism of a horizontal community and popular rule, furnished a substitute for religiously based communities.

What was it about modernization that gave birth to nations? Anderson identifies two key dynamics. First, the wide circulation of newspapers, magazines, journals, and novels (or what he refers to as "print capitalism") helped to produce a national community. How so? In the course of the eighteenth and nineteenth centuries, print materials increasingly used the language of ordinary folks, instead of Latin or some arcane, expert language. This created the possibility of a common public or a "people." At the same time, the mass production of print news in the vernacular made it possible for ordinary individuals in different towns, villages, cities, and regions of a territorial state to read about the same events and developments. Individuals could presume that others, all the anonymous others who also participate in a reading public, know the same things, share basic views about the past, present, and future, and accordingly develop a sense of being part of the same national community. In other words, print capitalism in an age of mass literacy helps to create a horizontal fellowship among citizens.

However, a popular reading public creates only the possibility of sharing a common world; this public must be mobilized and shaped to claim an identity as a nation. In other words, before a public becomes a nation, there must be a social group or movement that promotes the ideology of nationalism. Here we turn to the second part of Anderson's explanation. What was the driving force behind nationalism? Anderson's answer is: Creoles.

This term refers to Europeans who settled in the Americas roughly from the sixteenth through to the eighteenth centuries. During this time, Spain or the monarchy of Isabella and Francis aspired to become a world power that could rival Great Britain, France, and Holland. Spain set out to colonize the Americas. With its ships and guns, the Spanish monarchy sent settlers from all over Europe to conquer, plunder, settle, and civilize the Americas. Creoles are the descendants of the initial European settlers. They are the children of the colonizing European settlers in Mexico, Florida, Cuba, South and North America. Creoles inherited colonial privilege; they were prosperous and powerful and they brought their European Christian culture to the Americas. Over time Creoles came to think of themselves less as Spanish or Italian and more as citizens of the localities in the Americas that they called their home. But as powerful as some Creoles became, they were denied control over the levers of political power, which continued to lie in the hands of the Crown and its colonial administrators.

In colony after colony, all across the Americas, discontent was festering due to the rising economic and social power of the Creoles but their continued lack of political power. Discontent led to conflict and the desire for social change. Because the Creoles were relatively small in number, they forged alliances with segments of the native population, often leaders with large followings. In order to gain the support of the native population, the Creoles appealed to a nationalist ideology, or to the notion that the aim of revolt was to transfer power from the colonial authority to "the people." In other words, a rhetoric of nationalism gained widespread popular support. Thus, the anti-colonial revolts in the late eighteenth and early nineteenth centuries in the Americas were national liberation movements.

Ending colonial rule is but the first act in this transformative drama; the end-game is transferring political power and establishing a sovereign nation. This entails a transfer of the means of governance or the state from the colonizing authority to the colonized. Appropriating the state involves not only seizing control of the formal institutions of rulership; it also entails taking over a political culture in which the native population were mostly subjects, not citizens. In this regard, Anderson argues that colonial rule never operates simply by force or its threat; colonial states deploy various means to pacify and rule a resistant native population that represents an overwhelming majority. For example, many colonial regimes relied on a census, which provides a demographic mapping of the population (age, family size, region); the census may also divide the native population into distinct racial or ethnic groupings – classifications that may have been absent or only weakly present among the natives. Such classifications can then be used to divide the native population and fuel hostilities, as one group may be recruited to cooperate with the colonial state in return for local power and privileges. To summarize, however much a transfer of political power to the people is a triumphant moment, if there is not a parallel transformation of the political culture its colonial heritage will live on, creating all sorts of problems and challenges (as we will shortly see).

Anderson's ideas proved enormously influential, especially as scholars turned their attention to the history and sociology of postcolonial nationalism. Scholars have sought to assess his specific empirical claims about nationalism as well as consider his general theoretical ideas.

Briefly, since Anderson placed the Americas at the center of his account of nationalism, Latin Americanists have offered some of the most trenchant criticisms. By and large, they challenged a great deal of his historical analysis.[3] Contrary to Anderson, the independence movements (roughly 1810–25), sparked by the crisis of the Spanish monarchy as a result of Napoleon's occupation of Spain, was less about nationalism than about claiming a broad "American" identity against a kind of European chauvinism. Moreover, Anderson mistakenly downplayed or neglected the importance of local, regional, ethnic, provincial, and racial identities which were much more important than nationalistic aspirations. In fact, critics argue that a truly national consciousness didn't emerge until the mid-nineteenth century and then only among elites; it wasn't until the mid-twentieth century that the nation truly became an imagined community. And, while print capitalism played a role in the nineteenth century, it was well after independence. Many scholars place far more importance on the spread of cafes and salons, the role of clothes, music, food, accents, and civil and religious ceremonies and festivals in creating a sense of national identity. Finally, unlike in parts of Europe, in Latin America the state preceded the nation and was a significant social force in promoting nationalism in the decades after independence.

As significant as these empirical criticisms are, they do not necessarily challenge the theoretical core of his views. In *Nation and Fragments*, Partha Chatterjee addresses Anderson at a more theoretical level.[4] According to Chatterjee, Anderson at times seems to reduce the transformation of nationalism into nations as a political process or as entailing the transfer of a political–administrative apparatus (the state) from colonial powers to the native population. And, if he introduces a cultural dynamic, it is one that underscores that nationalists unwittingly absorbed much of the colonial culture. Chatterjee believes that Anderson fails to adequately understand the ways that nationalist movements in colonial nations differ from their Western counterparts. The former are often anti-Western; this means that anticolonial independence movements make the cultural construction of nationhood equally central to a political transformation. If a cultural project of change is central to postcolonial nationalism, this suggests that a native culture survives under colonial rule, something Anderson failed to consider. Natives may be compelled to surrender material power (e.g., control over land, labor, and the machinery of rulership) but they resist cultural colonialism. Despite the civilizing mission of much of European colonial governance, indigenous cultural traditions relating to kinship, gender, ideas of true self, religious belief, language, the arts, and so on persist. This "spiritual" realm survives colonialism and is the stuff from which nationhood is forged. Accordingly, postcolonial nations will then typically blend Western colonial political–administrative structures and native cultural traditions.

Chatterjee illustrates his notion of cultural resistance by referring to the way women were understood in India as markers of tradition and modernity. For the British colonizers, India's patriarchal traditions, often defended by nationalists, were seen as backward and oppressive. From their point of view, modernization through beneficent colonial "guidance" would liberate women, as it would give them new rights and entitlements.

Chatterjee takes issue with this polarizing debate. He argues that most nationalists imagined women as both part of a rich Indian tradition and as modern, but without collapsing "modern" into "Western." The new woman imagined by nationalists was traditional in respecting family or in being pious, but also modern in being educated and participating in public life. In short, nationalists sought a path to change, which imagined a postcolonial India in which traditional ideas of womanhood would blend with new ideas that were part of India's current transformation.

For some scholars, Anderson's idea of the nation as an imagined community and Chatterjee's "spiritual realm" lean too much on culturalist approaches. After all, a nation is not just an idea, but a material reality with territorial borders, citizens, institutions, laws, armies, and so on. Shouldn't these realities figure prominently in our accounts of nations? And, as much as discourses, representations, and narratives construct a nation, aren't nations also made through exclusions and repression? A young scholar (at the time), Joseph Massad made precisely this case. In *Colonial*

Effects, Massad aims to bring back the role of state institutions in shaping postcolonial nations.[5] Specifically, he emphasizes the role of law and the military, as both productive and repressive, in forging nations.

Massad proposes a "model" of new nation formation. He identifies four moments or phases. First, a foreign power establishes dominance. A colonial state is elaborated; borders are established, a governing apparatus is put in place, alliances are formed with sympathetic native elites, and so on. Second, an anticolonial independence movement emerges, demanding the transfer of political power. National sovereignty is staked out but the governing apparatus of the colonial state is largely retained. Third, the nation undergoes a contraction or expansion; new territories are annexed or lost; new populations are either incorporated or established citizens are excluded from nationhood status. Fourth, there is an extended period of social upheaval and conflict. There are struggles over national identity, over which groups best represent the nation, and which groups threaten nationhood. Sadly, civil war has all too often been the fate of postcolonial nations.

As a Middle East specialist, Massad uses Jordan to illustrate his ideas. Briefly, prior to World War I Jordan did not exist as a nation; it was a province of the Ottoman Empire. With the defeat of the Ottomans, the British were given the authority by the newly formed League of Nations to create a nation. In 1921, the new nation of TransJordan was created; the British proceeded to establish a colonial state. Jordan was to be a constitutional monarchy; Britain provided the laws, the borders, and installed King Abdullah who was a sympathetic ally. Native rebellions were defeated and by the 1930s the king had stabilized domestic affairs by relying on British military power and subsidies to key social groups such as Bedouins, In 1946, Jordan was officially granted sovereignty; populist revolts in the 1950s finally drove the British out of Jordan.

As we know, in 1948 the UN officially declared that the Palestinian territories should be divided between a Jewish and an Arab state. Palestinians rejected this decree and went to war with Israel (declared in May 1948). They were defeated and a deal was brokered between Israel and Jordan; the latter would annex the West Bank of the Palestinian territory. In other words, the Arab–Israeli war resulted in a considerable expansion of Jordan's national borders and the addition of hundred of thousands of new citizens; that is, those Palestinians who lived in the West Bank or took refuge after the war.

In the course of the 1960s the king sought to consolidate his rule by aligning himself with powerful Bedouin tribes. Although Palestinians were integrated and many prospered, there was a new militancy directed primarily at Israel but also at Jordanian rule over the West Bank. Palestinians believed that this land was part of their homeland. In 1970, a civil war erupted, pitting the king against the Palestinian militants. The latter were defeated and their leadership were forced to leave Jordan. In the aftermath of this war, the king relied on the military, law, and popular culture to create a Jordanian identity that was decidedly anti-Palestinian. In other words, Jordanian identity was imagined in a way that featured Bedouin culture, tribalism, public piety, and respect for the king. The Palestine became the Other – dangerous, aggressive, secular, and unruly. Law was used to define citizenship in ways that excluded or diminished Palestians; similarly the military became a key institution in producing Jordanian nationals who were loyal to the king and the nation.

Finally, as the Palestinian liberation movement became more powerful and gained international recognition as the legitimate representative of Palestinians, Jordan had to cede control of the West Bank to the Palestine Liberation Organization (PLO). There was then a contraction of the borders of Jordan along with a loss of citizens, as many Palestinians declared their loyalty to the Palestinian nation.

In this very rough sketch, we can appreciate that the making of nations is a extraordinarily complex process. Wars, civil strife, and regional politics as well as domestic power struggles shape the elementary features of a nation, such as its borders, demography, political culture, and collective identity. In the work of Anderson, Chatterjee, and Massad, we are also made aware that new nations are extremely fragile since the essentials of nationhood (borders, national identity, laws, political representation, and accountability) are the focus of sometimes heightened conflict and struggle. The dark side of new nations is the final theme of this chapter.

CRISES OF POSTCOLONIAL NATIONS: GENOCIDE AND CIVIL WAR

Once a transfer of sovereignty has been accomplished, the almost insurmountable challenge of functioning as an independent nation must be confronted. Among the key tasks to be addressed are: to establish a national identity, forge a domestic and international agenda, and to negotiate a relationship to both colonial and precolonial traditions. In the face of such challenges, postcolonial nations all too frequently succumb to civil violence. In this section we review two perspectives that try to explain the troubled histories of these nations.

If there is a central staging ground for new nations, it is Africa. Prior to 1880 there were no nation-states in Africa. Between 1880s and World War I, some 40 nation-states were carved out of the African continent by Great Britain, France, Belgium, Germany, and Italy (today, there are 54 African nations). By the late twentieth century, African colonialism had all been ended. Yet independence has often been sadly accompanied by tyranny, war, and genocide. The political scientist and Africanist Mahmood Mamdani has tried to explain some of this troubled history.[6]

The colonial powers created in almost every African nation a two-tiered political–administrative regime or colonial state. Colonialists were to be ruled by civil law and independent courts, and claimed full legal rights and citizenship status. By contrast, the colonized were subject to customary law. This requires some explanation. From the perspective of the colonial power, the only way to rule was by relying on native elites, who would receive privileges in return for delivering order. This mode of colonial rule is called "indirect rule." The countryside, which is where most natives lived, was divided into districts and tribes; each tribe was under the direct authority of a tribal notable or chieftain. They determined the customs of the tribe, which served as their laws. These tribal leaders were often ruthless; there were bitter rivalries between tribes, as they competed for scarce privileges and status under the colonial state.

In colonial Africa there was then a huge division separating colonists and natives. Whereas the former, who were European, Christian, and White, were rulers and citizens, natives were racialized, inferior colonial subjects. However, some natives were recruited to help administer the colonial state. Typically, the Europeans would rely on a specific tribe or ethnic group, further inflaming native divisions. In the eyes of the colonist, these native allies were still natives and still racialized, inferior subjects. But for those tribal or ethnic groups excluded from access to the restricted opportunities of the colonial state, native allies were scorned as if they were colonists.

This two-tier, colonial order was pervasive among African nations and persisted after independence. Mamdani believes that this colonial heritage explains much of the civil strife of contemporary Africa. In Rwanda, for example, Mamdani argues that the European colonists (France and Belgium) recruited the Tutsi people, an ethnic minority, to help govern because they were viewed as better educated and more trust-worthy than the majority Hutu. For decades the Tutsi had a privileged position among the colonized. The Hutu people viewed them as "settlers" or roughly equiva-lent to the Europeans. In other words, the colonized adopted the bifurcated racial-ized culture of the colonists. But now the Tutsi were being defined as "settlers" or colonists. As you can imagine, this cultural divide between the Tutsi and Hutu fueled hatred between these two ethnicities. When the Hutu revolted in 1994 the Tutsi, who were now a ruling elite in an independent Rwanda, became the enemy. What followed was unspeakable genocidal violence; almost one million people were slaugh-tered in some 100 days.

If genocide and ethnic cleansing occurred across Africa, civil war was a more common fate. Mamdani suggests that the colonial order, with its regime of indirect rule, helps to explain this outcome. African nationalist movements that succeeded were faced with a social order based on entrenched tribal divisions. Moreover, the various tribes and ethnicities of a nation had little or no history of living together; they shared few traditions, often not even sharing a common language. A sudden retreat of the colonial power left a political vacuum. How could a nation be forged in a soci-ety composed of rival tribes and ethnicities, where there is no or little history of citi-zenship and civic resolution of social conflicts?

In the best of cases, the postcolonial state deracialized the state, that is, all natives became citizens. Yet, a thin sense of citizenship was often overwhelmed by thick tribal and ethnic cultures where customary rule persisted. Independence did little to check tribal division and hostilities. The public arena of politics and civic life was vulnerable to becoming a space of heightened social strife and violence. In this condition, politics was often reduced to its worst forms, tyranny or civil war. Unless and until formal citizenship is combined with ending tribal and ethnic divisions, and the tradition of customary law, the likelihood that independence will bring civil progress is slim.

European colonialism altered the face of the globe. Some scholars estimate that by World War I some 80 percent of the civilized world was under the political dominance of a handful of European imperial states. In many respects, that world came to an end with World War I. Does that mean that colonialism came to an end? No, but the dynamic of colonialism and nationalism was quite different in the twentieth century. In *Inventing Iraq*, Toby Dodge, a British sociologist and Middle East specialist, explores this altered pattern.[7]

The territory of Iraq had been under the dominance of the Ottoman Empire until World War I. At this time, Iraq was not a nation but was composed of three Ottoman provinces – Mosul in the north, Bagdad in the center, and Basra in the south. Each province had its own culture and history. For example, Basra was predominantly Shiite, while Bagdad was Sunni and Mosul was heavily Sunni, but also contained mixed various ethnic groups, such as Arabs, Kurds, and Turkmen. Kurds are not Arabs; they have their own language and traditions.

After the defeat of the Ottomans in World War I, Britain and France wanted to annex the lands of the Middle East. To the victor, the spoils: this had been the guiding spirit of European colonialism. But, a new national power on the scene, the United States, ruled out old-style colonialism. President Wilson articulated a new principle that should govern the new world order: the sovereignty of all nations was to be respected. So, instead of colonizing the Arab lands, the newly formed League of Nations authorized Britain and France to create nations and guide their path to independence. A new system replaced colonialism: the mandate system. First-World states were to create new, ultimately sovereign, nations.

Britain was authorized to establish the nation of Iraq. Towards this end, Britain united the three provinces, seemingly ignorant that these regions represented very different ethnic, religious, and tribal identities and loyalties. Remember, these provinces had little or no basis for functioning as a nation. For example, though most were Muslim, Sunnis and Shias had a long history of antagonism and rivalry. Moreover, many Iraqi Shiites identified themselves as Persian, while many Sunnis were Arab nationalists. Moreover, Sunnis were further divided into Arabs and Kurds, representing different ethnic communities with different nationalist aspirations.

Apart from these regional, ethnic, and religious differences, there were deep tribal divisions. The British strengthened tribes by putting in place a system of indirect rule. The tribe became the cornerstone of its neocolonial agenda. Chieftans ruled the tribe, often with an iron fist. Tribes provided economic security and a sense of belonging. The British ruled Iraq in part through controlling powerful tribal chieftans.

Although the British created the nation of Iraq after the war (installed a king, created a constitution and laws, and so on), Iraq was in reality far from a nation. To become a nation this society would have to resolve deeply rooted tribal, sectarian, and ethnic antagonisms. Would Iraq be an Arab nation – what about the Kurds? – or a Muslim nation – what about the Christians and Jews, and the division between the Sunni and Shia? Would it be Western-oriented or an Arab nation?

In 1932, Iraq declared independence. The British withdrew but they left an ambiguous legacy. On the one hand, they strengthened the power of the tribes which were the bulwarks of order in the countryside. On the other hand, they created a powerful king and centralized state in order to provide a framework for national order. In the 1950s the monarchy gave way to a republic, but the stability and coherence of the nation continued to rely on a strong leader allied with key tribes. One autocrat after another ruled Iraq; Saddam Hussein was the last, and held power for almost 25 years. He accomplished this through elaborating a repressive security state, allying with Sunnis and key tribal leaders, promoting a cult of personality around himself, and using Iraq's considerable oil to sustain a corrupt patronage system.

Under Saddam, Iraq never became a nation. This became sadly apparent after the United States toppled Saddam, when sectarian, ethnic, and tribal hatreds erupted into a protracted civil war. This civil strife is very much a legacy of British colonialism.

Suggested Readings

Roger Brubaker, *Nationalism Reframed* (Cambridge: Cambridge University Press, 1996).
Partha Chatterjee, *Nationalist Thought and the Colonial World* (London: Zed Books, 1986).
Eric Hobsbawm, *Nation and Nationalism since 1780* (Cambridge: Cambridge University Press, 1990).
Jyoti Puri, *Encountering Nationalism* (Oxford: Blackwell, 2003).
Anthony Smith, *The Ethnic Origins of Nation* (Oxford: Blackwell, 1986).

References

1 Anthony Smith, *Nationalism and Modernism* (London: Macmillan, 1998) and *The Ethnic Origins of Nations* (Oxford: Blackwell, 1986).
2 Benedict Anderson, *Imagined Communities* (London: Verso, 1983).
3 For the Latin Americanist critics of Anderson, see Sara Castro-Klaren and John C. Chasteen, eds., *Beyond Imagined Communities* (Baltimore, MD: Johns Hopkins Press, 2003).
4 Partha Chatterjee, *The Nation and Its Fragments* (Princeton, NJ: Princeton University Press, 1993).
5 Joseph Massad, *Colonial Effects* (New York: Columbia University Press, 2001).
6 Mahmood Mamdani, *Citizen and Subject* (Princeton, NJ: Princeton University Press, 1996) and *When Victims Become Killers* (Princeton, NJ: Princeton University Press, 2002).
7 Toby Dodge, *Inventing Iraq* (New York: Columbia University Press, 2005).

Afterword to Part VII

As we've seen in this part and in Part VI, social theory is changing. As the world is becoming global and multicultural, as high-tech parks crowd out industrial manufacturing plants, as time and space are considerably altered through new high-speed communication and transportation systems, as the boundaries between nations, peoples, and cultures become porous, is it any wonder that the shape of social knowledge is also changing?

I've suggested one important change; the postdisciplinary organization of social knowledge. Although we still become sociologists or anthropologists, the scholarly debates and research problems we address, and the conceptual and methodological resources we use, are drawn from many disciplines. For many of us today, our identification as sociologists or political scientists tells us little about our actual theorizing and research.

In a postdisciplinary academic environment, scholarly debates are organized around dense clusters of key figures, texts, theoretical issues, research problems, and issues of contention, and are engaged in by scholars from a wide range of disciplines. Indeed, in some of these clusters the dividing line between academics and nonacademics is blurred as public intellectuals (e.g., journalists, social critics, independent scholars) participate in knowledge production. But there is an additional key feature of the postdisciplinary organization of social knowledge: a declining faith in the notion of an all-encompassing, unified social theory or system of social knowledge. The immense multiplication of perspectives, and the clash of theoretical and research languages that is a product of both a global, multicultural environment and a postdisciplinary academic culture, has compelled many scholars to reconsider their core beliefs about objectivity, universal knowledge, and the ideal of creating a theoretical system.

Faith in science has been at the heart of social thinking for a very long time. From Enlightenment thinkers such as Condorcet and Adam Smith to Marx and Durkheim and Parsons, Randall Collins, and Pierre Bourdieu, social thinkers have aspired to

Contested Knowledge: Social Theory Today, Fifth Edition. Steven Seidman.
© 2013 John Wiley & Sons, Ltd. Published 2013 by John Wiley & Sons, Ltd.

claim the status of being scientific for their social ideas. It wasn't just a cynical ploy to gain public authority or to defeat intellectual rivals. Many social thinkers, then and still today, believe that science is *the* path to objective knowledge. With its culture of methodological rigor and its public process of evaluating truth claims, science was thought to be able to fashion ideas that he world "as it really is." The social perspectives of ordinary folk, poets, religionists, or political activists are said to express their unique personal experience and values, or their political ideology. By contrast, science screens out, as it were, the particular values and interests of the scientist. To put it another way, the institution of science makes the scientist into a rational agent obeying general and impersonal rules of knowledge production and justification.

Whether or not you believe that science has been successful in yielding social truths, one thing seems clear: the desire to be scientific has pressured social thinkers to be rigorous, systematic, and critical of their own and others' ideas. The idea of a science of society has promoted a culture that is reflexive, rigorous, and methodical in thinking about concepts, evidence, and standards of truth. We would not want to surrender this aspect of scientific culture.

However, it seems clear that science has lost a good deal of its luster. Too much has happened in the last century for us to uncritically champion science: wars, scientific weaponry that threaten to end life itself, scientific torture, and scientific medicine meant to keep us alive but which also prolongs suffering. Science may indeed be a force promoting a better world; it can, though, just as easily lead us down the path of a social nightmare.

Doubts have been voiced, moreover, about the notion, almost unquestioned for two centuries, that science alone can yield objective social truths. Some critics have defended a new view of social knowledge: the idea of "situated knowledge."

Viewing knowledge as situated means that we know the world from a specific standpoint. A standpoint may indicate a gender or racial identity or a national or "civilizational" identity, as "Western" or "African" or "East Asian." A standpoint shapes how we see society – whether we focus on the individual or the group, whether we consider class or race or gender or colonialism to be important, or whether we focus on the isolated society or a network of societies. We never know the world apart from our standpoint; who we are matters in terms of what we can say or know about the world.

You might ask: how is knowledge possible if it is always related to a particular standpoint? The answer is that a standpoint makes knowledge possible, even if it also gives to it a partial character.

For example, according to some feminists, in many societies men's lives have been formed by their involvement in the public, institutional world, for example, the military or the government. This social standpoint shapes the way men view the world. Stated positively, men's public positioning enables them to develop complex ideas about public life. In this regard, it is not a coincidence that the chief contribution of the classical sociologists, all men, is their ideas about the economy, the division of labor, bureaucracy, or law. In fact, feminists would say that men have uncovered real social truths about the public, institutional world.

However, men's very social positioning in the public world has also meant that their ideas have been seriously flawed and partial. Men's social perspectives have basically written women out of the story of society and history. Until recently, women thinkers and cultural creators, and movements and organizations, have been absent from men's social and historical perspectives. The activities that have historically occupied women's lives, the making and caring for bodies, and the social organization of the household, have been absent from men's social thinking. Where is the analysis of sexuality, gender, reproduction, the care of children, or emotions in Comte or Marx or Durkheim? Most importantly, men's perspectives failed, until recently, to analyze the deeply gendered character of human behavior and the social world. Understanding the social making of gendered identities, practices, and the very divide between private and public life, was not part of the tradition of social theory. In much of classical and contemporary social thinking, gender was not a key lens through which to make sense of human life.

This neglect of gender was not innocent of political and moral meaning. To the extent that men benefitted from their association with public life while women were disadvantaged by their link to private life, masculine social knowledges have reinforced men's social dominance. And, feminists say, we should not be surprised! Like any privileged group, men have not been interested in exposing the social sources and rationales of their own power. By contrast, women do have an interest in trying to understand the social significance of gender and the social sources of gender difference and inequality. Women have been socially disadvantaged by existing gender orders. To improve their situation, they must challenge an ideology that makes gender difference and inequality a law of nature or God.

Approaching knowledge as situated does not deny the possibility of social truths. Rather, it suggests that we can only know the social world from a specific standpoint. A standpoint makes knowledge possible, but it also means our social ideas are always partial and perspectival. Perhaps we must give up the ideal of a comprehensive type of social knowledge. Social truths both reveal and obscure social reality. If we approach knowledge as situated, we should be attentive to the ways that knowledge shapes ourselves and social life. Knowledge is not only about representing reality but about constructing reality.

A culture that approaches social knowledge as situated and as fragmented into clustered debates will perhaps shy away from the quest for a system of social knowledge. Would anyone today dare to do what Comte or Parsons or even Habermas attempted – namely, to provide a system of sociology or a sort of comprehensive theory of society, history, and modernity? At least for the moment it seems that the era of systems, and the quest for a science of society that strides confidently towards universal truths, is less compelling to many of us. Perhaps something grand has been lost in surrendering this noble dream, and it may simply be a momentary loss of confidence as the West seems less sure of itself. But, whatever the fate of general theory, the spirit of science, its commitment to analytical rigor, its critical reflexivity, and an unrelenting questioning of the meaning of knowledge and social life, remains very much alive and well in our changing culture of social knowledge.

Index

Contested Knowledge: Social Theory Today, Fifth Edition. Steven Seidman.
© 2013 John Wiley & Sons, Ltd. Published 2013 by John Wiley & Sons, Ltd.